Grand Guignol orchestra

1

STORY AND ART BY

KAORI YUKI

Grand Guignol Orchestra

1

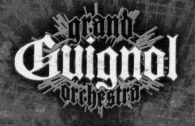

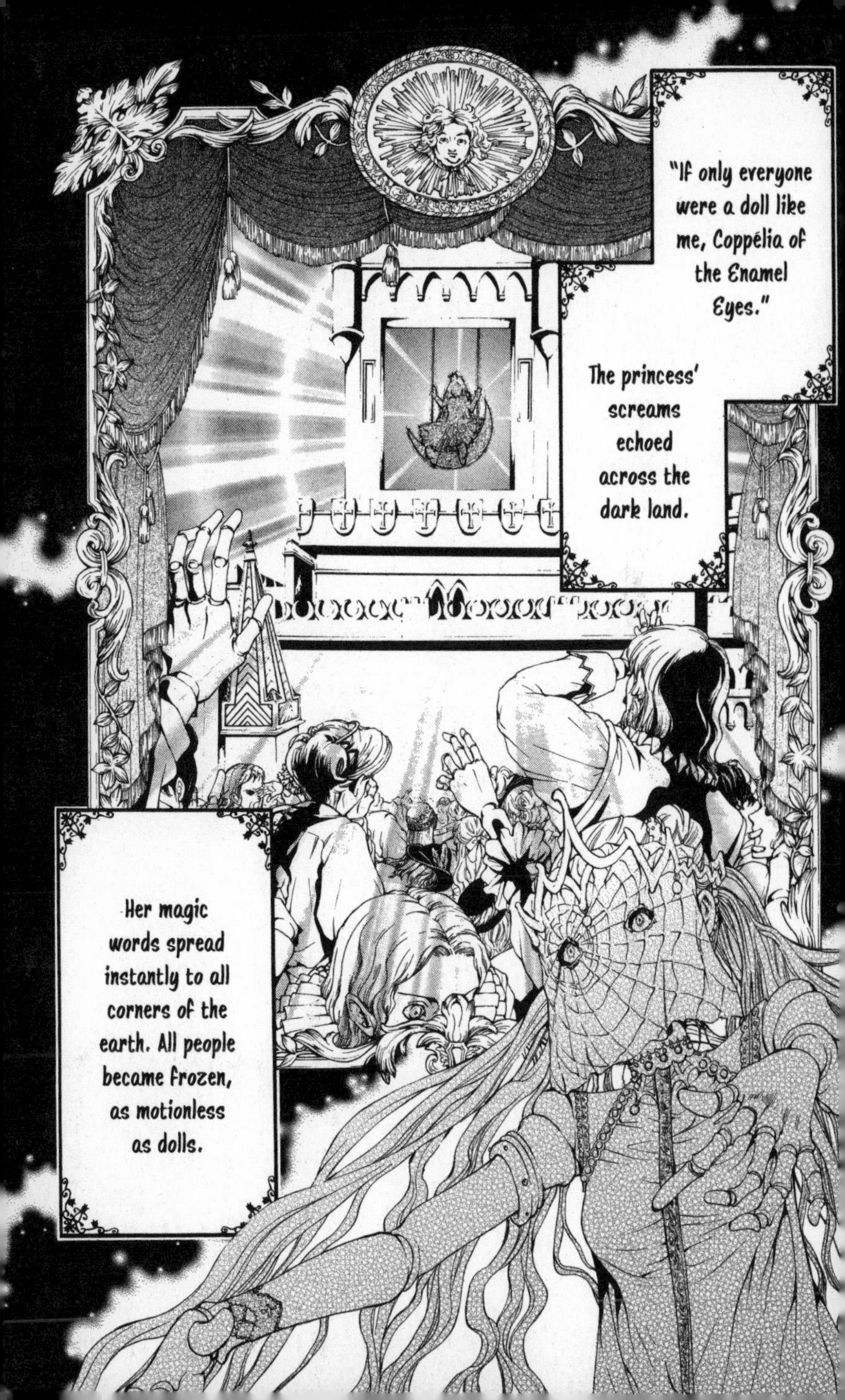
"If only everyone were a doll like me, Coppélia of the Enamel Eyes."
The princess' screams echoed across the dark land.
Her magic words spread instantly to all corners of the earth. All people became frozen, as motionless as dolls.

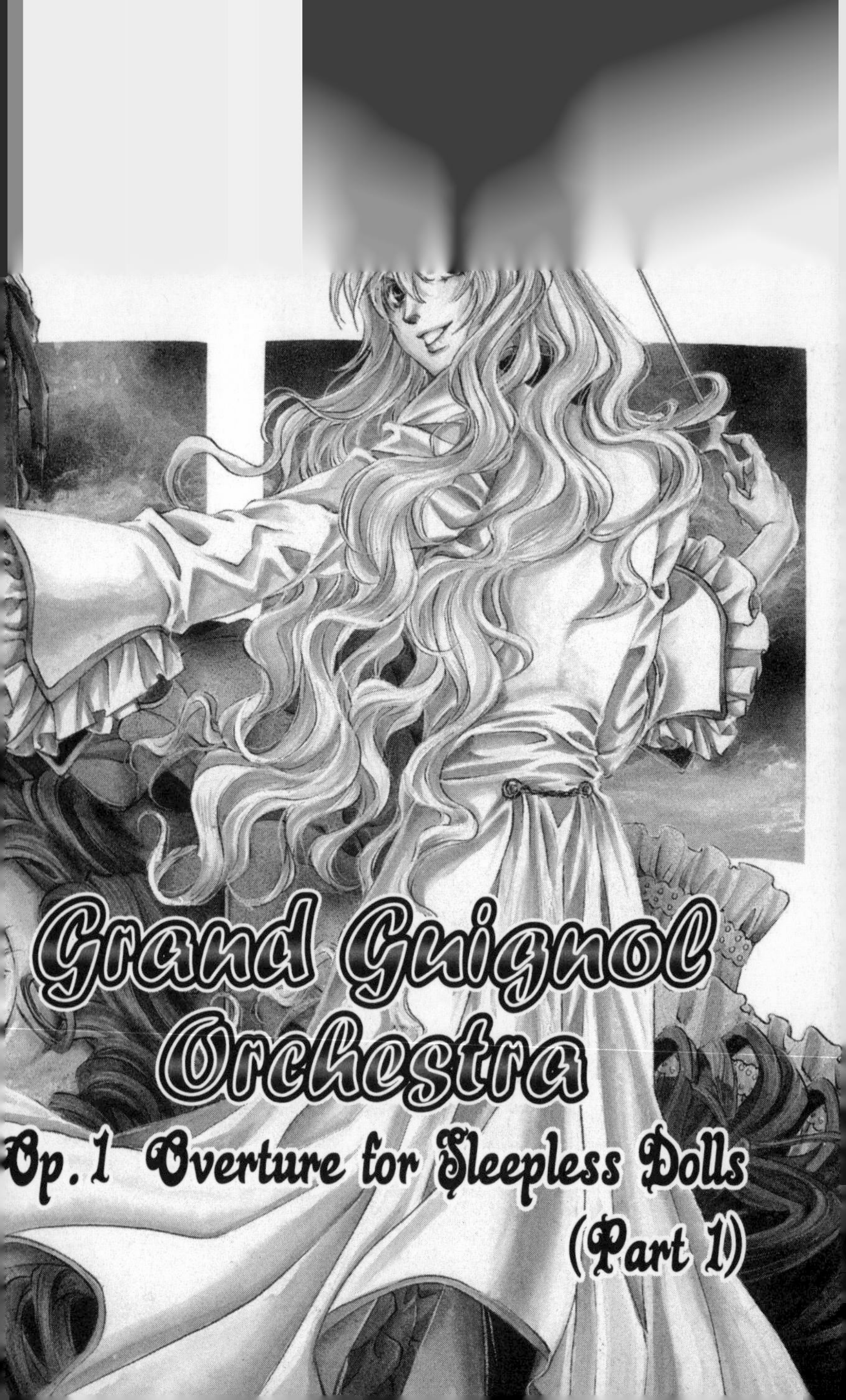
Grand Guignol Orchestra
Op.1 Overture for Sleepless Dolls
(Part 1)

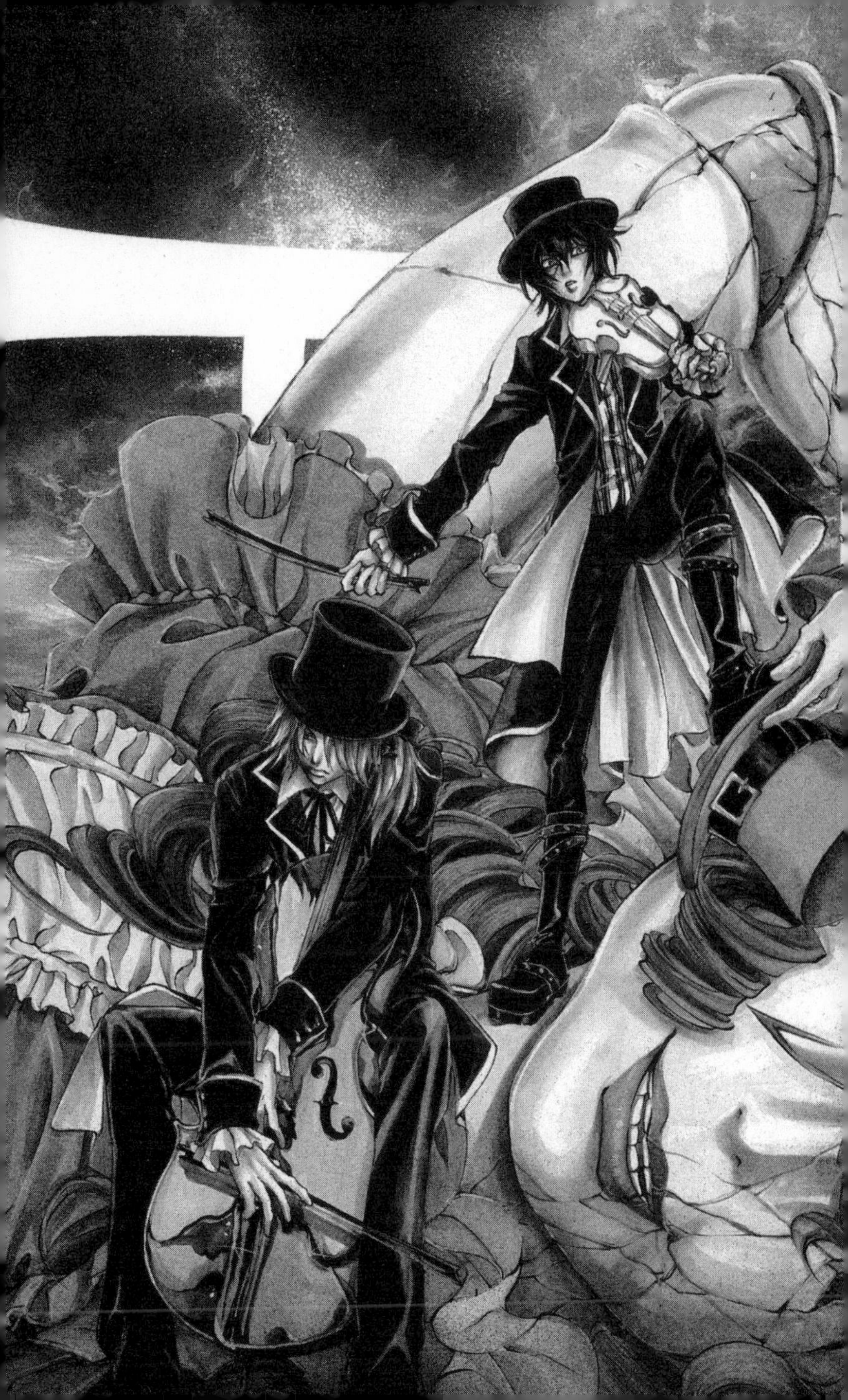

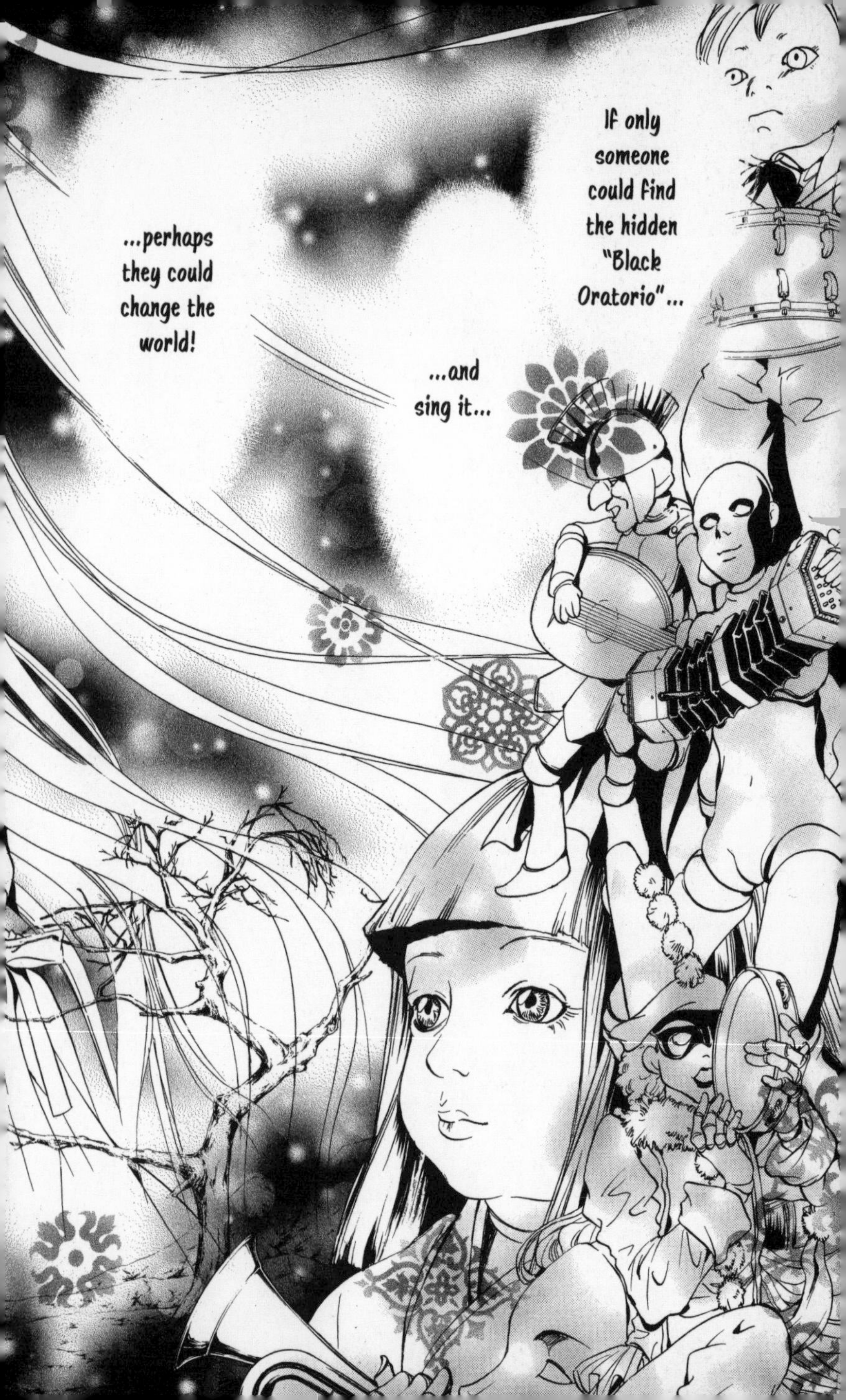
If only someone could find the hidden "Black Oratorio"...
...and sing it...
...perhaps they could change the world!

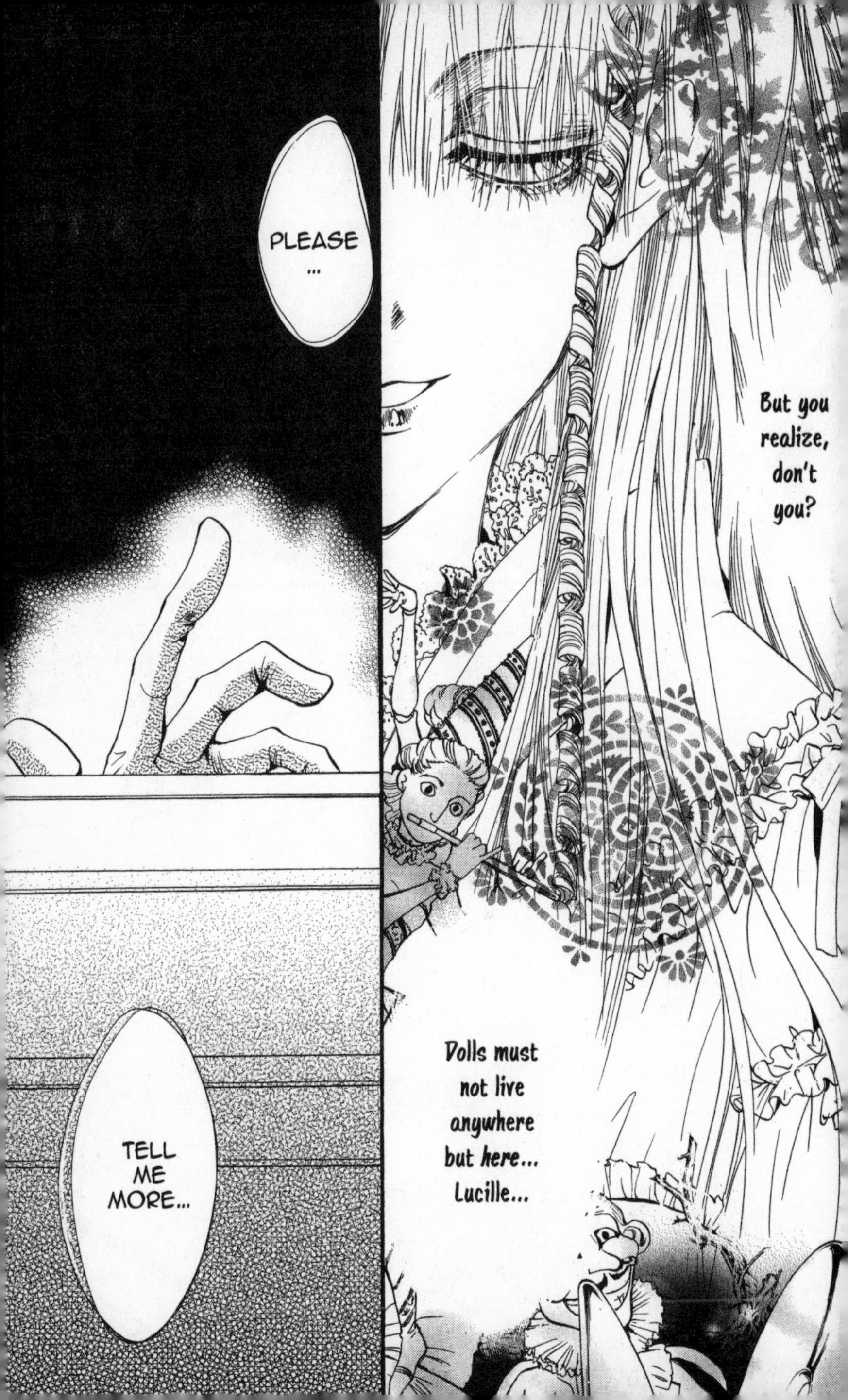
But you realize, don't you?
Dolls must not live anywhere but *here*... Lucille...
PLEASE ...
TELL ME MORE...

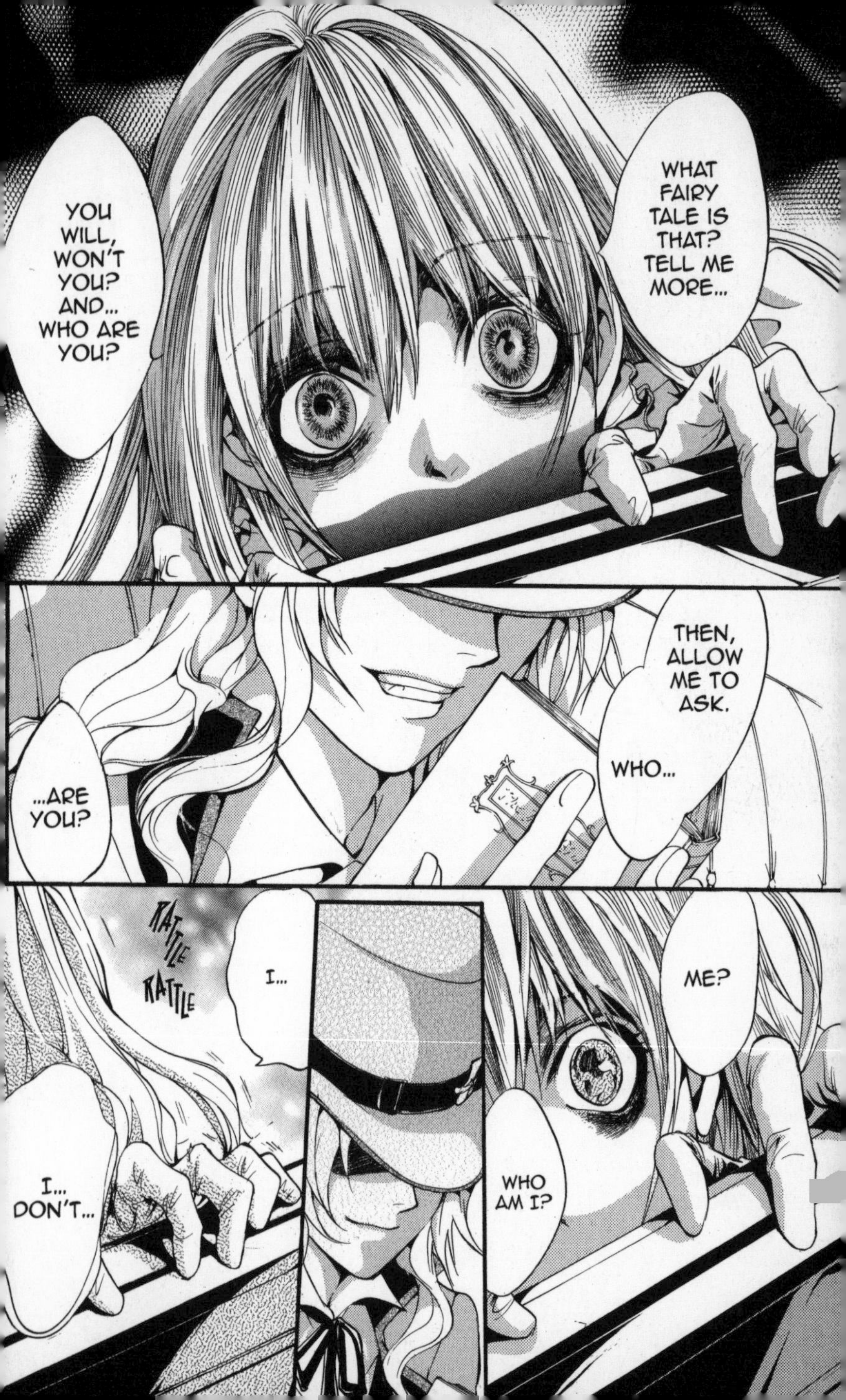
WHAT FAIRY TALE IS THAT? TELL ME MORE...
YOU WILL, WON'T YOU? AND... WHO ARE YOU?
THEN, ALLOW ME TO ASK.
WHO...
...ARE YOU?
ME?
WHO AM I?
I...
RATTLE RATTLE
I... DON'T...

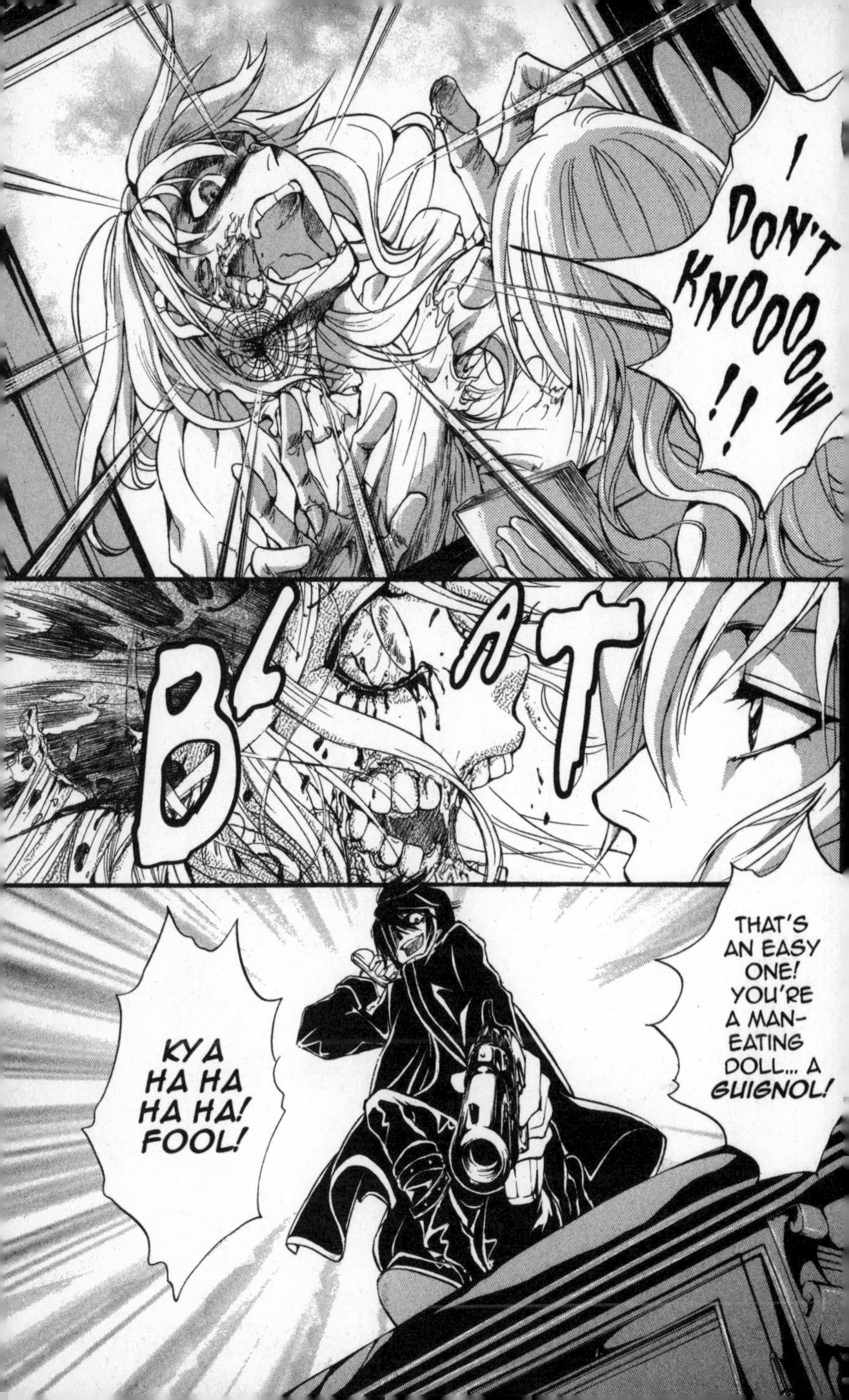
I DON'T KNOOOOOW!!
BLAT
THAT'S AN EASY ONE! YOU'RE A MAN-EATING DOLL... A GUIGNOL!
KYA HA HA HA HA! FOOL!

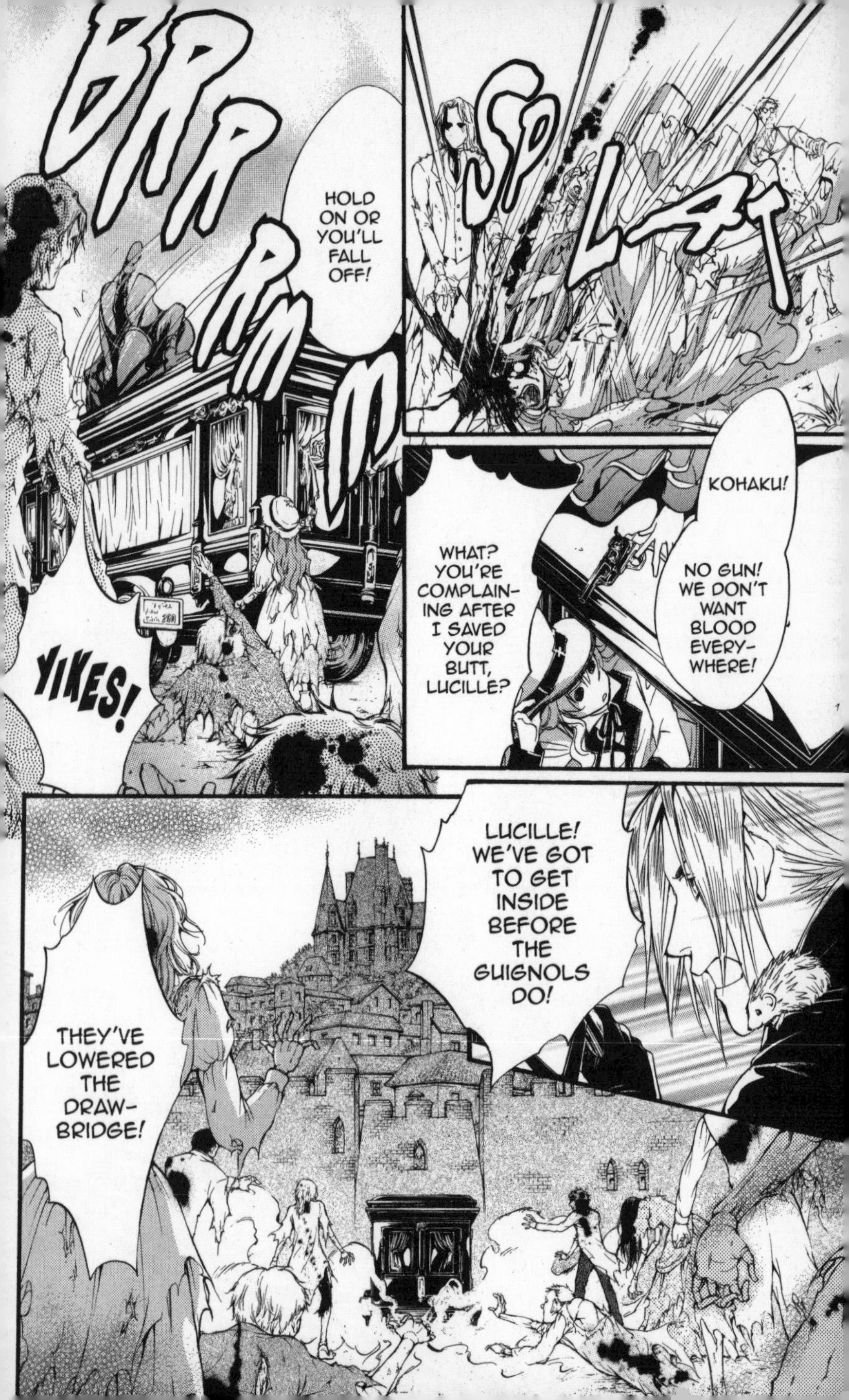
SPLAT
KOHAKU!
NO GUN! WE DON'T WANT BLOOD EVERY-WHERE!
WHAT? YOU'RE COMPLAIN-ING AFTER I SAVED YOUR BUTT, LUCILLE?
HOLD ON OR YOU'LL FALL OFF!
BRRRMMM
YIKES!
LUCILLE! WE'VE GOT TO GET INSIDE BEFORE THE GUIGNOLS DO!
THEY'VE LOWERED THE DRAW-BRIDGE!

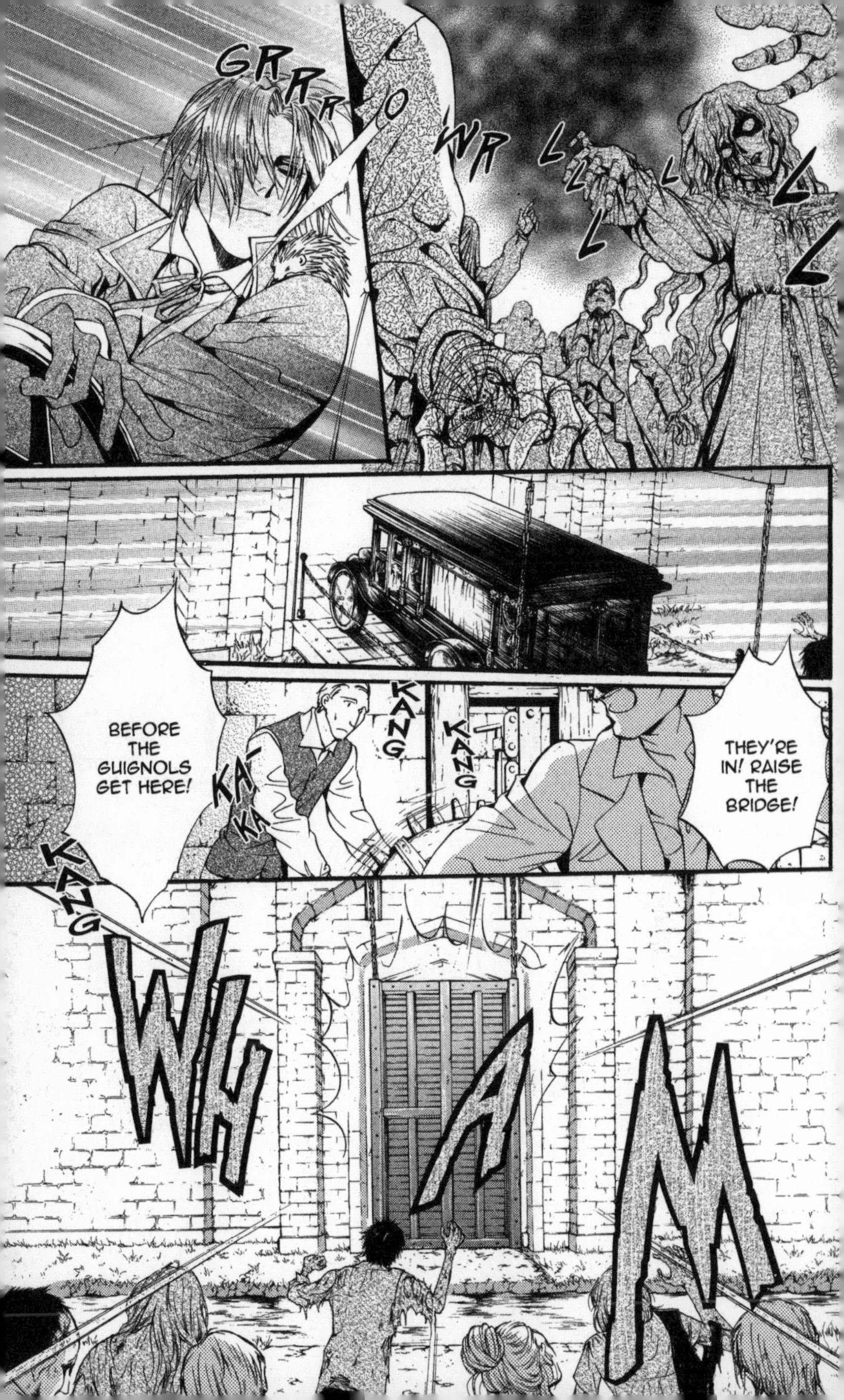
GRRRROWRLLLLLLL
THEY'RE IN! RAISE THE BRIDGE!
KANG
KANG
KA-KA
BEFORE THE GUIGNOLS GET HERE!
KANG
WHAM

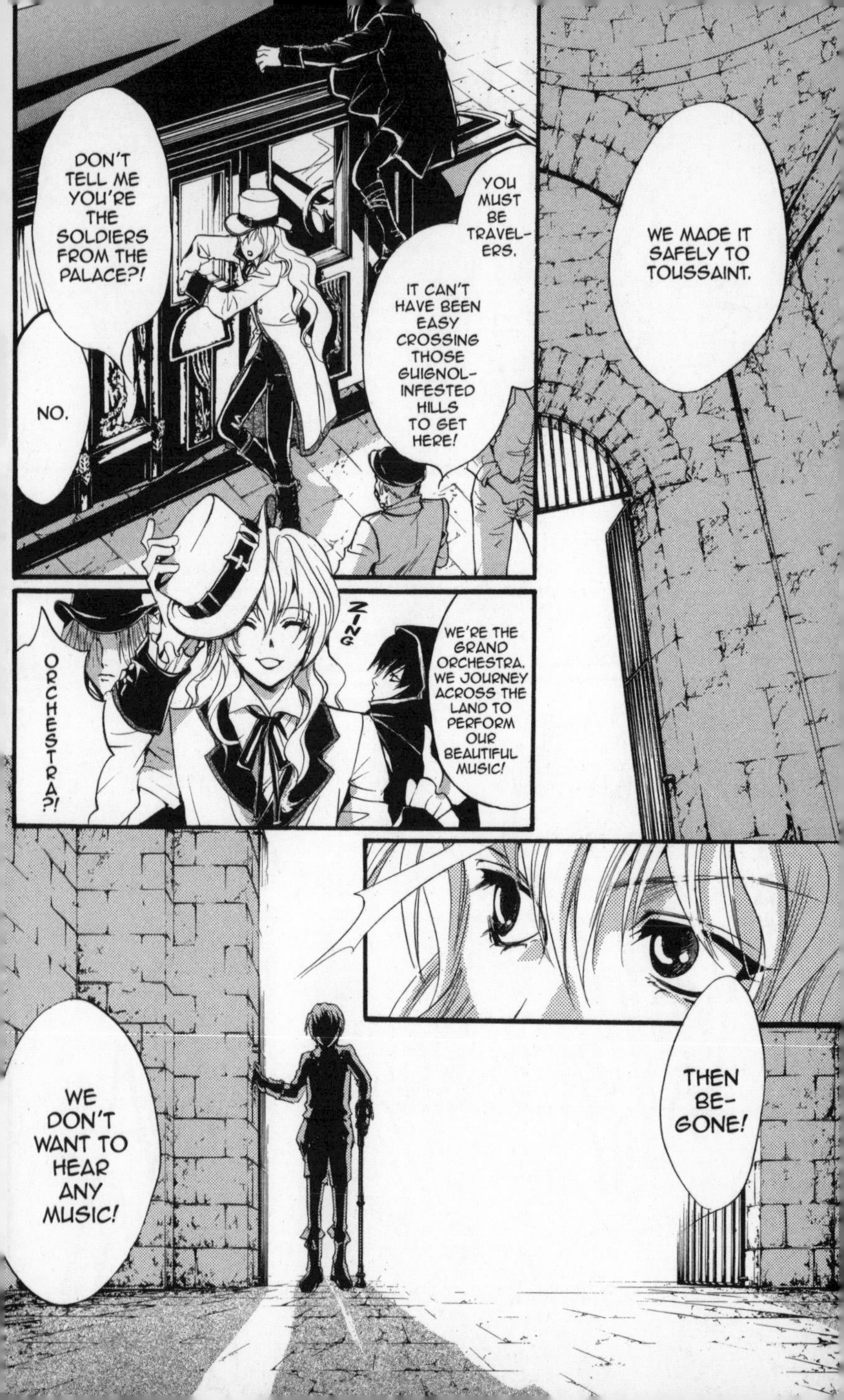
WE MADE IT SAFELY TO TOUSSAINT.
YOU MUST BE TRAVEL-ERS.
IT CAN'T HAVE BEEN EASY CROSSING THOSE GUIGNOL-INFESTED HILLS TO GET HERE!
DON'T TELL ME YOU'RE THE SOLDIERS FROM THE PALACE?!
NO.
WE'RE THE GRAND ORCHESTRA. WE JOURNEY ACROSS THE LAND TO PERFORM OUR BEAUTIFUL MUSIC!
ZING
ORCHESTRA?!
THEN BE-GONE!
WE DON'T WANT TO HEAR ANY MUSIC!

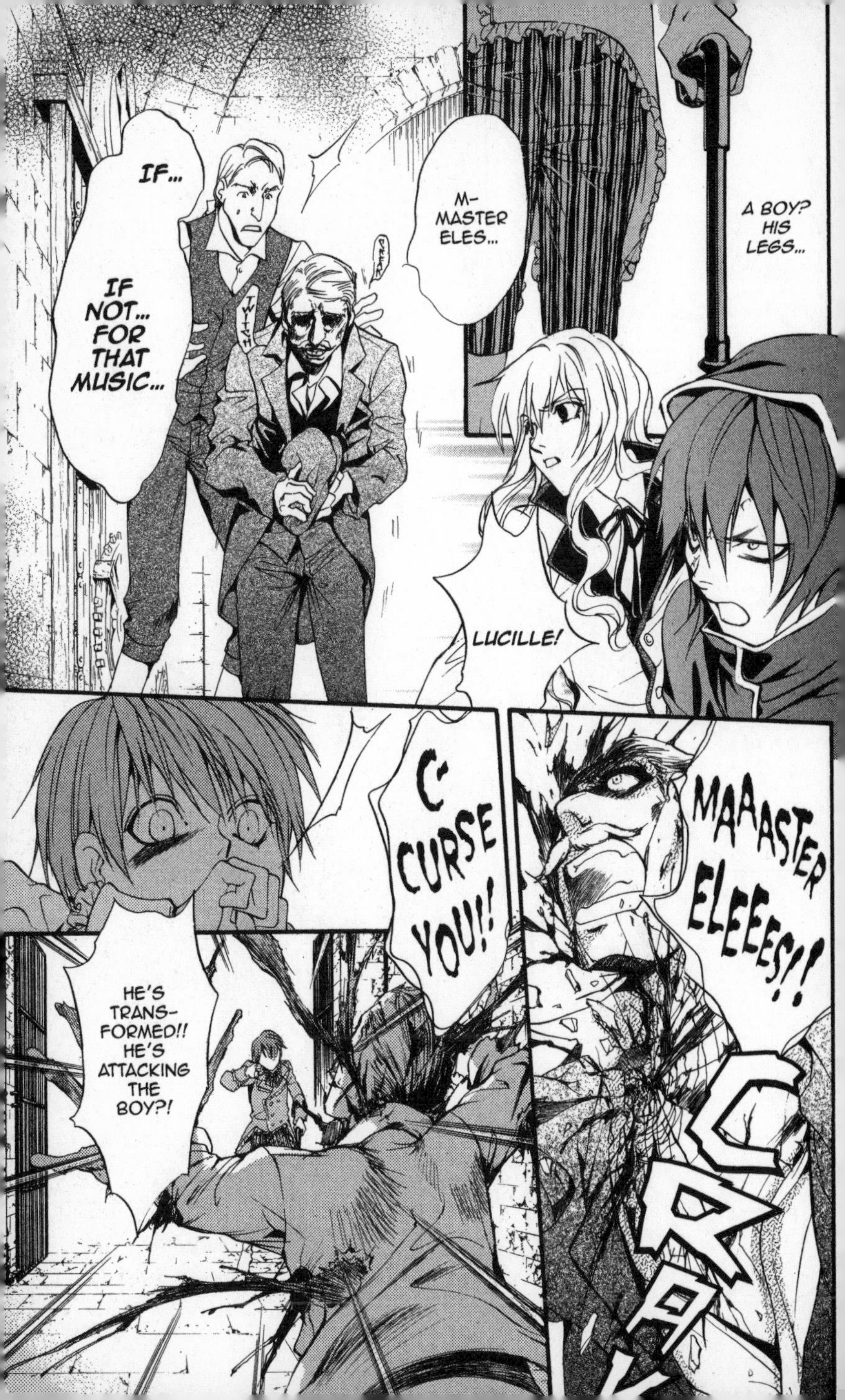
A BOY? HIS LEGS...
M-MASTER ELES...
CREAK
IF...
IF NOT... FOR THAT MUSIC...
TWITCH
LUCILLE!
MAAASTER ELEEES!!
C-CURSE YOU!!
CRA
HE'S TRANSFORMED!! HE'S ATTACKING THE BOY?!

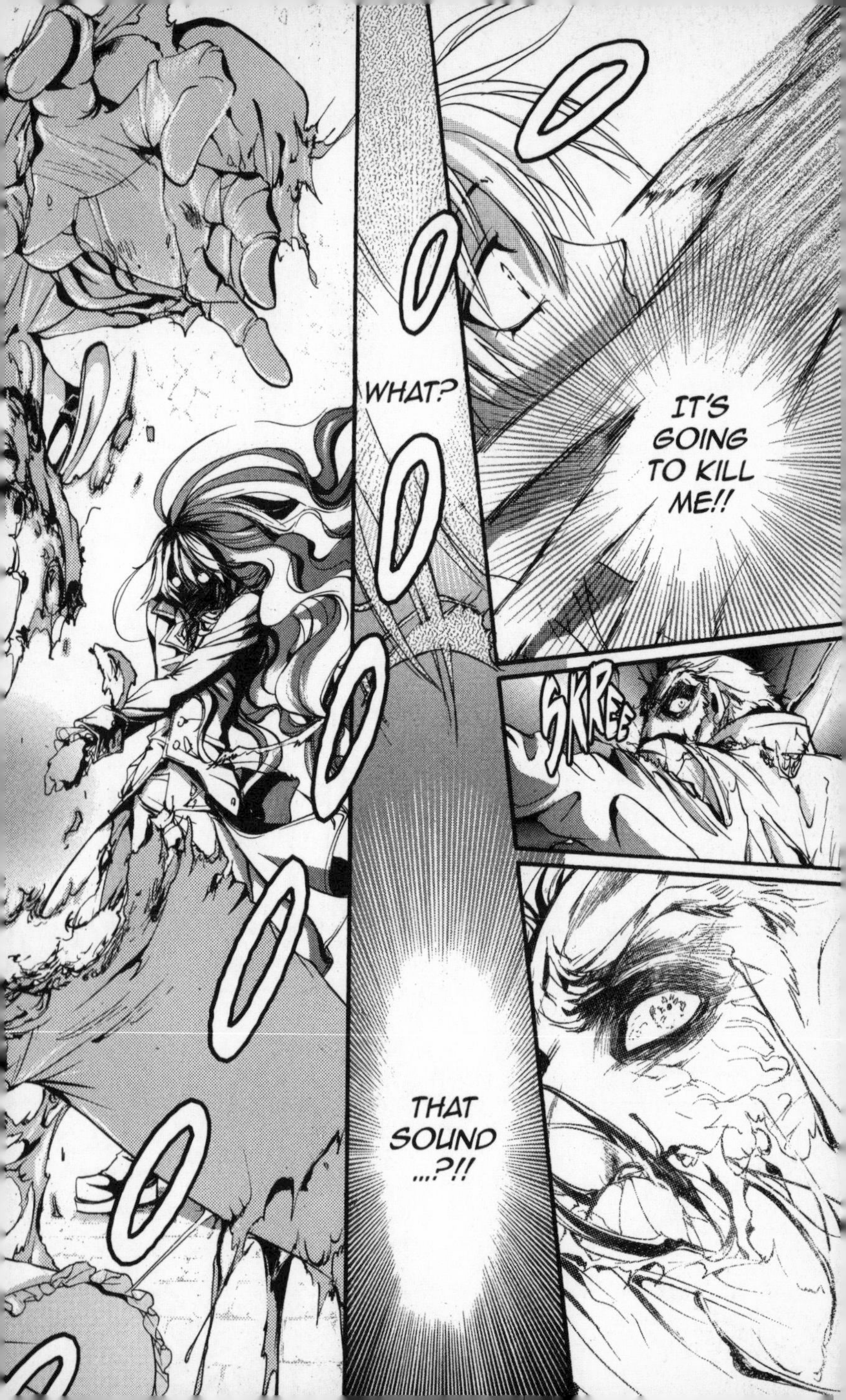
IT'S GOING TO KILL ME!!
SKREE
WHAT?
THAT SOUND ...?!!

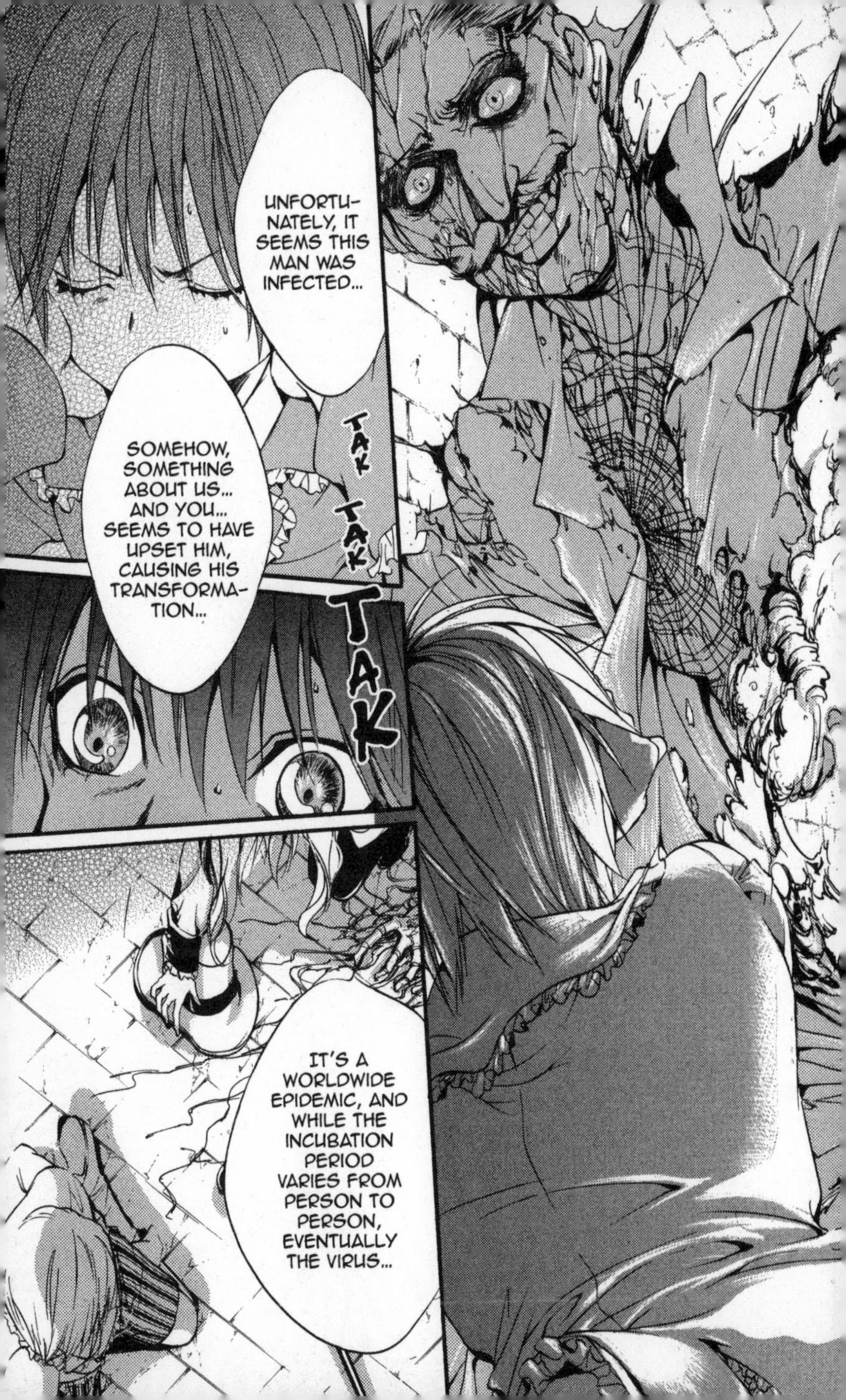
TAK TAK TAK
UNFORTUNATELY, IT SEEMS THIS MAN WAS INFECTED...
SOMEHOW, SOMETHING ABOUT US... AND YOU... SEEMS TO HAVE UPSET HIM, CAUSING HIS TRANSFORMATION...
IT'S A WORLDWIDE EPIDEMIC, AND WHILE THE INCUBATION PERIOD VARIES FROM PERSON TO PERSON, EVENTUALLY THE VIRUS...

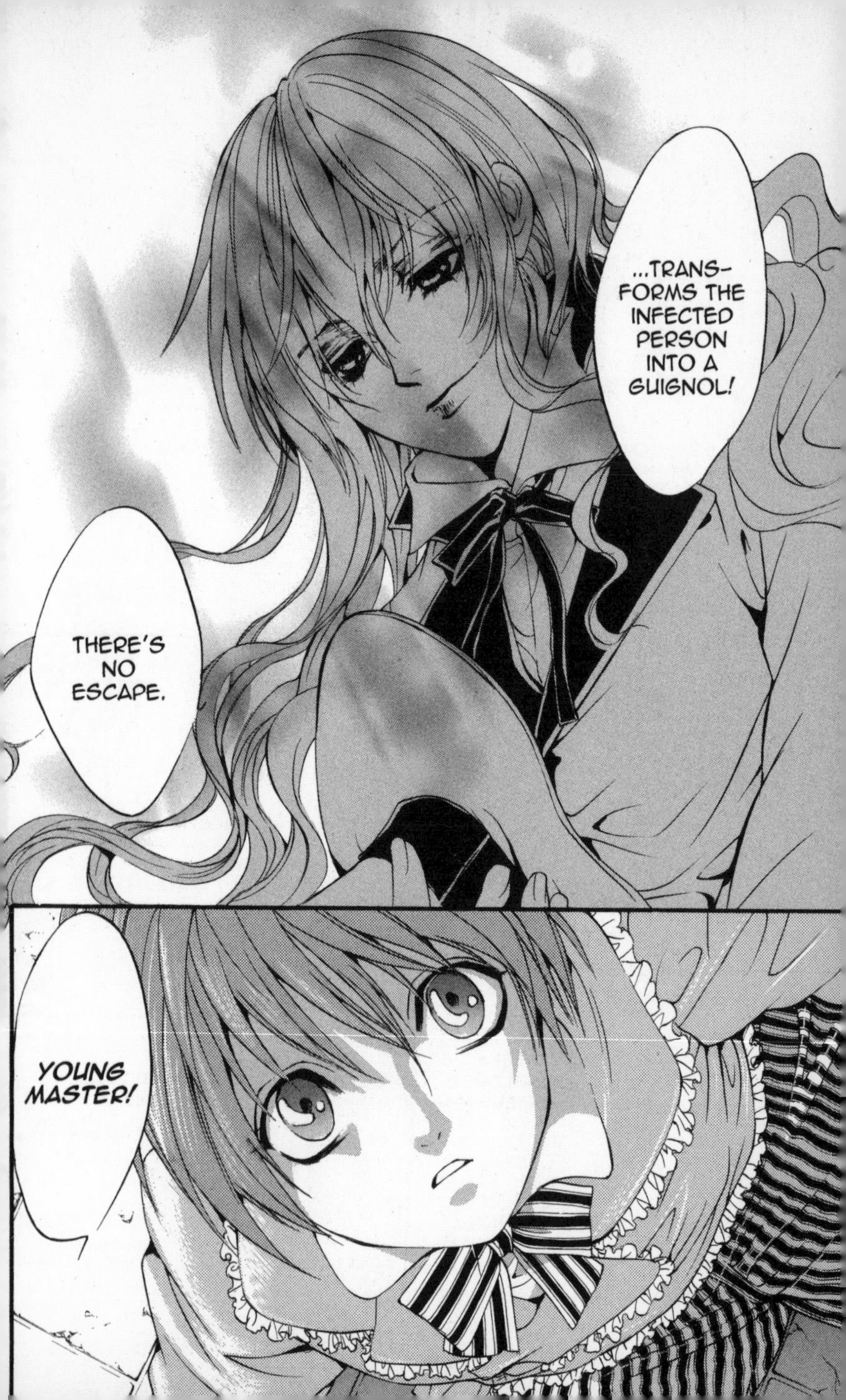
...TRANS-FORMS THE INFECTED PERSON INTO A GUIGNOL!
THERE'S NO ESCAPE.
YOUNG MASTER!

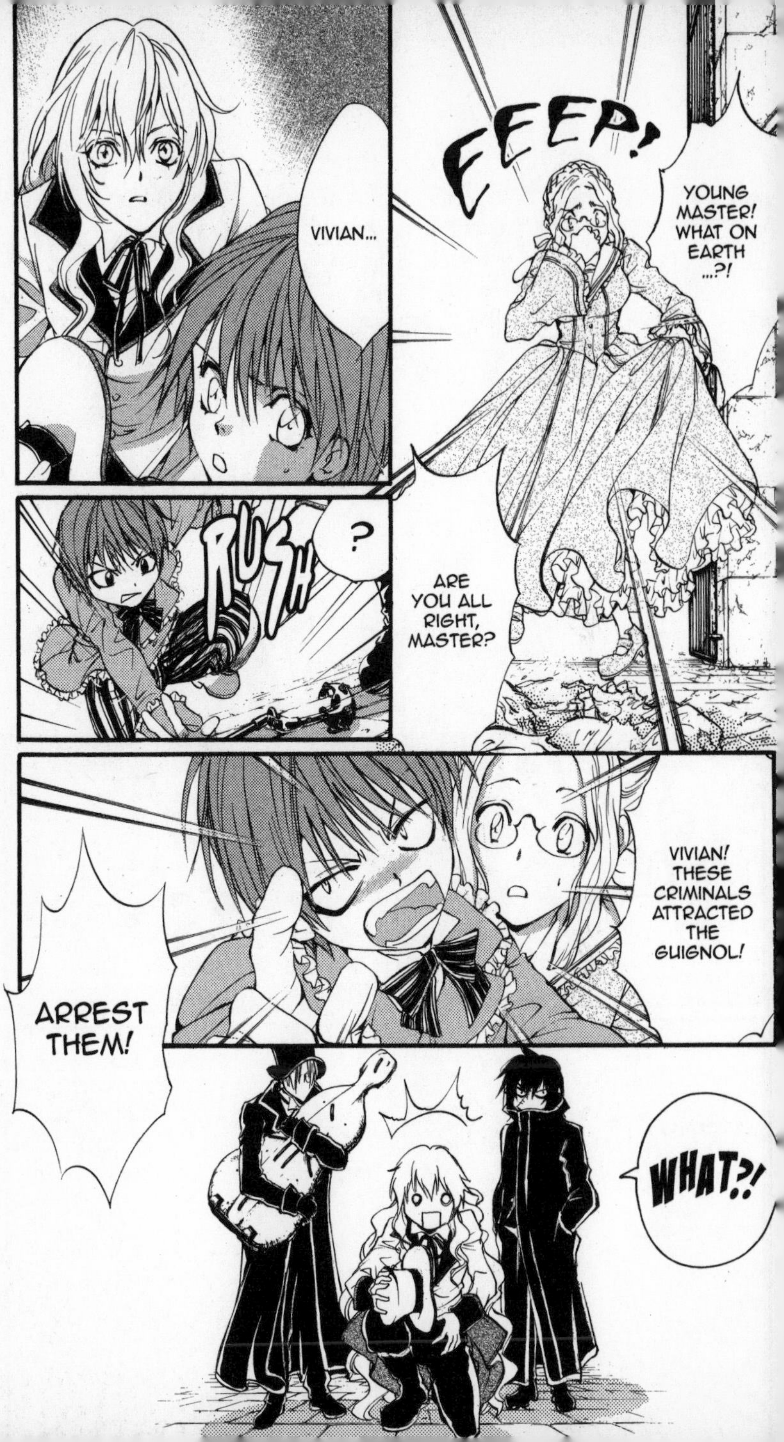
EEEP!
YOUNG MASTER! WHAT ON EARTH ...?!
ARE YOU ALL RIGHT, MASTER?
VIVIAN...
?
RUSH
VIVIAN! THESE CRIMINALS ATTRACTED THE GUIGNOL!
ARREST THEM!
WHAT?!

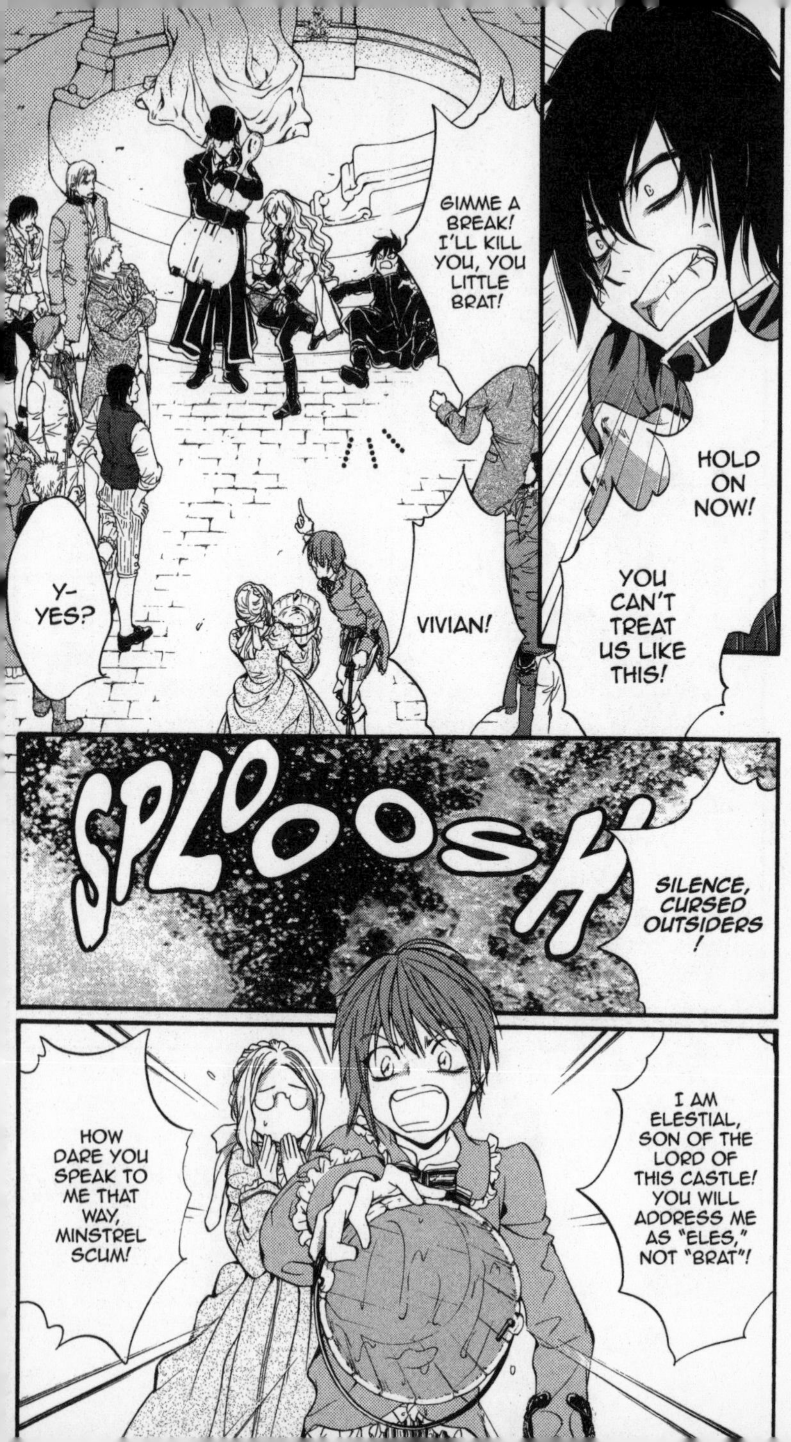
HOLD ON NOW!
YOU CAN'T TREAT US LIKE THIS!
GIMME A BREAK! I'LL KILL YOU, YOU LITTLE BRAT!
...
VIVIAN!
Y-YES?
SPLOOSH
SILENCE, CURSED OUTSIDERS!
I AM ELESTIAL, SON OF THE LORD OF THIS CASTLE! YOU WILL ADDRESS ME AS "ELES," NOT "BRAT"!
HOW DARE YOU SPEAK TO ME THAT WAY, MINSTREL SCUM!

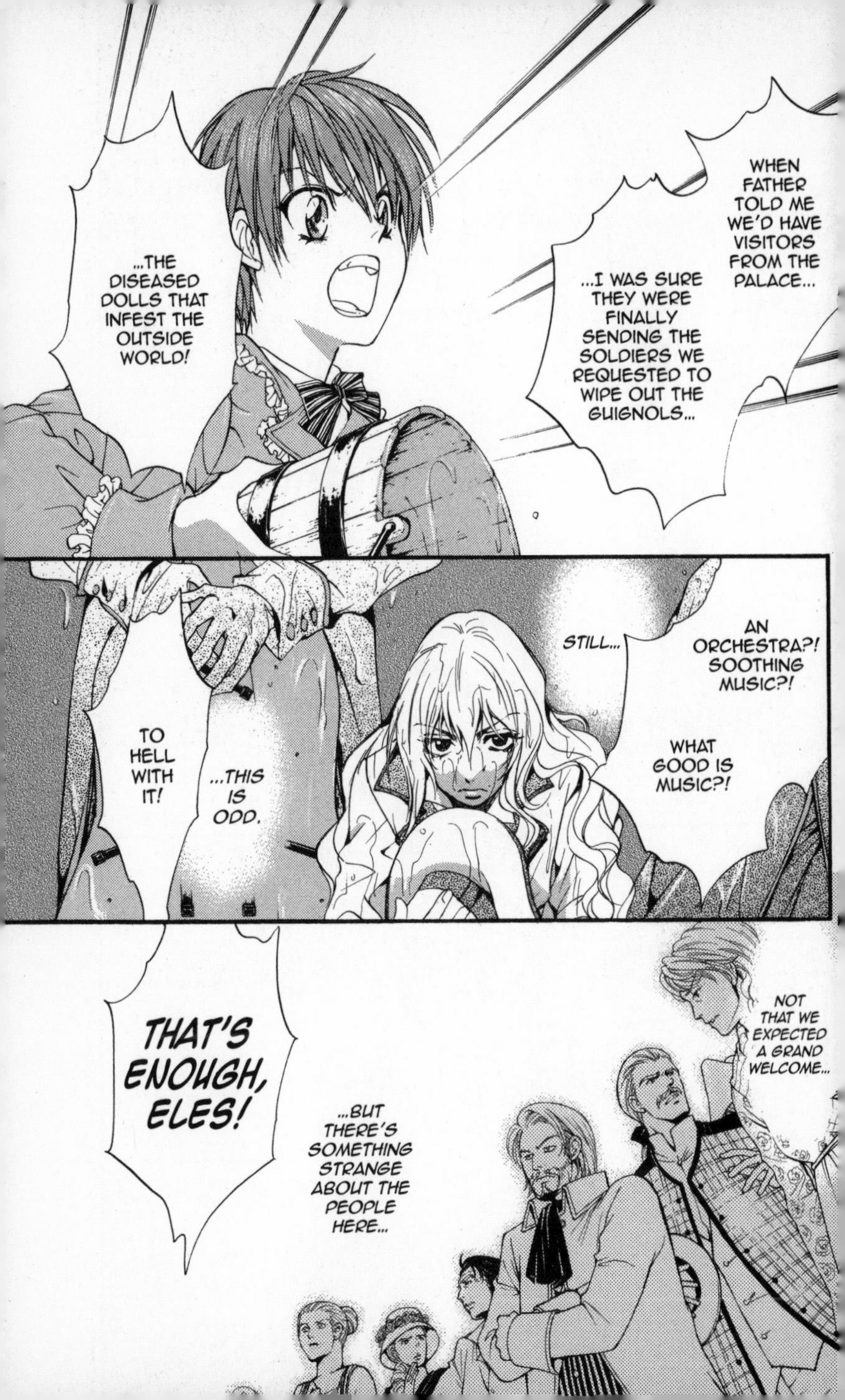
WHEN FATHER TOLD ME WE'D HAVE VISITORS FROM THE PALACE...
...I WAS SURE THEY WERE FINALLY SENDING THE SOLDIERS WE REQUESTED TO WIPE OUT THE GUIGNOLS...
...THE DISEASED DOLLS THAT INFEST THE OUTSIDE WORLD!
AN ORCHESTRA?! SOOTHING MUSIC?!
WHAT GOOD IS MUSIC?!
STILL...
...THIS IS ODD.
TO HELL WITH IT!
NOT THAT WE EXPECTED A GRAND WELCOME...
...BUT THERE'S SOMETHING STRANGE ABOUT THE PEOPLE HERE...
THAT'S ENOUGH, ELES!

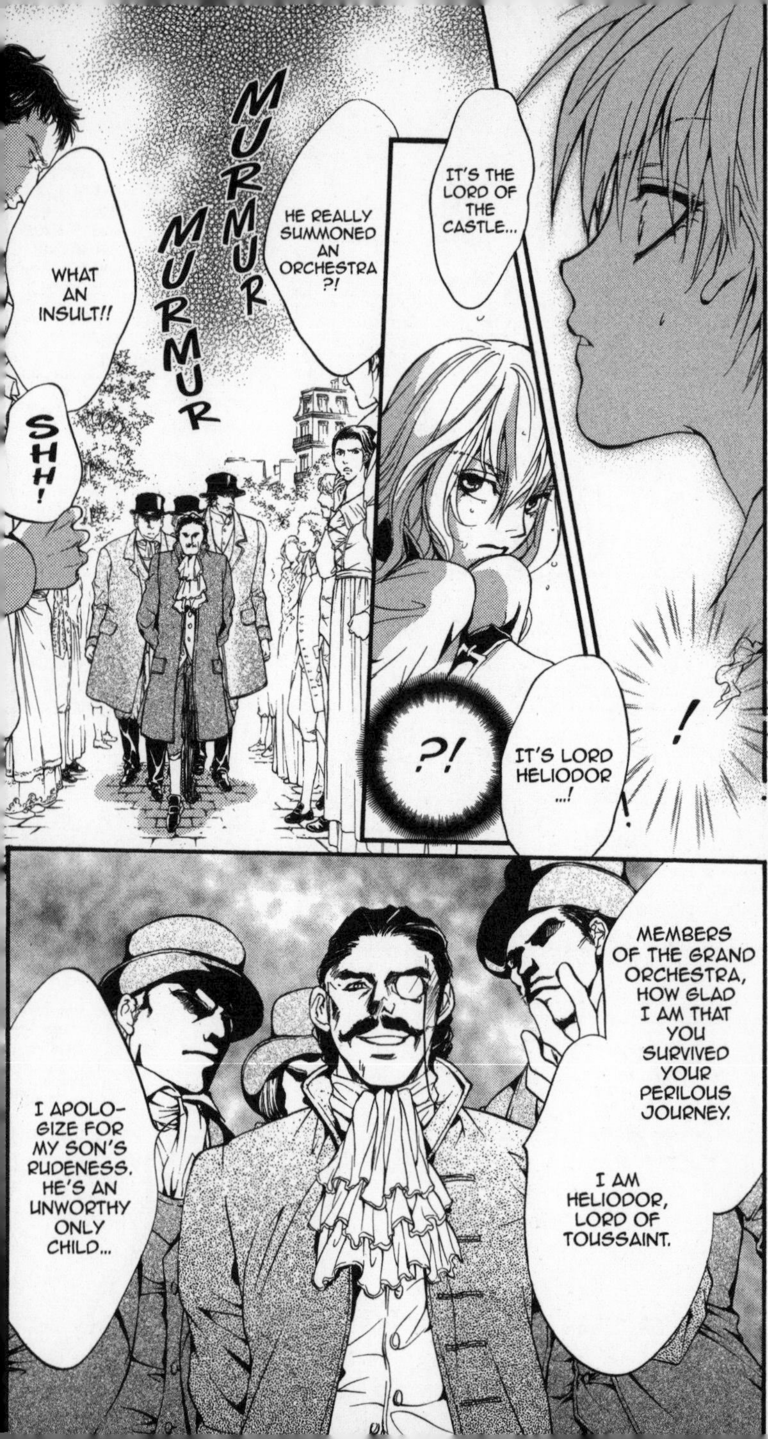
IT'S THE LORD OF THE CASTLE...
!
IT'S LORD HELIODOR ...!
?!
HE REALLY SUMMONED AN ORCHESTRA ?!
MURMUR
MURMUR
WHAT AN INSULT!!
SHH!
MEMBERS OF THE GRAND ORCHESTRA, HOW GLAD I AM THAT YOU SURVIVED YOUR PERILOUS JOURNEY.
I AM HELIODOR, LORD OF TOUSSAINT.
I APOLO-GIZE FOR MY SON'S RUDENESS. HE'S AN UNWORTHY ONLY CHILD...

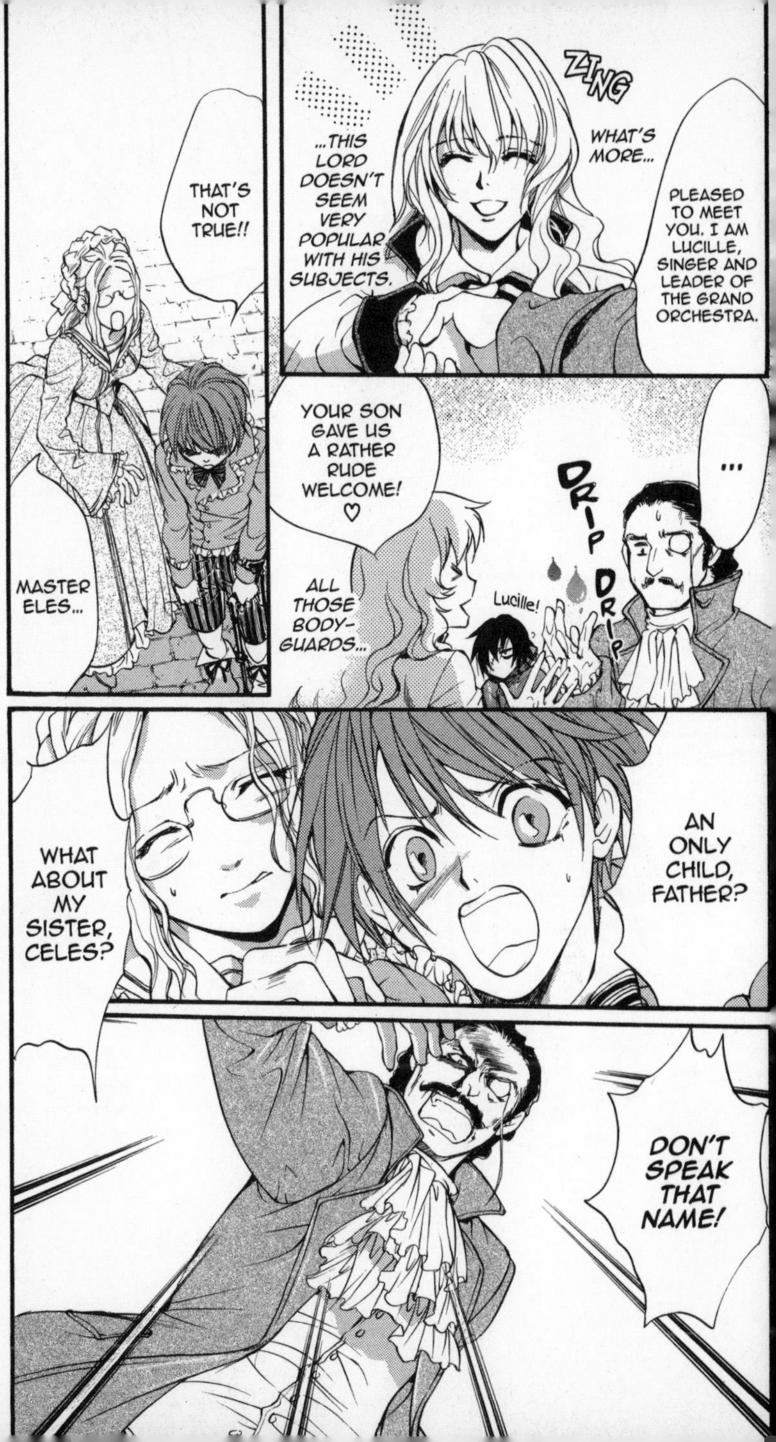
ZING
PLEASED TO MEET YOU. I AM LUCILLE, SINGER AND LEADER OF THE GRAND ORCHESTRA.
WHAT'S MORE...
...THIS LORD DOESN'T SEEM VERY POPULAR WITH HIS SUBJECTS.
...
DRIP DRIP
YOUR SON GAVE US A RATHER RUDE WELCOME! ♡
ALL THOSE BODY-GUARDS...
Lucille!
THAT'S NOT TRUE!!
MASTER ELES...
AN ONLY CHILD, FATHER?
WHAT ABOUT MY SISTER, CELES?
DON'T SPEAK THAT NAME!

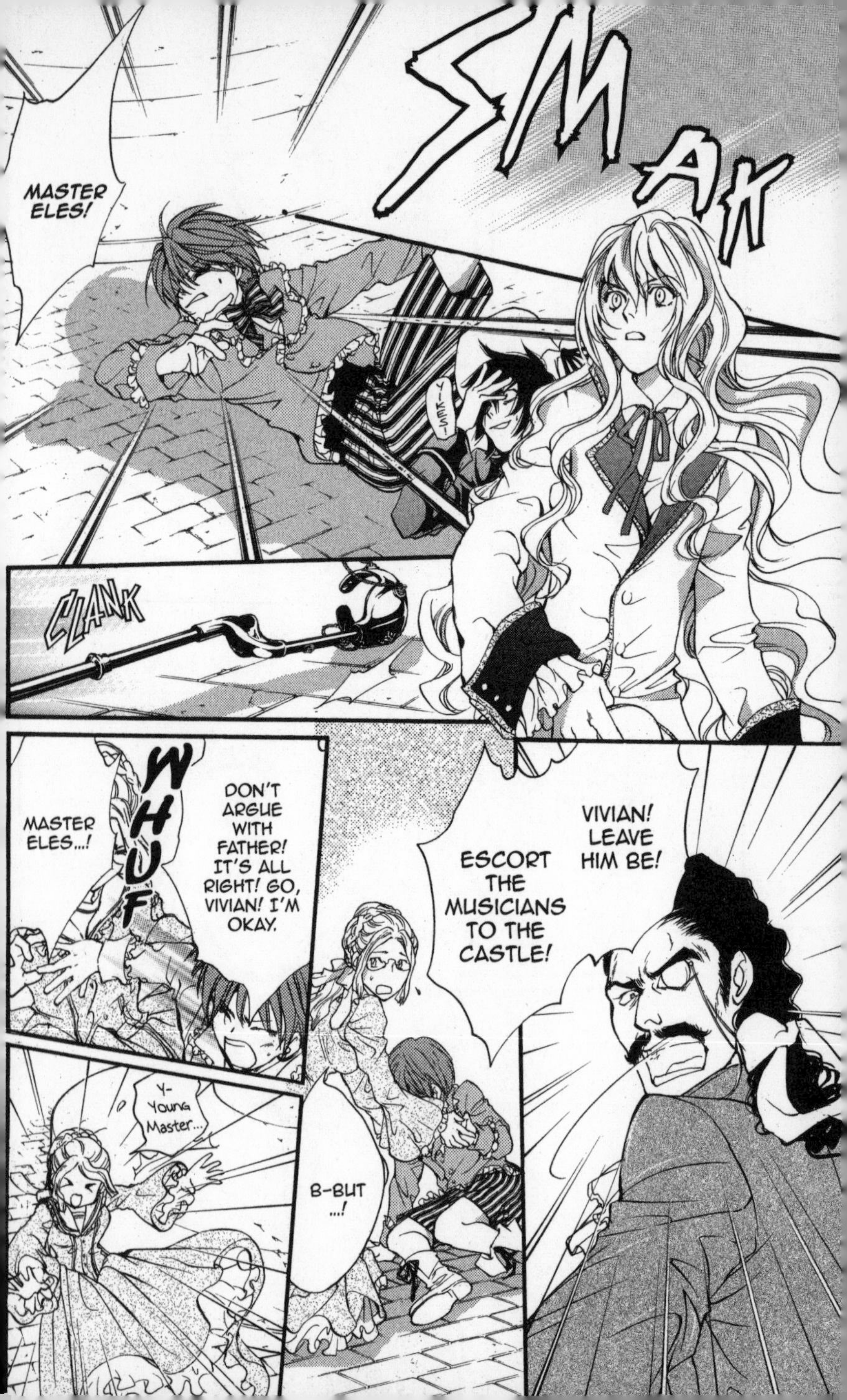
SMAK
MASTER ELES!
YIKES!
CLANK
VIVIAN! LEAVE HIM BE!
ESCORT THE MUSICIANS TO THE CASTLE!
DON'T ARGUE WITH FATHER! IT'S ALL RIGHT! GO, VIVIAN! I'M OKAY.
WHUF
MASTER ELES...!
B-BUT ...!
Y-Young Master...

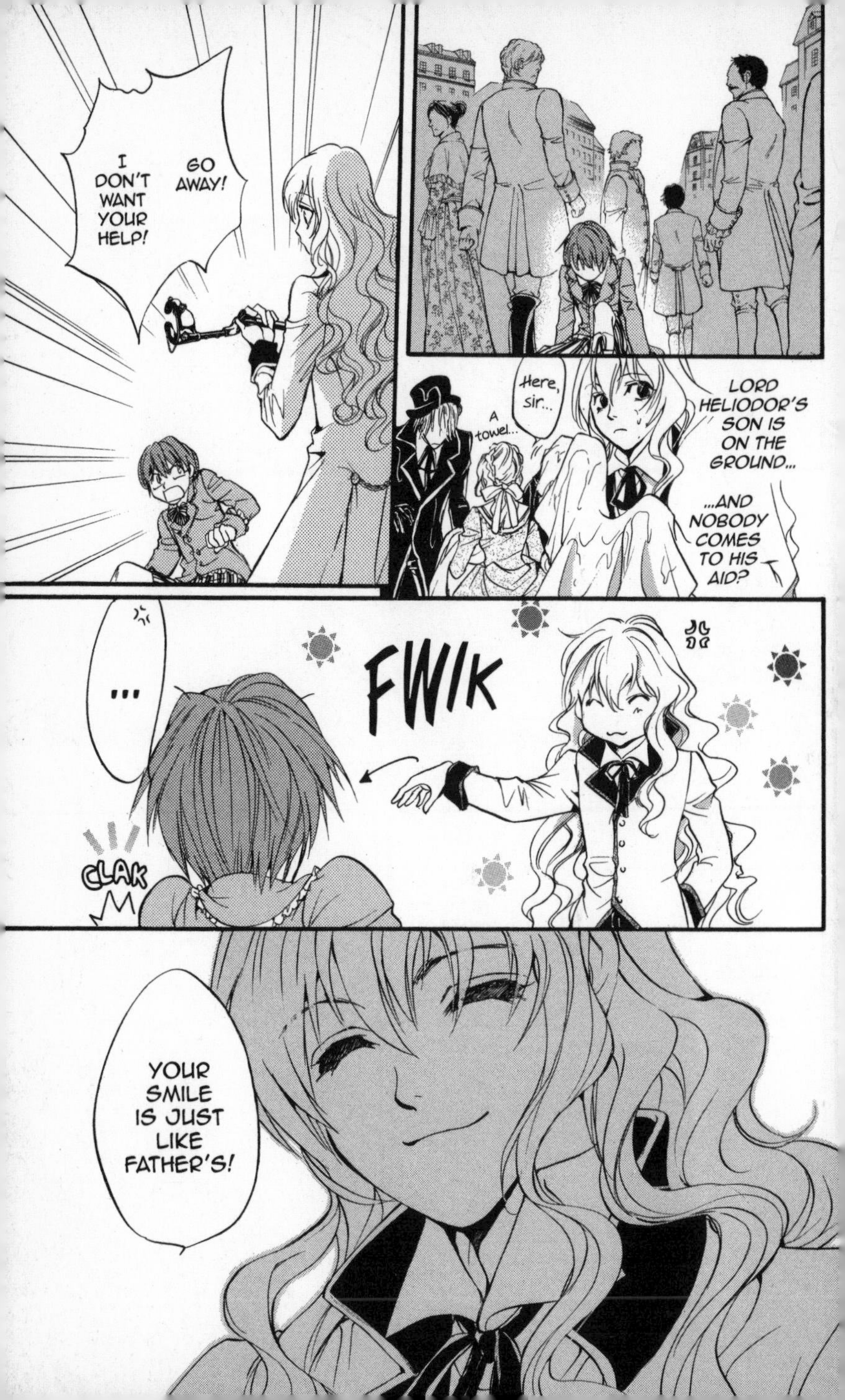
LORD HELIODOR'S SON IS ON THE GROUND...
...AND NOBODY COMES TO HIS AID?
Here, sir...
A towel...
GO AWAY!
I DON'T WANT YOUR HELP!
FWIK
...
CLAK
YOUR SMILE IS JUST LIKE FATHER'S!

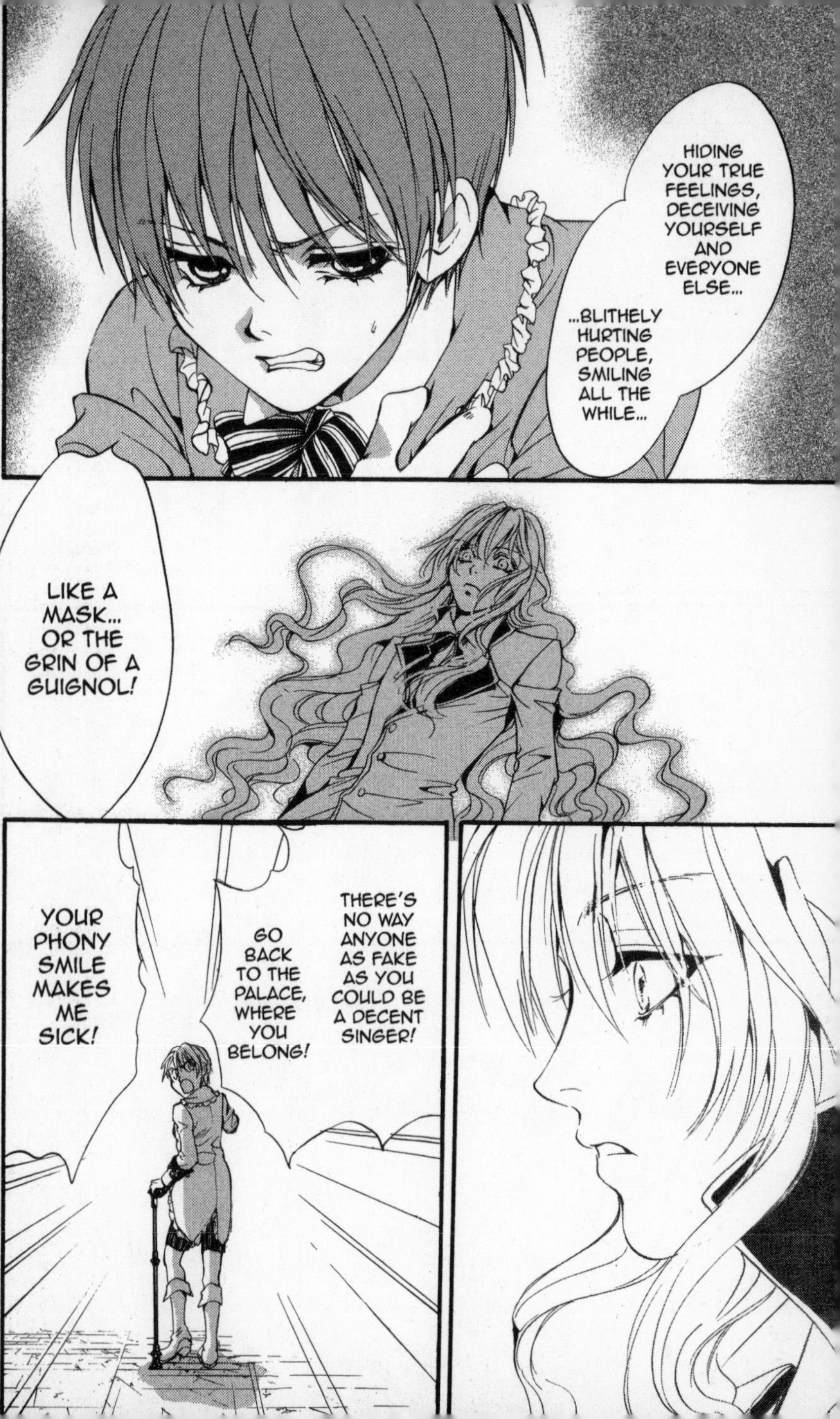
HIDING YOUR TRUE FEELINGS, DECEIVING YOURSELF AND EVERYONE ELSE...
...BLITHELY HURTING PEOPLE, SMILING ALL THE WHILE...
LIKE A MASK... OR THE GRIN OF A GUIGNOL!
THERE'S NO WAY ANYONE AS FAKE AS YOU COULD BE A DECENT SINGER!
GO BACK TO THE PALACE, WHERE YOU BELONG!
YOUR PHONY SMILE MAKES ME SICK!

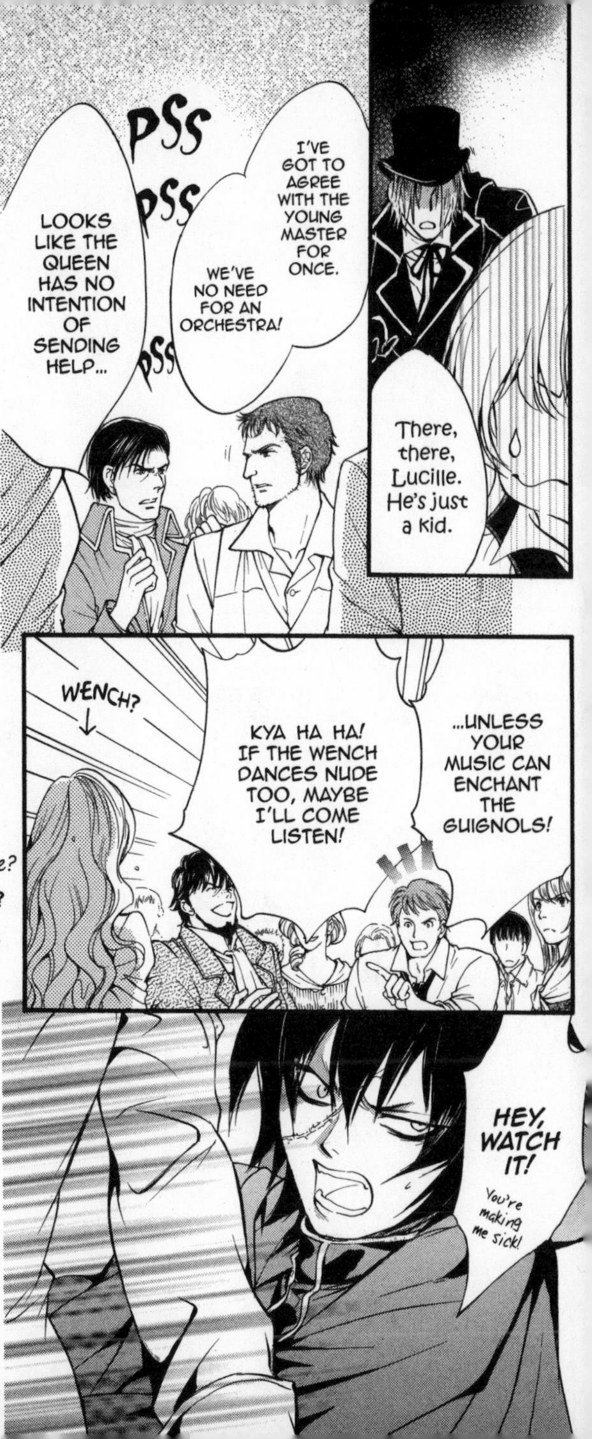
There, there, Lucille. He's just a kid.
I'VE GOT TO AGREE WITH THE YOUNG MASTER FOR ONCE.
WE'VE NO NEED FOR AN ORCHESTRA!
PSS
PSS
PSS
LOOKS LIKE THE QUEEN HAS NO INTENTION OF SENDING HELP...
...UNLESS YOUR MUSIC CAN ENCHANT THE GUIGNOLS!
KYA HA HA! IF THE WENCH DANCES NUDE TOO, MAYBE I'LL COME LISTEN!
WENCH? ↓
HEY, WATCH IT!
You're making me sick!

This is my first new volume in a while. How have you been? Thanks for reading my work again. I love you. No, really!

I have two kids. As expected, it's really hard juggling the kids, housework and work. I'm sleep deprived every day. ZZZZZ

So, this is a story about a group of traveling musicians who continue to spread songs of love in a desolate world overrun by dolls called Guignols.

...What? Is that true? Maybe? Maybe?

Well anyway, please read it.

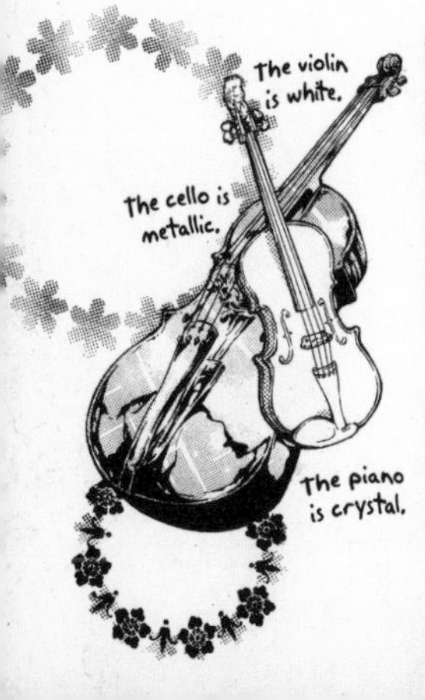
The violin is white.
The cello is metallic.
The piano is crystal.

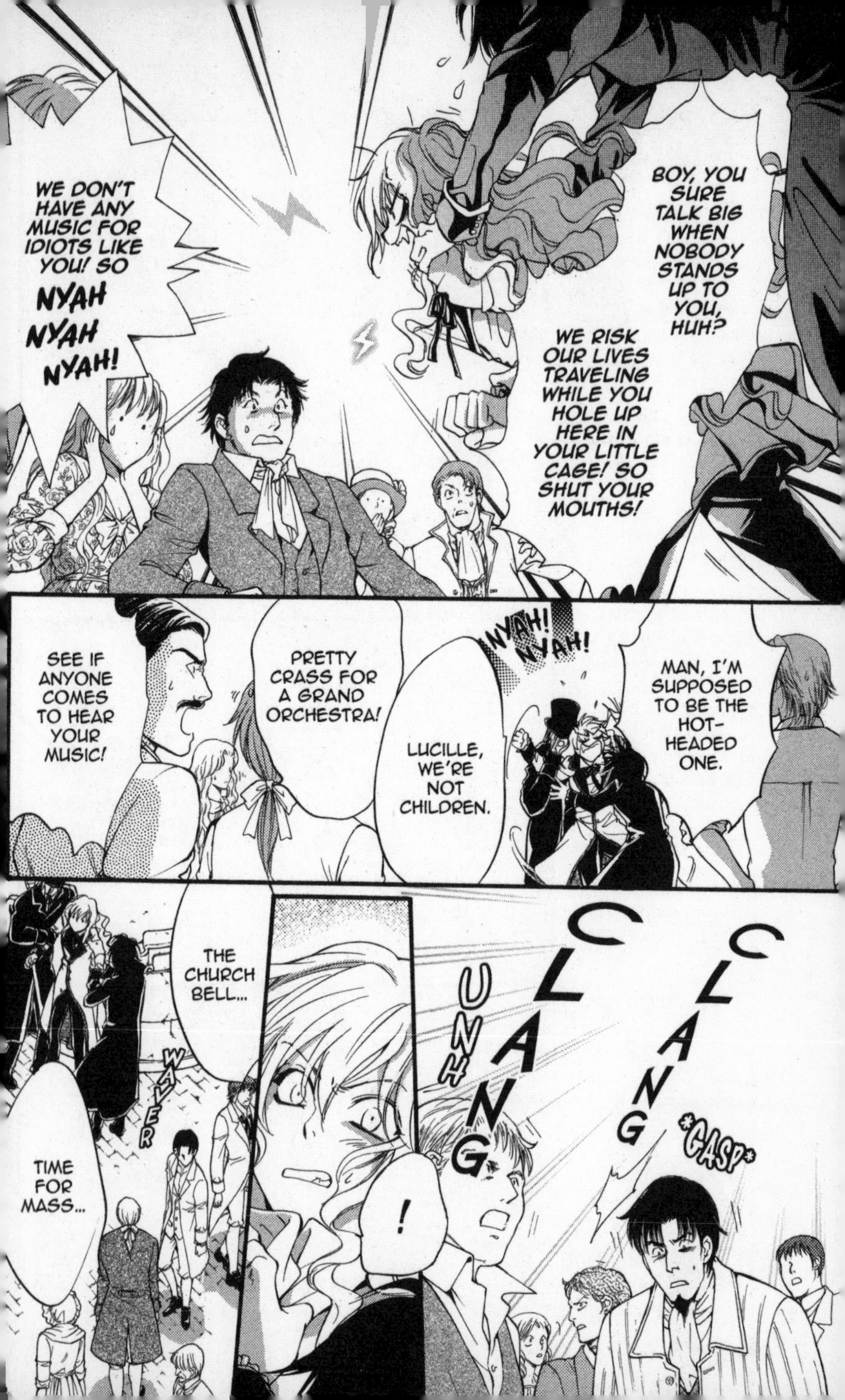
BOY, YOU SURE TALK BIG WHEN NOBODY STANDS UP TO YOU, HUH?
WE RISK OUR LIVES TRAVELING WHILE YOU HOLE UP HERE IN YOUR LITTLE CAGE! SO SHUT YOUR MOUTHS!
WE DON'T HAVE ANY MUSIC FOR IDIOTS LIKE YOU! SO NYAH NYAH NYAH!
MAN, I'M SUPPOSED TO BE THE HOT-HEADED ONE.
NYAH! NYAH!
LUCILLE, WE'RE NOT CHILDREN.
PRETTY CRASS FOR A GRAND ORCHESTRA!
SEE IF ANYONE COMES TO HEAR YOUR MUSIC!
CLANG
CLANG
GASP
UNHH
!
THE CHURCH BELL...
WAVER
TIME FOR MASS...

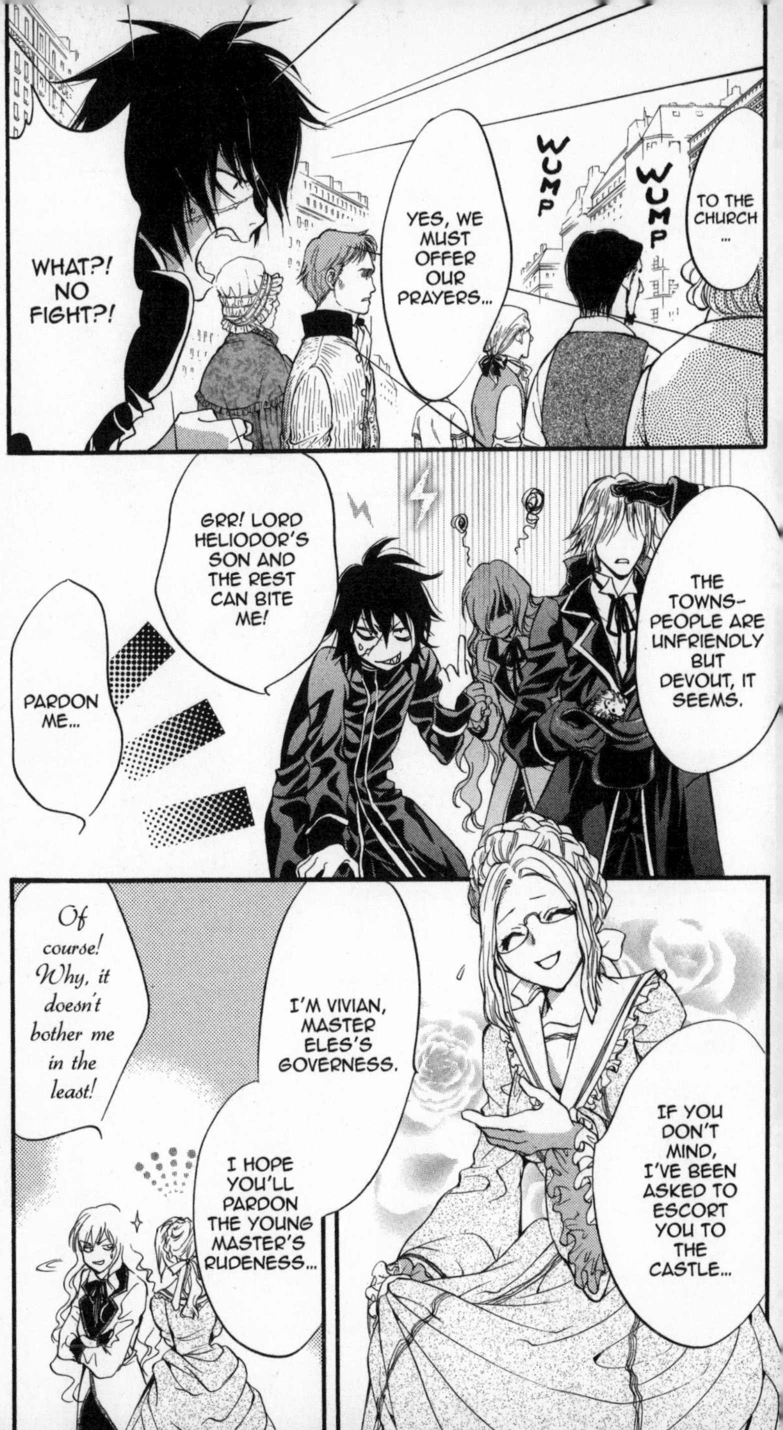
TO THE CHURCH ...
WUMP
WUMP
YES, WE MUST OFFER OUR PRAYERS...
WHAT?! NO FIGHT?!
THE TOWNS-PEOPLE ARE UNFRIENDLY BUT DEVOUT, IT SEEMS.
GRR! LORD HELIODOR'S SON AND THE REST CAN BITE ME!
PARDON ME...
IF YOU DON'T MIND, I'VE BEEN ASKED TO ESCORT YOU TO THE CASTLE...
I'M VIVIAN, MASTER ELES'S GOVERNESS.
I HOPE YOU'LL PARDON THE YOUNG MASTER'S RUDENESS...
Of course! Why, it doesn't bother me in the least!

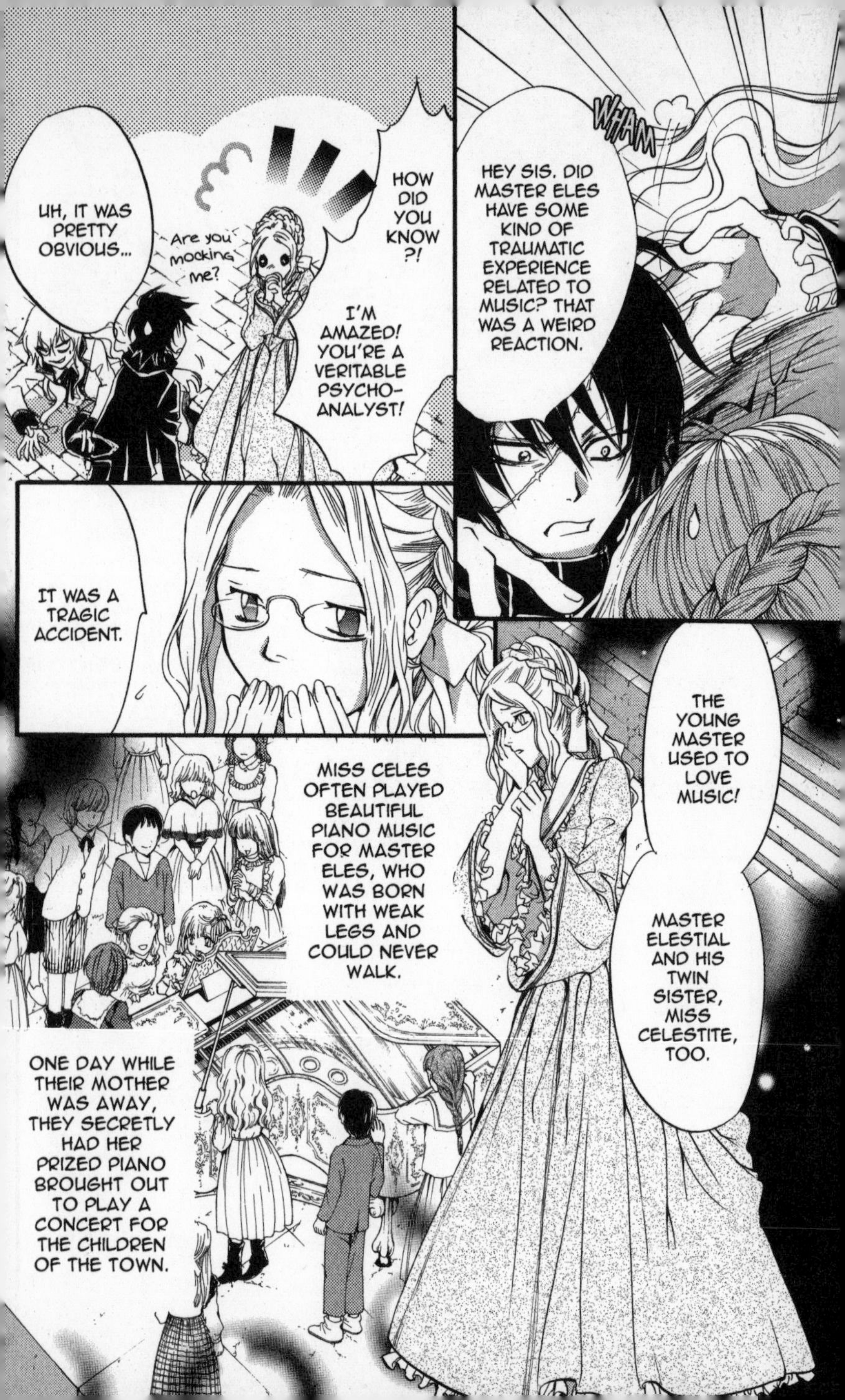
WHAM
HEY SIS. DID MASTER ELES HAVE SOME KIND OF TRAUMATIC EXPERIENCE RELATED TO MUSIC? THAT WAS A WEIRD REACTION.
HOW DID YOU KNOW?!
I'M AMAZED! YOU'RE A VERITABLE PSYCHO-ANALYST!
UH, IT WAS PRETTY OBVIOUS...
Are you mocking me?
IT WAS A TRAGIC ACCIDENT.
THE YOUNG MASTER USED TO LOVE MUSIC!
MASTER ELESTIAL AND HIS TWIN SISTER, MISS CELESTITE, TOO.
MISS CELES OFTEN PLAYED BEAUTIFUL PIANO MUSIC FOR MASTER ELES, WHO WAS BORN WITH WEAK LEGS AND COULD NEVER WALK.
ONE DAY WHILE THEIR MOTHER WAS AWAY, THEY SECRETLY HAD HER PRIZED PIANO BROUGHT OUT TO PLAY A CONCERT FOR THE CHILDREN OF THE TOWN.

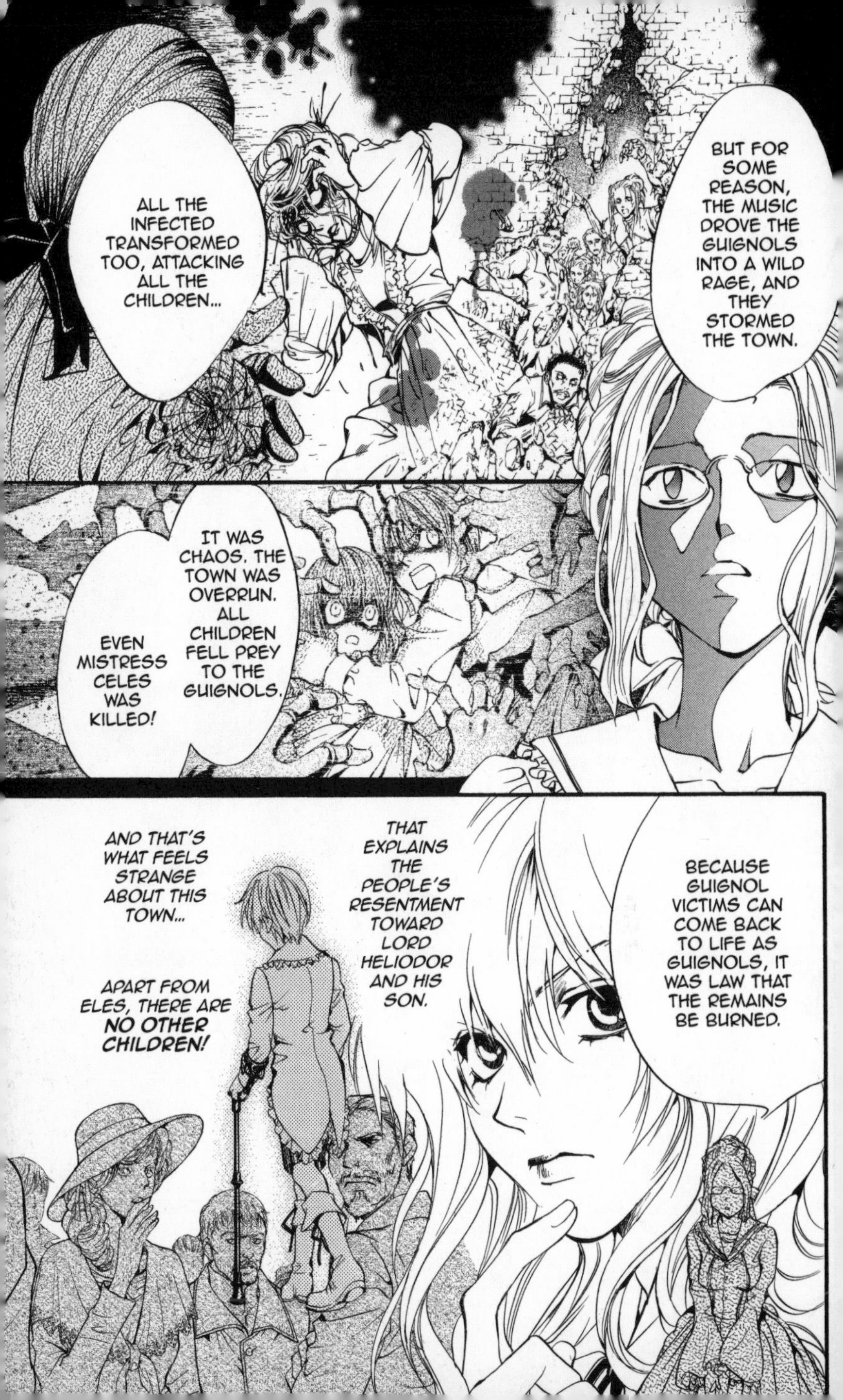
BUT FOR SOME REASON, THE MUSIC DROVE THE GUIGNOLS INTO A WILD RAGE, AND THEY STORMED THE TOWN.
ALL THE INFECTED TRANSFORMED TOO, ATTACKING ALL THE CHILDREN...
IT WAS CHAOS. THE TOWN WAS OVERRUN. ALL CHILDREN FELL PREY TO THE GUIGNOLS.
EVEN MISTRESS CELES WAS KILLED!
BECAUSE GUIGNOL VICTIMS CAN COME BACK TO LIFE AS GUIGNOLS, IT WAS LAW THAT THE REMAINS BE BURNED.
THAT EXPLAINS THE PEOPLE'S RESENTMENT TOWARD LORD HELIODOR AND HIS SON.
AND THAT'S WHAT FEELS STRANGE ABOUT THIS TOWN...
APART FROM ELES, THERE ARE **NO OTHER CHILDREN!**

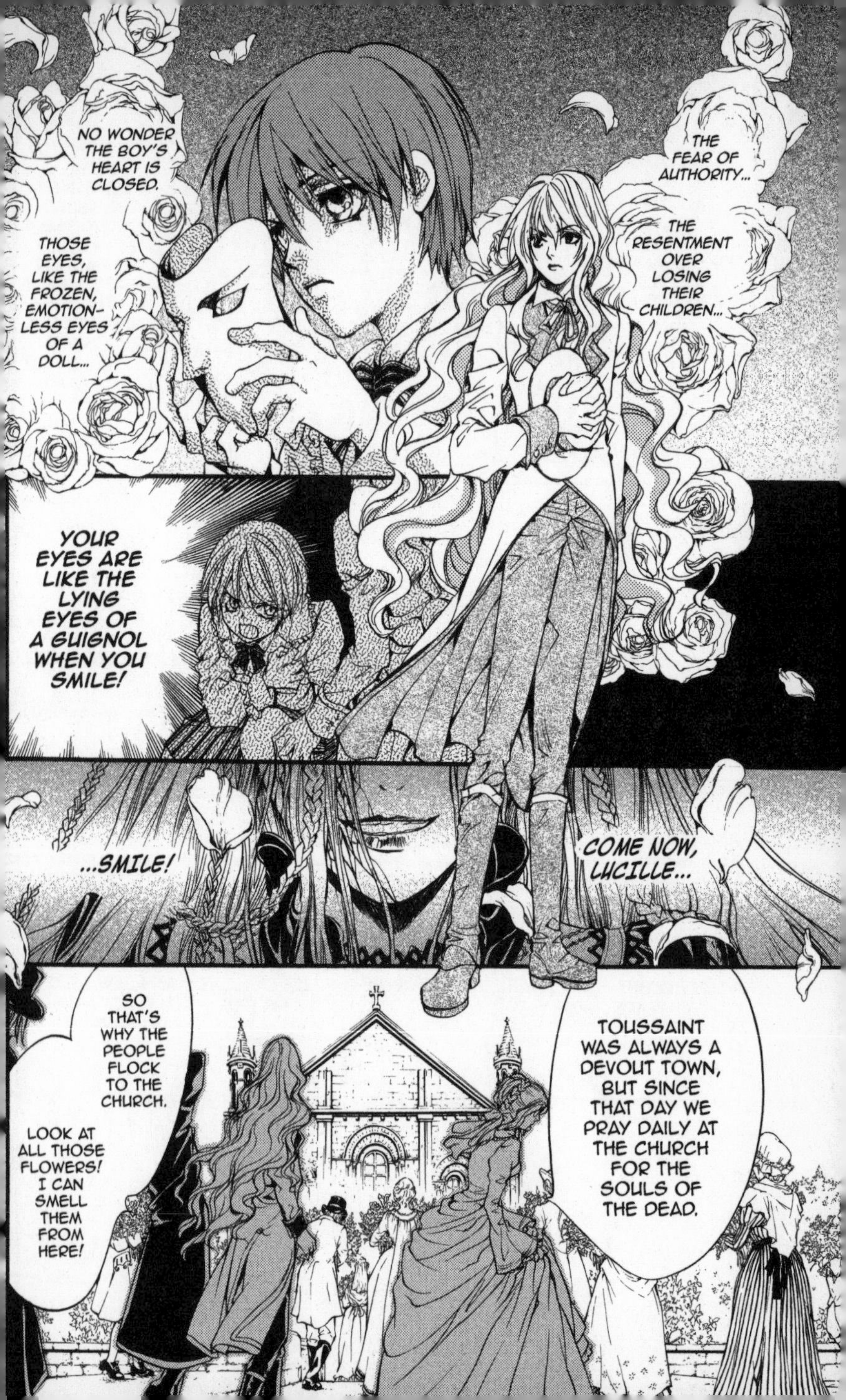
THE FEAR OF AUTHORITY...
THE RESENTMENT OVER LOSING THEIR CHILDREN...
NO WONDER THE BOY'S HEART IS CLOSED.
THOSE EYES, LIKE THE FROZEN, EMOTIONLESS EYES OF A DOLL...
YOUR EYES ARE LIKE THE LYING EYES OF A GUIGNOL WHEN YOU SMILE!
COME NOW, LUCILLE...
...SMILE!
TOUSSAINT WAS ALWAYS A DEVOUT TOWN, BUT SINCE THAT DAY WE PRAY DAILY AT THE CHURCH FOR THE SOULS OF THE DEAD.
SO THAT'S WHY THE PEOPLE FLOCK TO THE CHURCH.
LOOK AT ALL THOSE FLOWERS! I CAN SMELL THEM FROM HERE!

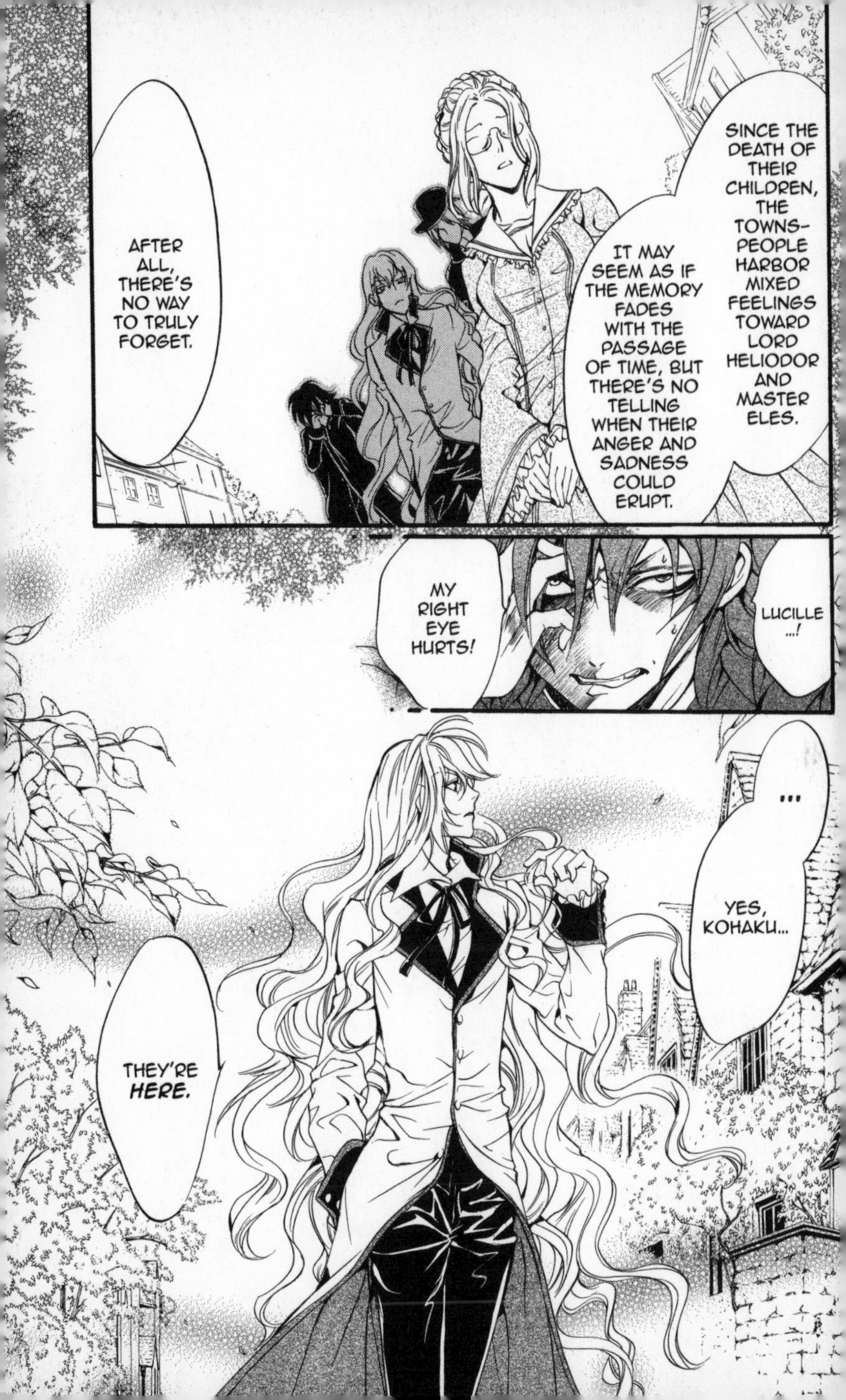
SINCE THE DEATH OF THEIR CHILDREN, THE TOWNSPEOPLE HARBOR MIXED FEELINGS TOWARD LORD HELIODOR AND MASTER ELES.
IT MAY SEEM AS IF THE MEMORY FADES WITH THE PASSAGE OF TIME, BUT THERE'S NO TELLING WHEN THEIR ANGER AND SADNESS COULD ERUPT.
AFTER ALL, THERE'S NO WAY TO TRULY FORGET.
LUCILLE ...!
MY RIGHT EYE HURTS!
...
YES, KOHAKU...
THEY'RE *HERE.*

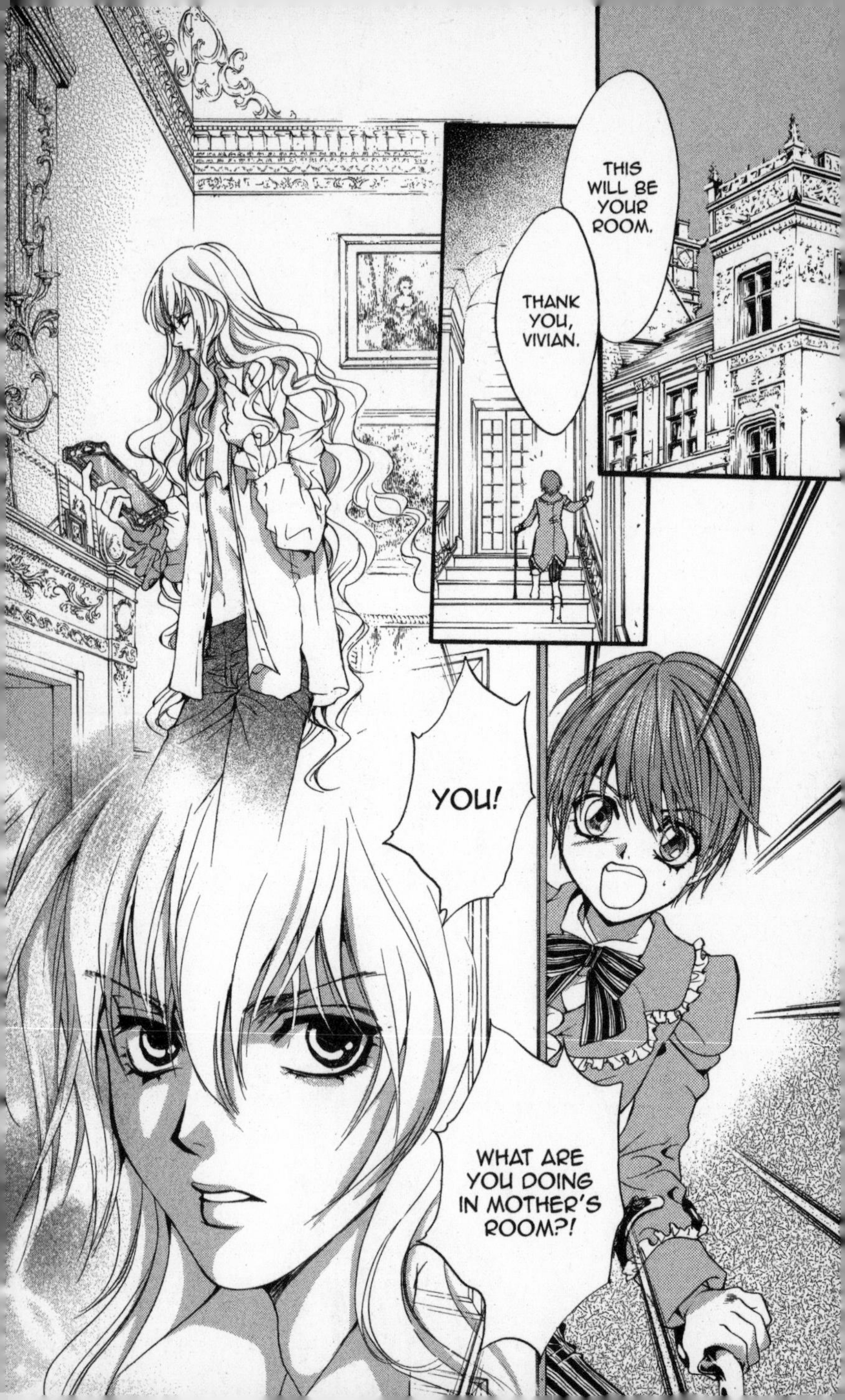
THIS WILL BE YOUR ROOM.
THANK YOU, VIVIAN.
YOU!
WHAT ARE YOU DOING IN MOTHER'S ROOM?!

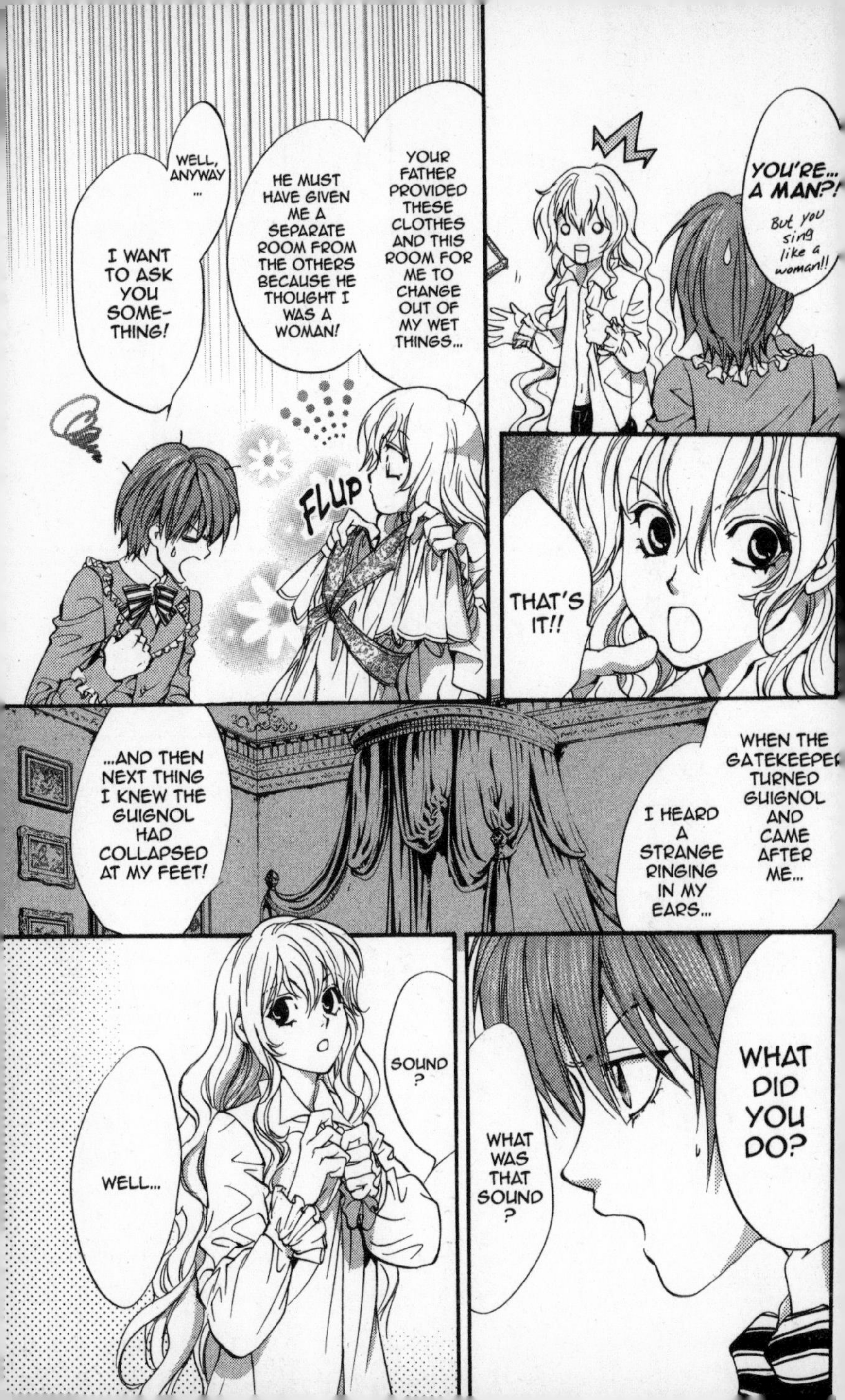
YOU'RE... A MAN?!
But you sing like a woman!!
THAT'S IT!!
YOUR FATHER PROVIDED THESE CLOTHES AND THIS ROOM FOR ME TO CHANGE OUT OF MY WET THINGS...
HE MUST HAVE GIVEN ME A SEPARATE ROOM FROM THE OTHERS BECAUSE HE THOUGHT I WAS A WOMAN!
WELL, ANYWAY ...
I WANT TO ASK YOU SOME-THING!
FLUP
WHEN THE GATEKEEPER TURNED GUIGNOL AND CAME AFTER ME...
I HEARD A STRANGE RINGING IN MY EARS...
...AND THEN NEXT THING I KNEW THE GUIGNOL HAD COLLAPSED AT MY FEET!
WHAT DID YOU DO?
WHAT WAS THAT SOUND ?
SOUND ?
WELL...

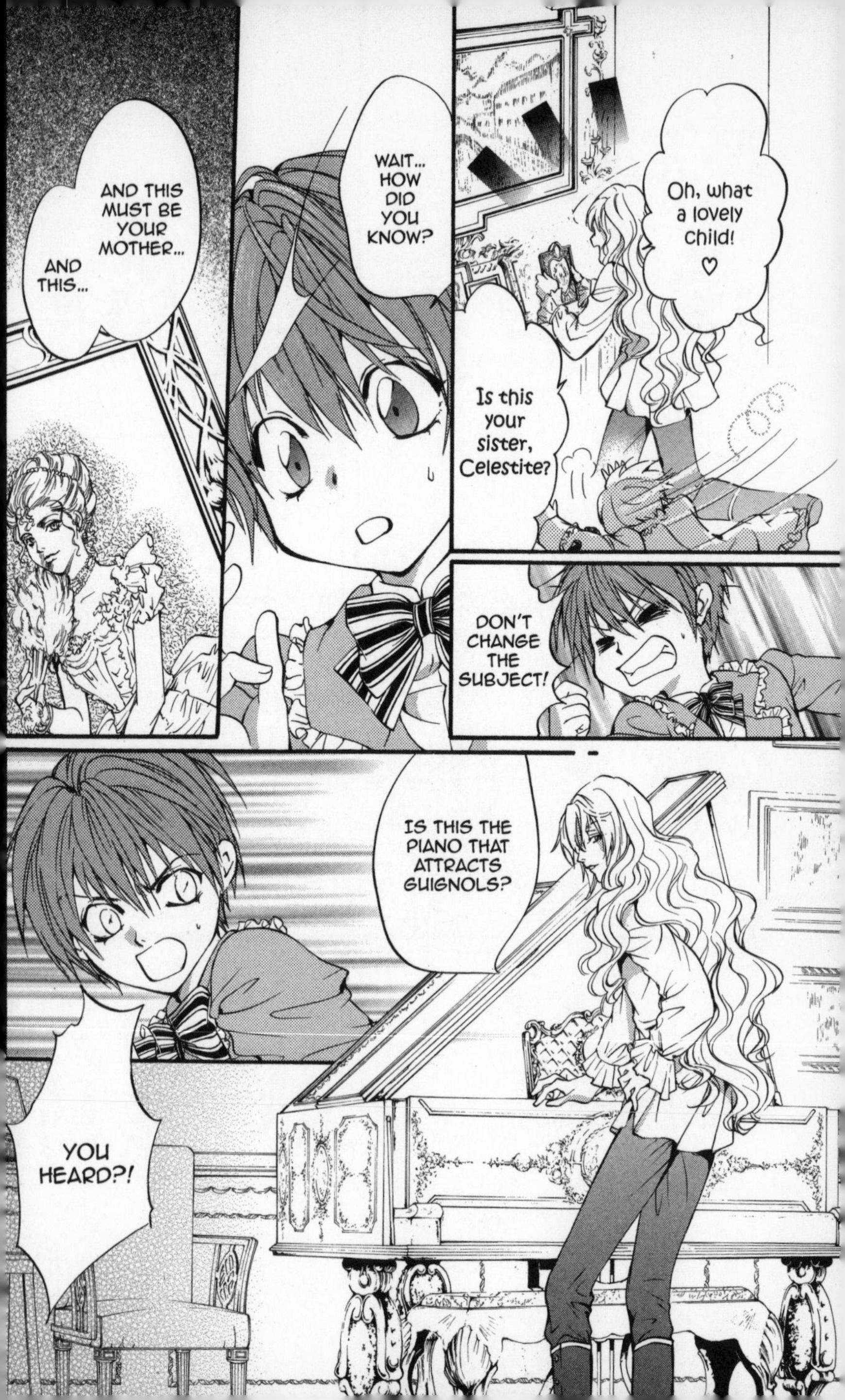
Oh, what a lovely child! ♡
Is this your sister, Celestite?
DON'T CHANGE THE SUBJECT!
WAIT... HOW DID YOU KNOW?
AND THIS MUST BE YOUR MOTHER...
AND THIS...
IS THIS THE PIANO THAT ATTRACTS GUIGNOLS?
YOU HEARD?!

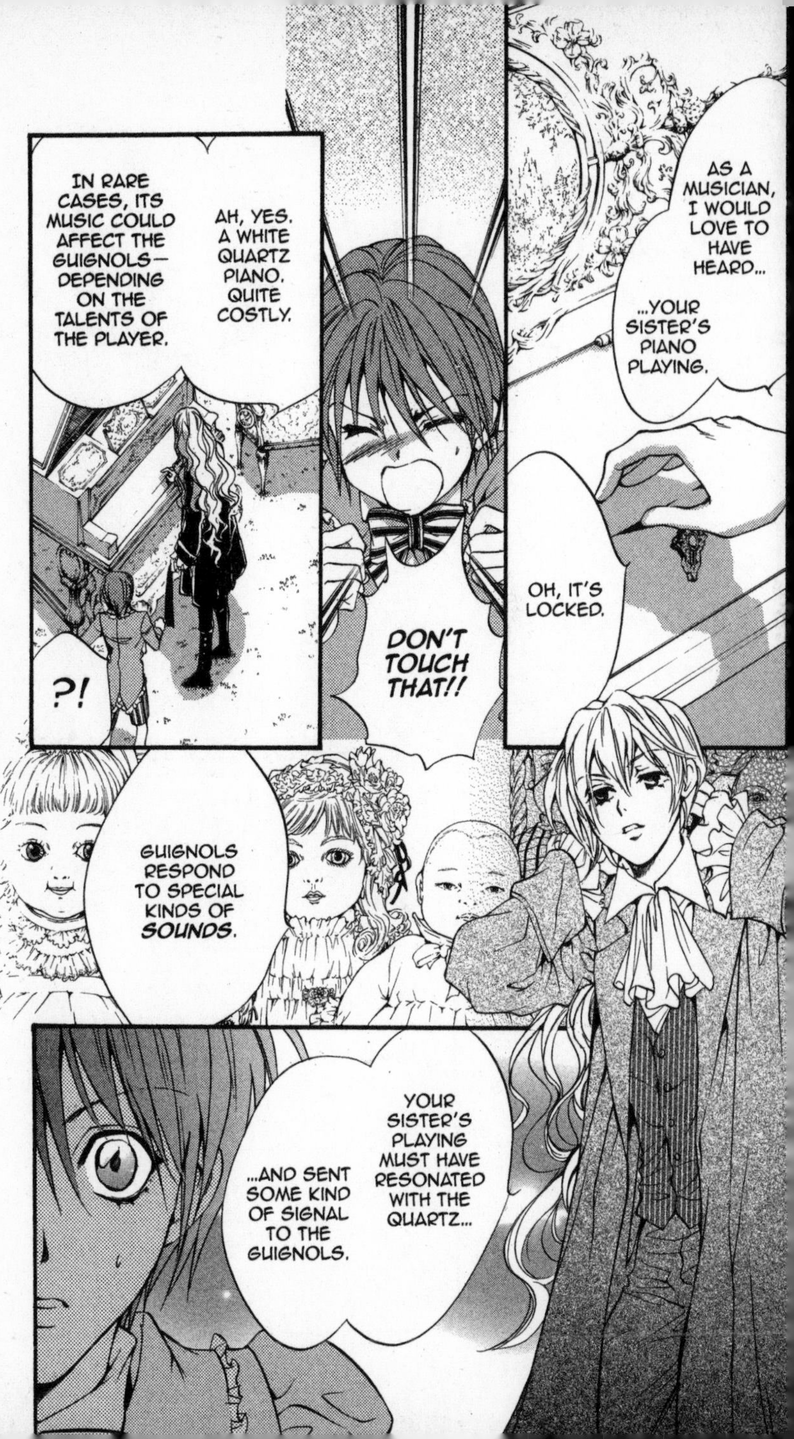
AS A MUSICIAN, I WOULD LOVE TO HAVE HEARD...
...YOUR SISTER'S PIANO PLAYING.
OH, IT'S LOCKED.
DON'T TOUCH THAT!!
AH, YES. A WHITE QUARTZ PIANO. QUITE COSTLY.
IN RARE CASES, ITS MUSIC COULD AFFECT THE GUIGNOLS—DEPENDING ON THE TALENTS OF THE PLAYER.
?!
GUIGNOLS RESPOND TO SPECIAL KINDS OF SOUNDS.
YOUR SISTER'S PLAYING MUST HAVE RESONATED WITH THE QUARTZ...
...AND SENT SOME KIND OF SIGNAL TO THE GUIGNOLS.

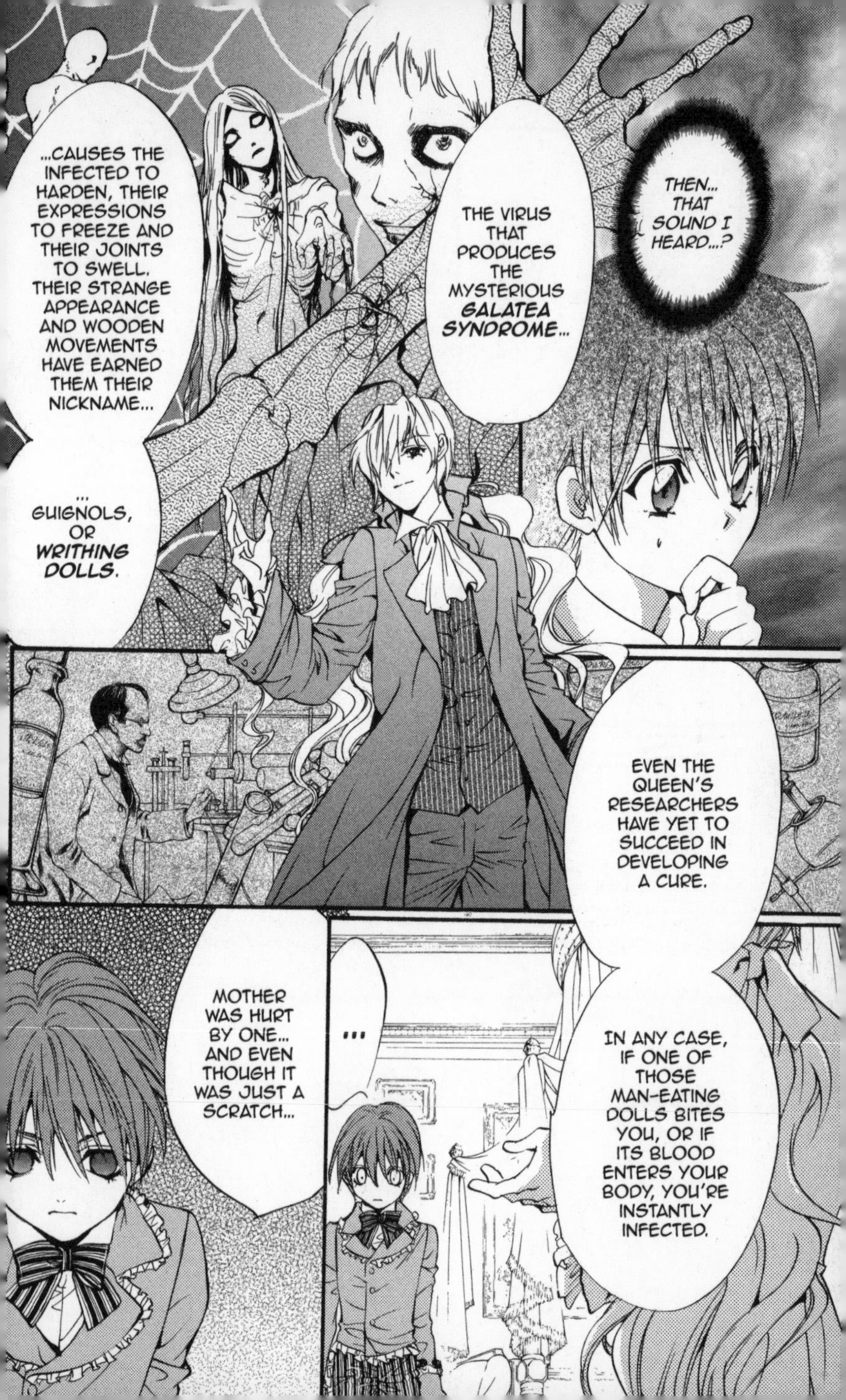
THEN... THAT SOUND I HEARD...?
THE VIRUS THAT PRODUCES THE MYSTERIOUS *GALATEA SYNDROME*...
...CAUSES THE INFECTED TO HARDEN, THEIR EXPRESSIONS TO FREEZE AND THEIR JOINTS TO SWELL. THEIR STRANGE APPEARANCE AND WOODEN MOVEMENTS HAVE EARNED THEM THEIR NICKNAME...
... GUIGNOLS, OR *WRITHING DOLLS*.
EVEN THE QUEEN'S RESEARCHERS HAVE YET TO SUCCEED IN DEVELOPING A CURE.
IN ANY CASE, IF ONE OF THOSE MAN-EATING DOLLS BITES YOU, OR IF ITS BLOOD ENTERS YOUR BODY, YOU'RE INSTANTLY INFECTED.
...
MOTHER WAS HURT BY ONE... AND EVEN THOUGH IT WAS JUST A SCRATCH...

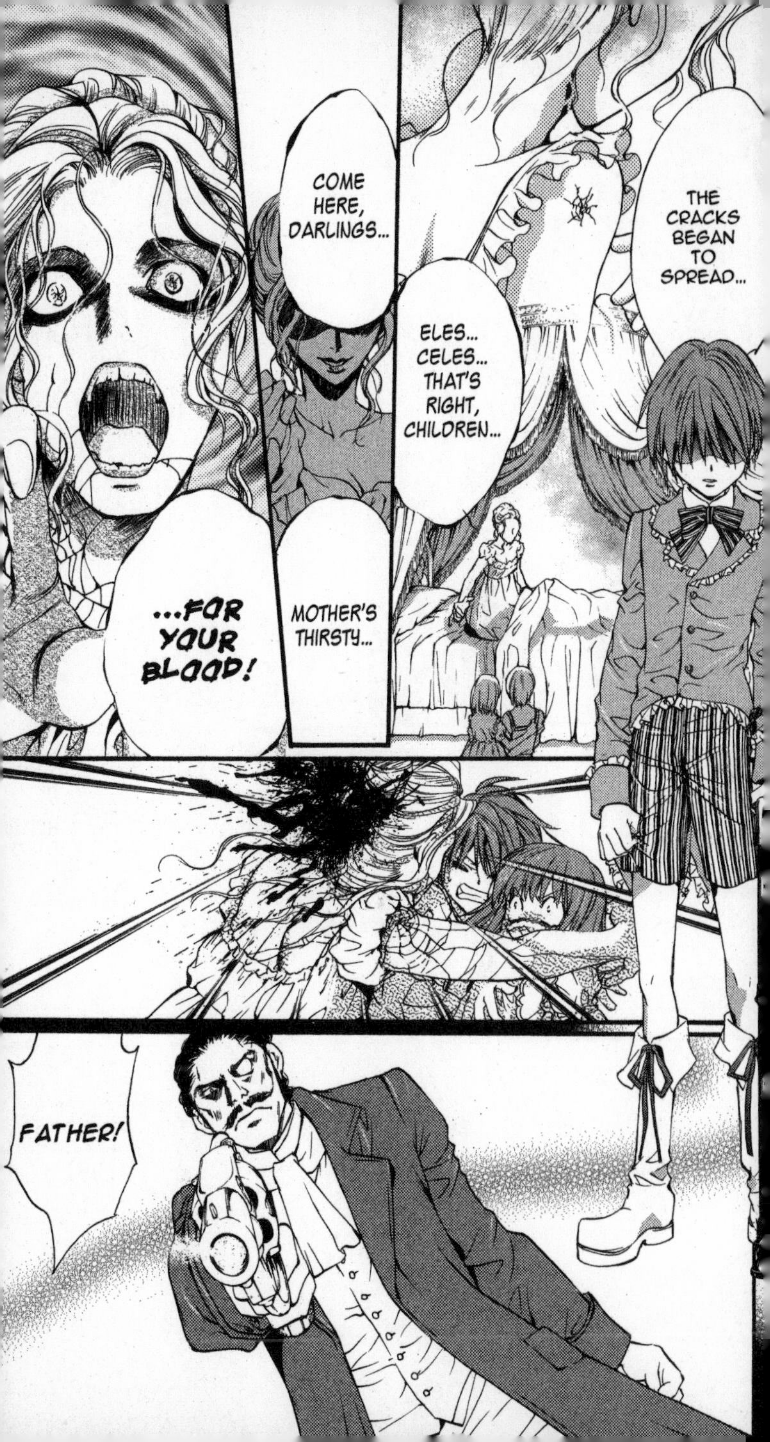
THE CRACKS BEGAN TO SPREAD...
ELES... CELES... THAT'S RIGHT, CHILDREN...
COME HERE, DARLINGS...
MOTHER'S THIRSTY...
...FOR YOUR BLOOD!
FATHER!

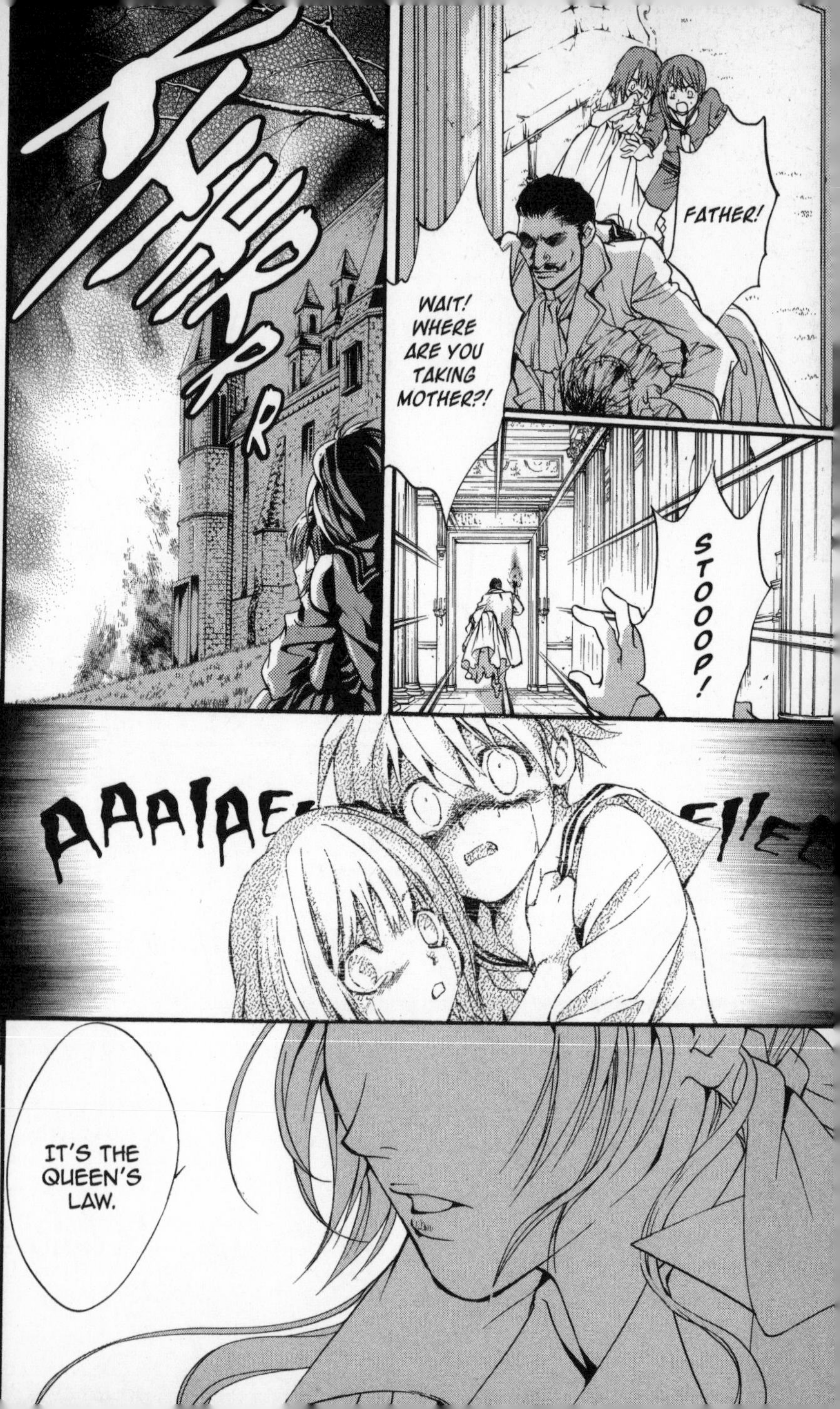
FATHER!
WAIT! WHERE ARE YOU TAKING MOTHER?!
STOOOOP!
AAAIAE
IT'S THE QUEEN'S LAW.

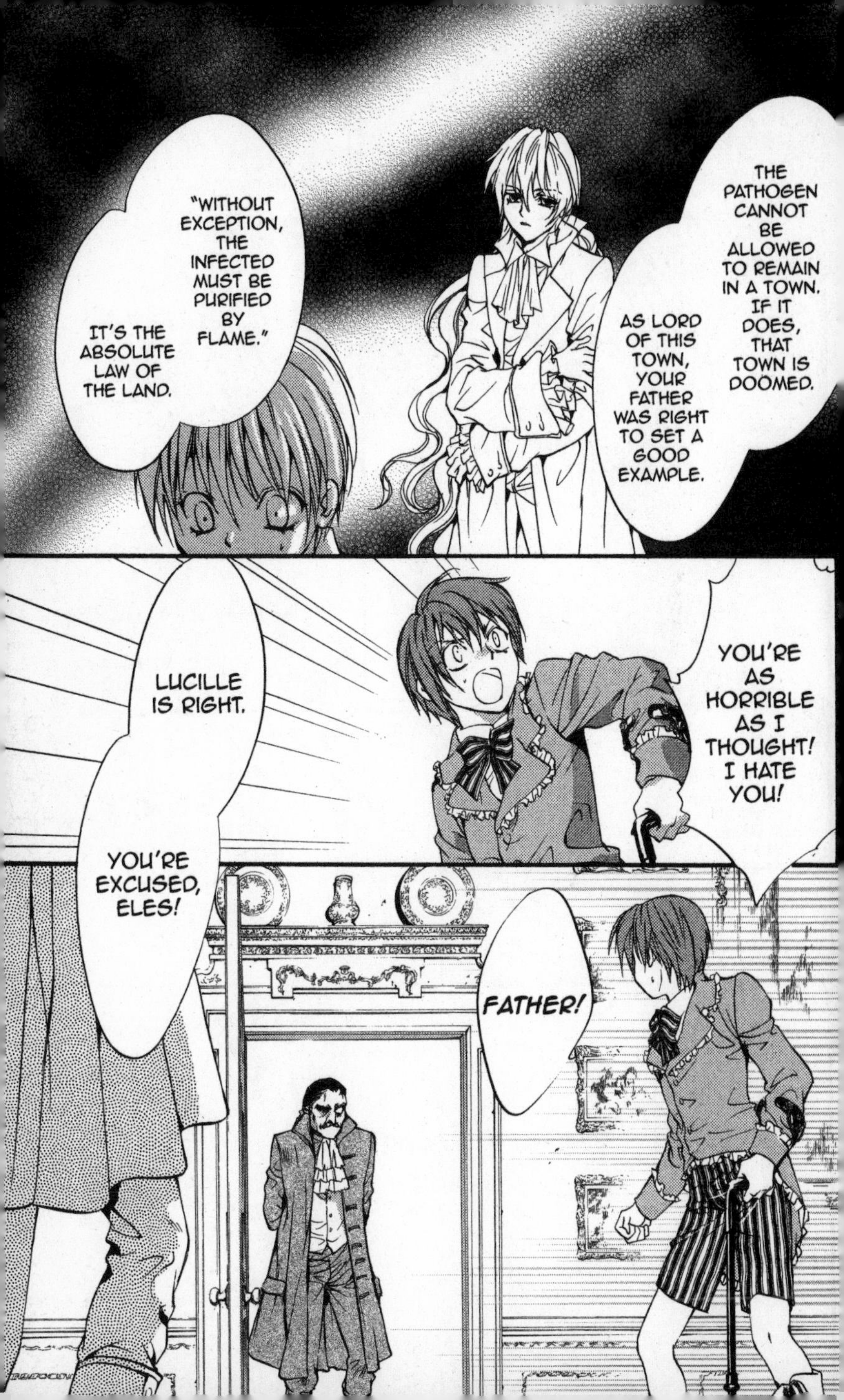
THE PATHOGEN CANNOT BE ALLOWED TO REMAIN IN A TOWN. IF IT DOES, THAT TOWN IS DOOMED.
AS LORD OF THIS TOWN, YOUR FATHER WAS RIGHT TO SET A GOOD EXAMPLE.
"WITHOUT EXCEPTION, THE INFECTED MUST BE PURIFIED BY FLAME."
IT'S THE ABSOLUTE LAW OF THE LAND.
YOU'RE AS HORRIBLE AS I THOUGHT! I HATE YOU!
LUCILLE IS RIGHT.
YOU'RE EXCUSED, ELES!
FATHER!

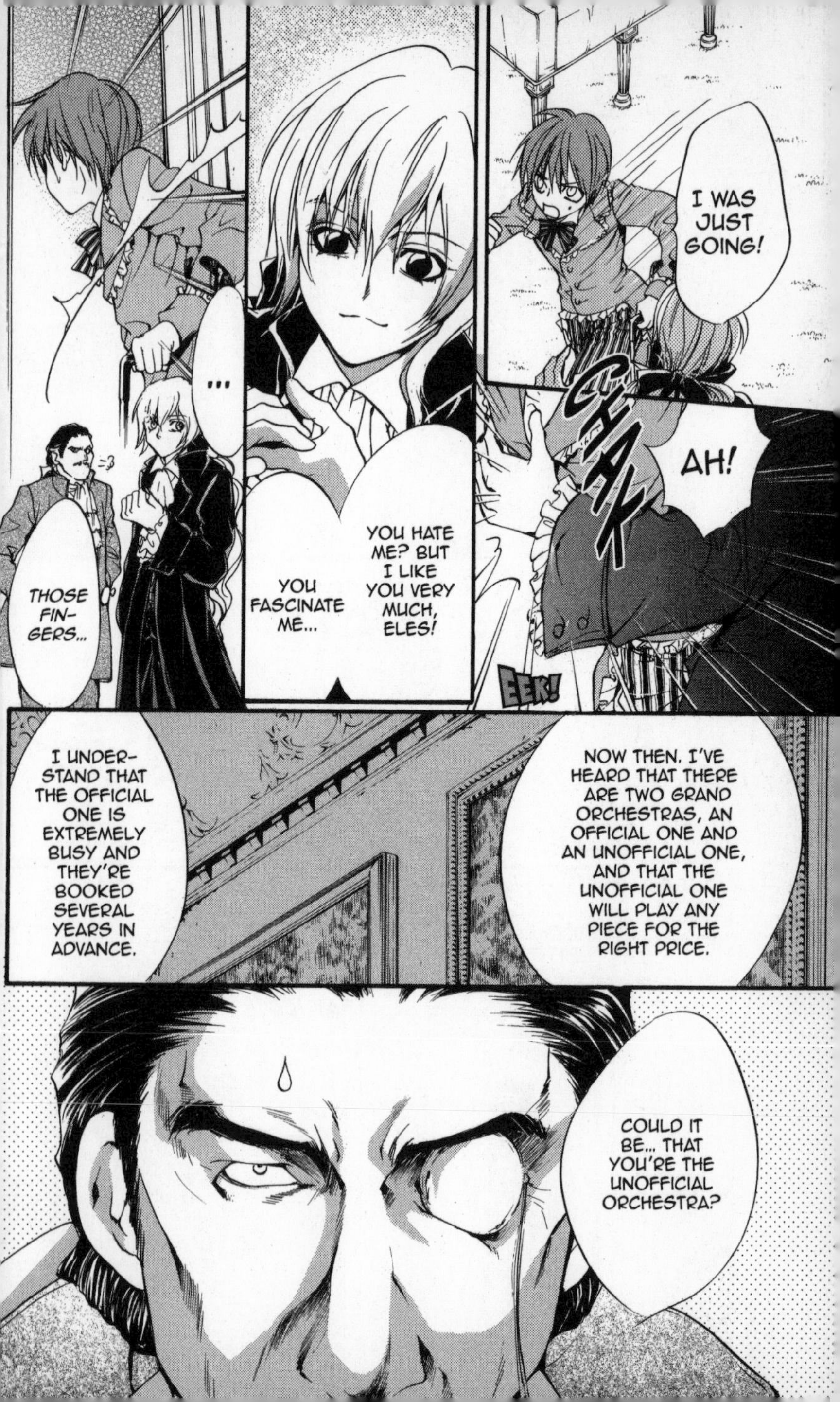
I WAS JUST GOING!
CHAK
AH!
EEK!
YOU HATE ME? BUT I LIKE YOU VERY MUCH, ELES!
YOU FASCINATE ME...
...
THOSE FIN-GERS...
NOW THEN. I'VE HEARD THAT THERE ARE TWO GRAND ORCHESTRAS, AN OFFICIAL ONE AND AN UNOFFICIAL ONE, AND THAT THE UNOFFICIAL ONE WILL PLAY ANY PIECE FOR THE RIGHT PRICE.
I UNDER-STAND THAT THE OFFICIAL ONE IS EXTREMELY BUSY AND THEY'RE BOOKED SEVERAL YEARS IN ADVANCE.
COULD IT BE... THAT YOU'RE THE UNOFFICIAL ORCHESTRA?

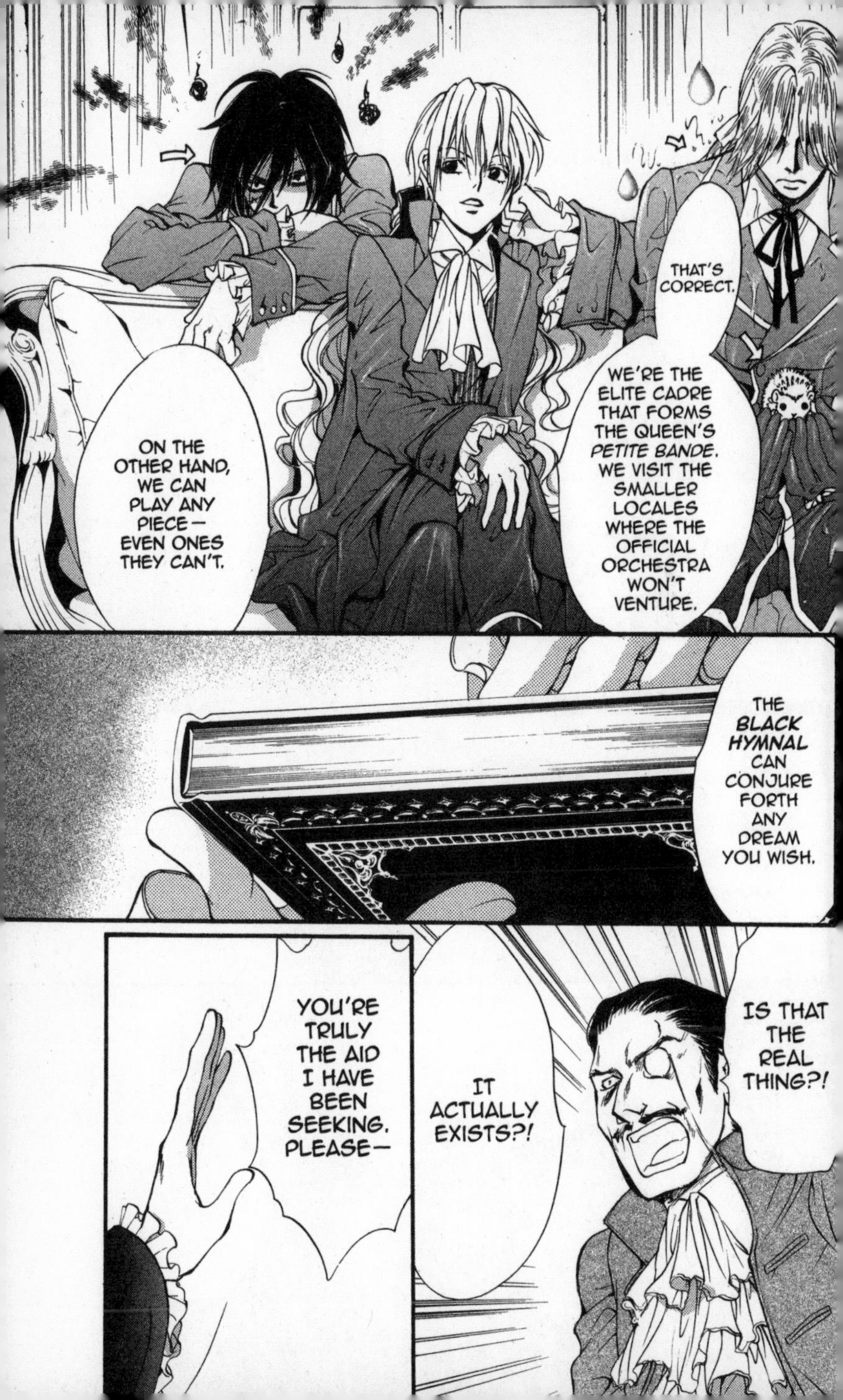
THAT'S CORRECT.
WE'RE THE ELITE CADRE THAT FORMS THE QUEEN'S *PETITE BANDE*. WE VISIT THE SMALLER LOCALES WHERE THE OFFICIAL ORCHESTRA WON'T VENTURE.
ON THE OTHER HAND, WE CAN PLAY ANY PIECE—EVEN ONES THEY CAN'T.
THE ***BLACK HYMNAL*** CAN CONJURE FORTH ANY DREAM YOU WISH.
IS THAT THE REAL THING?!
IT ACTUALLY EXISTS?!
YOU'RE TRULY THE AID I HAVE BEEN SEEKING. PLEASE—

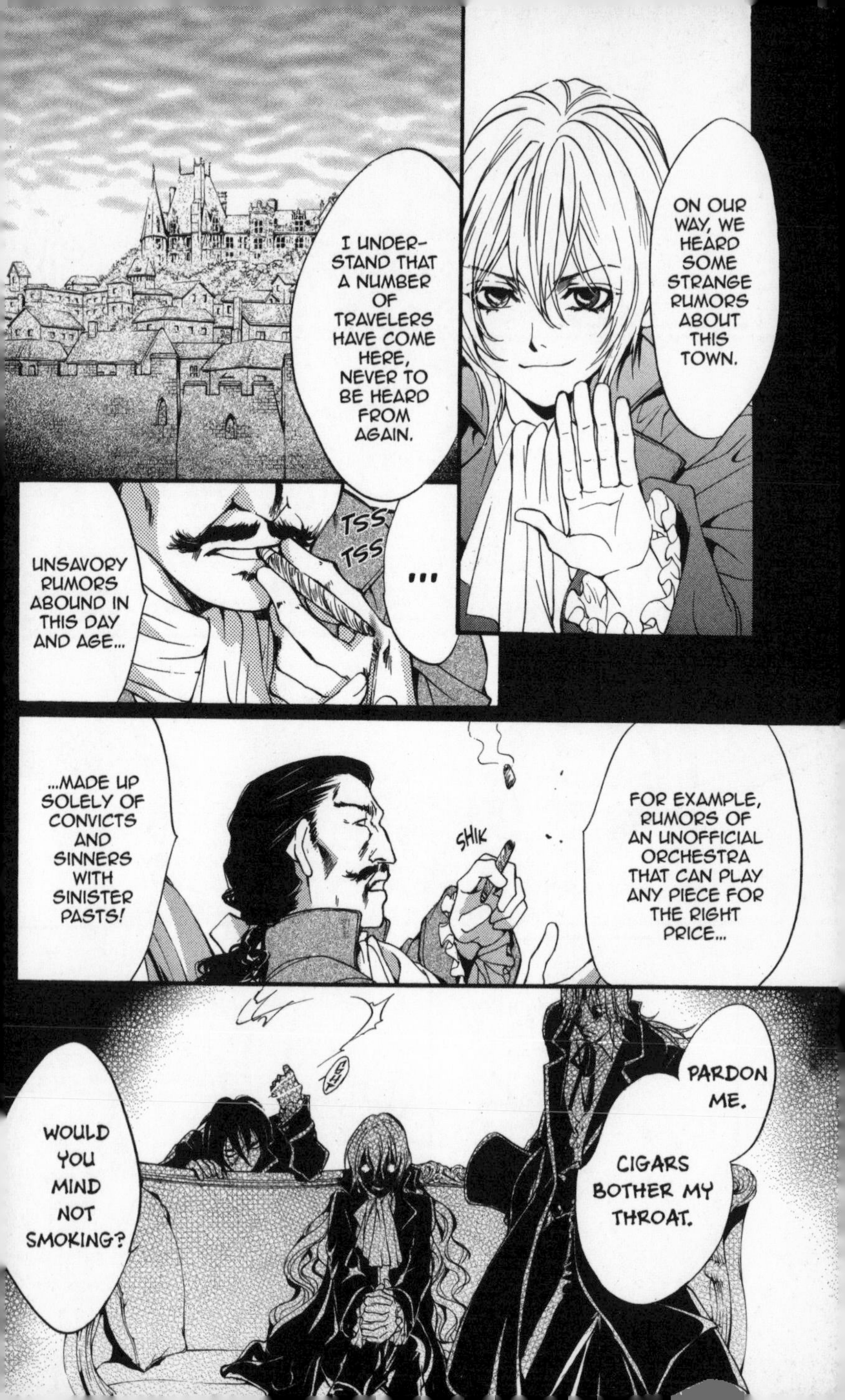
ON OUR WAY, WE HEARD SOME STRANGE RUMORS ABOUT THIS TOWN.
I UNDER-STAND THAT A NUMBER OF TRAVELERS HAVE COME HERE, NEVER TO BE HEARD FROM AGAIN.
TSS TSS
...
UNSAVORY RUMORS ABOUND IN THIS DAY AND AGE...
FOR EXAMPLE, RUMORS OF AN UNOFFICIAL ORCHESTRA THAT CAN PLAY ANY PIECE FOR THE RIGHT PRICE...
SHIK
...MADE UP SOLELY OF CONVICTS AND SINNERS WITH SINISTER PASTS!
PARDON ME.
CIGARS BOTHER MY THROAT.
WOULD YOU MIND NOT SMOKING?

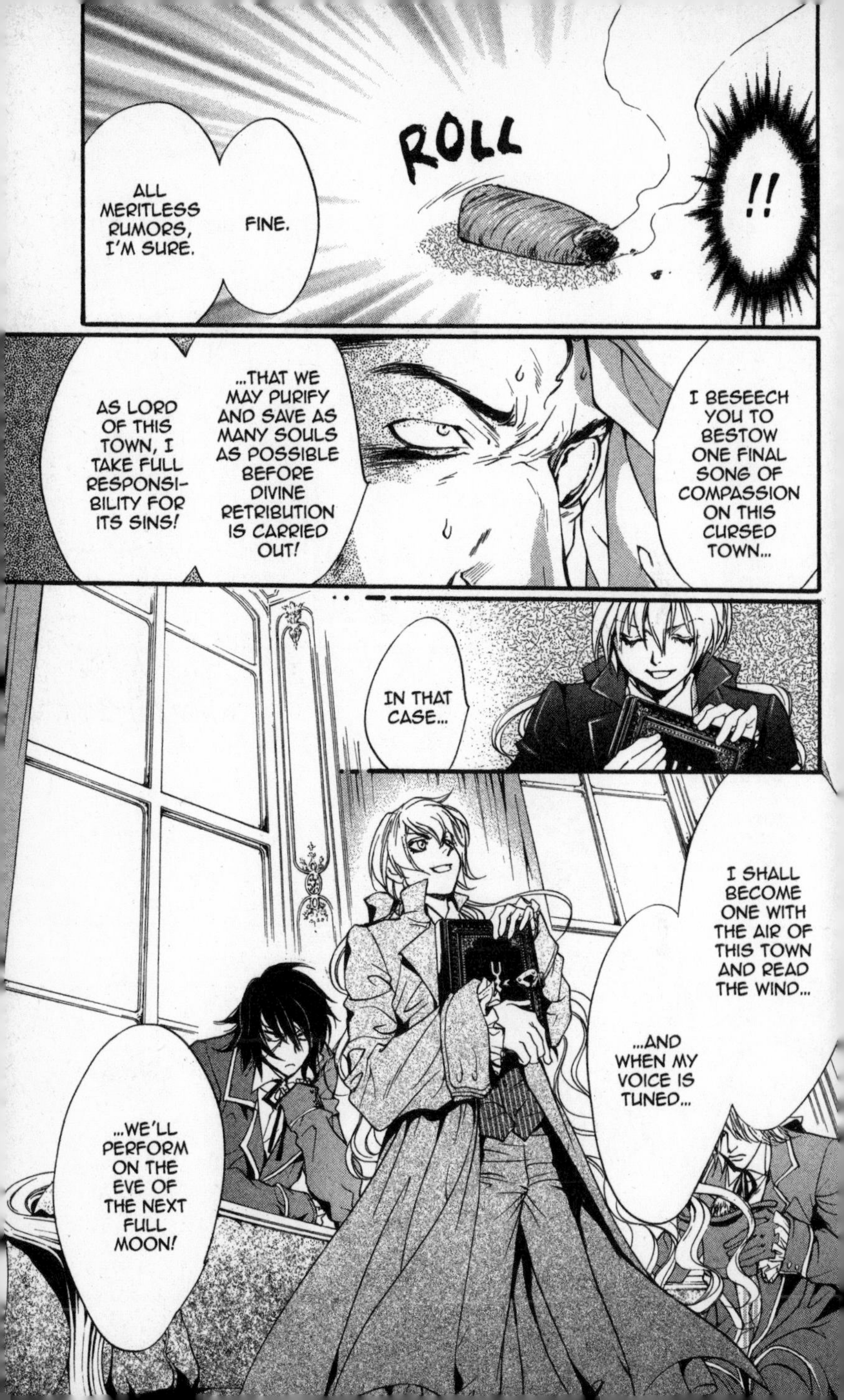
!!
ROLL
FINE.
ALL MERITLESS RUMORS, I'M SURE.
I BESEECH YOU TO BESTOW ONE FINAL SONG OF COMPASSION ON THIS CURSED TOWN...
...THAT WE MAY PURIFY AND SAVE AS MANY SOULS AS POSSIBLE BEFORE DIVINE RETRIBUTION IS CARRIED OUT!
AS LORD OF THIS TOWN, I TAKE FULL RESPONSI-BILITY FOR ITS SINS!
IN THAT CASE...
I SHALL BECOME ONE WITH THE AIR OF THIS TOWN AND READ THE WIND...
...AND WHEN MY VOICE IS TUNED...
...WE'LL PERFORM ON THE EVE OF THE NEXT FULL MOON!

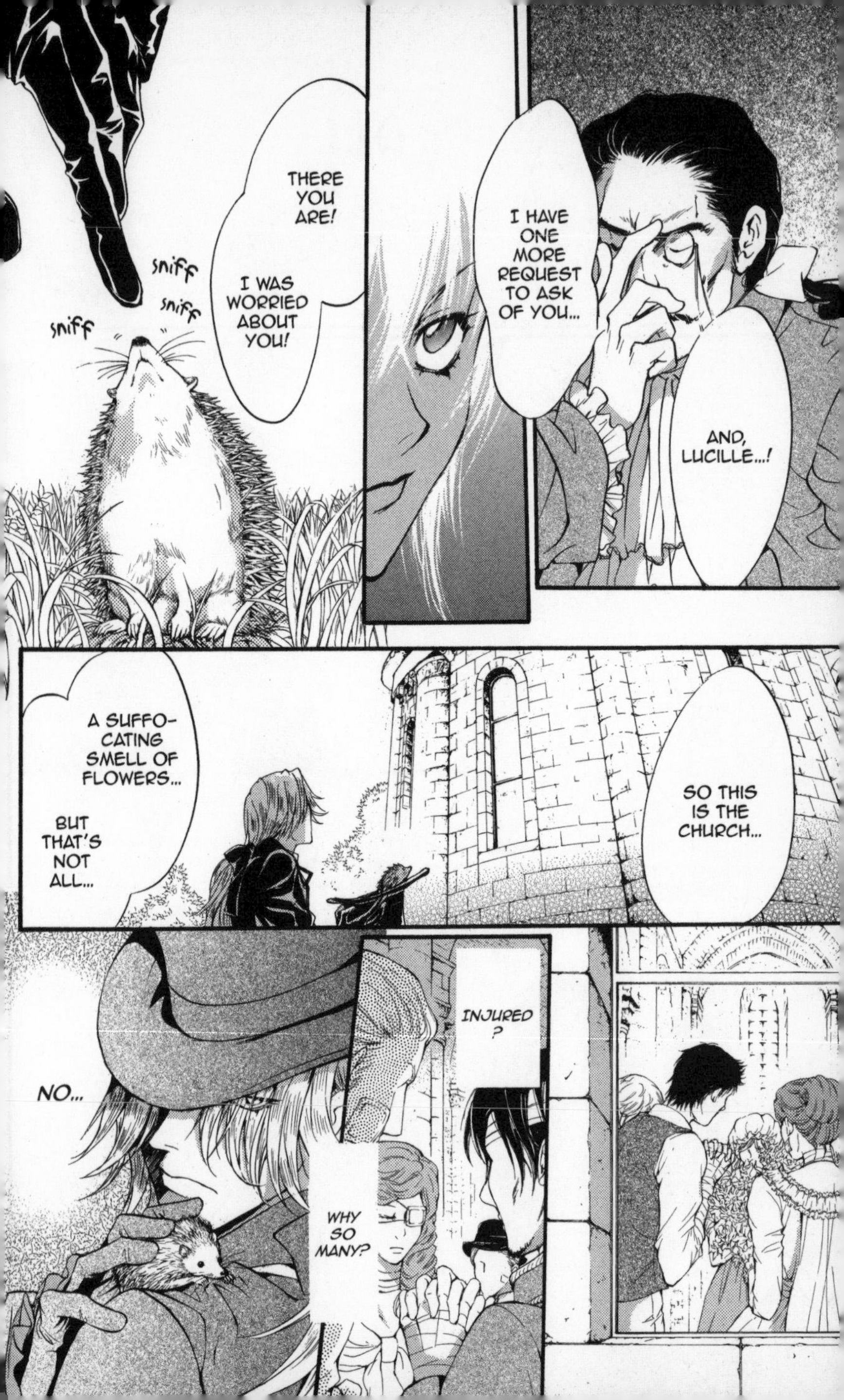
I HAVE ONE MORE REQUEST TO ASK OF YOU...
AND, LUCILLE...!
THERE YOU ARE!
I WAS WORRIED ABOUT YOU!
sniff
sniff
sniff
SO THIS IS THE CHURCH...
A SUFFOCATING SMELL OF FLOWERS...
BUT THAT'S NOT ALL...
INJURED?
WHY SO MANY?
NO...

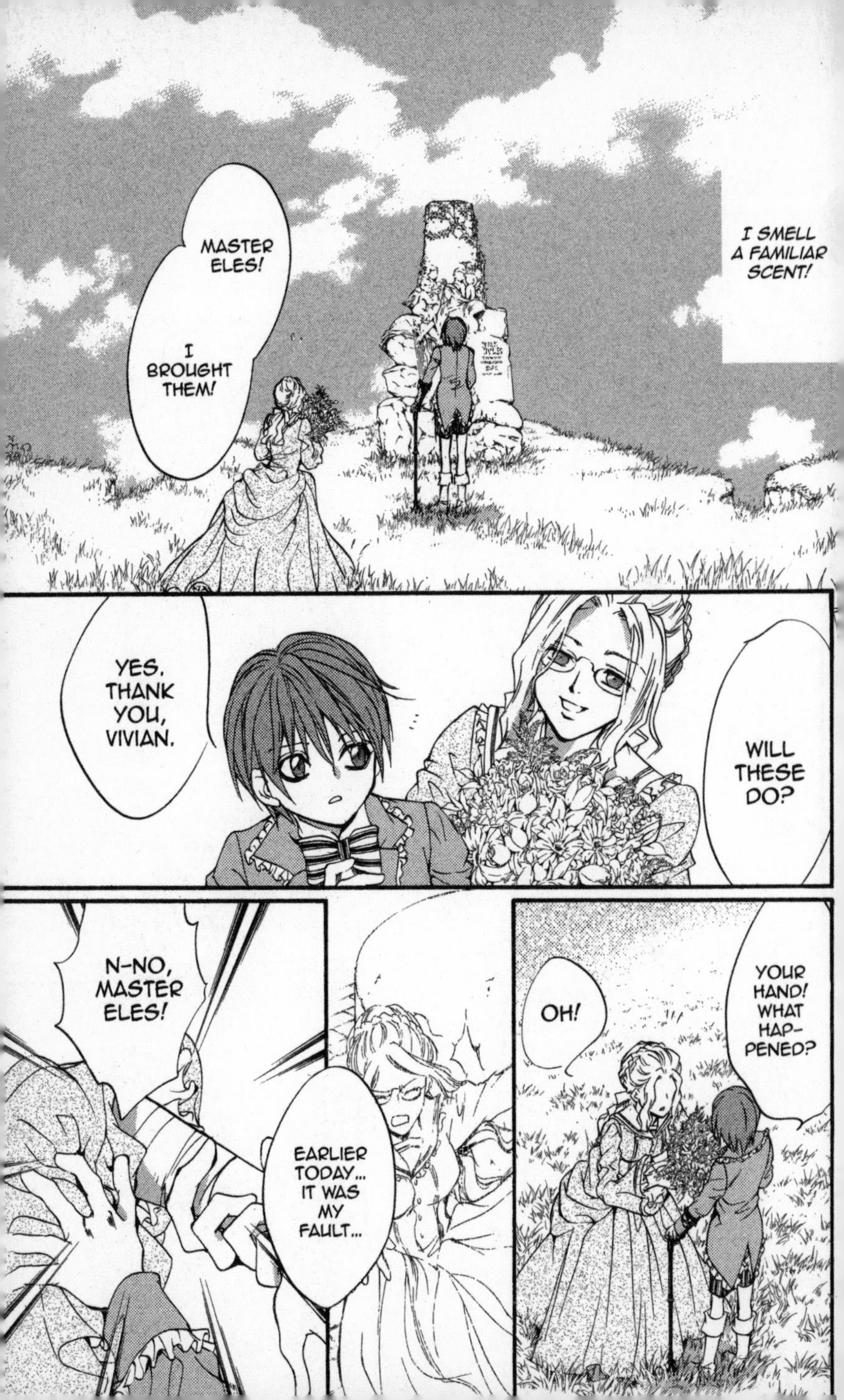
I SMELL A FAMILIAR SCENT!
MASTER ELES!
I BROUGHT THEM!
WILL THESE DO?
YES. THANK YOU, VIVIAN.
YOUR HAND! WHAT HAP-PENED?
OH!
N-NO, MASTER ELES!
EARLIER TODAY... IT WAS MY FAULT...

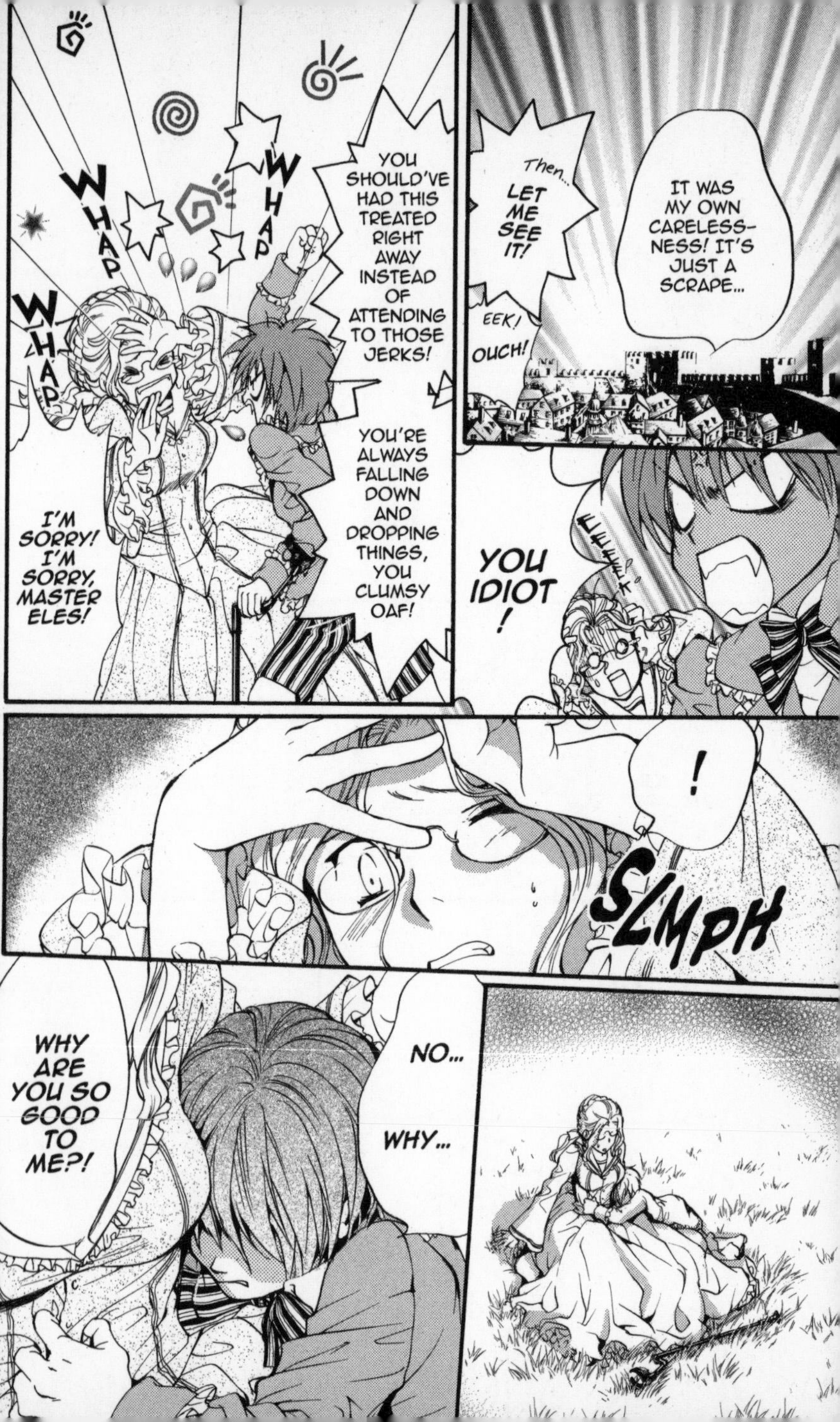
IT WAS MY OWN CARELESS-NESS! IT'S JUST A SCRAPE...
Then... LET ME SEE IT!
EEK!
OUCH!
EEEEK
YOU IDIOT!
YOU SHOULD'VE HAD THIS TREATED RIGHT AWAY INSTEAD OF ATTENDING TO THOSE JERKS!
WHAP
WHAP
YOU'RE ALWAYS FALLING DOWN AND DROPPING THINGS, YOU CLUMSY OAF!
WHAP
I'M SORRY! I'M SORRY, MASTER ELES!
!
SLMPH
NO... WHY...
WHY ARE YOU SO GOOD TO ME?!

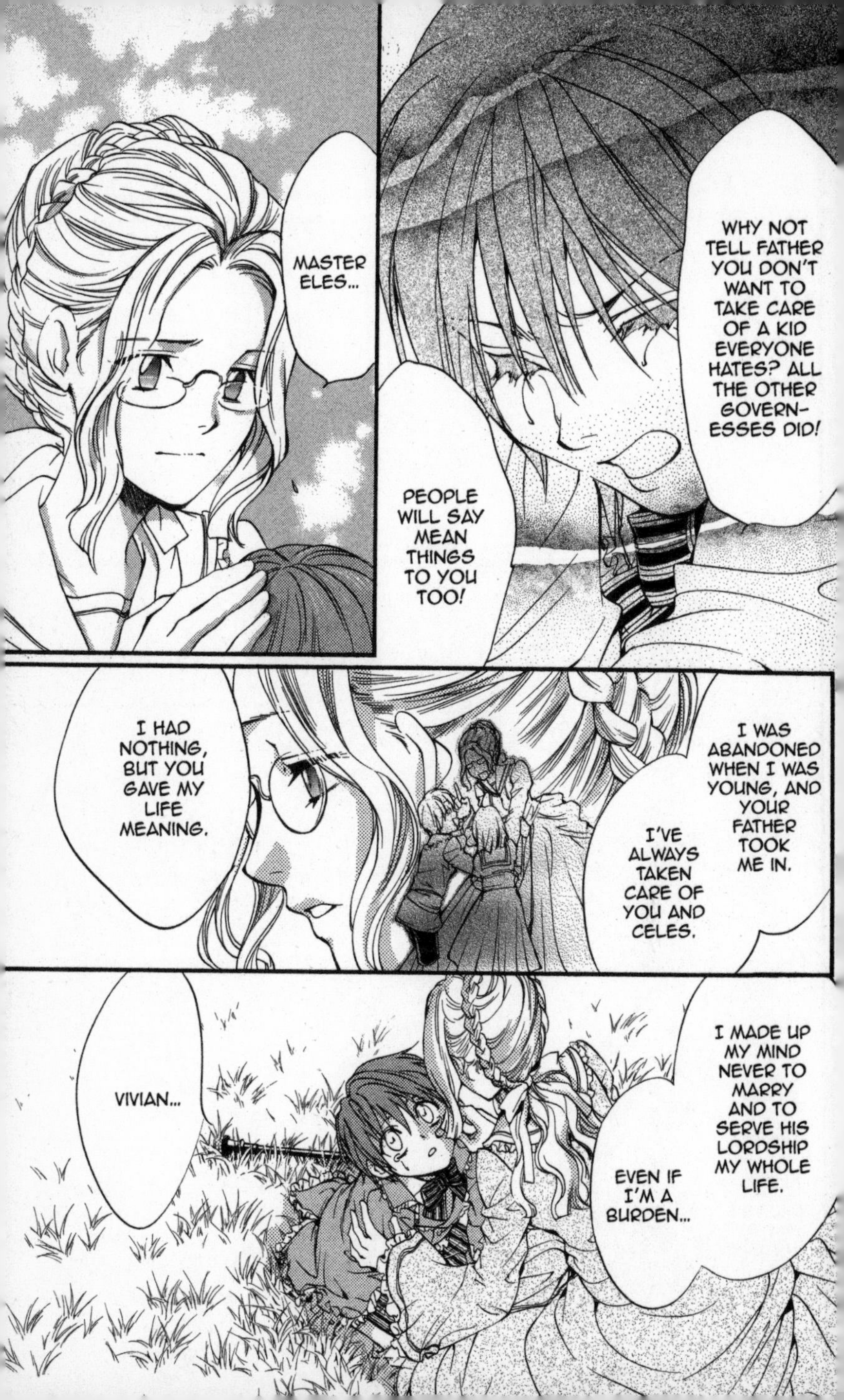
WHY NOT TELL FATHER YOU DON'T WANT TO TAKE CARE OF A KID EVERYONE HATES? ALL THE OTHER GOVERN-ESSES DID!
PEOPLE WILL SAY MEAN THINGS TO YOU TOO!
MASTER ELES...
I WAS ABANDONED WHEN I WAS YOUNG, AND YOUR FATHER TOOK ME IN.
I'VE ALWAYS TAKEN CARE OF YOU AND CELES.
I HAD NOTHING, BUT YOU GAVE MY LIFE MEANING.
I MADE UP MY MIND NEVER TO MARRY AND TO SERVE HIS LORDSHIP MY WHOLE LIFE.
EVEN IF I'M A BURDEN...
VIVIAN...

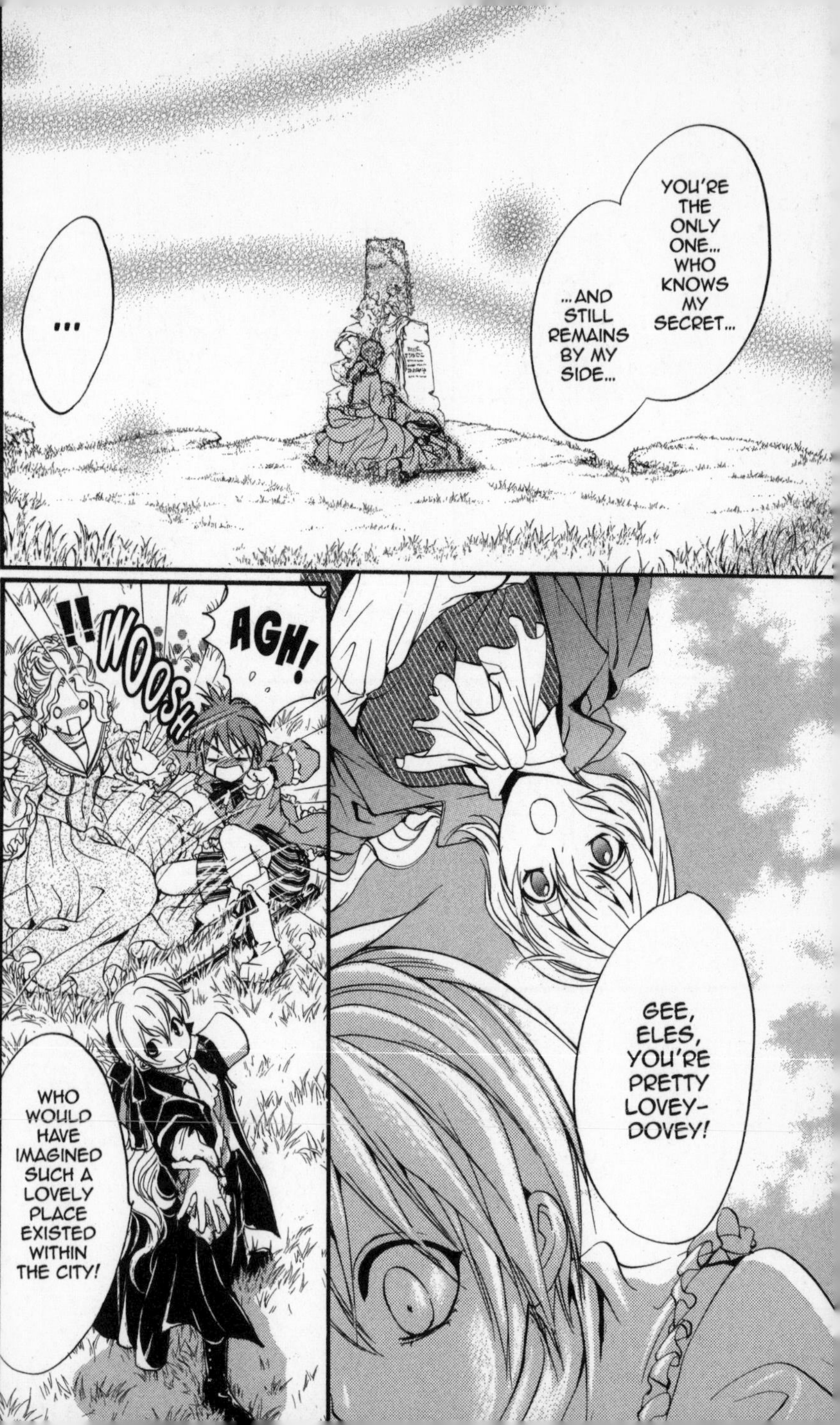
YOU'RE THE ONLY ONE... WHO KNOWS MY SECRET...
...AND STILL REMAINS BY MY SIDE...
...
GEE, ELES, YOU'RE PRETTY LOVEY-DOVEY!
AGH!
WOOSH
!!
WHO WOULD HAVE IMAGINED SUCH A LOVELY PLACE EXISTED WITHIN THE CITY!

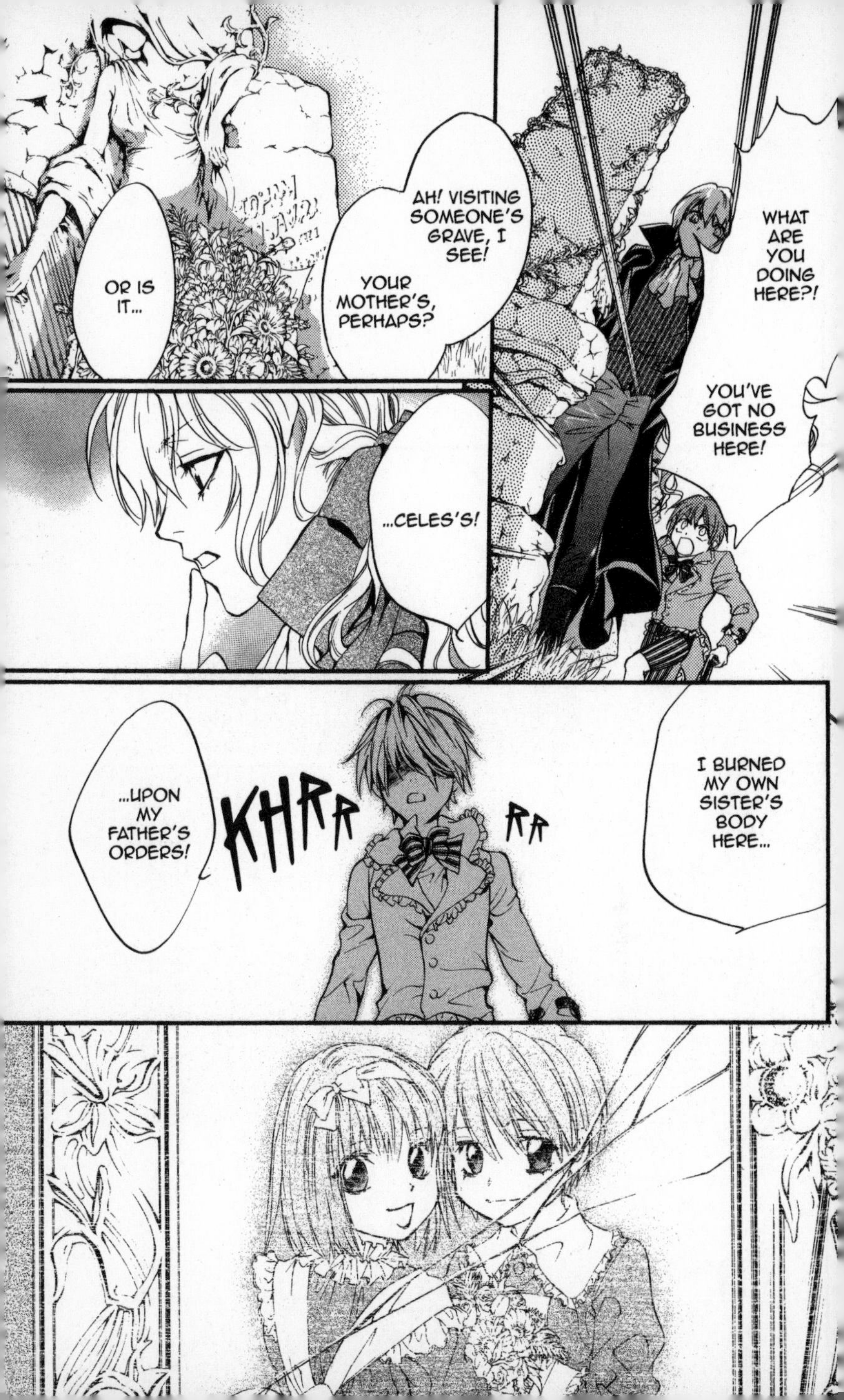
WHAT ARE YOU DOING HERE?!
YOU'VE GOT NO BUSINESS HERE!
AH! VISITING SOMEONE'S GRAVE, I SEE!
YOUR MOTHER'S, PERHAPS?
OR IS IT...
...CELES'S!
I BURNED MY OWN SISTER'S BODY HERE...
KHRR RR
...UPON MY FATHER'S ORDERS!

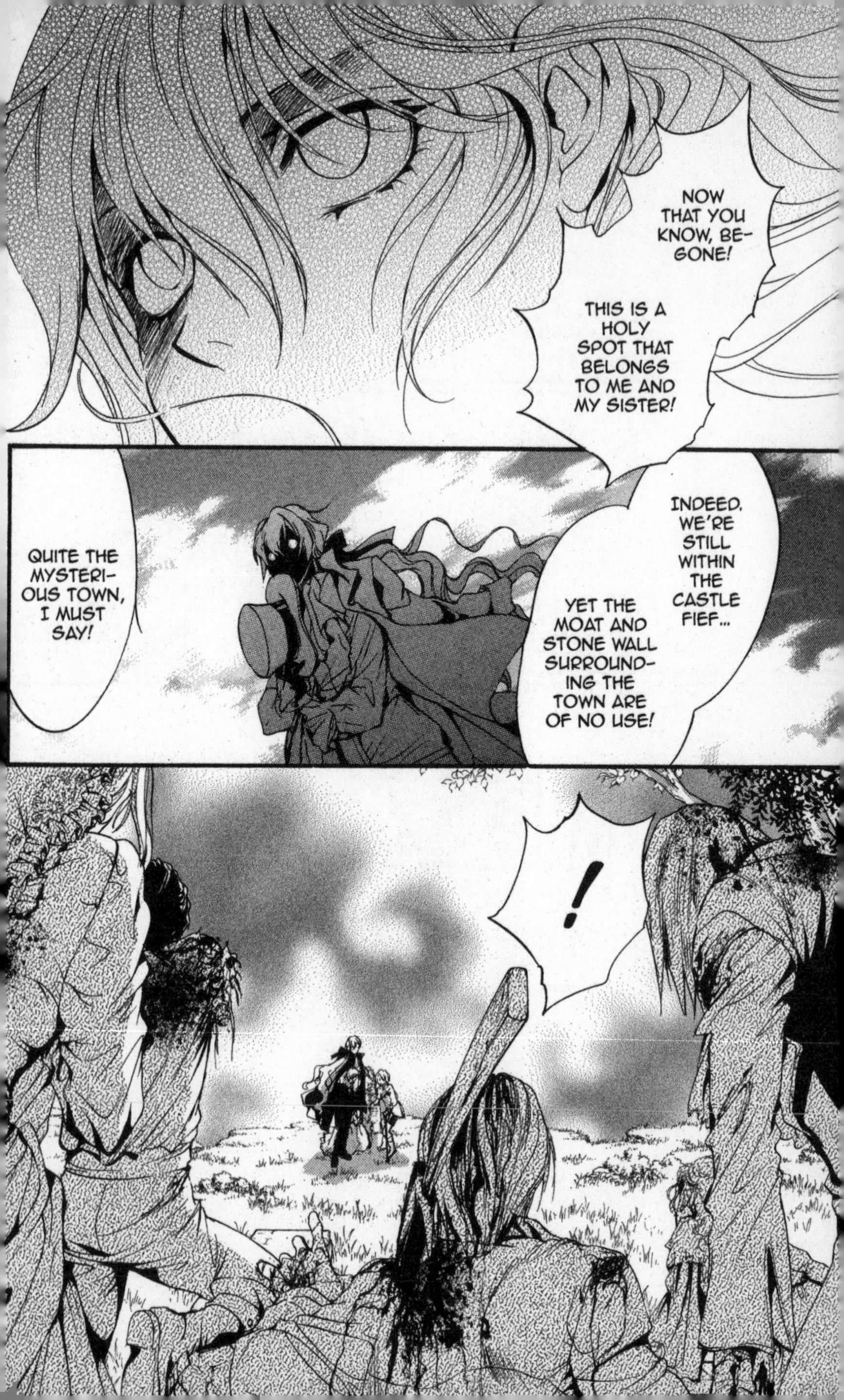
NOW THAT YOU KNOW, BEGONE!
THIS IS A HOLY SPOT THAT BELONGS TO ME AND MY SISTER!
INDEED. WE'RE STILL WITHIN THE CASTLE FIEF...
YET THE MOAT AND STONE WALL SURROUNDING THE TOWN ARE OF NO USE!
QUITE THE MYSTERIOUS TOWN, I MUST SAY!
!

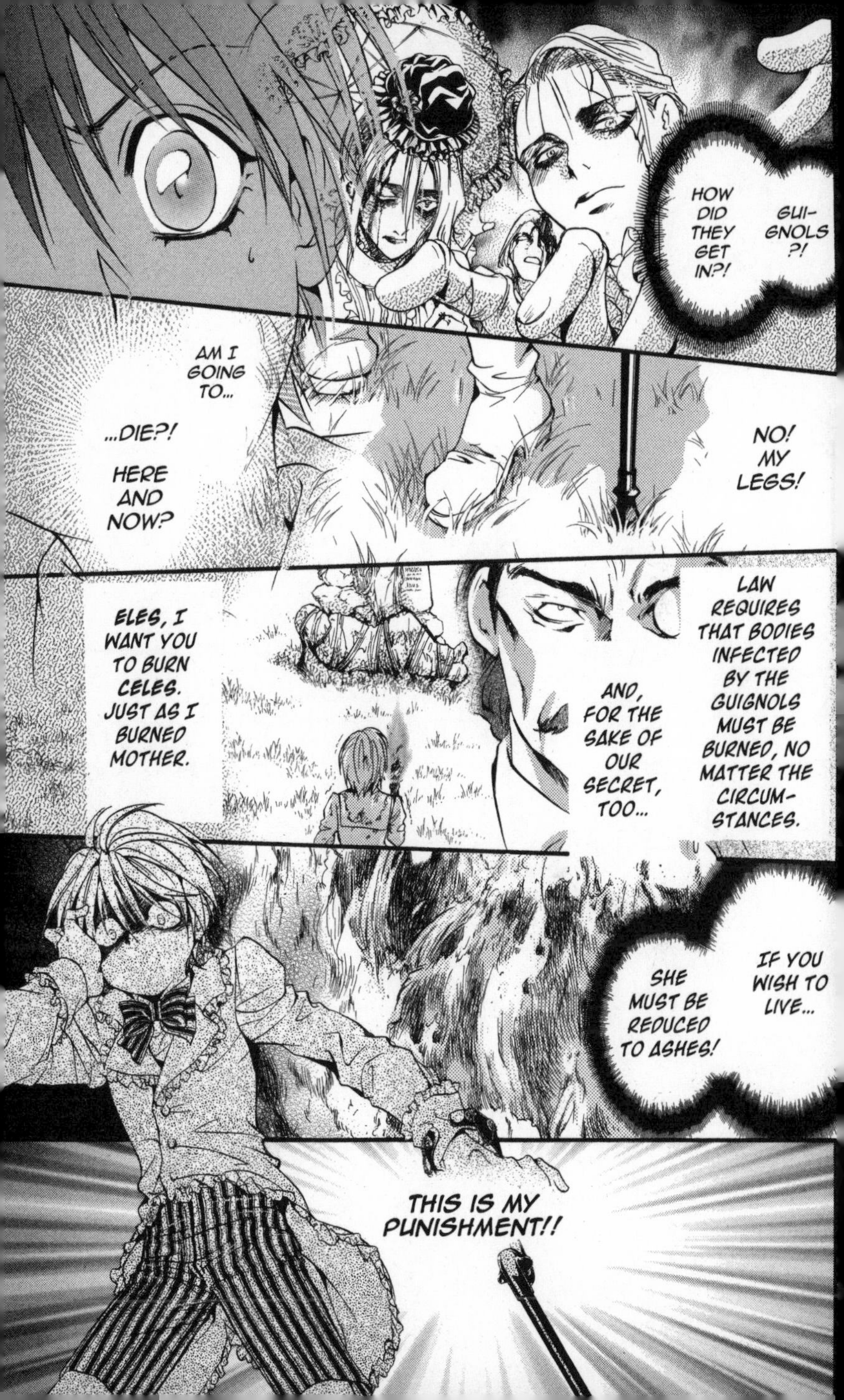
GUI-GNOLS?!
HOW DID THEY GET IN?!
NO! MY LEGS!
AM I GOING TO...
...DIE?!
HERE AND NOW?
LAW REQUIRES THAT BODIES INFECTED BY THE GUIGNOLS MUST BE BURNED, NO MATTER THE CIRCUMSTANCES.
AND, FOR THE SAKE OF OUR SECRET, TOO...
ELES, I WANT YOU TO BURN CELES. JUST AS I BURNED MOTHER.
IF YOU WISH TO LIVE...
SHE MUST BE REDUCED TO ASHES!
THIS IS MY PUNISHMENT!!

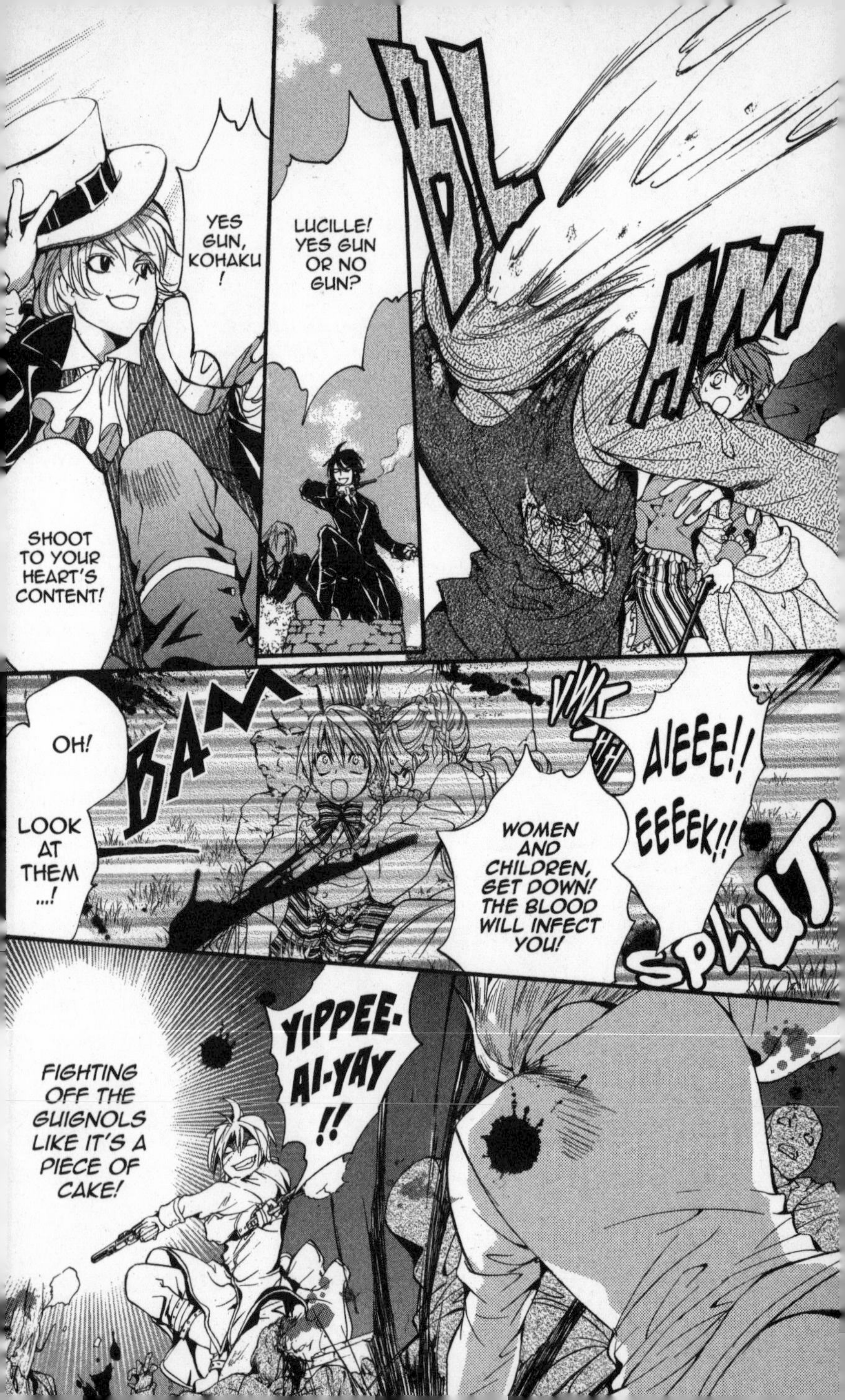
BLAM
LUCILLE! YES GUN OR NO GUN?
YES GUN, KOHAKU!
SHOOT TO YOUR HEART'S CONTENT!
SPLUT
AIEEE!! EEEEK!!
WOMEN AND CHILDREN, GET DOWN! THE BLOOD WILL INFECT YOU!
BAM
OH!
LOOK AT THEM ...!
YIPPEE-AI-YAY!!
FIGHTING OFF THE GUIGNOLS LIKE IT'S A PIECE OF CAKE!

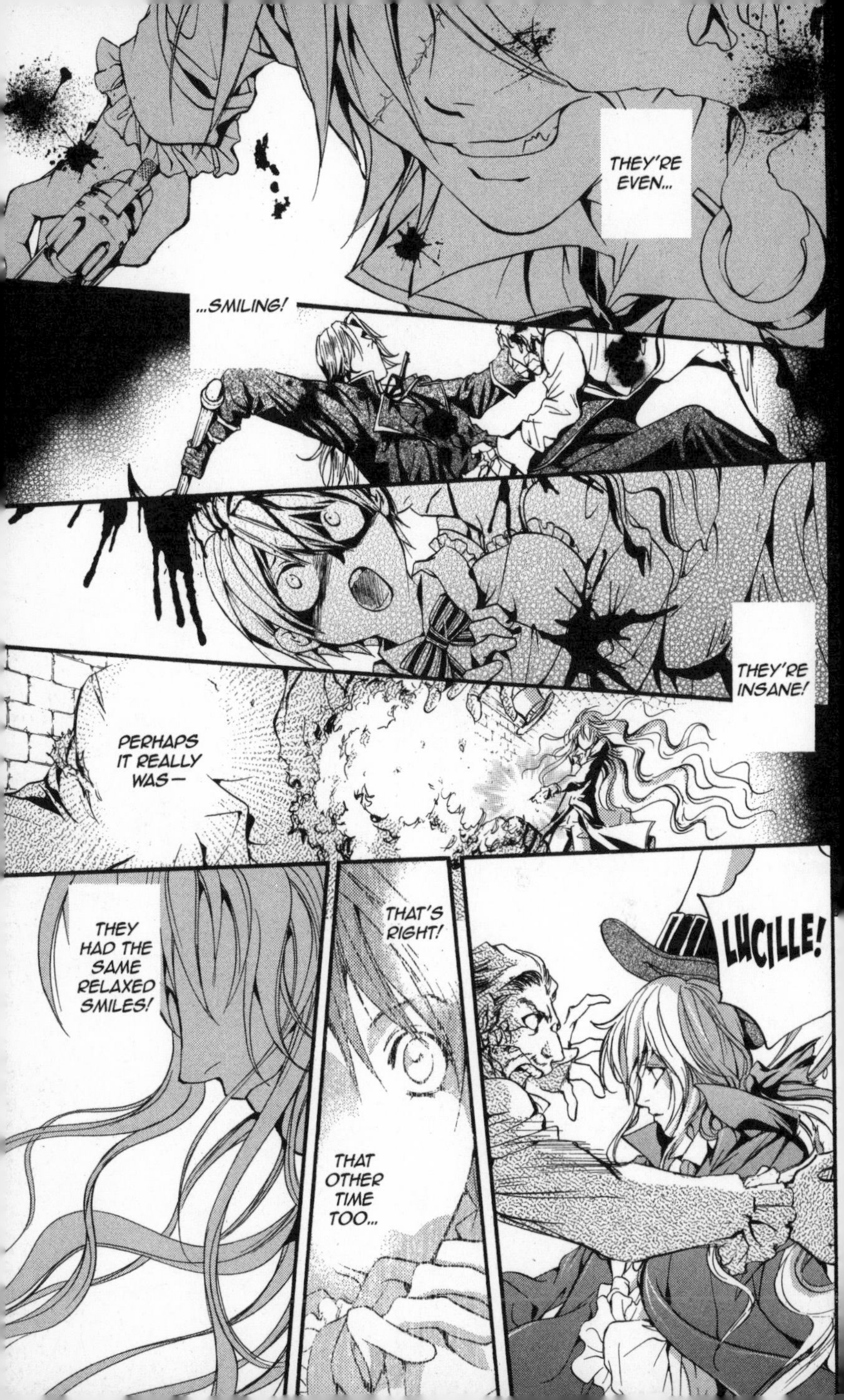
THEY'RE EVEN...
...SMILING!
THEY'RE INSANE!
PERHAPS IT REALLY WAS—
LUCILLE!
THAT'S RIGHT!
THAT OTHER TIME TOO...
THEY HAD THE SAME RELAXED SMILES!

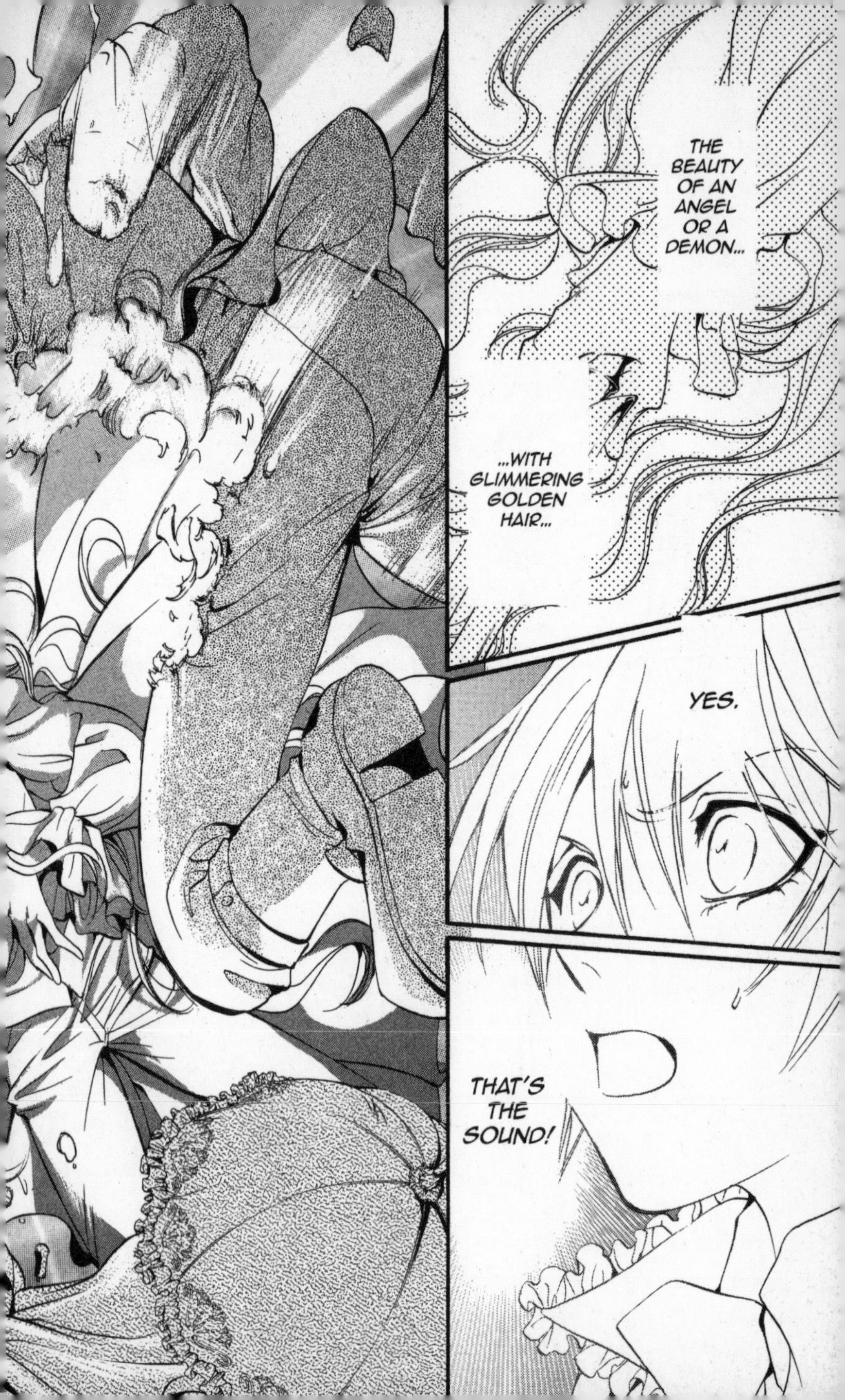
THE BEAUTY OF AN ANGEL OR A DEMON...
...WITH GLIMMERING GOLDEN HAIR...
YES.
THAT'S THE SOUND!

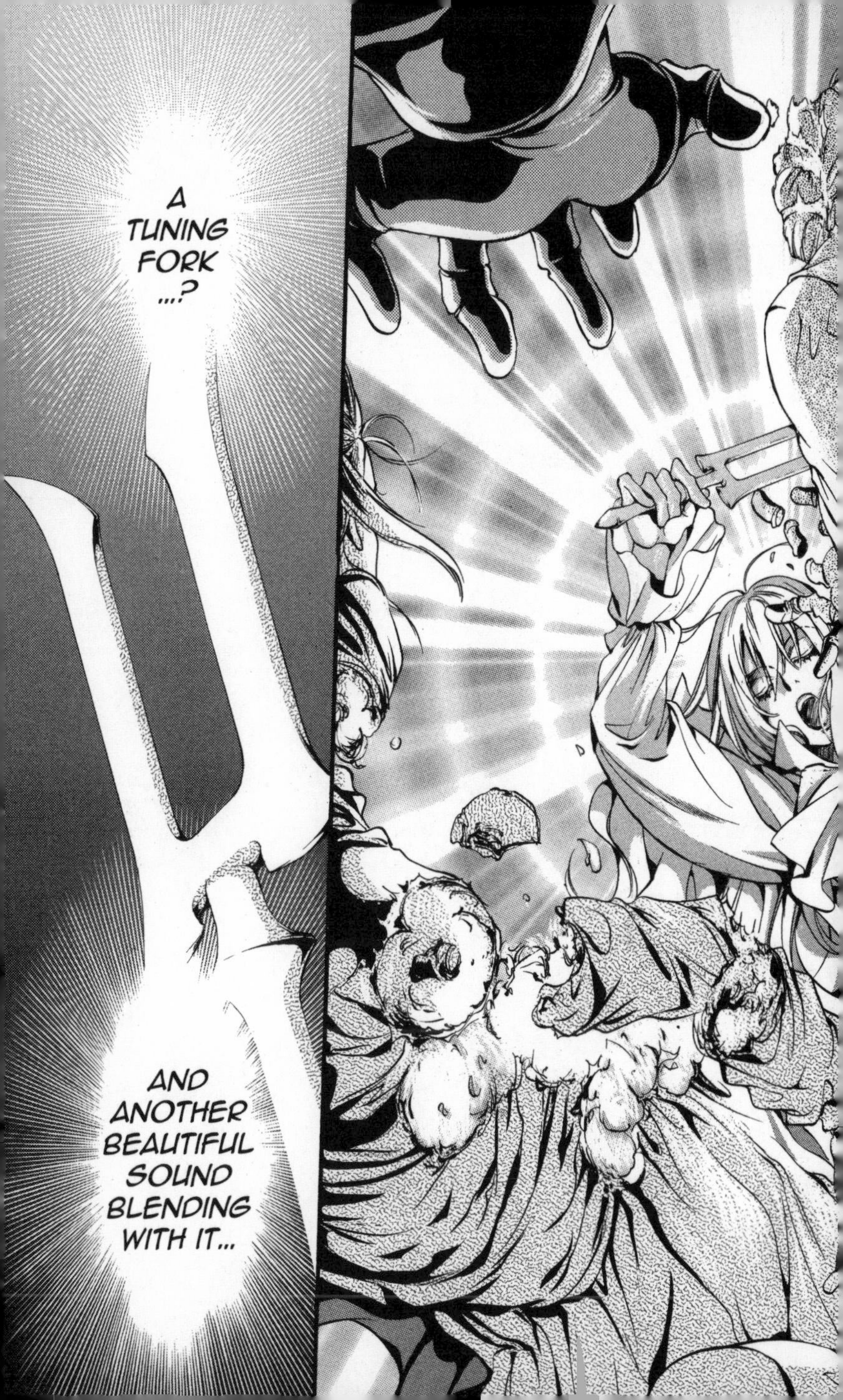
A TUNING FORK ...?
AND ANOTHER BEAUTIFUL SOUND BLENDING WITH IT...

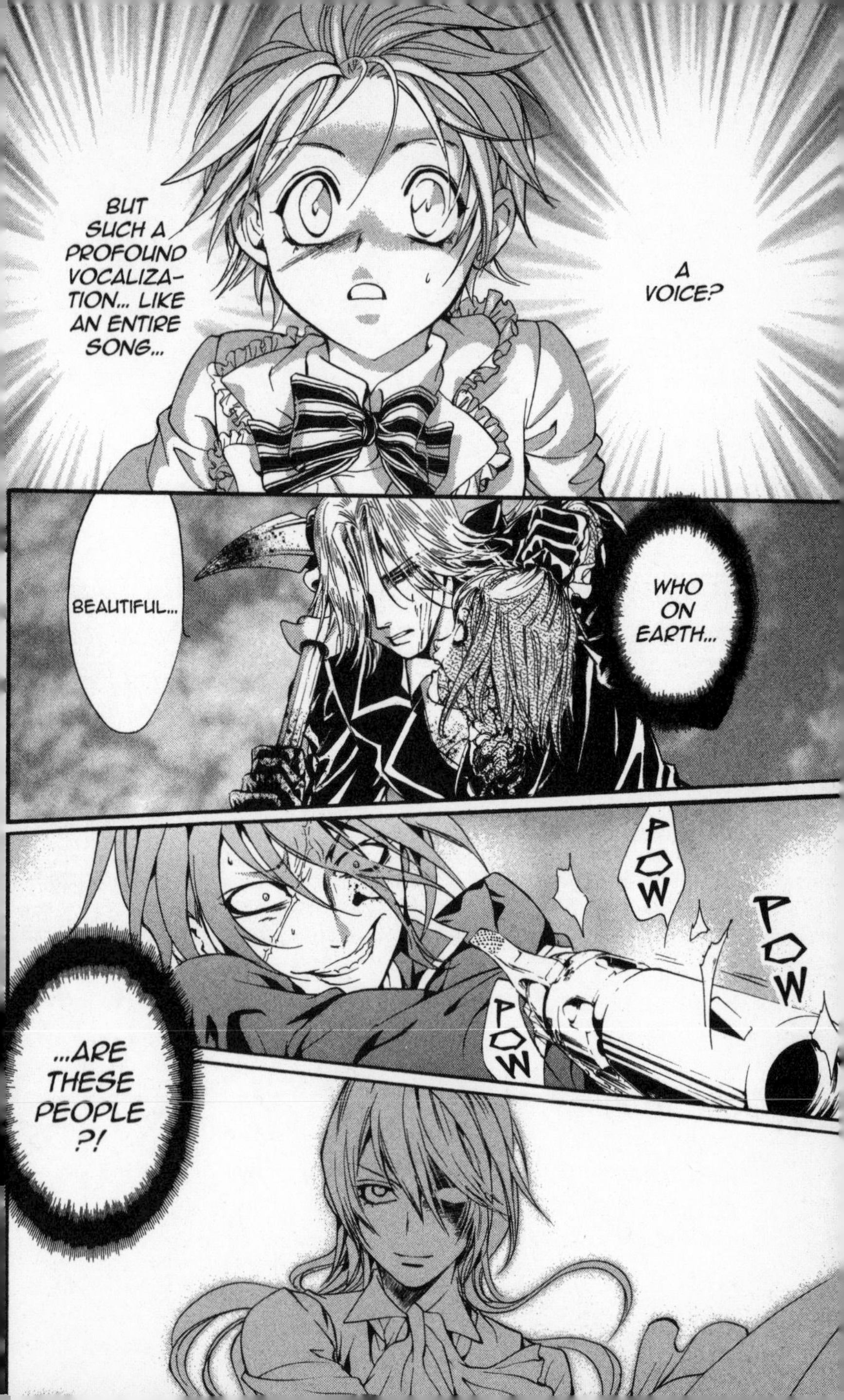
A VOICE?
BUT SUCH A PROFOUND VOCALIZATION... LIKE AN ENTIRE SONG...
WHO ON EARTH...
BEAUTIFUL...
POW
POW
POW
...ARE THESE PEOPLE ?!

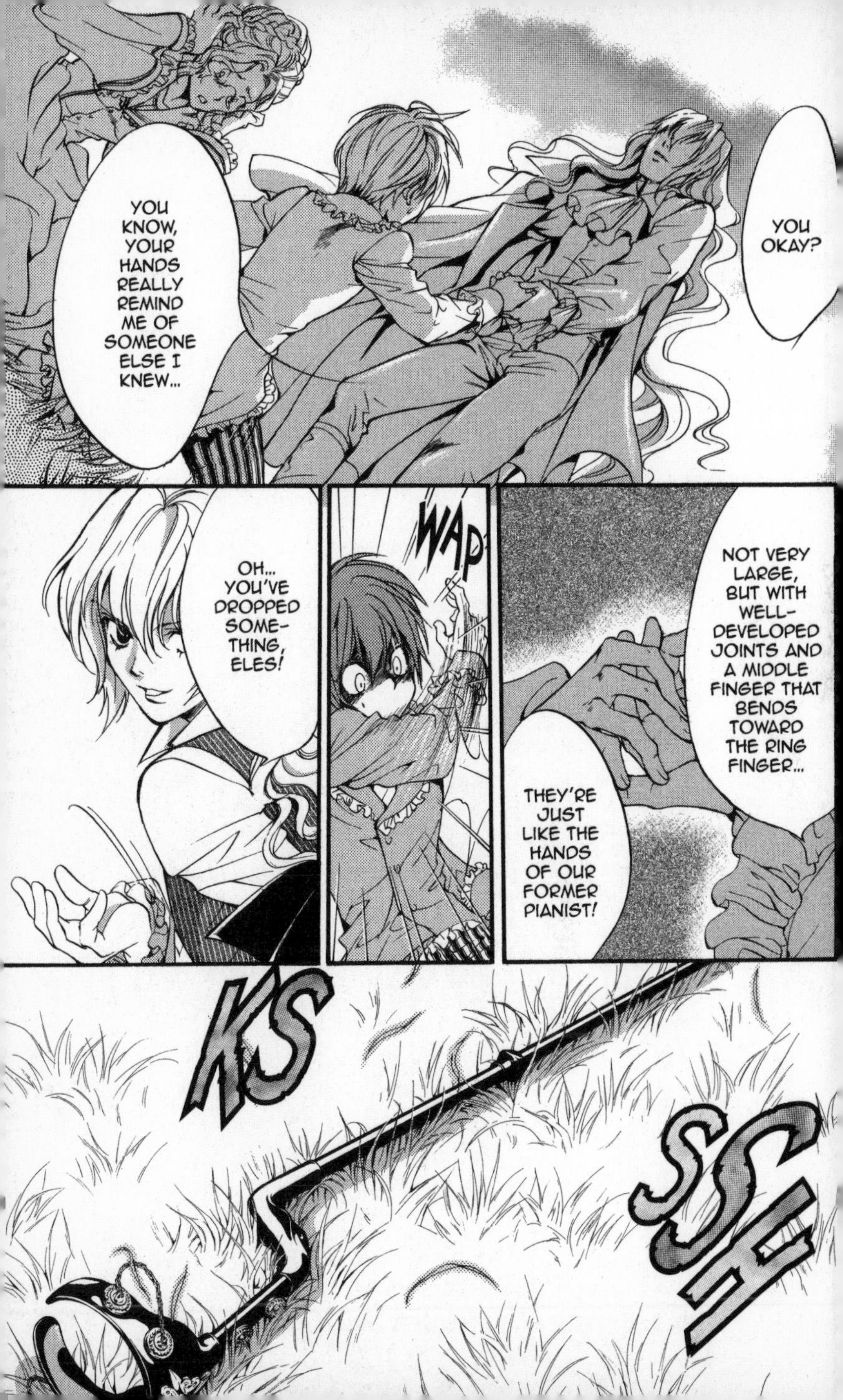
YOU OKAY?
YOU KNOW, YOUR HANDS REALLY REMIND ME OF SOMEONE ELSE I KNEW...
NOT VERY LARGE, BUT WITH WELL-DEVELOPED JOINTS AND A MIDDLE FINGER THAT BENDS TOWARD THE RING FINGER...
THEY'RE JUST LIKE THE HANDS OF OUR FORMER PIANIST!
WAP
OH... YOU'VE DROPPED SOME-THING, ELES!
KS
SSH

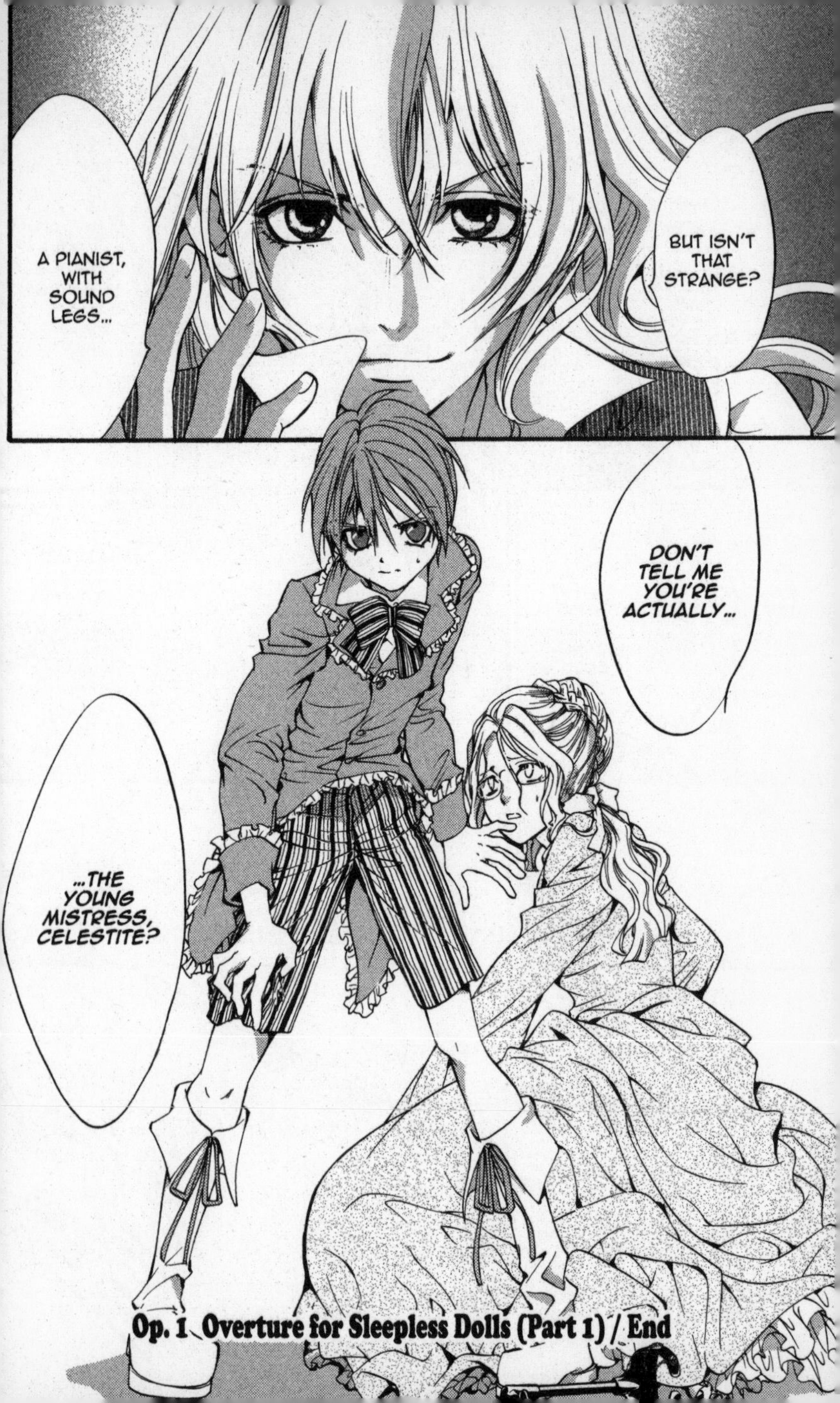
BUT ISN'T THAT STRANGE?
A PIANIST, WITH SOUND LEGS...
DON'T TELL ME YOU'RE ACTUALLY...
...THE YOUNG MISTRESS, CELESTITE?

Op. 1 Overture for Sleepless Dolls (Part 1) / End

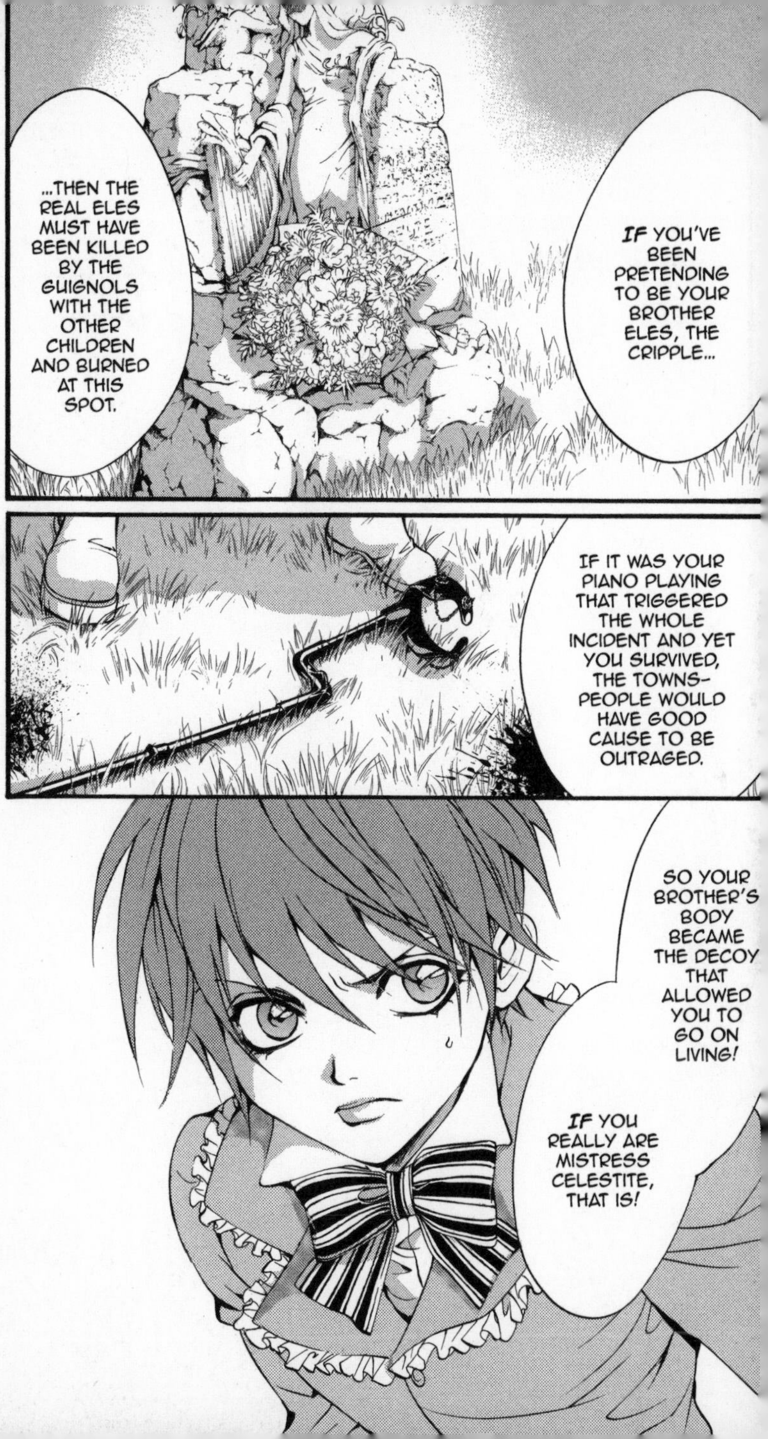
IF YOU'VE BEEN PRETENDING TO BE YOUR BROTHER ELES, THE CRIPPLE...
...THEN THE REAL ELES MUST HAVE BEEN KILLED BY THE GUIGNOLS WITH THE OTHER CHILDREN AND BURNED AT THIS SPOT.
IF IT WAS YOUR PIANO PLAYING THAT TRIGGERED THE WHOLE INCIDENT AND YET YOU SURVIVED, THE TOWNS-PEOPLE WOULD HAVE GOOD CAUSE TO BE OUTRAGED.
SO YOUR BROTHER'S BODY BECAME THE DECOY THAT ALLOWED YOU TO GO ON LIVING!
IF YOU REALLY ARE MISTRESS CELESTITE, THAT IS!

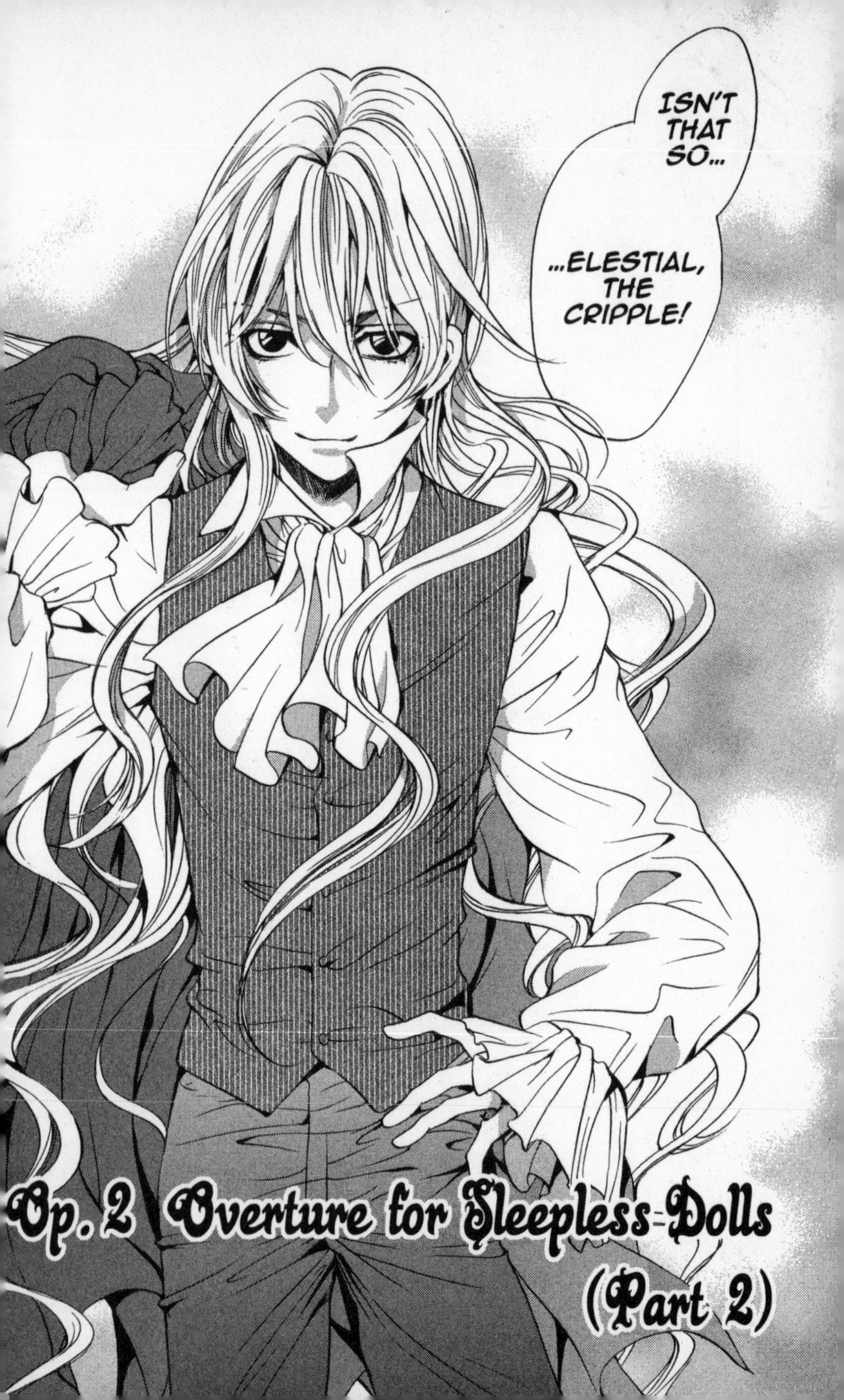
ISN'T THAT SO...
...ELESTIAL, THE CRIPPLE!
Op. 2 Overture for Sleepless=Dolls (Part 2)

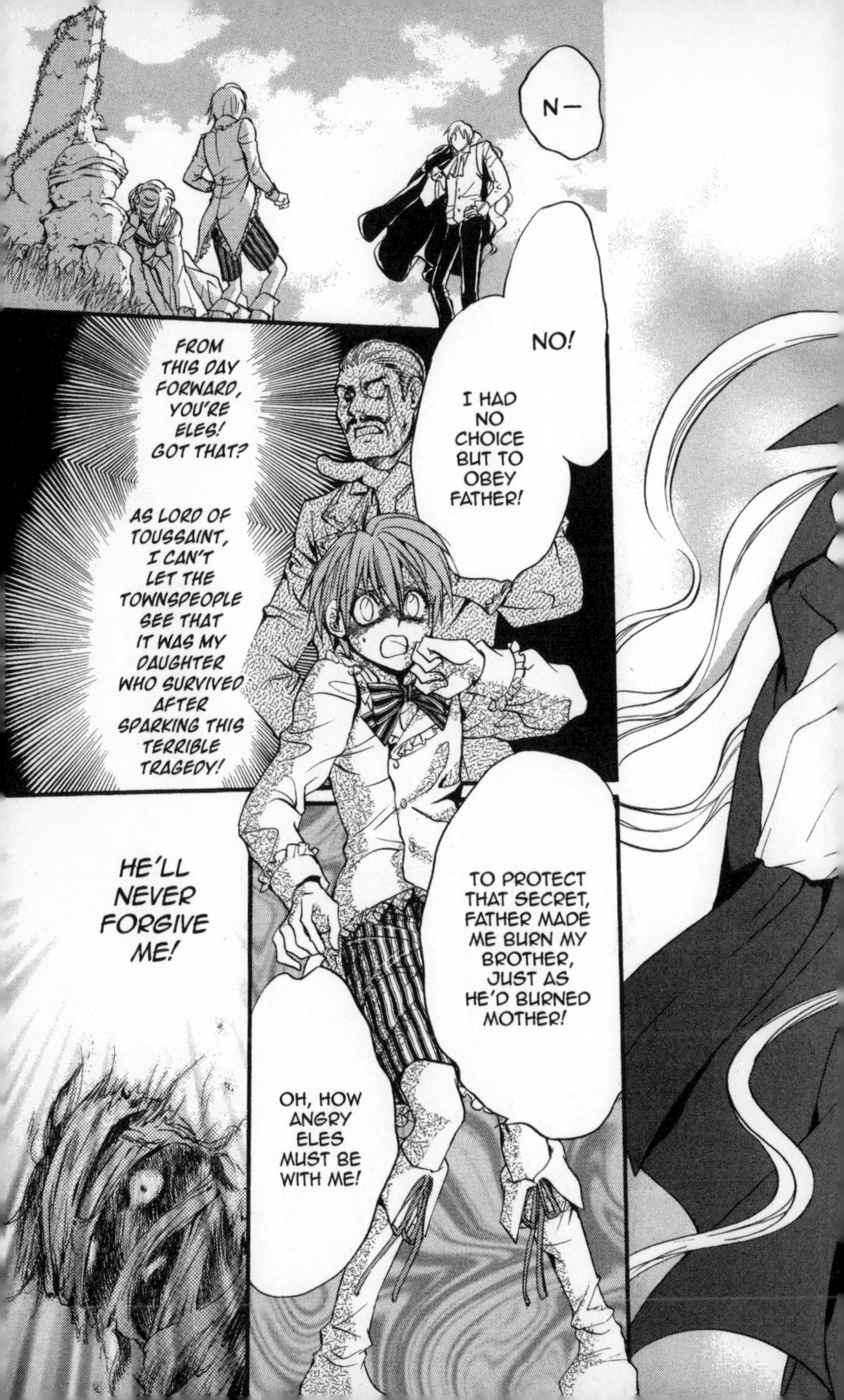
N—
NO!
I HAD NO CHOICE BUT TO OBEY FATHER!
FROM THIS DAY FORWARD, YOU'RE ELES! GOT THAT?
AS LORD OF TOUSSAINT, I CAN'T LET THE TOWNSPEOPLE SEE THAT IT WAS MY DAUGHTER WHO SURVIVED AFTER SPARKING THIS TERRIBLE TRAGEDY!
TO PROTECT THAT SECRET, FATHER MADE ME BURN MY BROTHER, JUST AS HE'D BURNED MOTHER!
OH, HOW ANGRY ELES MUST BE WITH ME!
HE'LL NEVER FORGIVE ME!

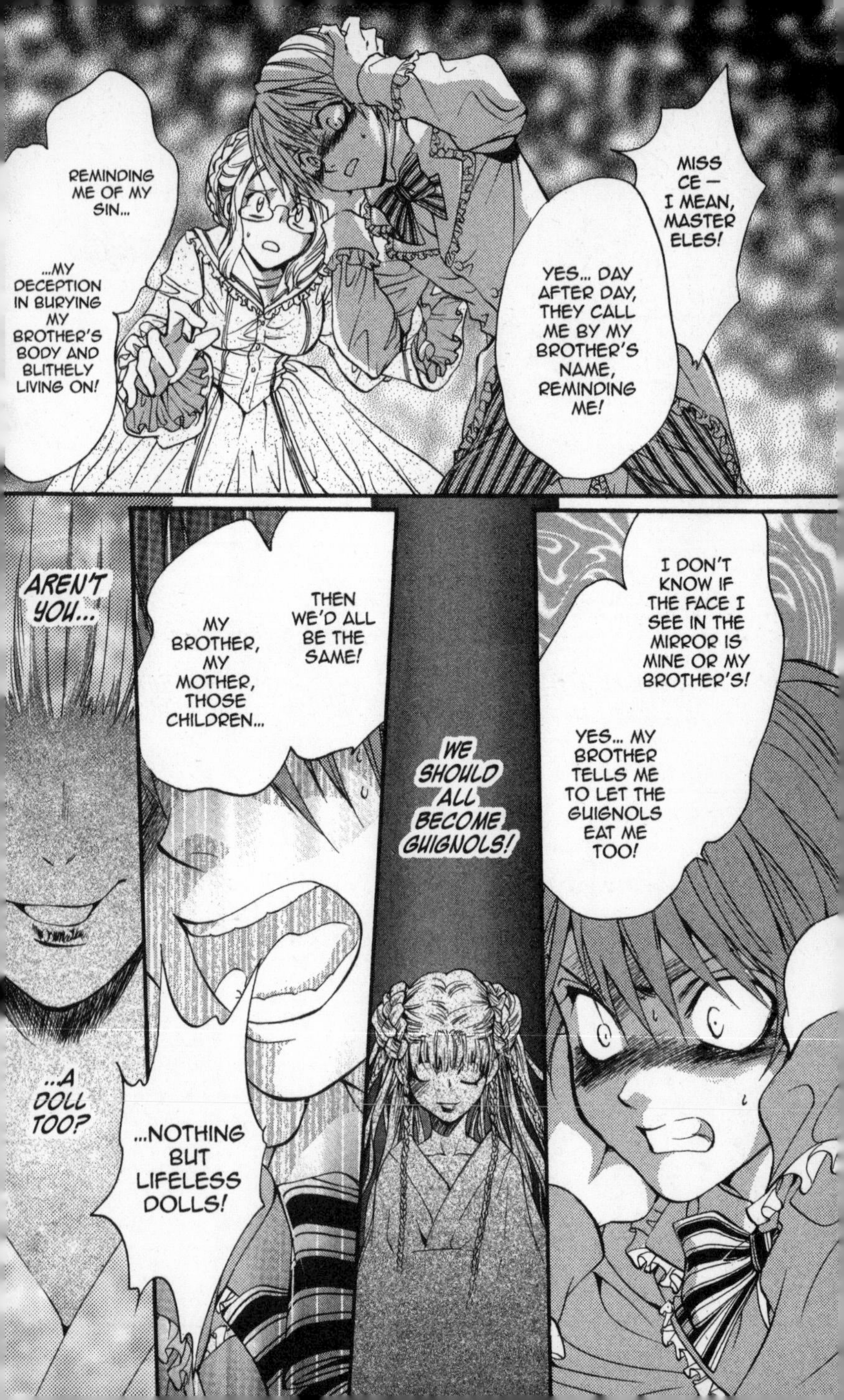
MISS CE— I MEAN, MASTER ELES!
YES... DAY AFTER DAY, THEY CALL ME BY MY BROTHER'S NAME, REMINDING ME!
REMINDING ME OF MY SIN...
...MY DECEPTION IN BURYING MY BROTHER'S BODY AND BLITHELY LIVING ON!
I DON'T KNOW IF THE FACE I SEE IN THE MIRROR IS MINE OR MY BROTHER'S!
YES... MY BROTHER TELLS ME TO LET THE GUIGNOLS EAT ME TOO!
WE SHOULD ALL BECOME GUIGNOLS!
THEN WE'D ALL BE THE SAME!
MY BROTHER, MY MOTHER, THOSE CHILDREN...
...NOTHING BUT LIFELESS DOLLS!
AREN'T YOU...
...A DOLL TOO?

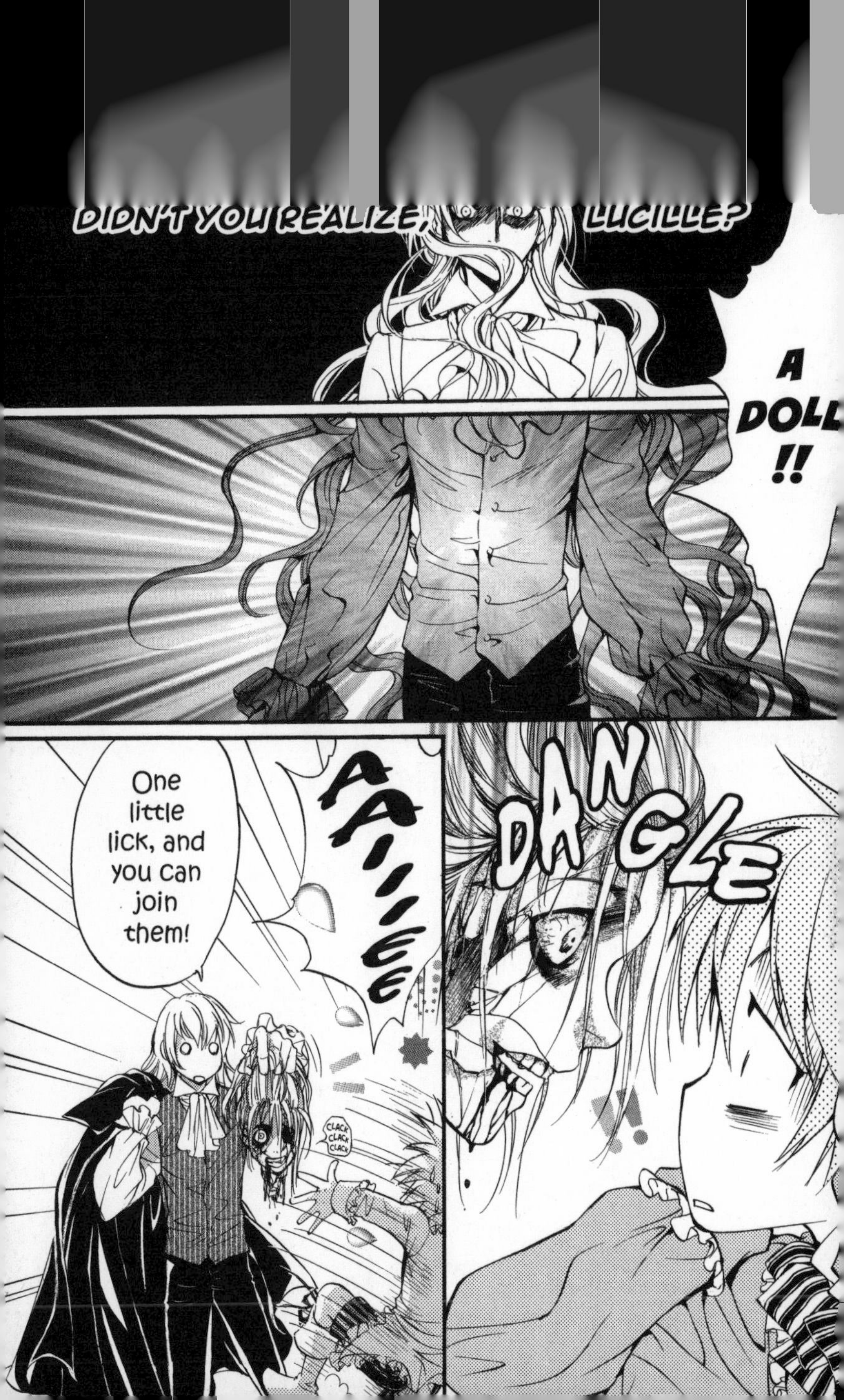
DIDN'T YOU REALIZE, LUCILLE?
A DOLL!!
DANGLE
!!
AAIIIEEE
One little lick, and you can join them!
CLACK CLACK CLACK

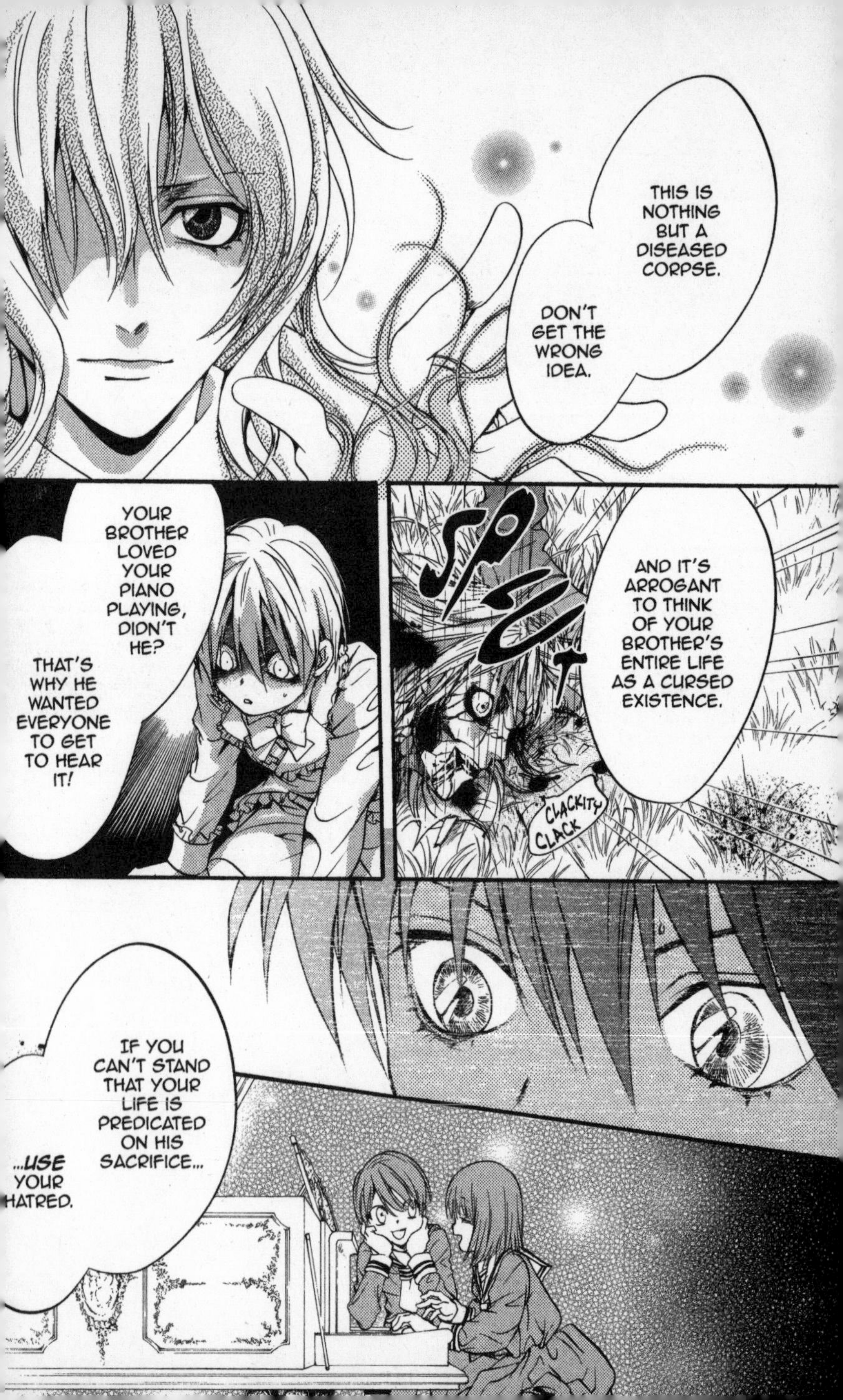
THIS IS NOTHING BUT A DISEASED CORPSE.
DON'T GET THE WRONG IDEA.
SPLUT
AND IT'S ARROGANT TO THINK OF YOUR BROTHER'S ENTIRE LIFE AS A CURSED EXISTENCE.
CLACKITY CLACK
YOUR BROTHER LOVED YOUR PIANO PLAYING, DIDN'T HE?
THAT'S WHY HE WANTED EVERYONE TO GET TO HEAR IT!
IF YOU CAN'T STAND THAT YOUR LIFE IS PREDICATED ON HIS SACRIFICE...
...USE YOUR HATRED.

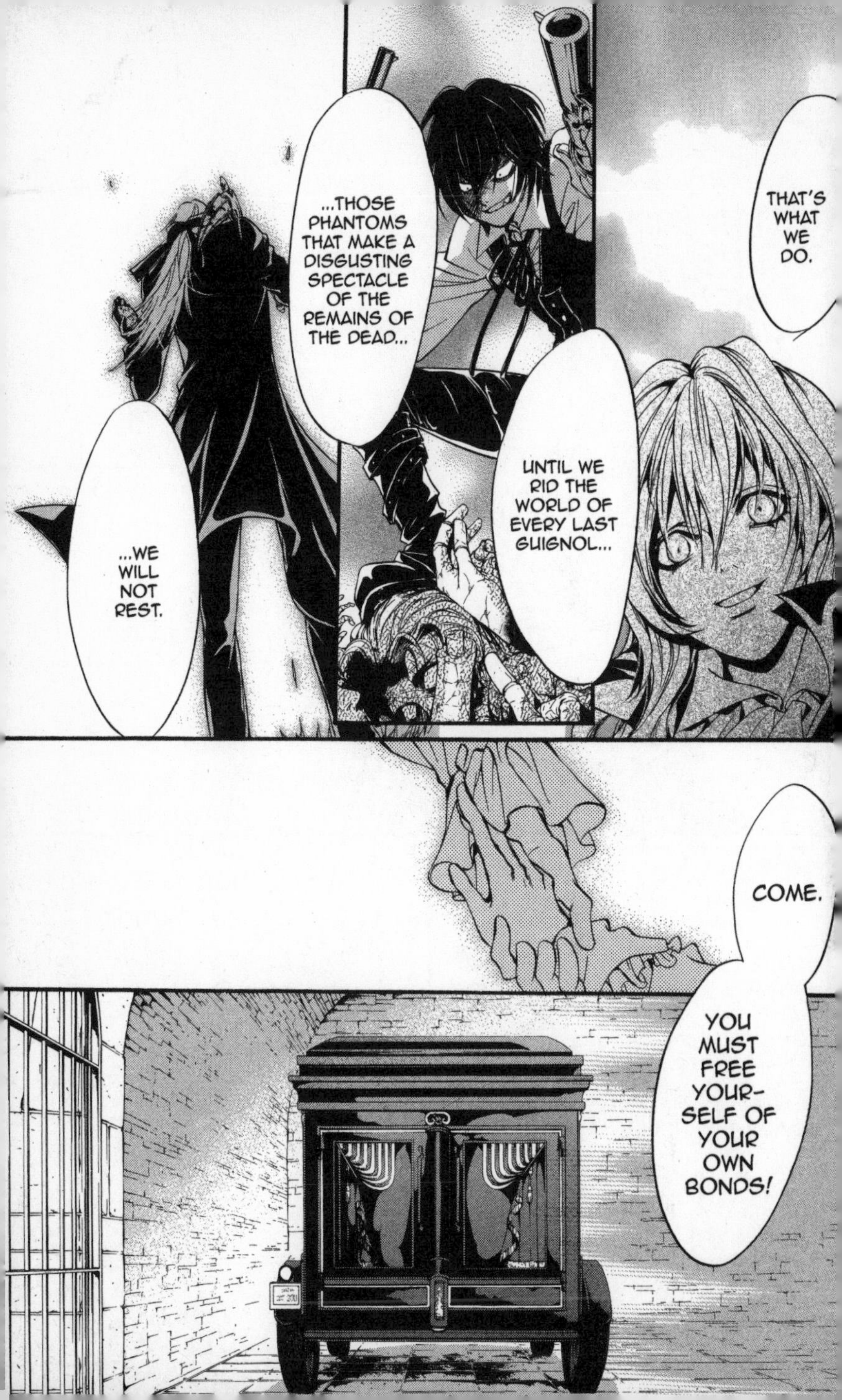
THAT'S WHAT WE DO.
...THOSE PHANTOMS THAT MAKE A DISGUSTING SPECTACLE OF THE REMAINS OF THE DEAD...
UNTIL WE RID THE WORLD OF EVERY LAST GUIGNOL...
...WE WILL NOT REST.
COME.
YOU MUST FREE YOUR-SELF OF YOUR OWN BONDS!

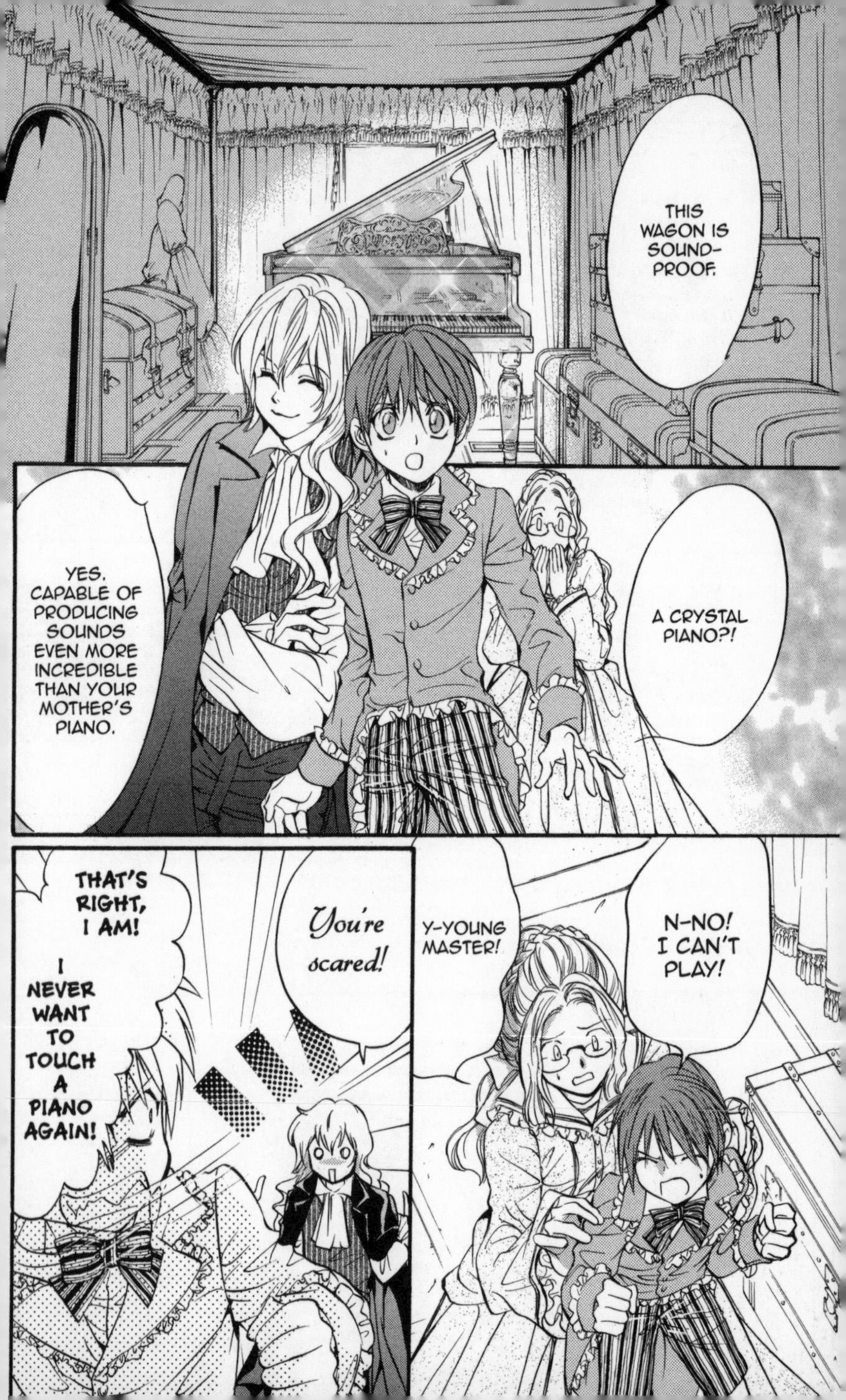
THIS WAGON IS SOUND-PROOF.
A CRYSTAL PIANO?!
YES. CAPABLE OF PRODUCING SOUNDS EVEN MORE INCREDIBLE THAN YOUR MOTHER'S PIANO.
N-NO! I CAN'T PLAY!
Y-YOUNG MASTER!
You're scared!
THAT'S RIGHT, I AM!
I NEVER WANT TO TOUCH A PIANO AGAIN!

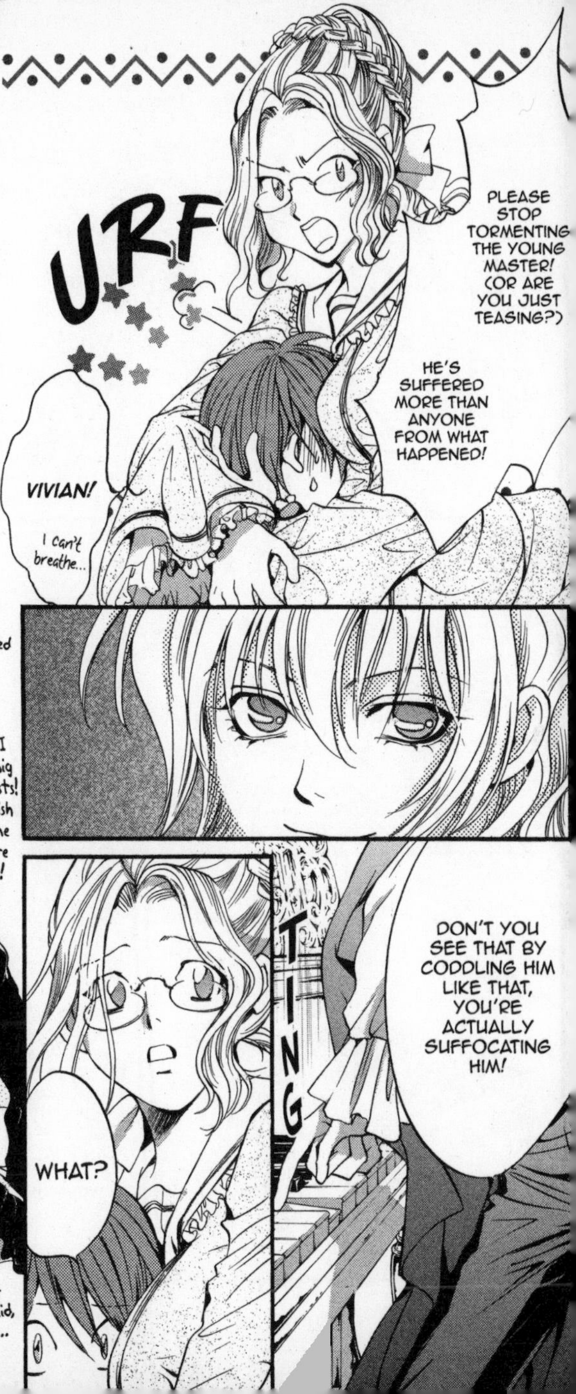
PLEASE STOP TORMENTING THE YOUNG MASTER! (OR ARE YOU JUST TEASING?)
HE'S SUFFERED MORE THAN ANYONE FROM WHAT HAPPENED!
URF
VIVIAN!
I can't breathe...
DON'T YOU SEE THAT BY CODDLING HIM LIKE THAT, YOU'RE ACTUALLY SUFFOCATING HIM!
TING
WHAT?

The dolls in this story are called **Guignols**, and I guess the title *Grand Guignol Orchestra* is misleading because it sounds like an orchestra of Guignols. The word **guignol** refers to a hand puppet doll, so they're actually different from marionettes, but I used the word because I liked its ring.

It's just like the Grand Guignol Theater that existed in the 19th century.

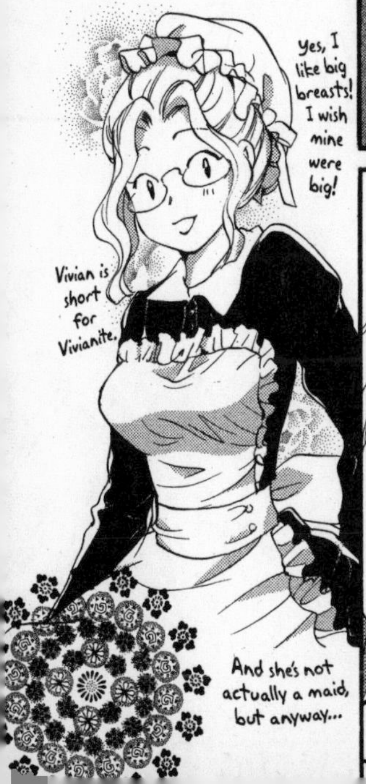
Yes, I like big breasts! I wish mine were big!
Vivian is short for Vivianite.
And she's not actually a maid, but anyway...

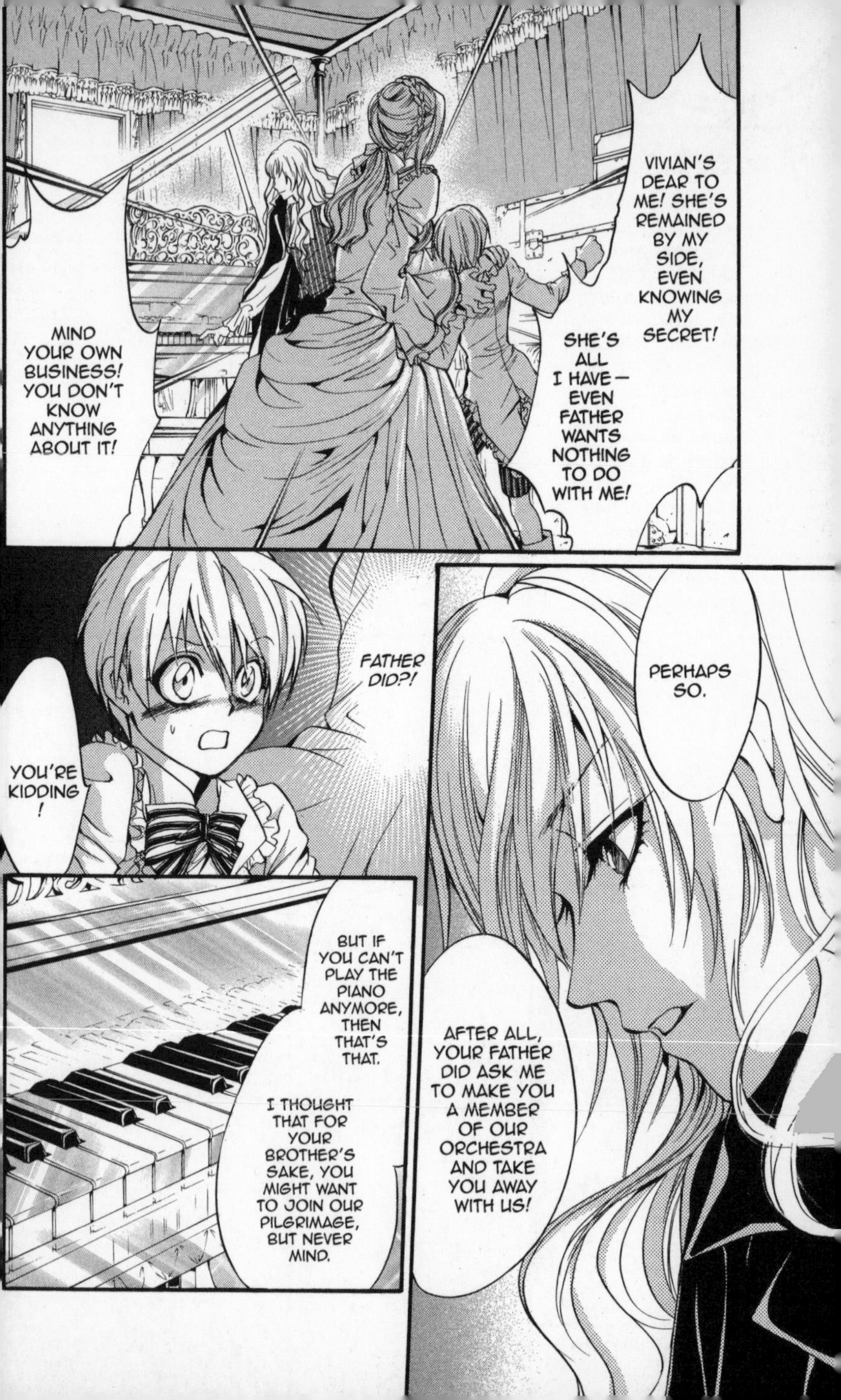
VIVIAN'S DEAR TO ME! SHE'S REMAINED BY MY SIDE, EVEN KNOWING MY SECRET!
SHE'S ALL I HAVE—EVEN FATHER WANTS NOTHING TO DO WITH ME!
MIND YOUR OWN BUSINESS! YOU DON'T KNOW ANYTHING ABOUT IT!
PERHAPS SO.
AFTER ALL, YOUR FATHER DID ASK ME TO MAKE YOU A MEMBER OF OUR ORCHESTRA AND TAKE YOU AWAY WITH US!
FATHER DID?!
YOU'RE KIDDING!
BUT IF YOU CAN'T PLAY THE PIANO ANYMORE, THEN THAT'S THAT.
I THOUGHT THAT FOR YOUR BROTHER'S SAKE, YOU MIGHT WANT TO JOIN OUR PILGRIMAGE, BUT NEVER MIND.

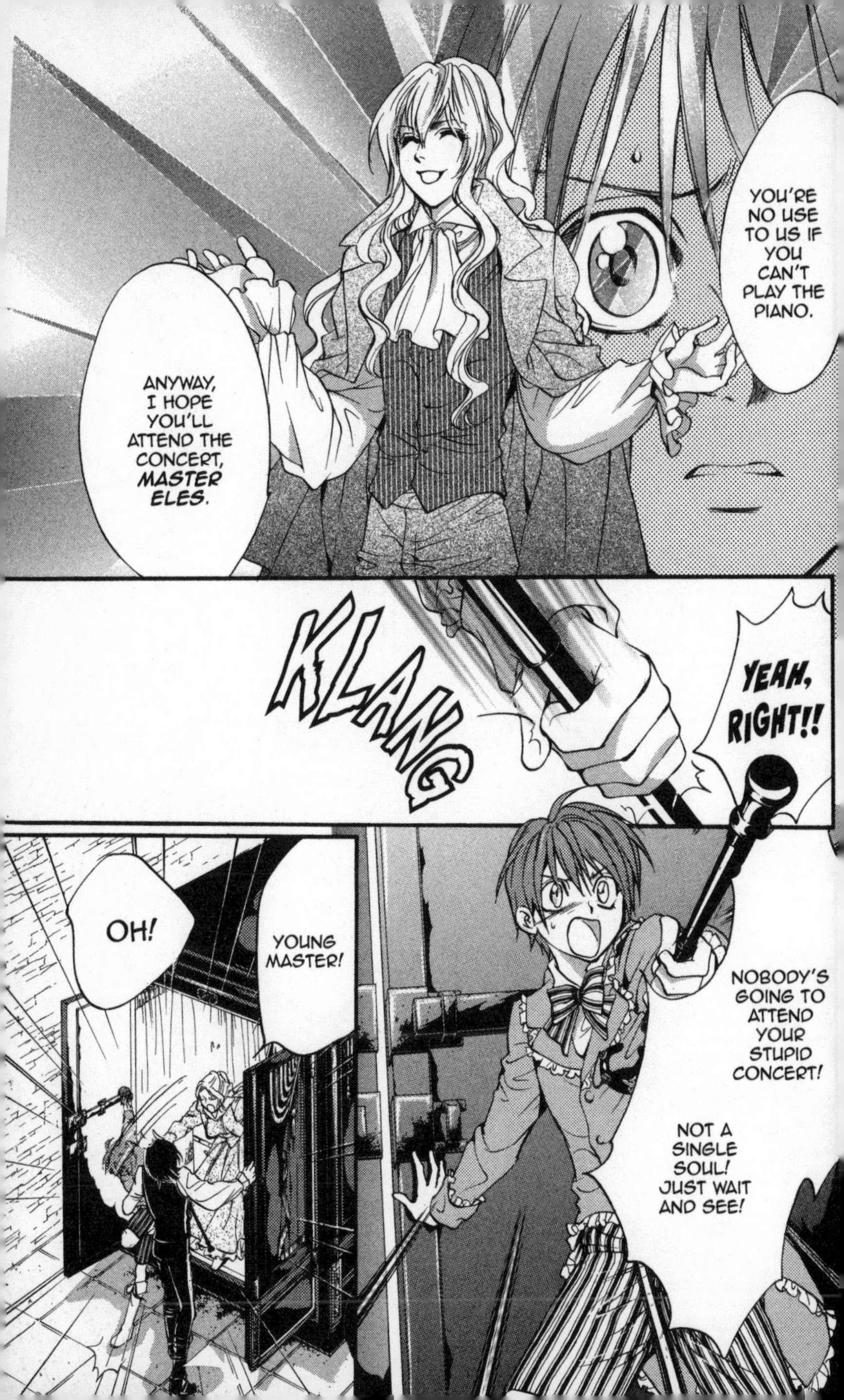
YOU'RE NO USE TO US IF YOU CAN'T PLAY THE PIANO.
ANYWAY, I HOPE YOU'LL ATTEND THE CONCERT, MASTER ELES.
YEAH, RIGHT!!
KLANG
NOBODY'S GOING TO ATTEND YOUR STUPID CONCERT!
NOT A SINGLE SOUL! JUST WAIT AND SEE!
YOUNG MASTER!
OH!

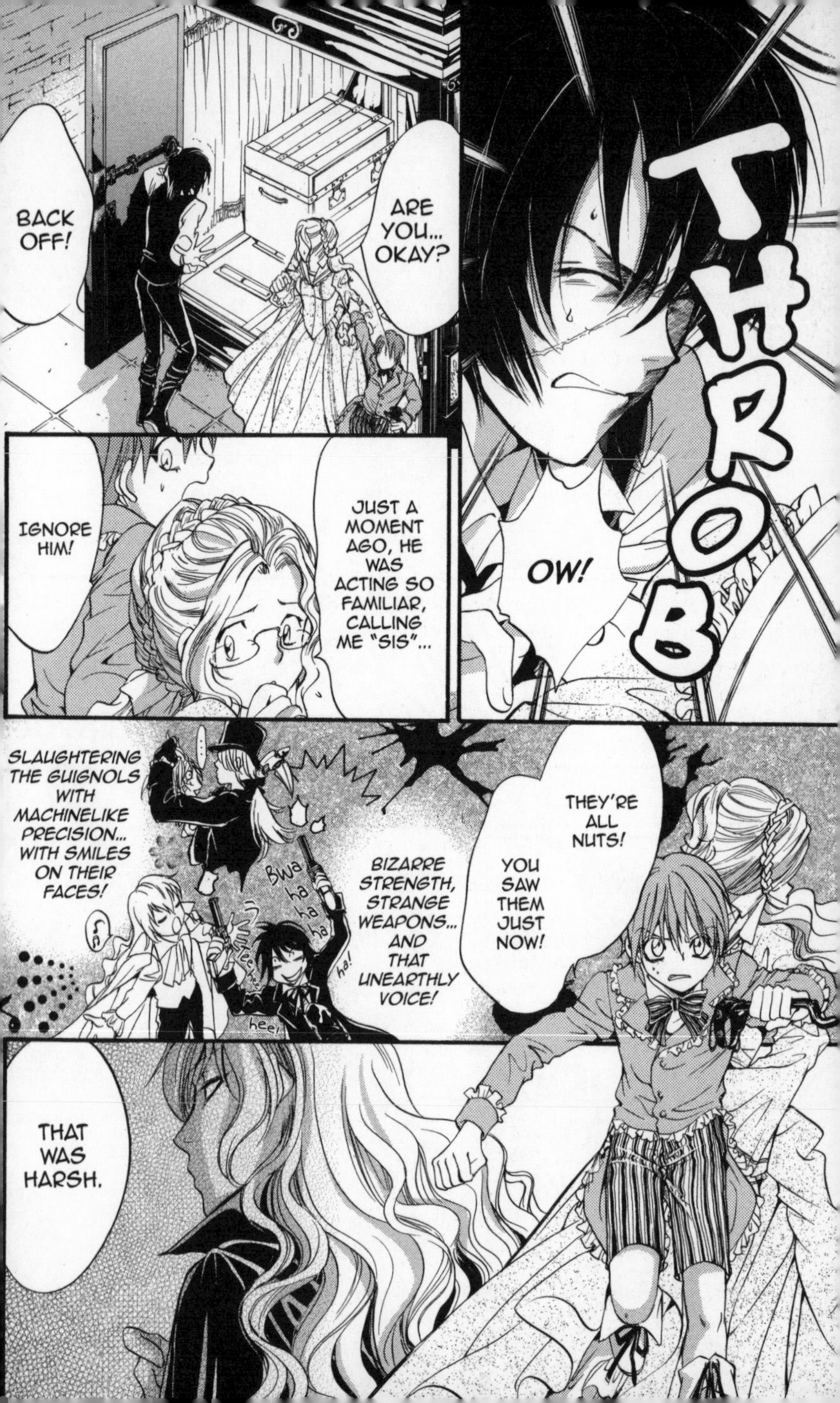
THROB
OW!
ARE YOU... OKAY?
BACK OFF!
JUST A MOMENT AGO, HE WAS ACTING SO FAMILIAR, CALLING ME "SIS"...
IGNORE HIM!
THEY'RE ALL NUTS!
YOU SAW THEM JUST NOW!
BIZARRE STRENGTH, STRANGE WEAPONS... AND THAT UNEARTHLY VOICE!
SLAUGHTERING THE GUIGNOLS WITH MACHINELIKE PRECISION... WITH SMILES ON THEIR FACES!
Bwa ha ha ha
ha!
hee!
THAT WAS HARSH.

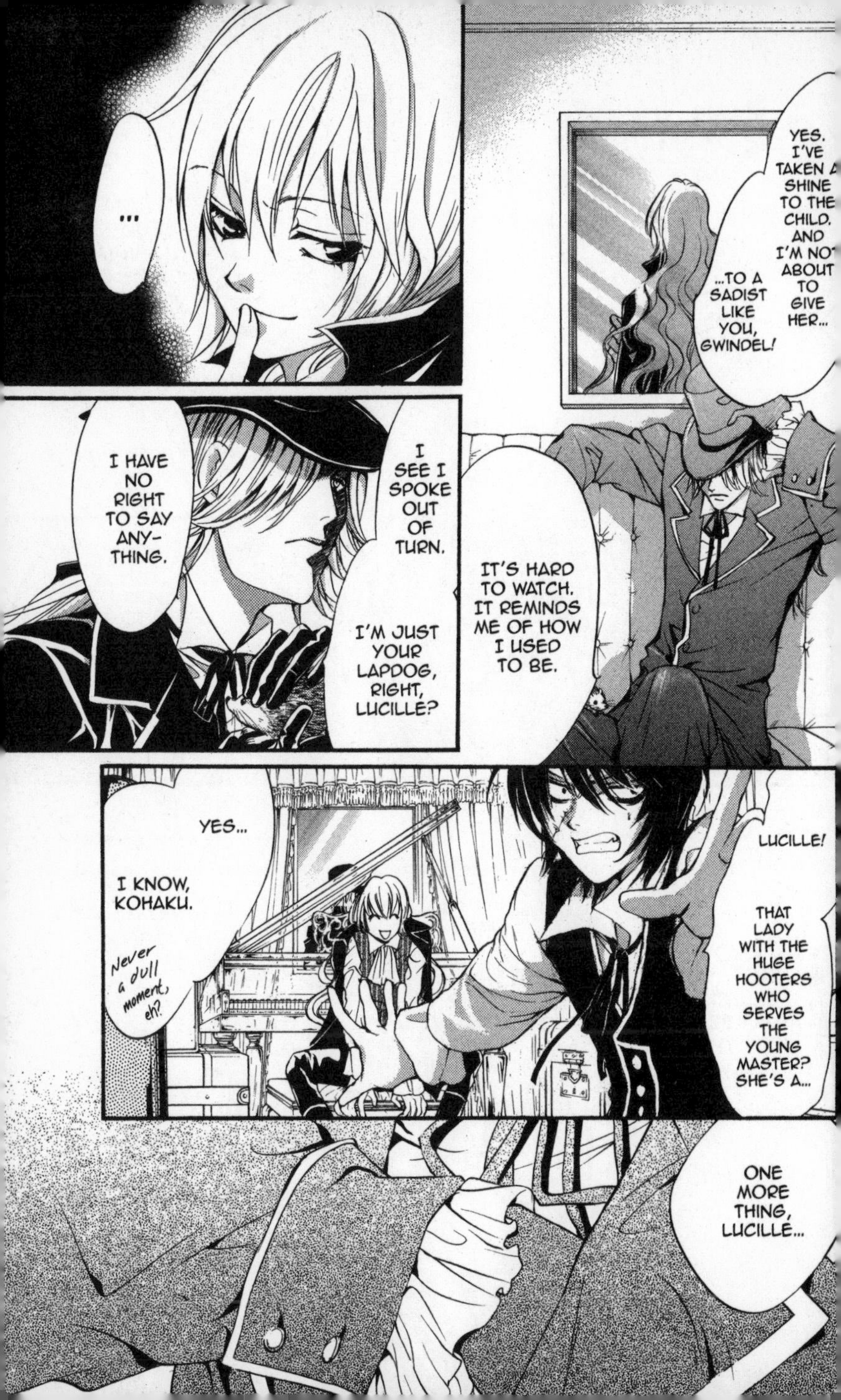
YES. I'VE TAKEN A SHINE TO THE CHILD. AND I'M NOT ABOUT TO GIVE HER...
...TO A SADIST LIKE YOU, GWINDEL!
...
IT'S HARD TO WATCH. IT REMINDS ME OF HOW I USED TO BE.
I SEE I SPOKE OUT OF TURN.
I'M JUST YOUR LAPDOG, RIGHT, LUCILLE?
I HAVE NO RIGHT TO SAY ANY-THING.
LUCILLE!
THAT LADY WITH THE HUGE HOOTERS WHO SERVES THE YOUNG MASTER? SHE'S A...
YES...
I KNOW, KOHAKU.
Never a dull moment, eh?
ONE MORE THING, LUCILLE...

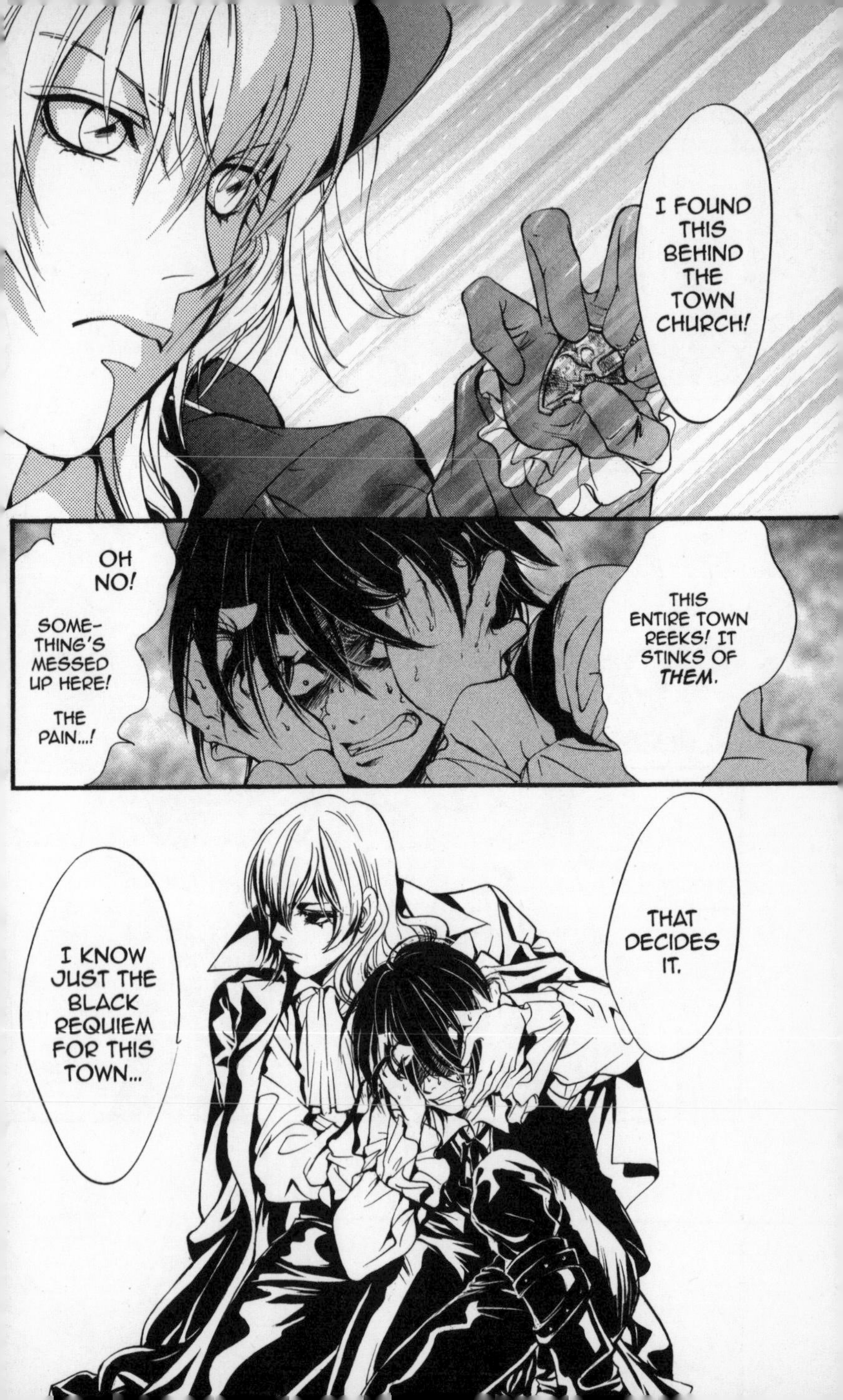
I FOUND THIS BEHIND THE TOWN CHURCH!
THIS ENTIRE TOWN REEKS! IT STINKS OF *THEM*.
OH NO!
SOME-THING'S MESSED UP HERE!
THE PAIN...!
THAT DECIDES IT.
I KNOW JUST THE BLACK REQUIEM FOR THIS TOWN...

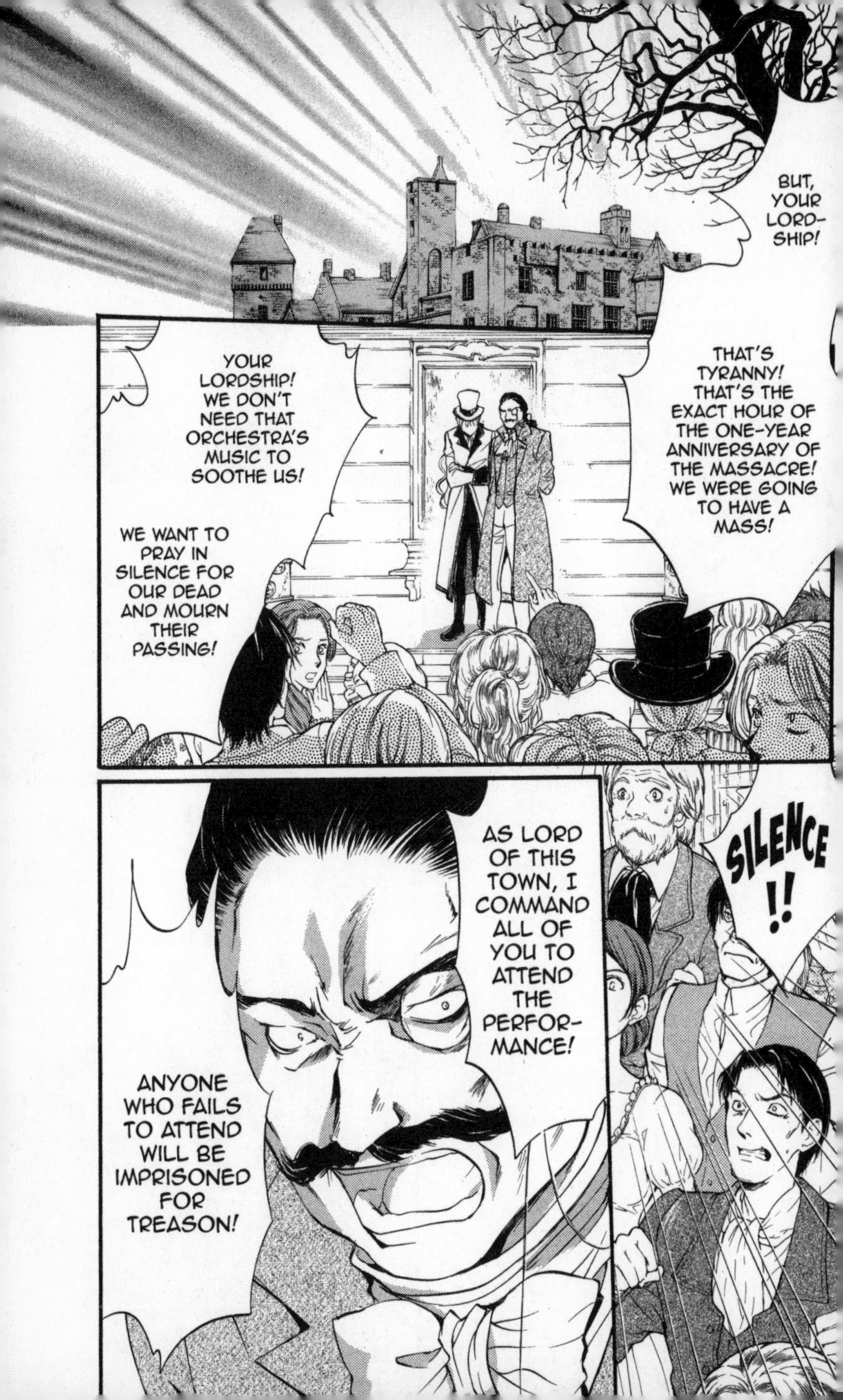
BUT, YOUR LORDSHIP!
THAT'S TYRANNY! THAT'S THE EXACT HOUR OF THE ONE-YEAR ANNIVERSARY OF THE MASSACRE! WE WERE GOING TO HAVE A MASS!
YOUR LORDSHIP! WE DON'T NEED THAT ORCHESTRA'S MUSIC TO SOOTHE US!
WE WANT TO PRAY IN SILENCE FOR OUR DEAD AND MOURN THEIR PASSING!
SILENCE!!
AS LORD OF THIS TOWN, I COMMAND ALL OF YOU TO ATTEND THE PERFORMANCE!
ANYONE WHO FAILS TO ATTEND WILL BE IMPRISONED FOR TREASON!

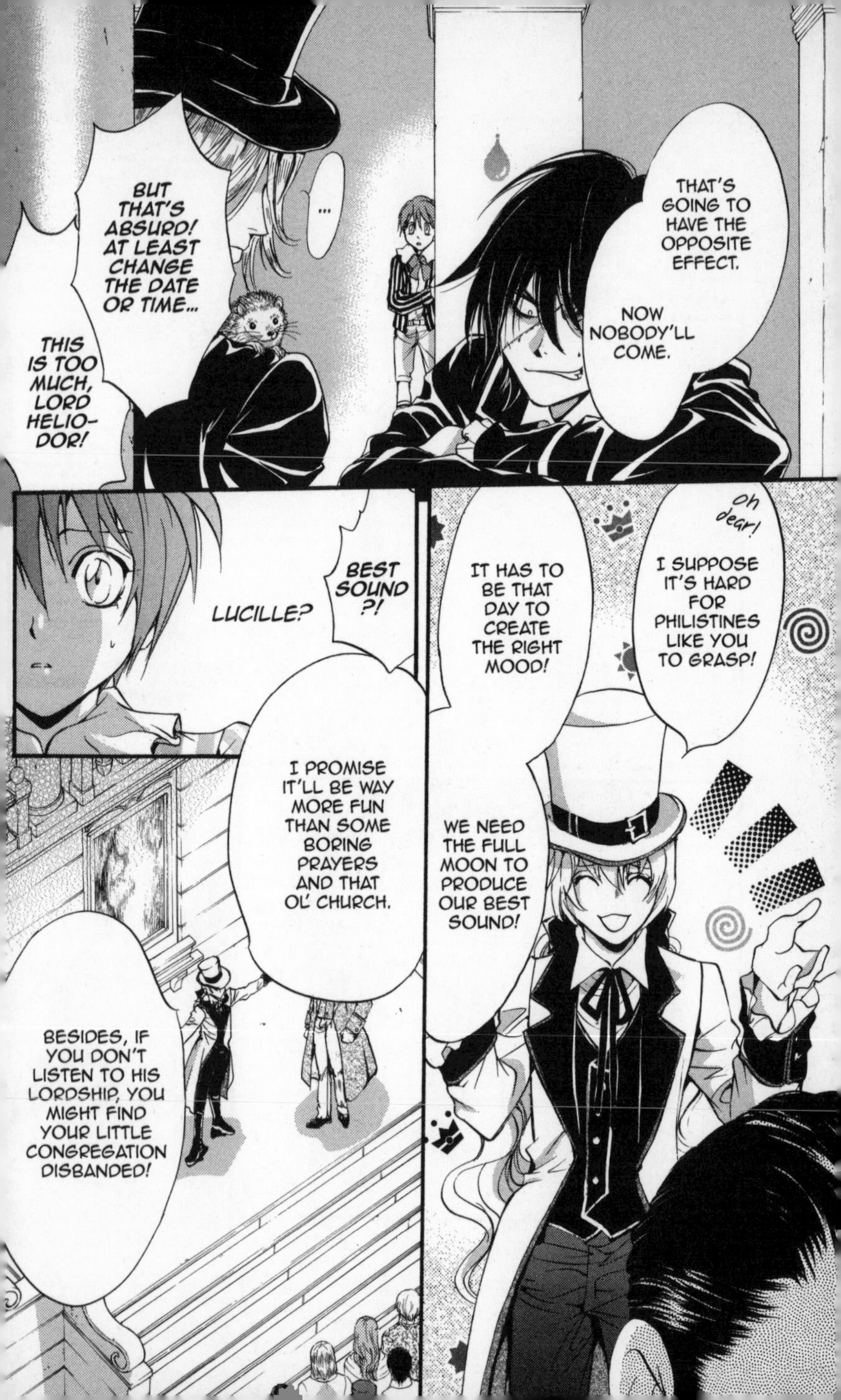
THAT'S GOING TO HAVE THE OPPOSITE EFFECT.
NOW NOBODY'LL COME.
...
BUT THAT'S ABSURD! AT LEAST CHANGE THE DATE OR TIME...
THIS IS TOO MUCH, LORD HELIODOR!
oh dear!
I SUPPOSE IT'S HARD FOR PHILISTINES LIKE YOU TO GRASP!
IT HAS TO BE THAT DAY TO CREATE THE RIGHT MOOD!
WE NEED THE FULL MOON TO PRODUCE OUR BEST SOUND!
BEST SOUND?!
LUCILLE?
I PROMISE IT'LL BE WAY MORE FUN THAN SOME BORING PRAYERS AND THAT OL' CHURCH.
BESIDES, IF YOU DON'T LISTEN TO HIS LORDSHIP, YOU MIGHT FIND YOUR LITTLE CONGREGATION DISBANDED!

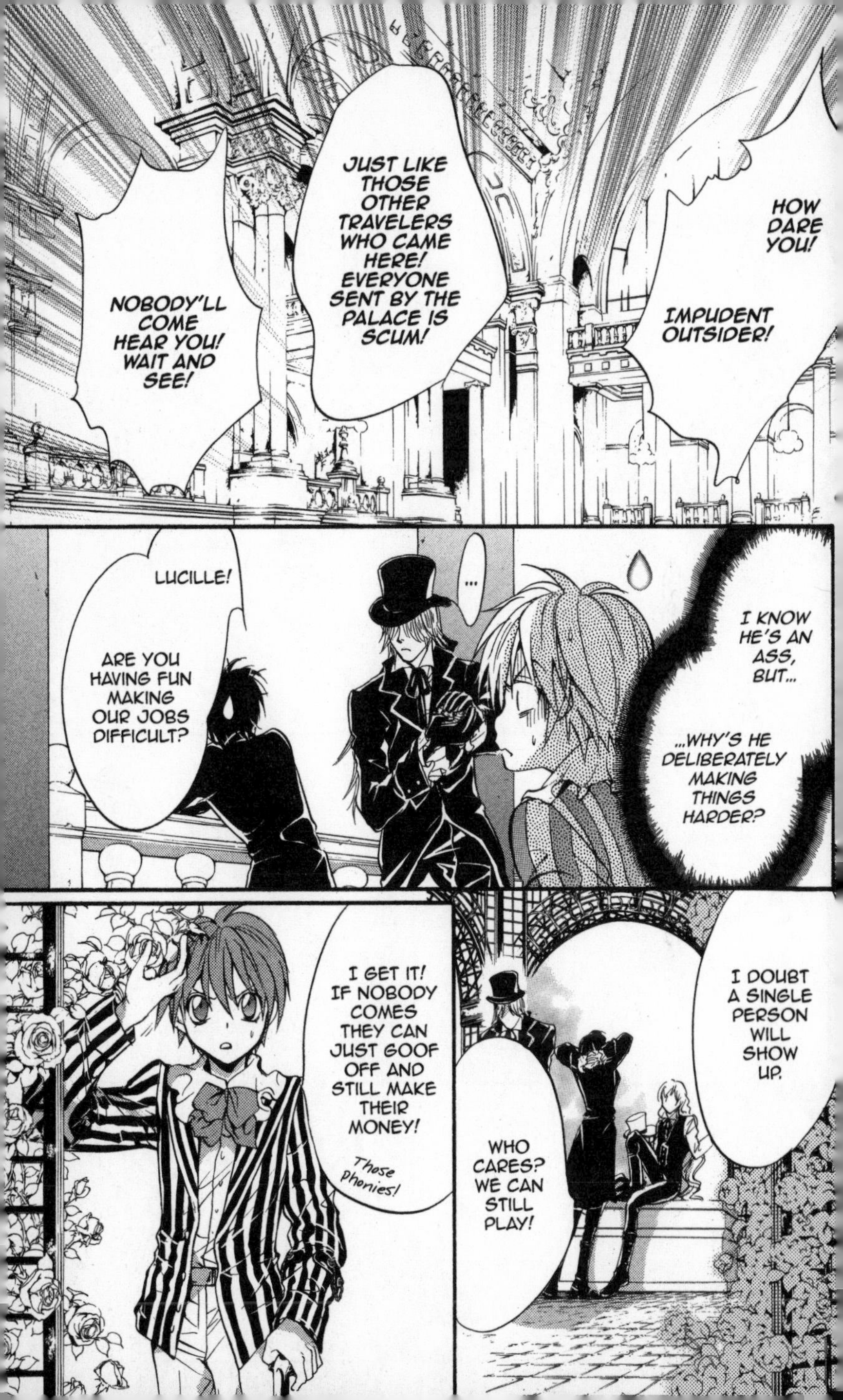
HOW DARE YOU!
IMPUDENT OUTSIDER!
JUST LIKE THOSE OTHER TRAVELERS WHO CAME HERE! EVERYONE SENT BY THE PALACE IS SCUM!
NOBODY'LL COME HEAR YOU! WAIT AND SEE!
I KNOW HE'S AN ASS, BUT...
...WHY'S HE DELIBERATELY MAKING THINGS HARDER?
...
LUCILLE!
ARE YOU HAVING FUN MAKING OUR JOBS DIFFICULT?
I DOUBT A SINGLE PERSON WILL SHOW UP.
WHO CARES? WE CAN STILL PLAY!
I GET IT! IF NOBODY COMES THEY CAN JUST GOOF OFF AND STILL MAKE THEIR MONEY!
Those Phonies!

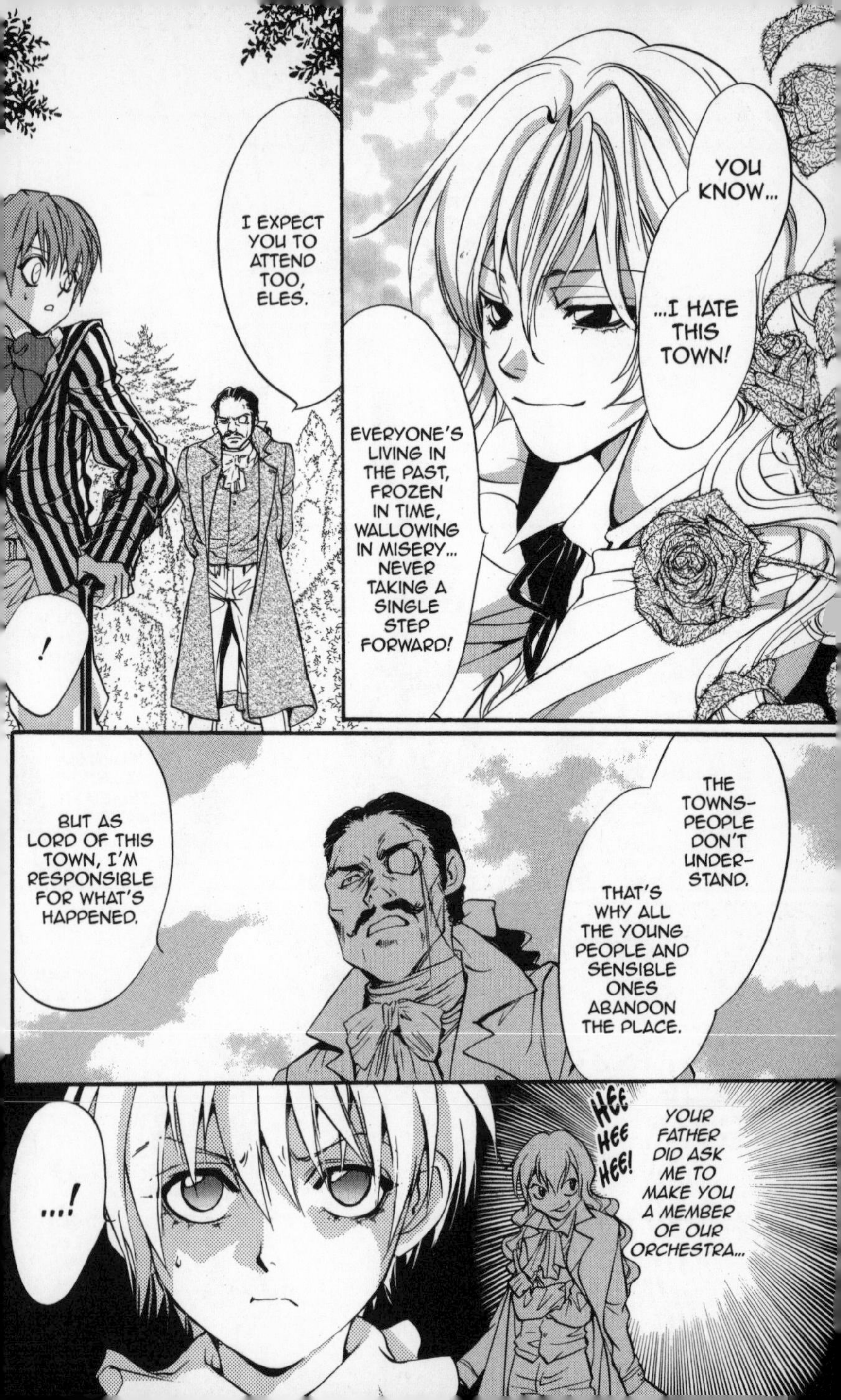
YOU KNOW...
...I HATE THIS TOWN!
EVERYONE'S LIVING IN THE PAST, FROZEN IN TIME, WALLOWING IN MISERY... NEVER TAKING A SINGLE STEP FORWARD!
I EXPECT YOU TO ATTEND TOO, ELES.
!
THE TOWNS-PEOPLE DON'T UNDER-STAND.
THAT'S WHY ALL THE YOUNG PEOPLE AND SENSIBLE ONES ABANDON THE PLACE.
BUT AS LORD OF THIS TOWN, I'M RESPONSIBLE FOR WHAT'S HAPPENED.
YOUR FATHER DID ASK ME TO MAKE YOU A MEMBER OF OUR ORCHESTRA...
HEE HEE HEE!
...!

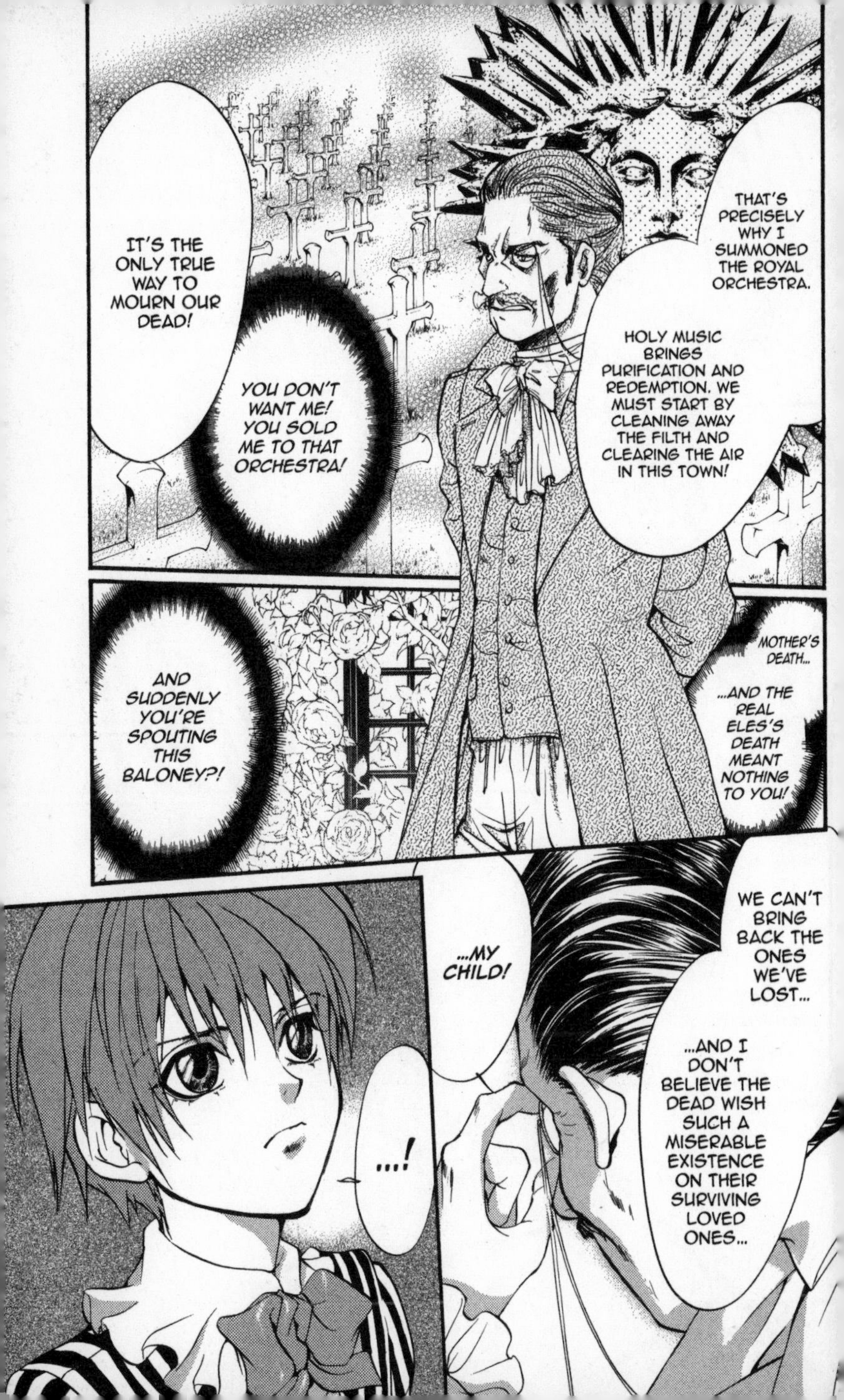
THAT'S PRECISELY WHY I SUMMONED THE ROYAL ORCHESTRA.
HOLY MUSIC BRINGS PURIFICATION AND REDEMPTION. WE MUST START BY CLEANING AWAY THE FILTH AND CLEARING THE AIR IN THIS TOWN!
IT'S THE ONLY TRUE WAY TO MOURN OUR DEAD!
YOU DON'T WANT ME! YOU SOLD ME TO THAT ORCHESTRA!
MOTHER'S DEATH...
...AND THE REAL ELES'S DEATH MEANT NOTHING TO YOU!
AND SUDDENLY YOU'RE SPOUTING THIS BALONEY?!
WE CAN'T BRING BACK THE ONES WE'VE LOST...
...AND I DON'T BELIEVE THE DEAD WISH SUCH A MISERABLE EXISTENCE ON THEIR SURVIVING LOVED ONES...
...MY CHILD!
...!

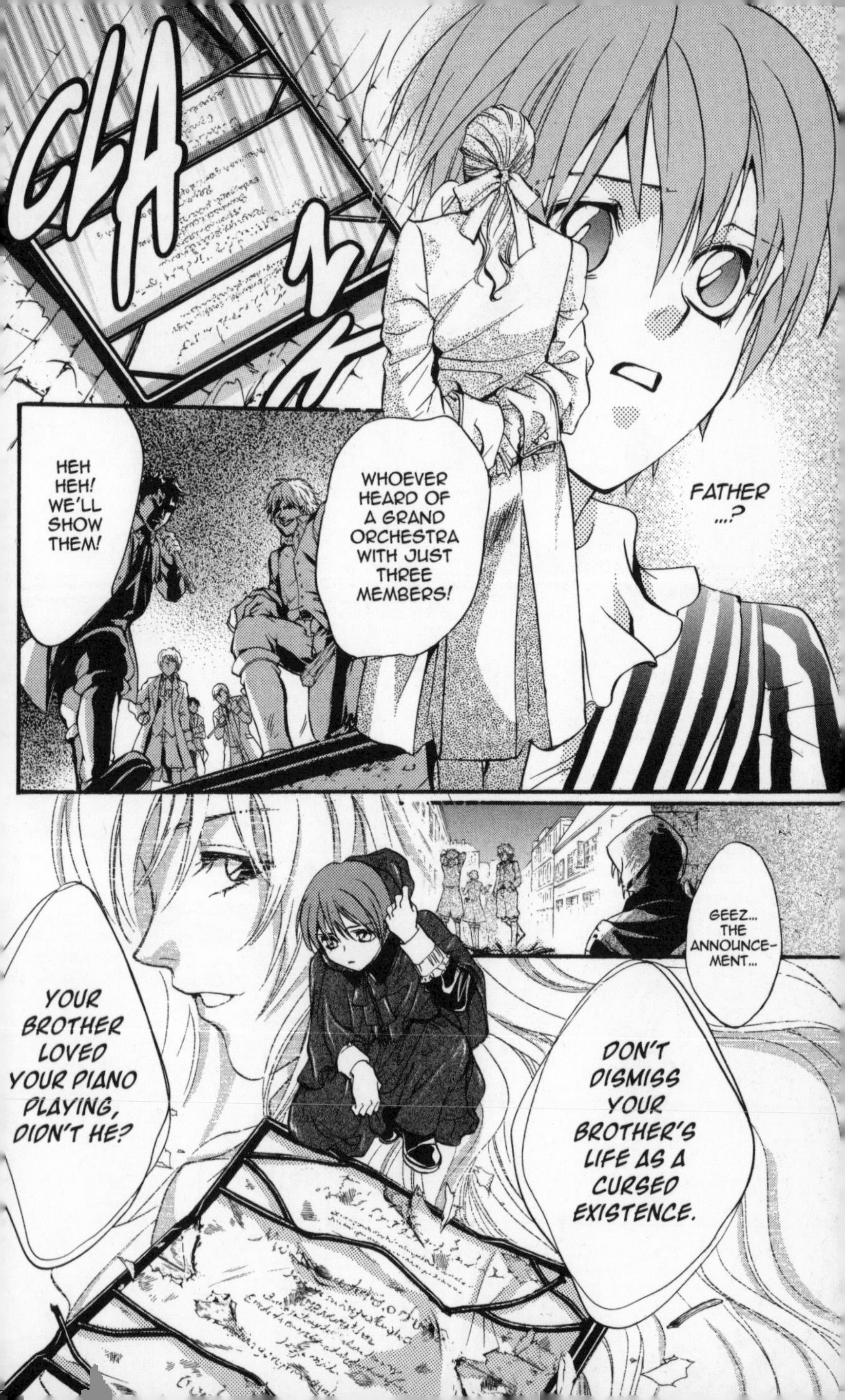
CLANK
FATHER ...?
WHOEVER HEARD OF A GRAND ORCHESTRA WITH JUST THREE MEMBERS!
HEH HEH! WE'LL SHOW THEM!
GEEZ... THE ANNOUNCE-MENT...
DON'T DISMISS YOUR BROTHER'S LIFE AS A CURSED EXISTENCE.
YOUR BROTHER LOVED YOUR PIANO PLAYING, DIDN'T HE?

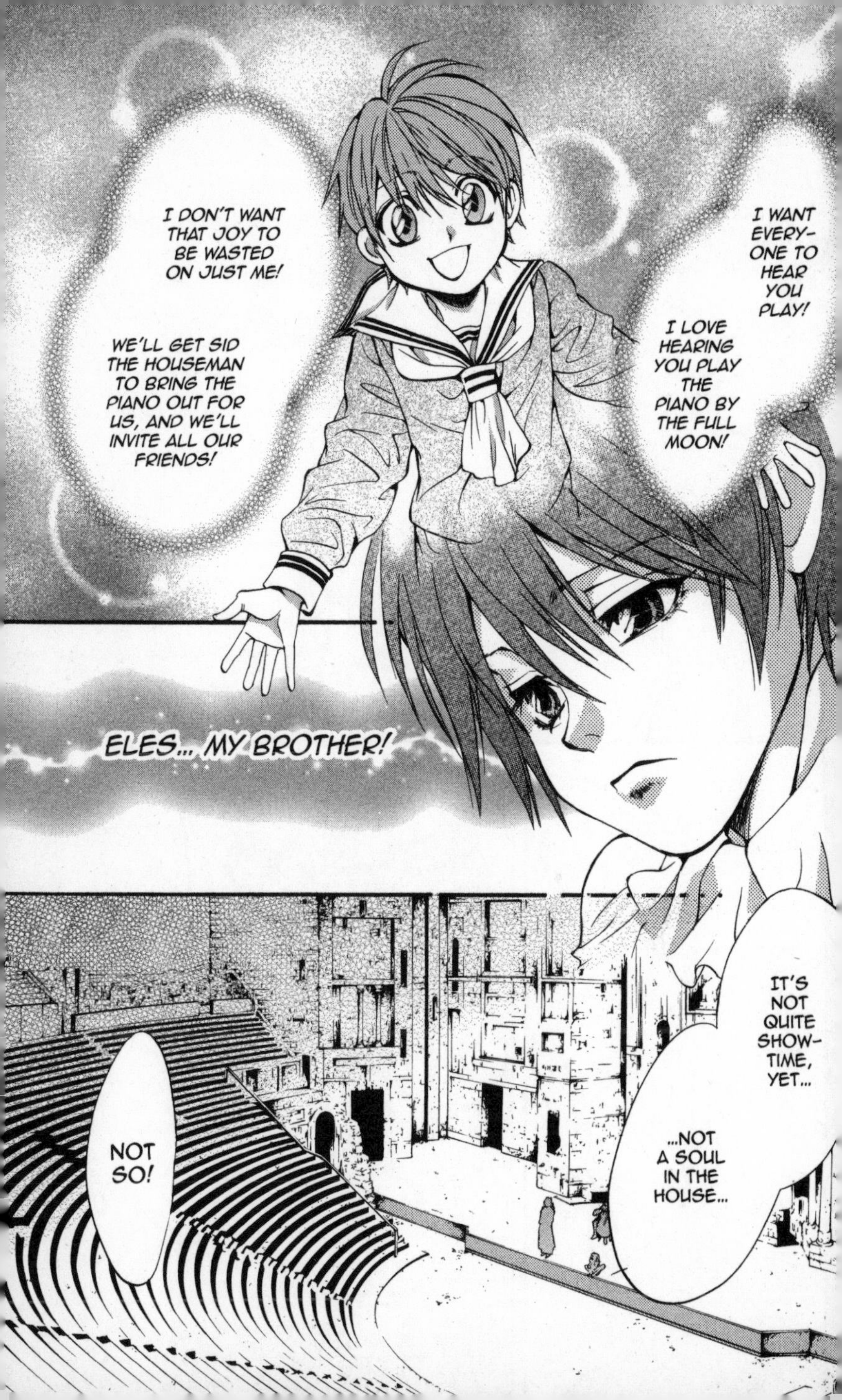
I WANT EVERY-ONE TO HEAR YOU PLAY!
I LOVE HEARING YOU PLAY THE PIANO BY THE FULL MOON!
I DON'T WANT THAT JOY TO BE WASTED ON JUST ME!
WE'LL GET SID THE HOUSEMAN TO BRING THE PIANO OUT FOR US, AND WE'LL INVITE ALL OUR FRIENDS!
ELES... MY BROTHER!
IT'S NOT QUITE SHOW-TIME, YET...
...NOT A SOUL IN THE HOUSE...
NOT SO!

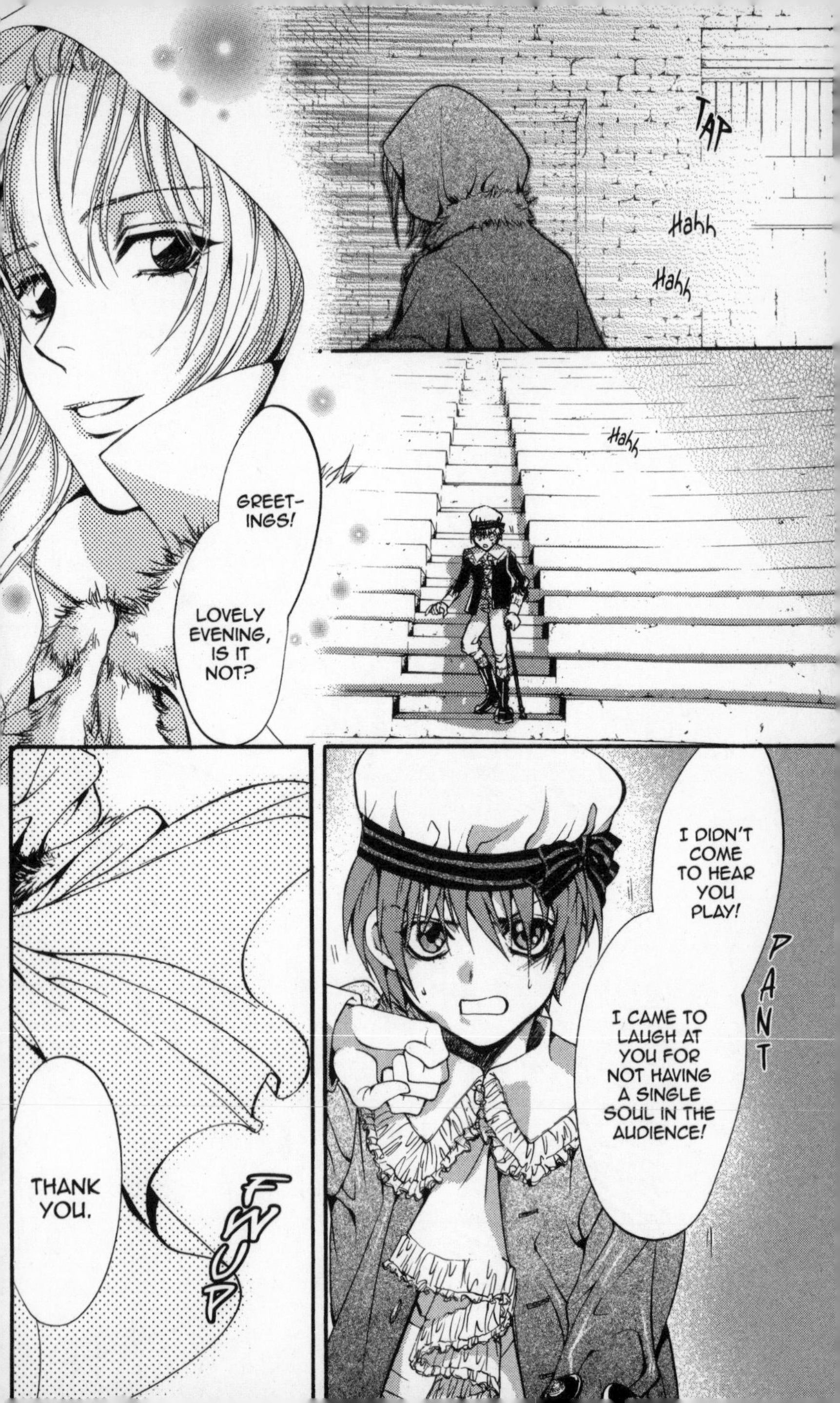
TAP
Hahh
Hahh
Hahh
GREET-INGS!
LOVELY EVENING, IS IT NOT?
I DIDN'T COME TO HEAR YOU PLAY!
I CAME TO LAUGH AT YOU FOR NOT HAVING A SINGLE SOUL IN THE AUDIENCE!
PANT
THANK YOU.
FWUP

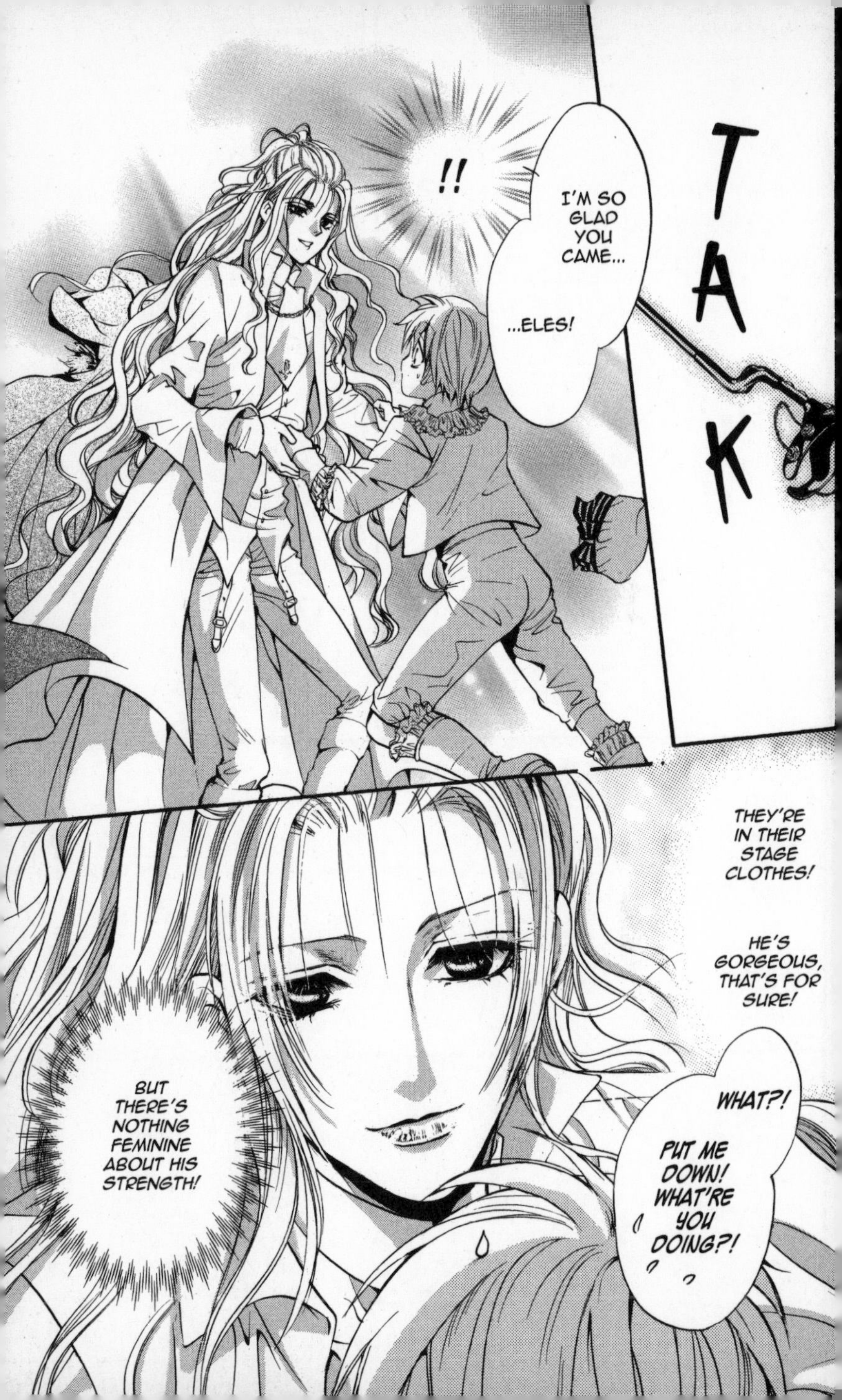
TAK
I'M SO GLAD YOU CAME... ...ELES!
!!
THEY'RE IN THEIR STAGE CLOTHES!
HE'S GORGEOUS, THAT'S FOR SURE!
WHAT?! PUT ME DOWN! WHAT'RE YOU DOING?!
BUT THERE'S NOTHING FEMININE ABOUT HIS STRENGTH!

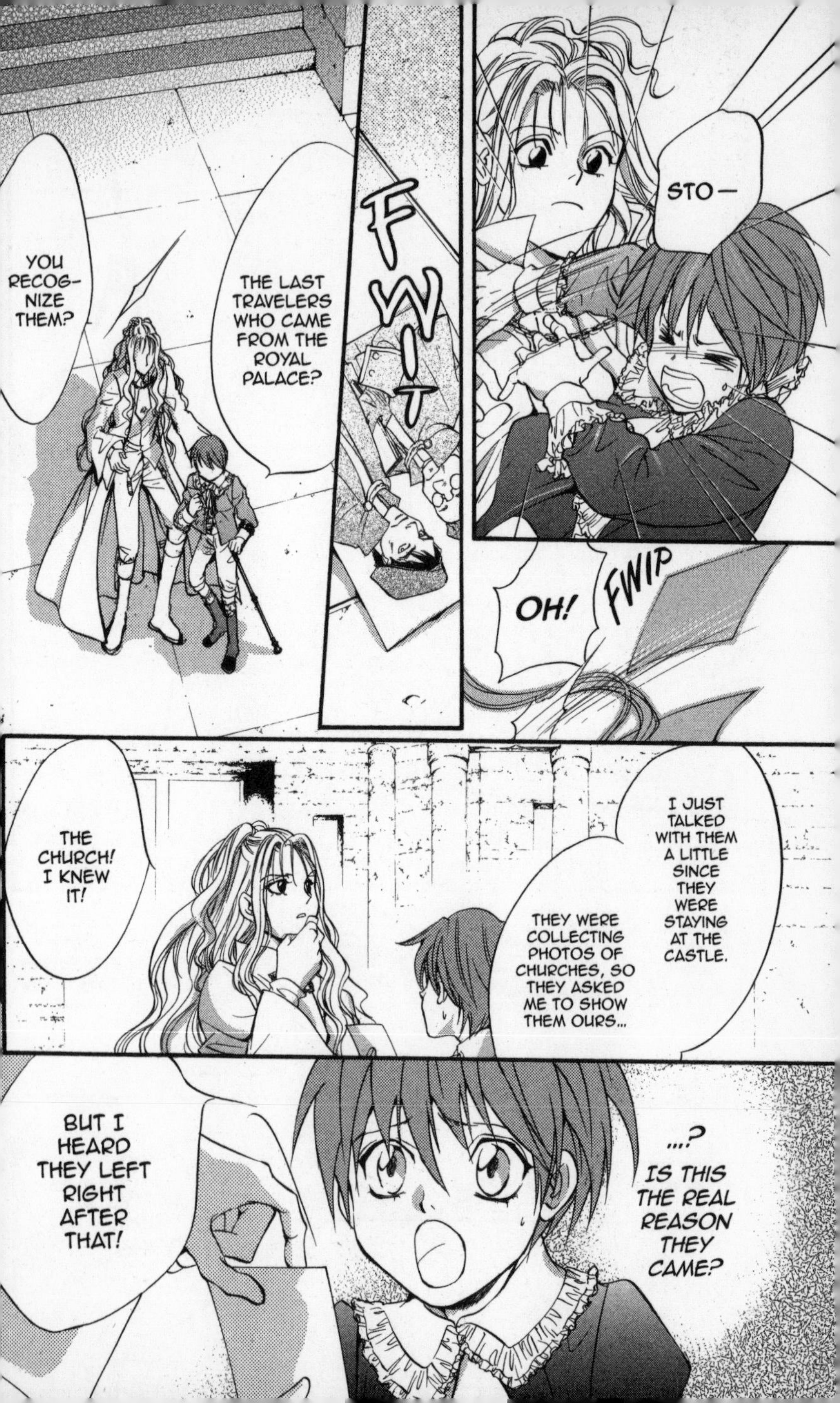

STO—
OH!
FWIP
FWIT
THE LAST TRAVELERS WHO CAME FROM THE ROYAL PALACE?
YOU RECOG-NIZE THEM?
I JUST TALKED WITH THEM A LITTLE SINCE THEY WERE STAYING AT THE CASTLE.
THEY WERE COLLECTING PHOTOS OF CHURCHES, SO THEY ASKED ME TO SHOW THEM OURS...
THE CHURCH! I KNEW IT!
...? IS THIS THE REAL REASON THEY CAME?
BUT I HEARD THEY LEFT RIGHT AFTER THAT!

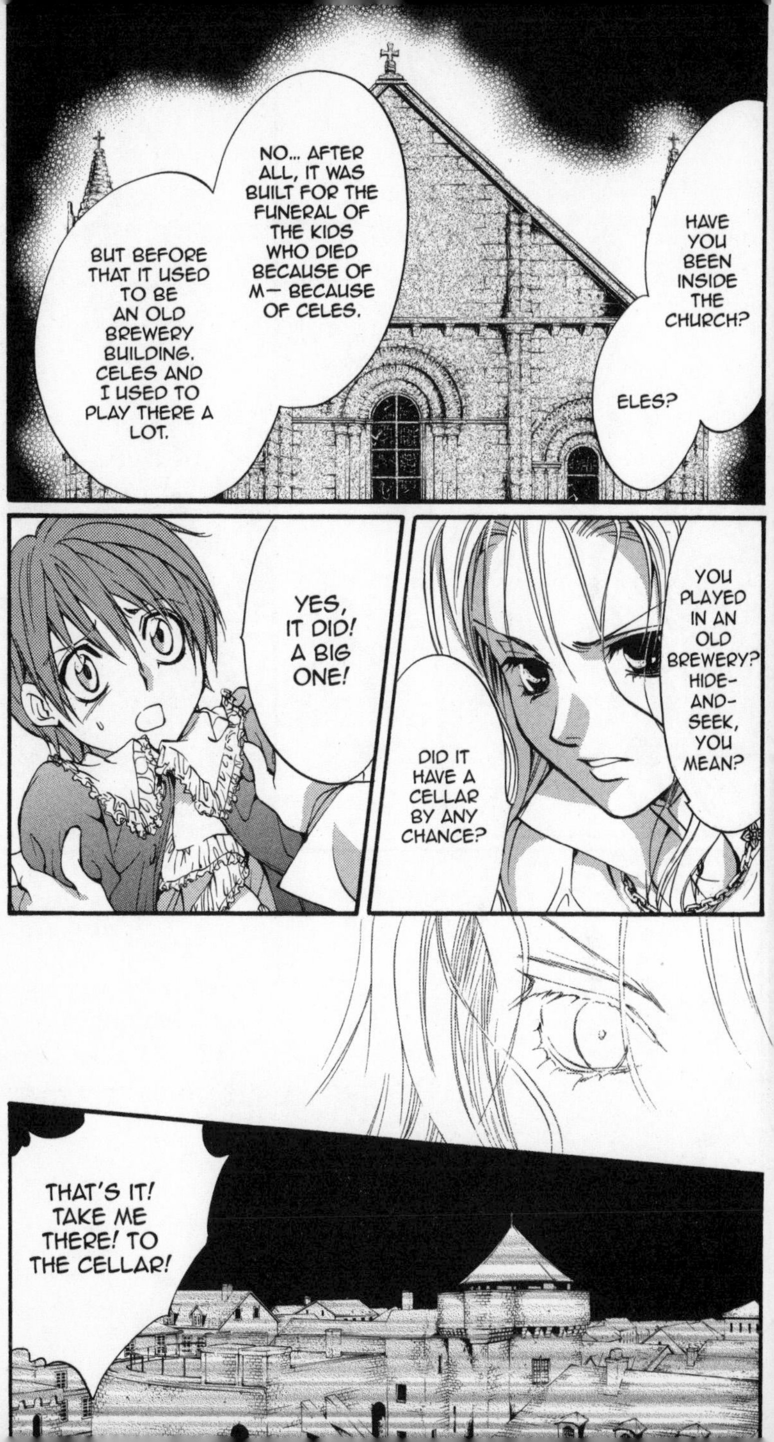
HAVE YOU BEEN INSIDE THE CHURCH?
ELES?
NO... AFTER ALL, IT WAS BUILT FOR THE FUNERAL OF THE KIDS WHO DIED BECAUSE OF M— BECAUSE OF CELES.
BUT BEFORE THAT IT USED TO BE AN OLD BREWERY BUILDING. CELES AND I USED TO PLAY THERE A LOT.
YOU PLAYED IN AN OLD BREWERY? HIDE-AND-SEEK, YOU MEAN?
DID IT HAVE A CELLAR BY ANY CHANCE?
YES, IT DID! A BIG ONE!
THAT'S IT! TAKE ME THERE! TO THE CELLAR!

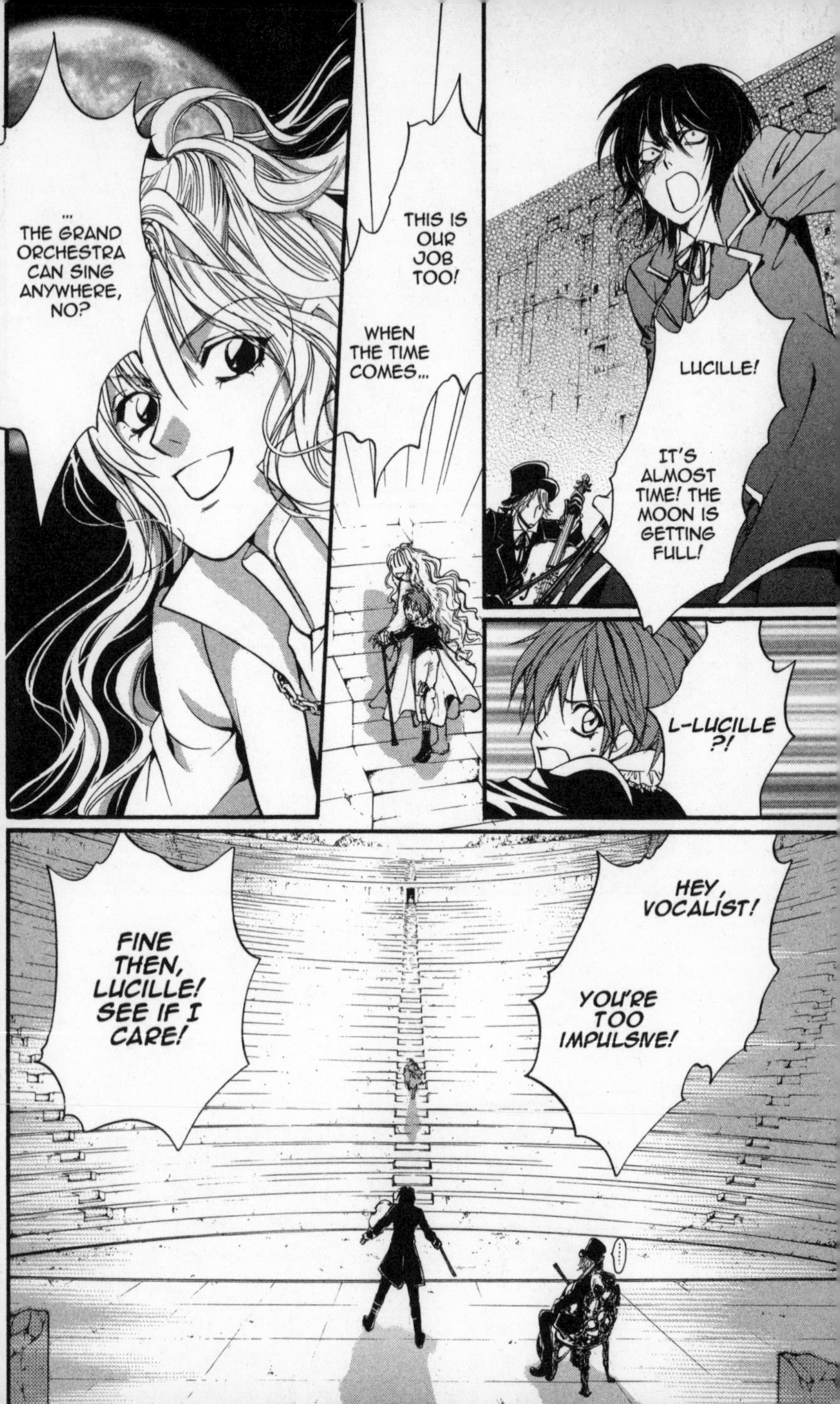
LUCILLE!
IT'S ALMOST TIME! THE MOON IS GETTING FULL!
L-LUCILLE ?!
THIS IS OUR JOB TOO!
WHEN THE TIME COMES...
... THE GRAND ORCHESTRA CAN SING ANYWHERE, NO?
HEY, VOCALIST!
YOU'RE TOO IMPULSIVE!
FINE THEN, LUCILLE! SEE IF I CARE!
.....

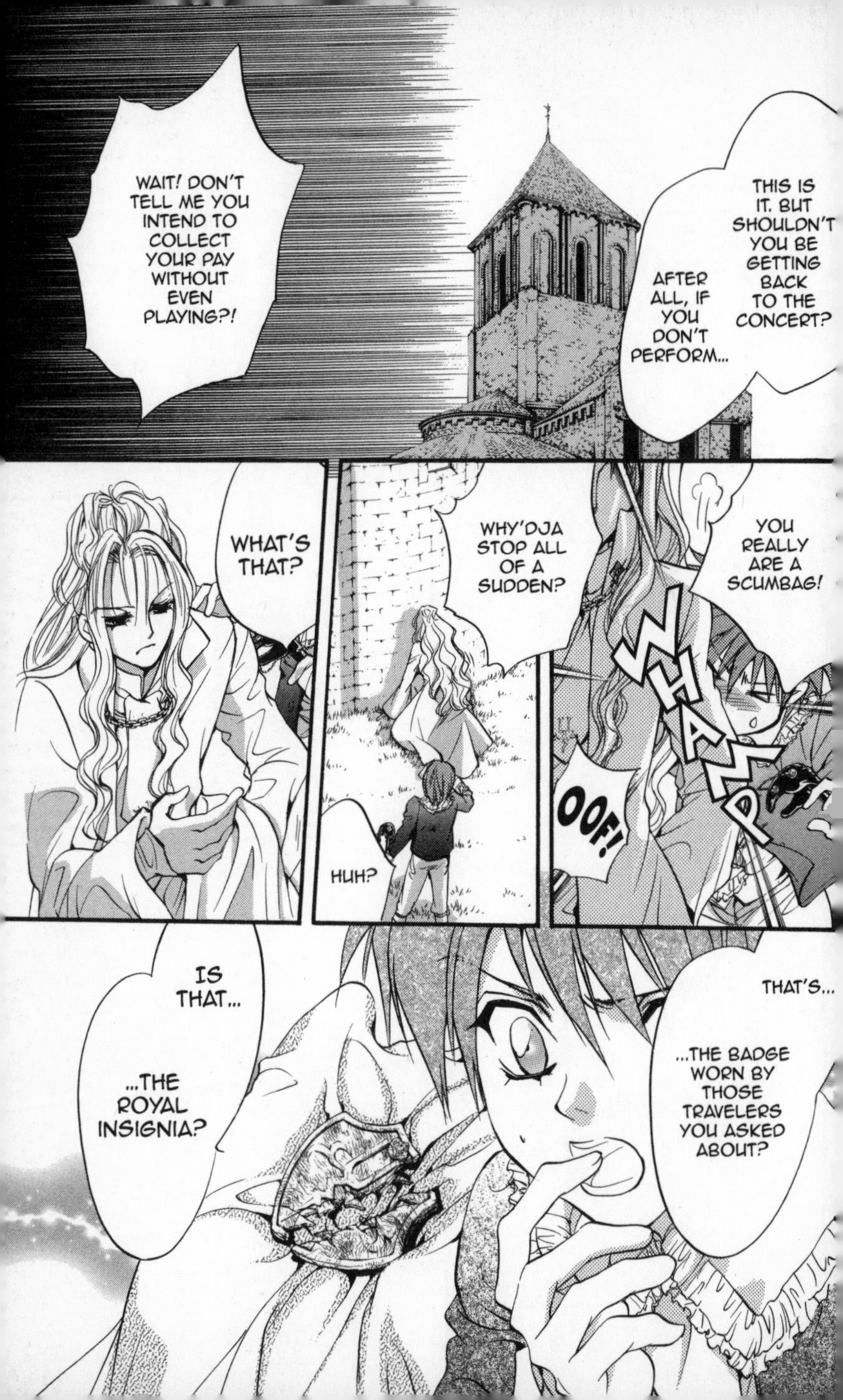
THIS IS IT. BUT SHOULDN'T YOU BE GETTING BACK TO THE CONCERT?
AFTER ALL, IF YOU DON'T PERFORM...
WAIT! DON'T TELL ME YOU INTEND TO COLLECT YOUR PAY WITHOUT EVEN PLAYING?!
YOU REALLY ARE A SCUMBAG!
WHAMP
OOF!
WHY'DJA STOP ALL OF A SUDDEN?
HUH?
WHAT'S THAT?
THAT'S...
...THE BADGE WORN BY THOSE TRAVELERS YOU ASKED ABOUT?
IS THAT...
...THE ROYAL INSIGNIA?

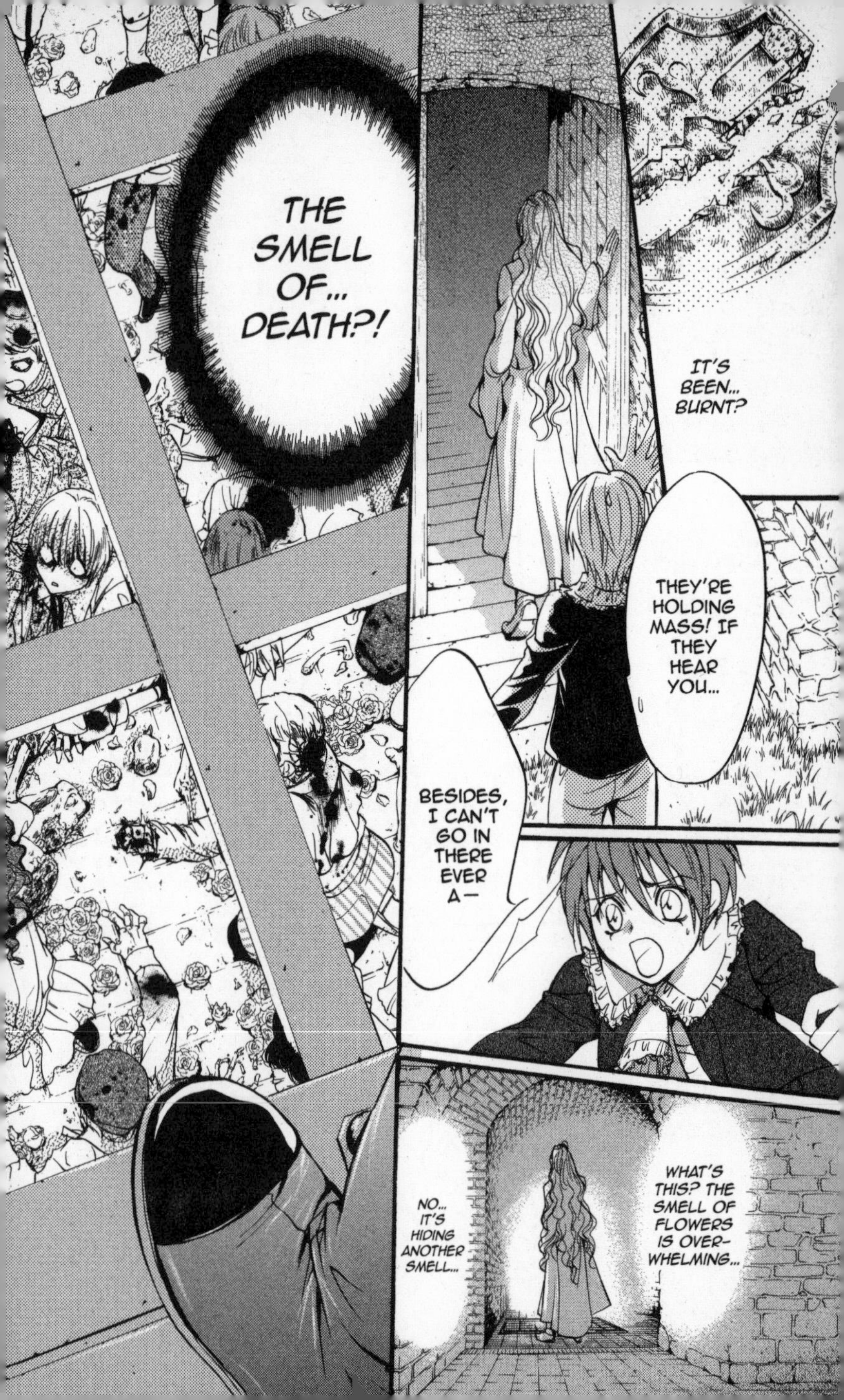
IT'S BEEN... BURNT?
THEY'RE HOLDING MASS! IF THEY HEAR YOU...
BESIDES, I CAN'T GO IN THERE EVER A—
WHAT'S THIS? THE SMELL OF FLOWERS IS OVER-WHELMING...
NO... IT'S HIDING ANOTHER SMELL...
THE SMELL OF... DEATH?!

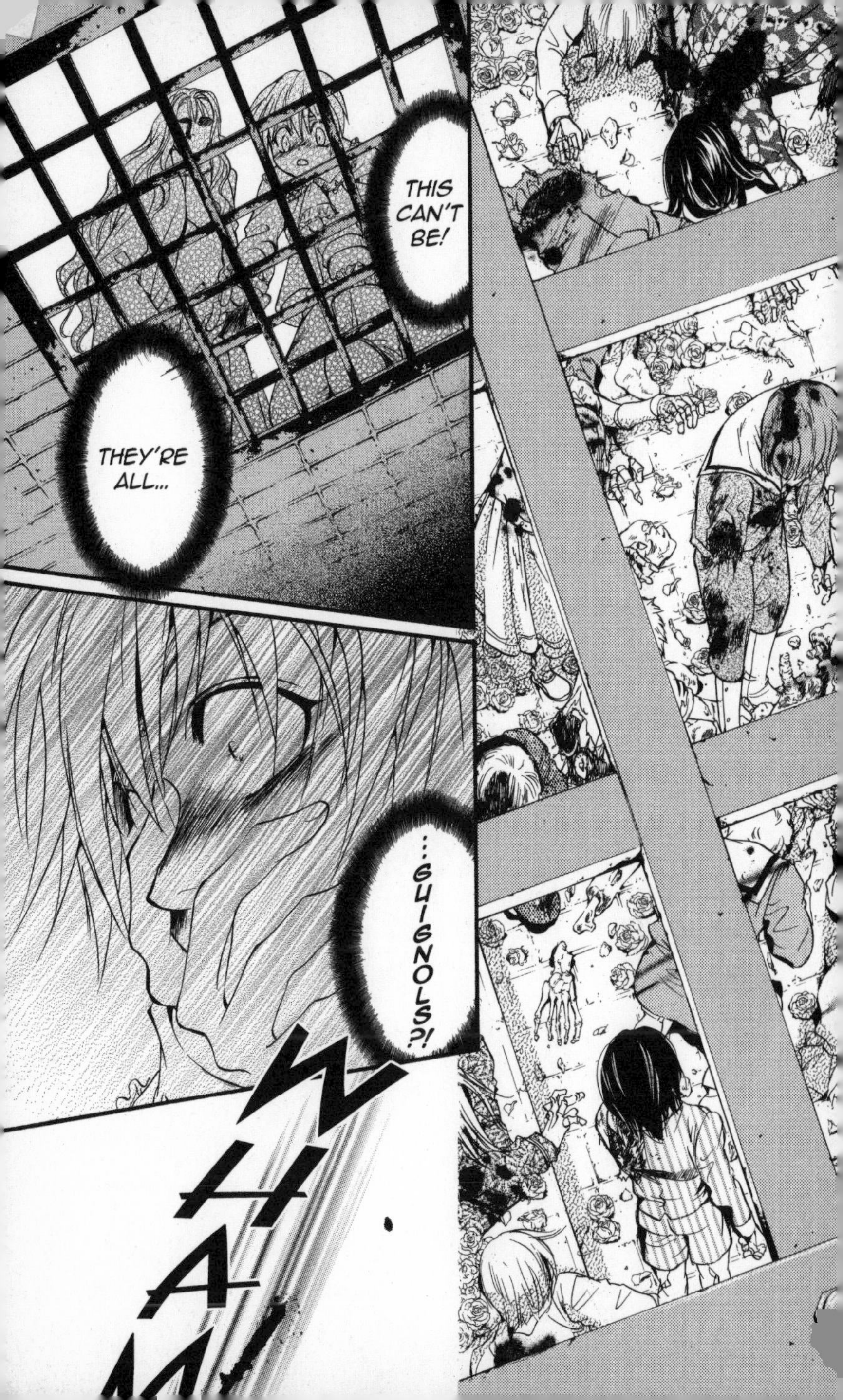
THIS CAN'T BE!
THEY'RE ALL...
...GUIGNOLS?!
WHAM

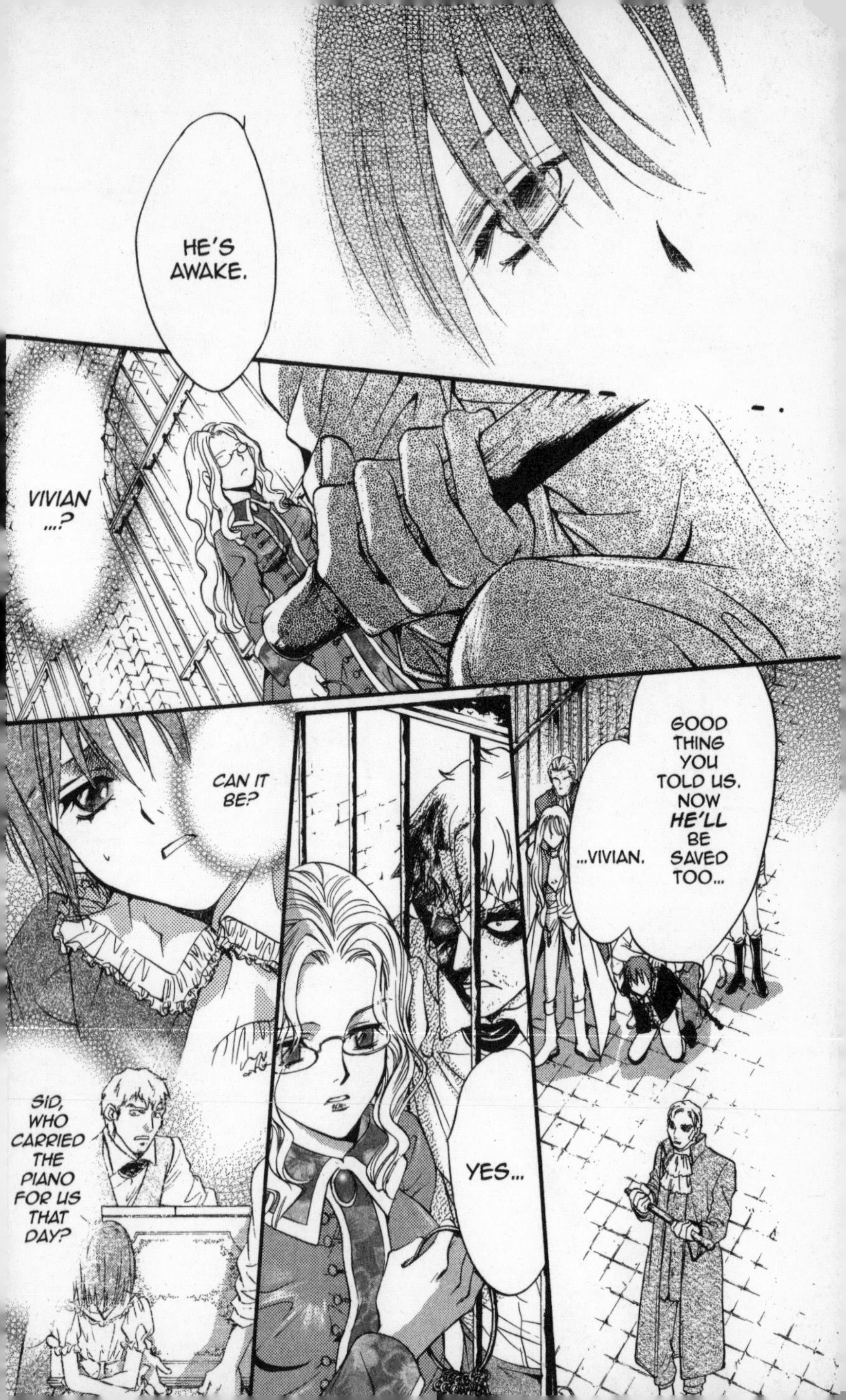
HE'S AWAKE.
VIVIAN ...?
GOOD THING YOU TOLD US. NOW HE'LL BE SAVED TOO...
...VIVIAN.
CAN IT BE?
SID, WHO CARRIED THE PIANO FOR US THAT DAY?
YES...

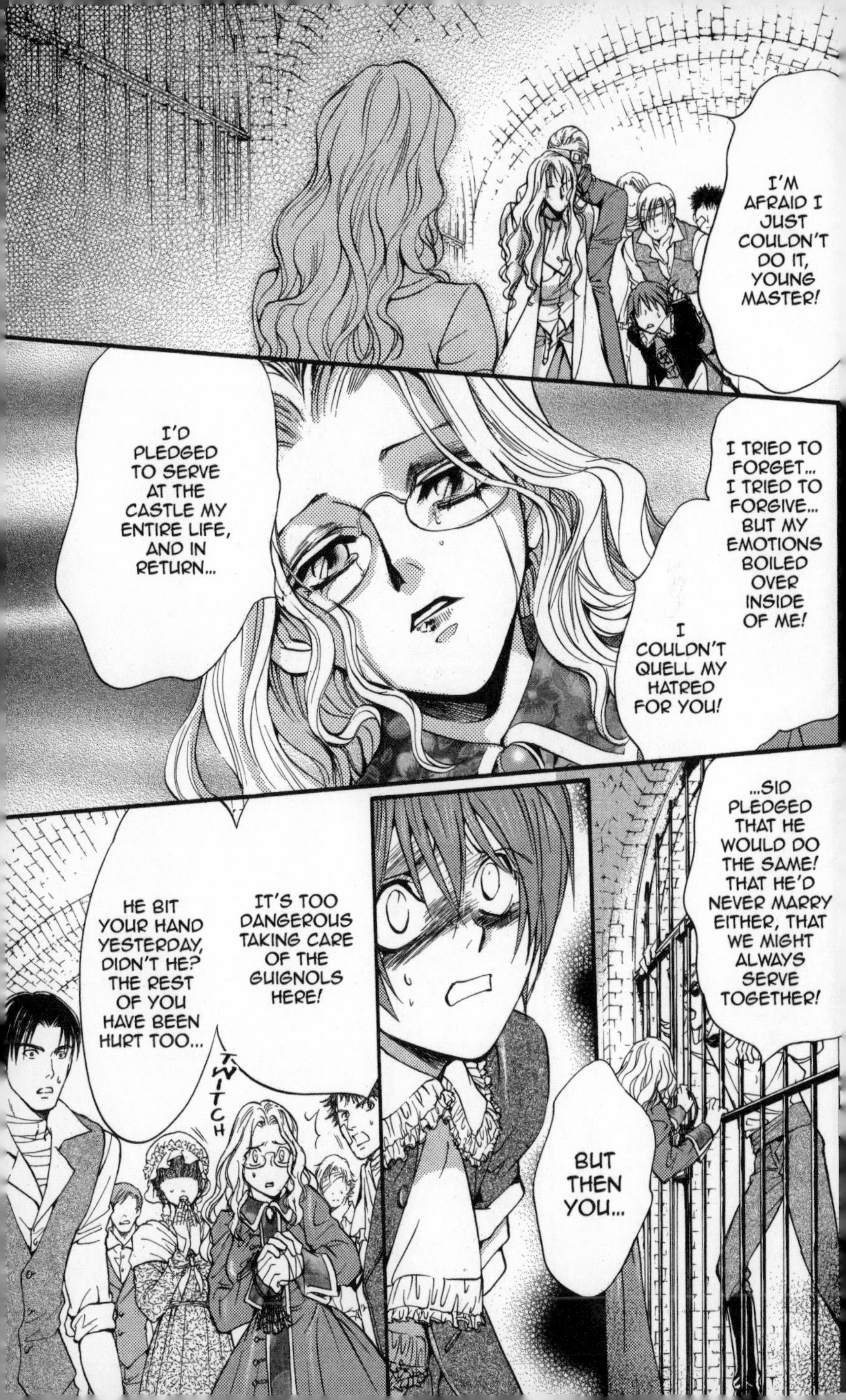
I'M AFRAID I JUST COULDN'T DO IT, YOUNG MASTER!
I TRIED TO FORGET... I TRIED TO FORGIVE... BUT MY EMOTIONS BOILED OVER INSIDE OF ME!
I COULDN'T QUELL MY HATRED FOR YOU!
I'D PLEDGED TO SERVE AT THE CASTLE MY ENTIRE LIFE, AND IN RETURN...
...SID PLEDGED THAT HE WOULD DO THE SAME! THAT HE'D NEVER MARRY EITHER, THAT WE MIGHT ALWAYS SERVE TOGETHER!
BUT THEN YOU...
IT'S TOO DANGEROUS TAKING CARE OF THE GUIGNOLS HERE!
HE BIT YOUR HAND YESTERDAY, DIDN'T HE? THE REST OF YOU HAVE BEEN HURT TOO...
TWITCH

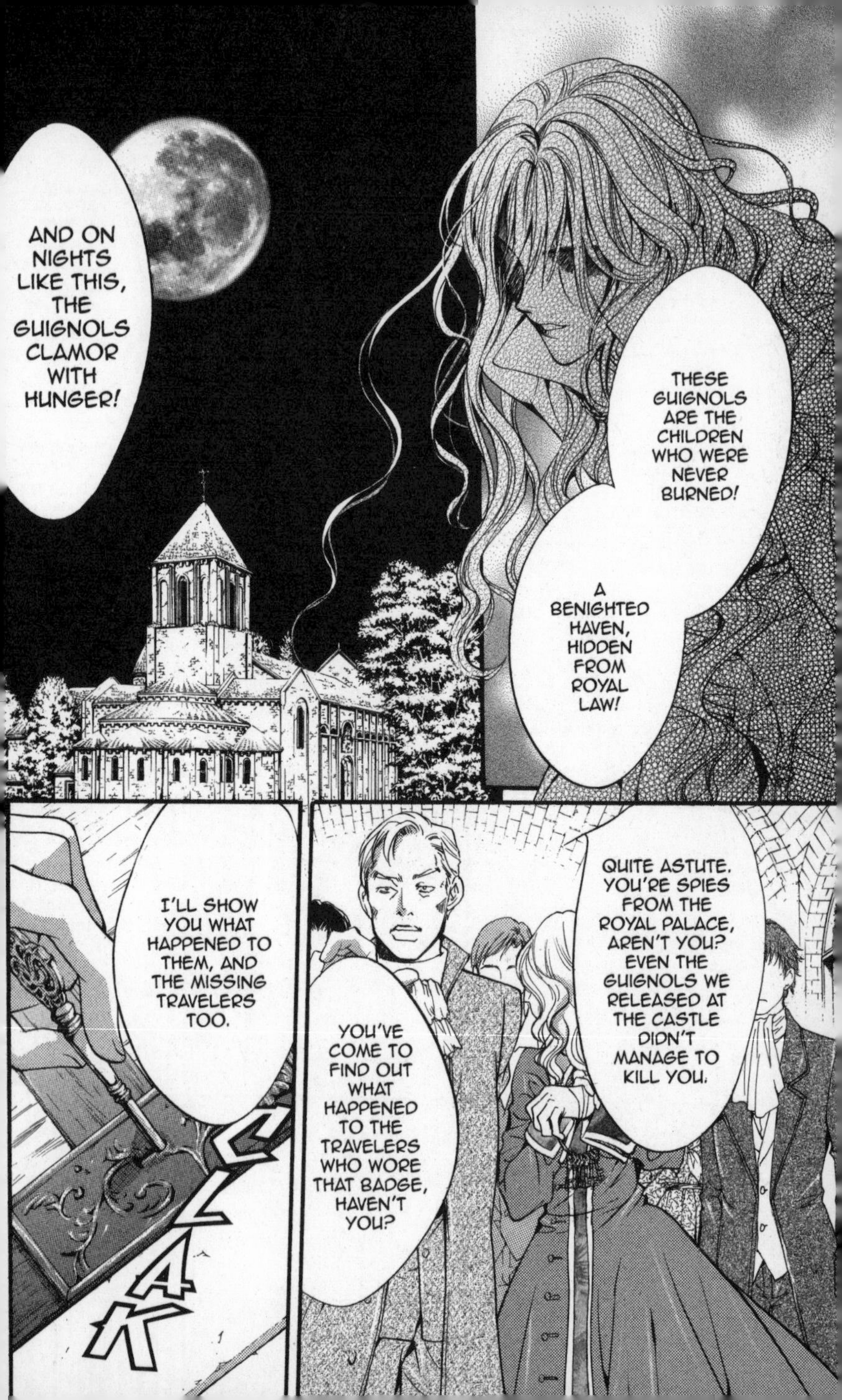
THESE GUIGNOLS ARE THE CHILDREN WHO WERE NEVER BURNED!
A BENIGHTED HAVEN, HIDDEN FROM ROYAL LAW!
AND ON NIGHTS LIKE THIS, THE GUIGNOLS CLAMOR WITH HUNGER!
QUITE ASTUTE. YOU'RE SPIES FROM THE ROYAL PALACE, AREN'T YOU? EVEN THE GUIGNOLS WE RELEASED AT THE CASTLE DIDN'T MANAGE TO KILL YOU.
YOU'VE COME TO FIND OUT WHAT HAPPENED TO THE TRAVELERS WHO WORE THAT BADGE, HAVEN'T YOU?
I'LL SHOW YOU WHAT HAPPENED TO THEM, AND THE MISSING TRAVELERS TOO.
CLAK

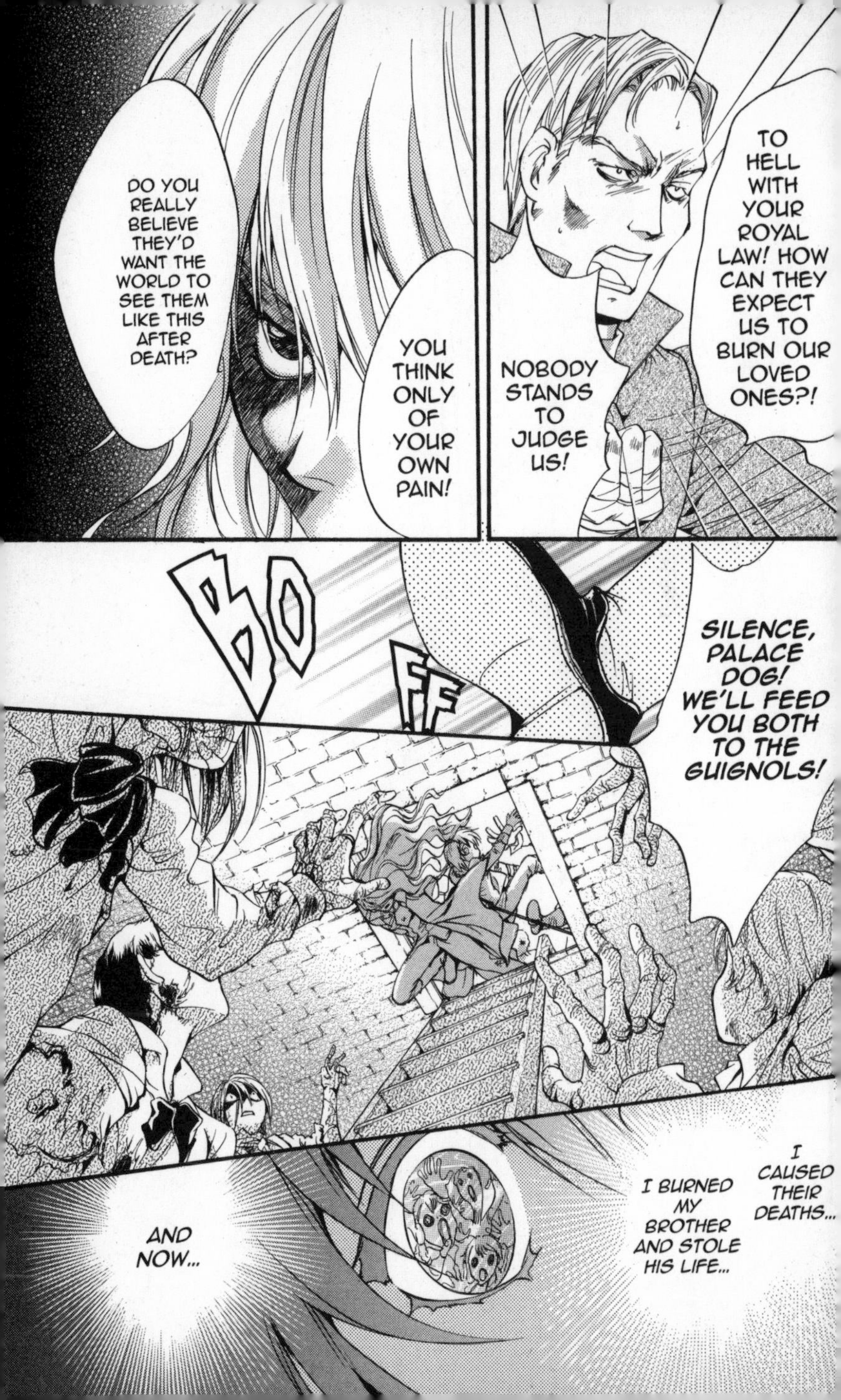
TO HELL WITH YOUR ROYAL LAW! HOW CAN THEY EXPECT US TO BURN OUR LOVED ONES?!
NOBODY STANDS TO JUDGE US!
YOU THINK ONLY OF YOUR OWN PAIN!
DO YOU REALLY BELIEVE THEY'D WANT THE WORLD TO SEE THEM LIKE THIS AFTER DEATH?
SILENCE, PALACE DOG! WE'LL FEED YOU BOTH TO THE GUIGNOLS!
BOFF
I CAUSED THEIR DEATHS...
I BURNED MY BROTHER AND STOLE HIS LIFE...
AND NOW...

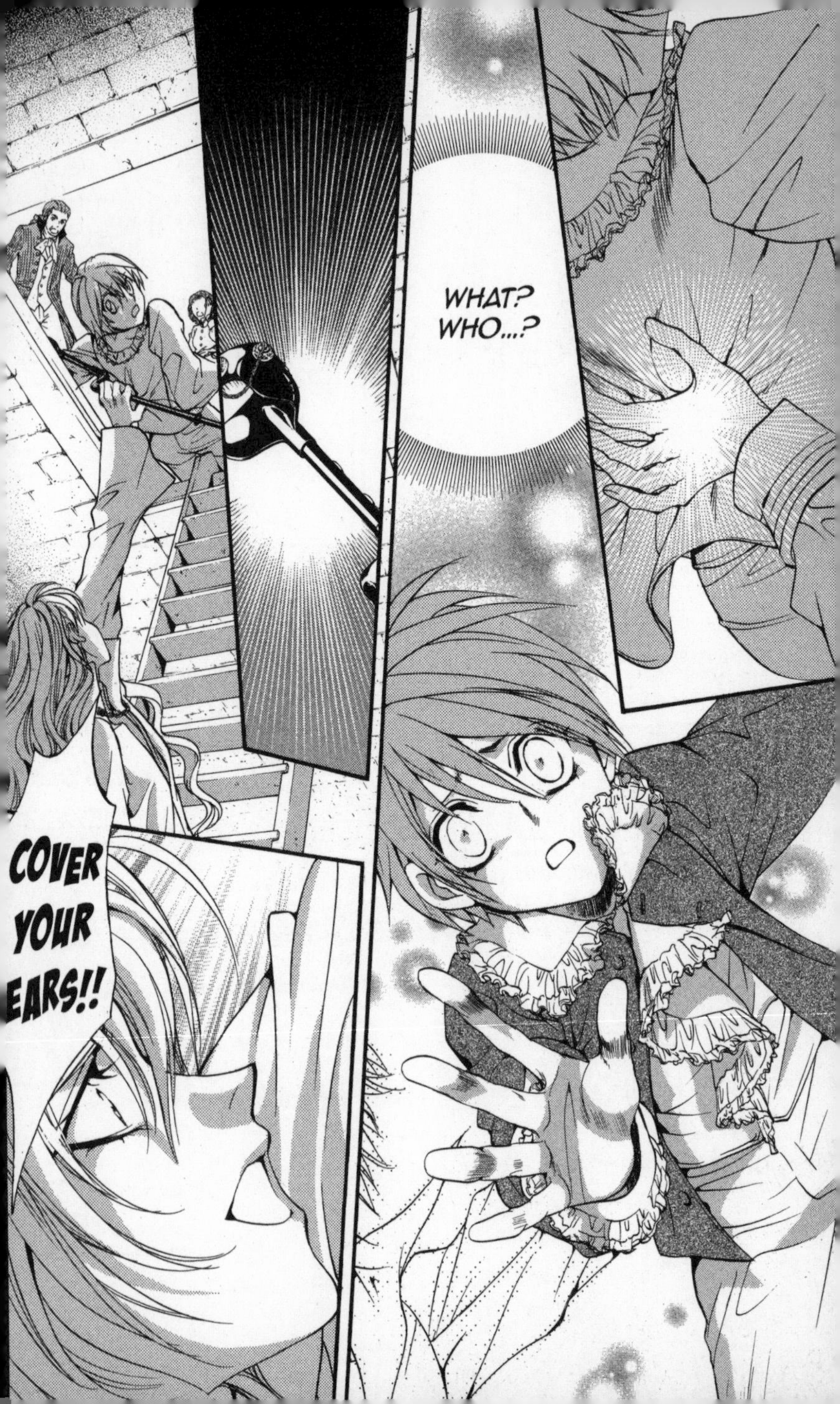
WHAT? WHO...?
COVER YOUR EARS!!

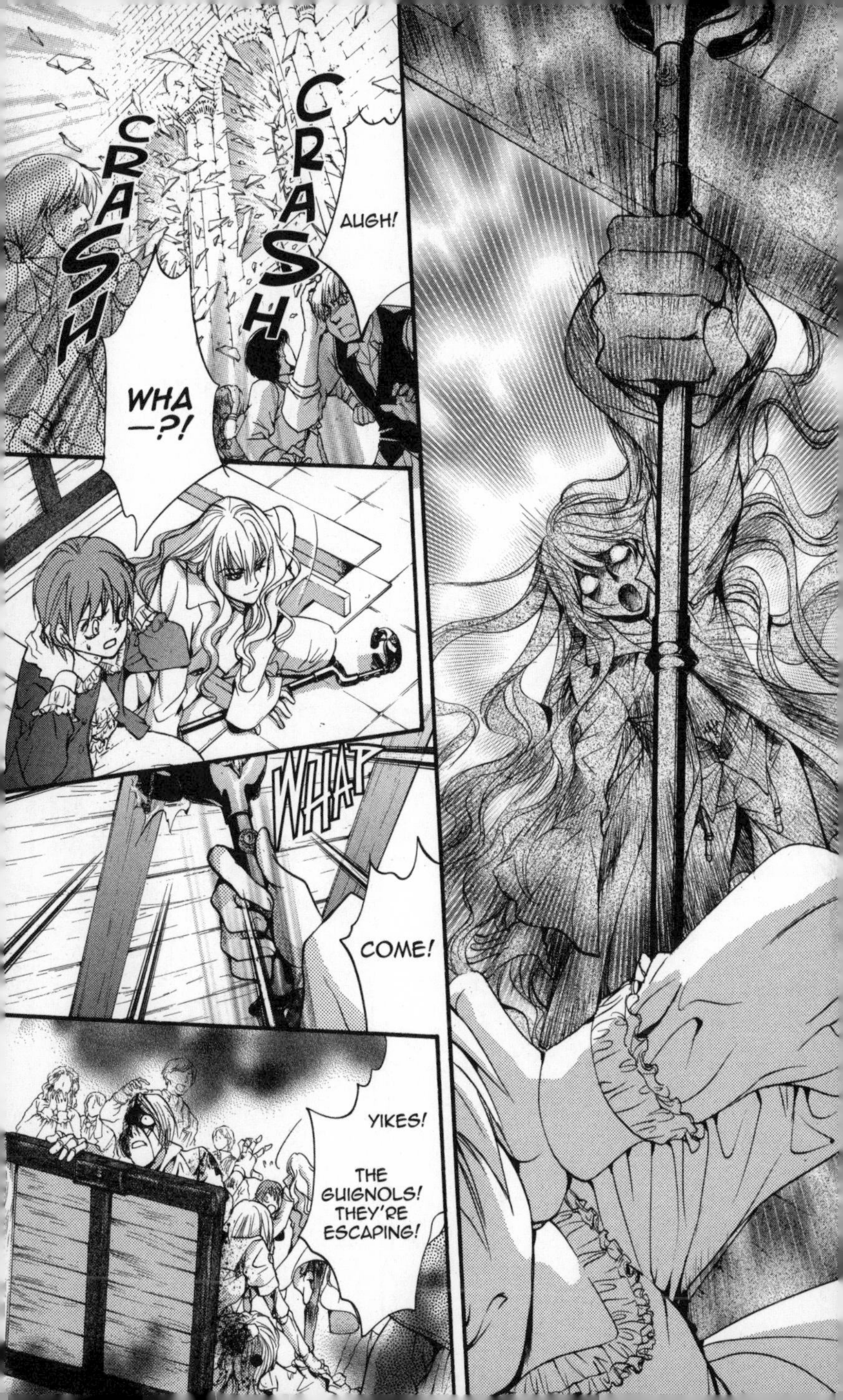
CRASH
AUGH!
CRASH
WHA —?!
WHAP
COME!
YIKES!
THE GUIGNOLS! THEY'RE ESCAPING!

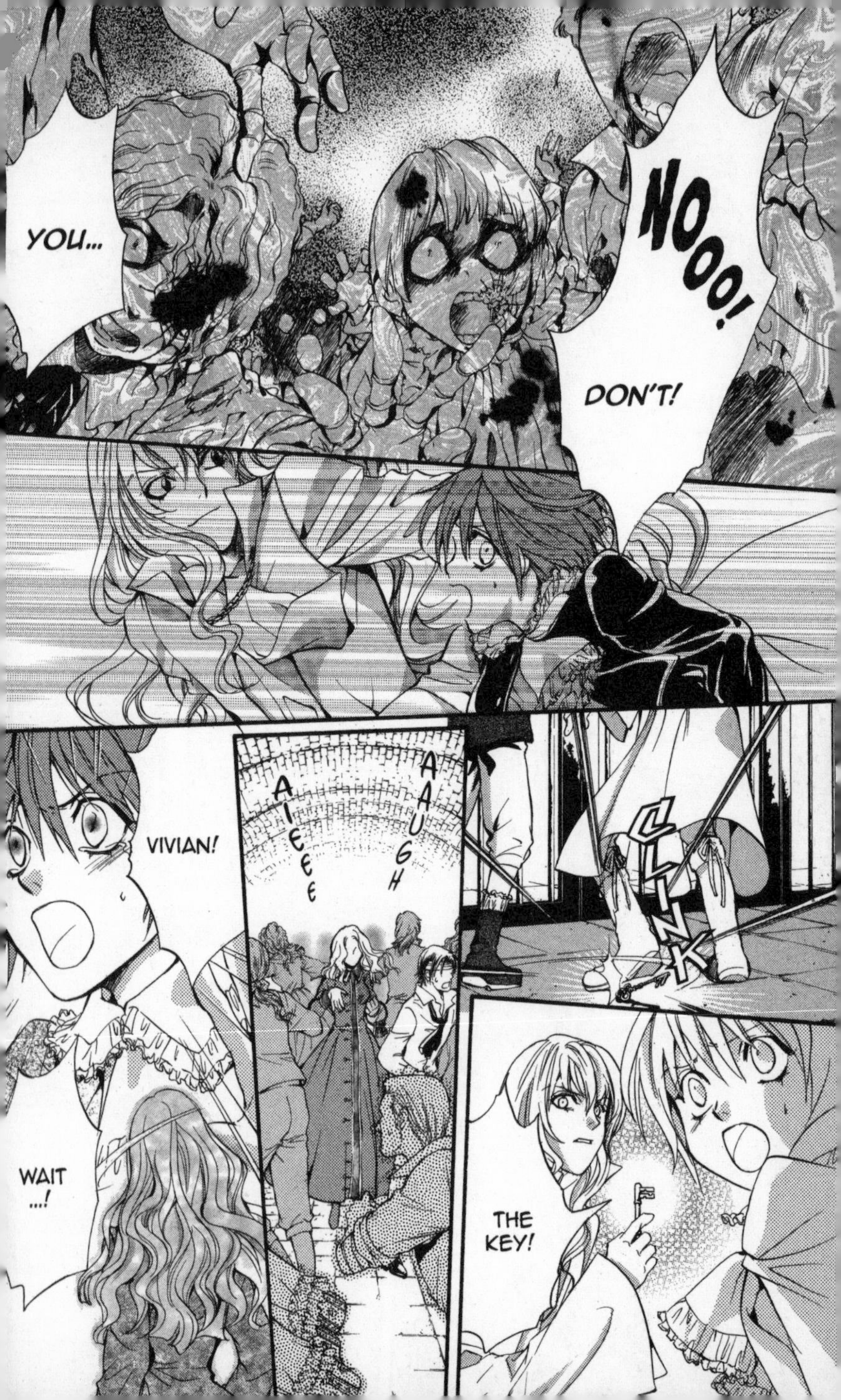

NOOO!
DON'T!
YOU...
CLINK
THE KEY!
AAUGH
AIEEE
VIVIAN!
WAIT ...!

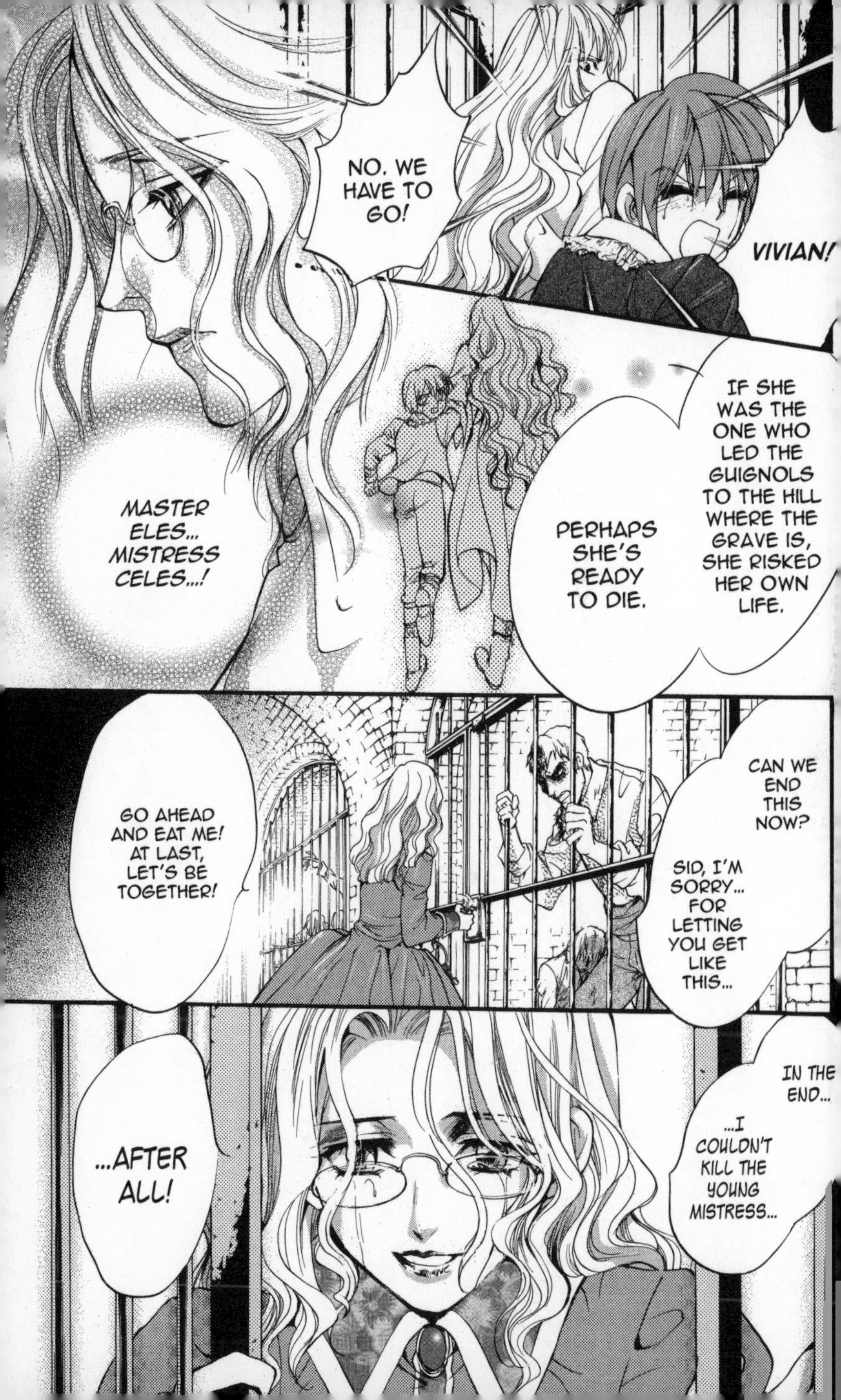
VIVIAN!
NO. WE HAVE TO GO!
IF SHE WAS THE ONE WHO LED THE GUIGNOLS TO THE HILL WHERE THE GRAVE IS, SHE RISKED HER OWN LIFE.
PERHAPS SHE'S READY TO DIE.
MASTER ELES... MISTRESS CELES...!
CAN WE END THIS NOW?
SID, I'M SORRY... FOR LETTING YOU GET LIKE THIS...
GO AHEAD AND EAT ME! AT LAST, LET'S BE TOGETHER!
IN THE END...
...I COULDN'T KILL THE YOUNG MISTRESS...
...AFTER ALL!

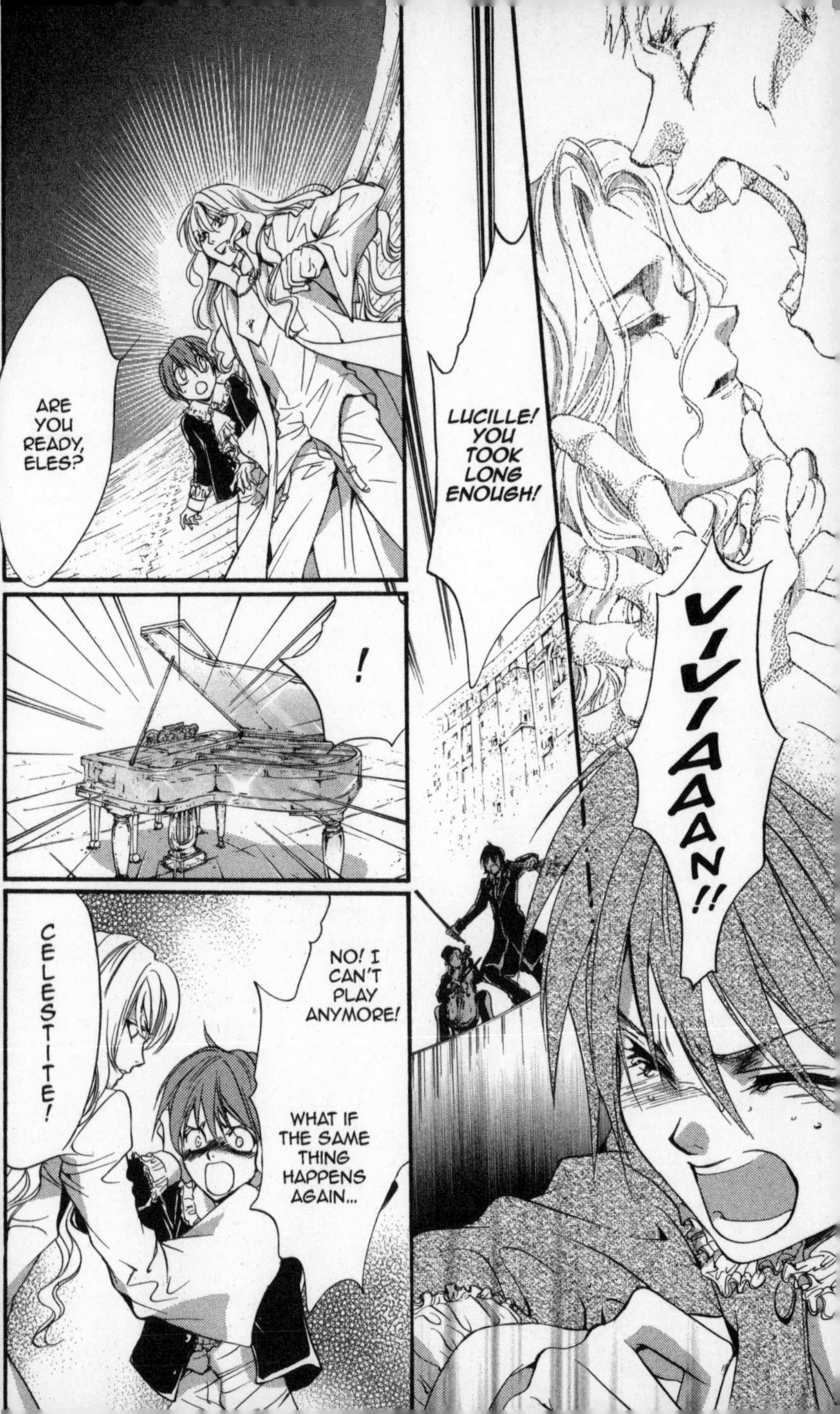
LUCILLE! YOU TOOK LONG ENOUGH!
VIVIAAAN!!
ARE YOU READY, ELES?
!
NO! I CAN'T PLAY ANYMORE!
WHAT IF THE SAME THING HAPPENS AGAIN...
CELESTITE!

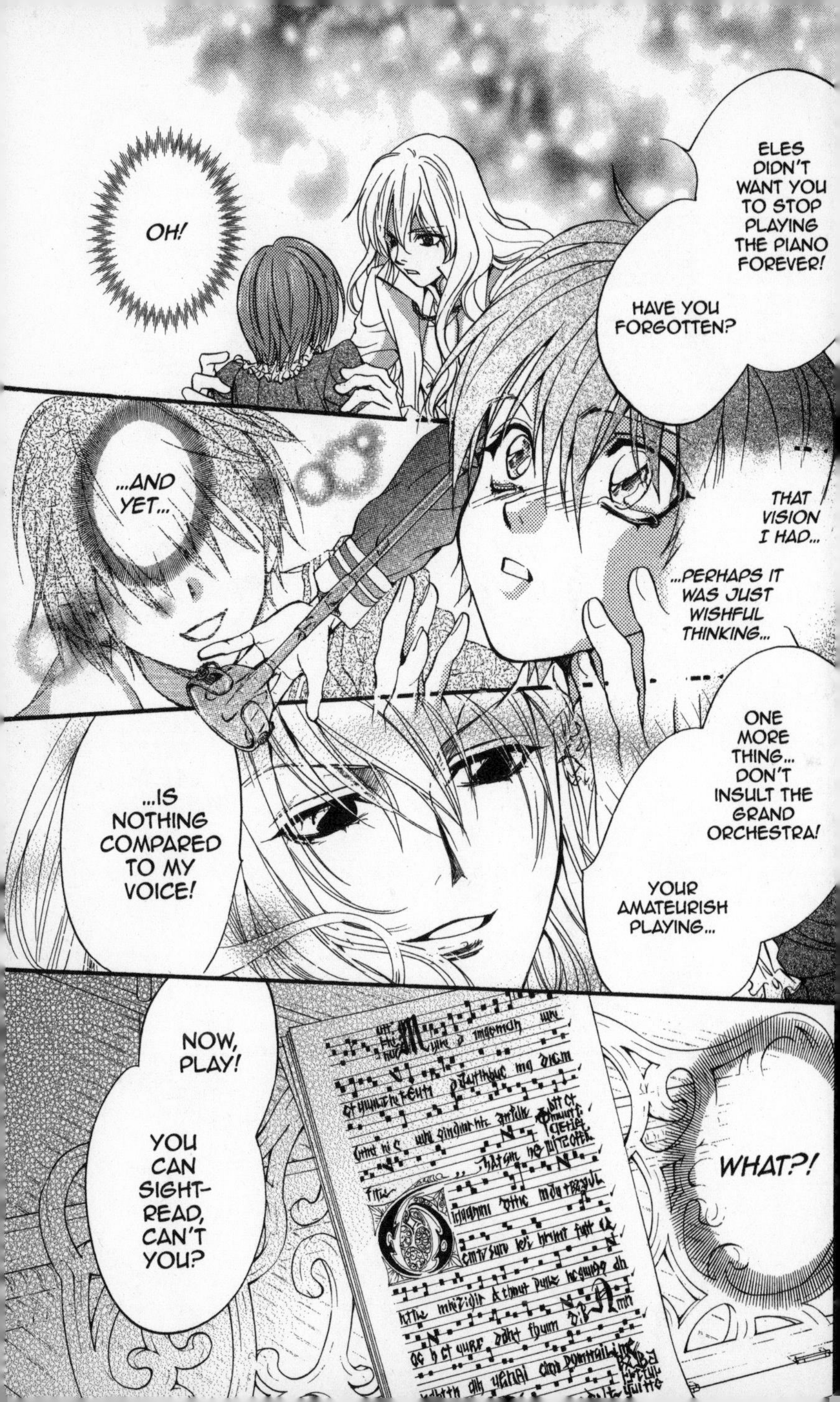
ELES DIDN'T WANT YOU TO STOP PLAYING THE PIANO FOREVER!
HAVE YOU FORGOTTEN?
OH!
THAT VISION I HAD...
...PERHAPS IT WAS JUST WISHFUL THINKING...
...AND YET...
ONE MORE THING... DON'T INSULT THE GRAND ORCHESTRA!
YOUR AMATEURISH PLAYING...
...IS NOTHING COMPARED TO MY VOICE!
WHAT?!
NOW, PLAY!
YOU CAN SIGHT-READ, CAN'T YOU?

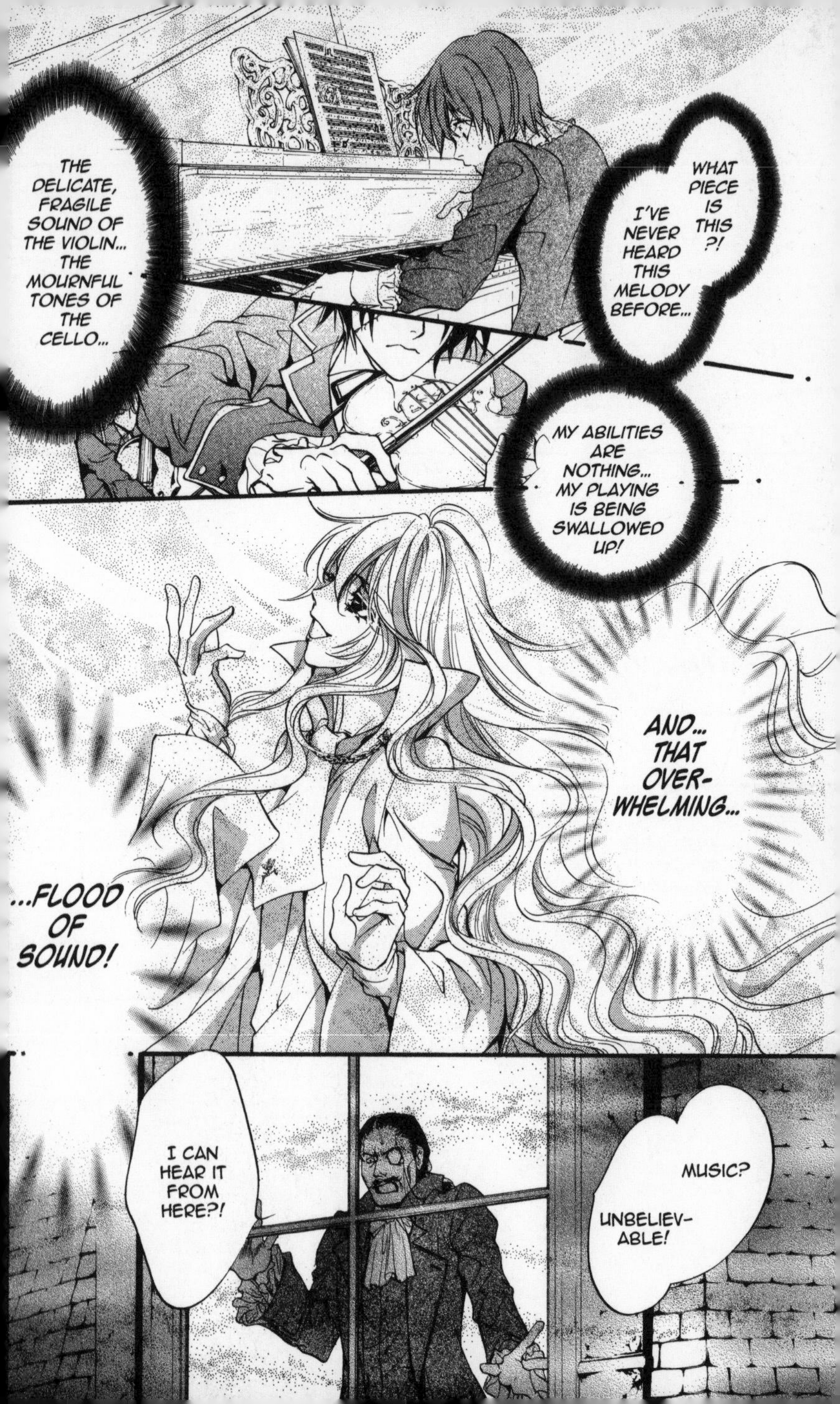
WHAT PIECE IS THIS?!
I'VE NEVER HEARD THIS MELODY BEFORE...
THE DELICATE, FRAGILE SOUND OF THE VIOLIN... THE MOURNFUL TONES OF THE CELLO...
MY ABILITIES ARE NOTHING... MY PLAYING IS BEING SWALLOWED UP!
AND... THAT OVER-WHELMING...
...FLOOD OF SOUND!
MUSIC?
UNBELIEV-ABLE!
I CAN HEAR IT FROM HERE?!

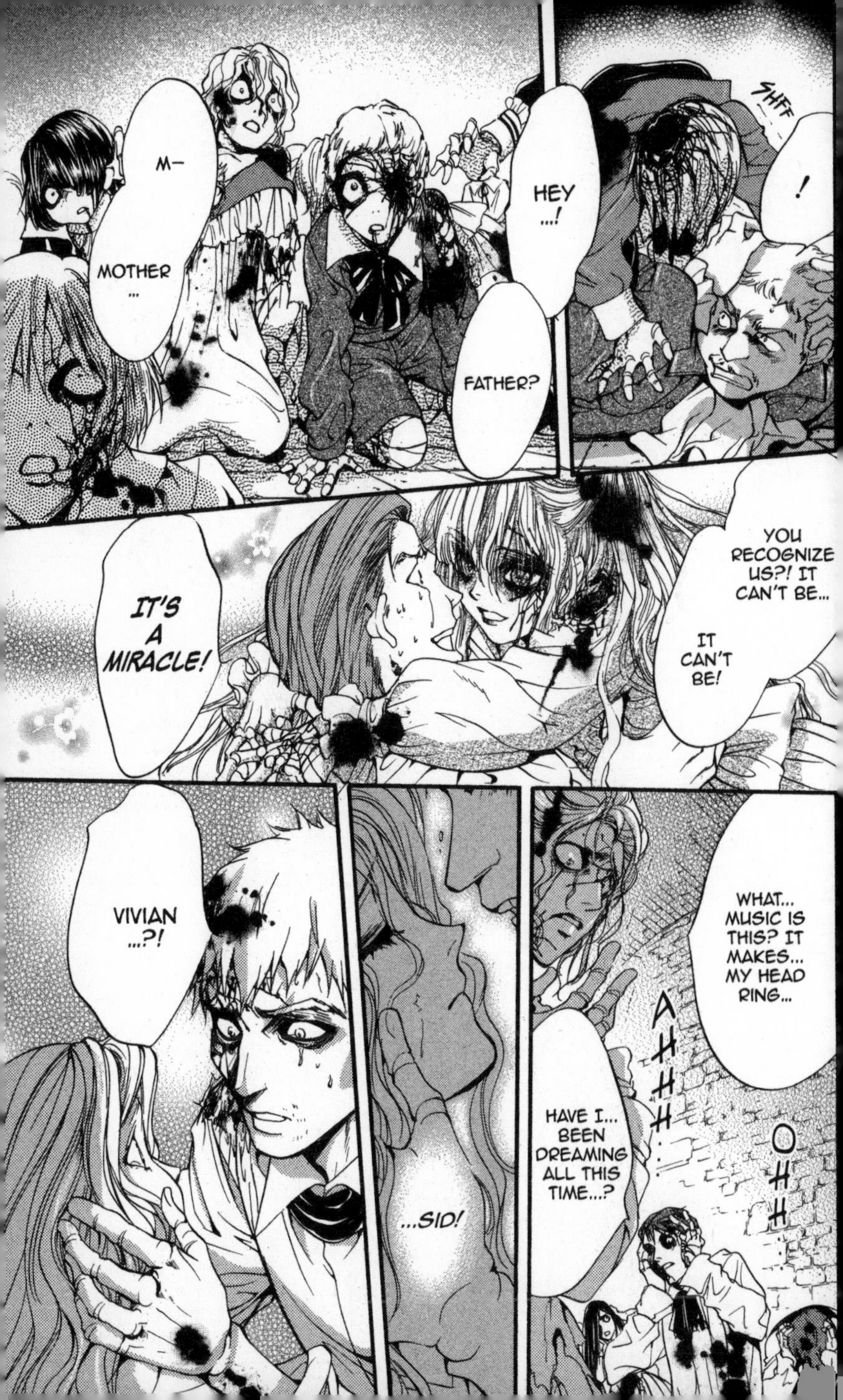
SHFF
!
HEY ...!
FATHER?
M—
MOTHER ...
YOU RECOGNIZE US?! IT CAN'T BE...
IT CAN'T BE!
IT'S A MIRACLE!
WHAT... MUSIC IS THIS? IT MAKES... MY HEAD RING...
OHH
AHHH...
HAVE I... BEEN DREAMING ALL THIS TIME...?
...SID!
VIVIAN ...?!

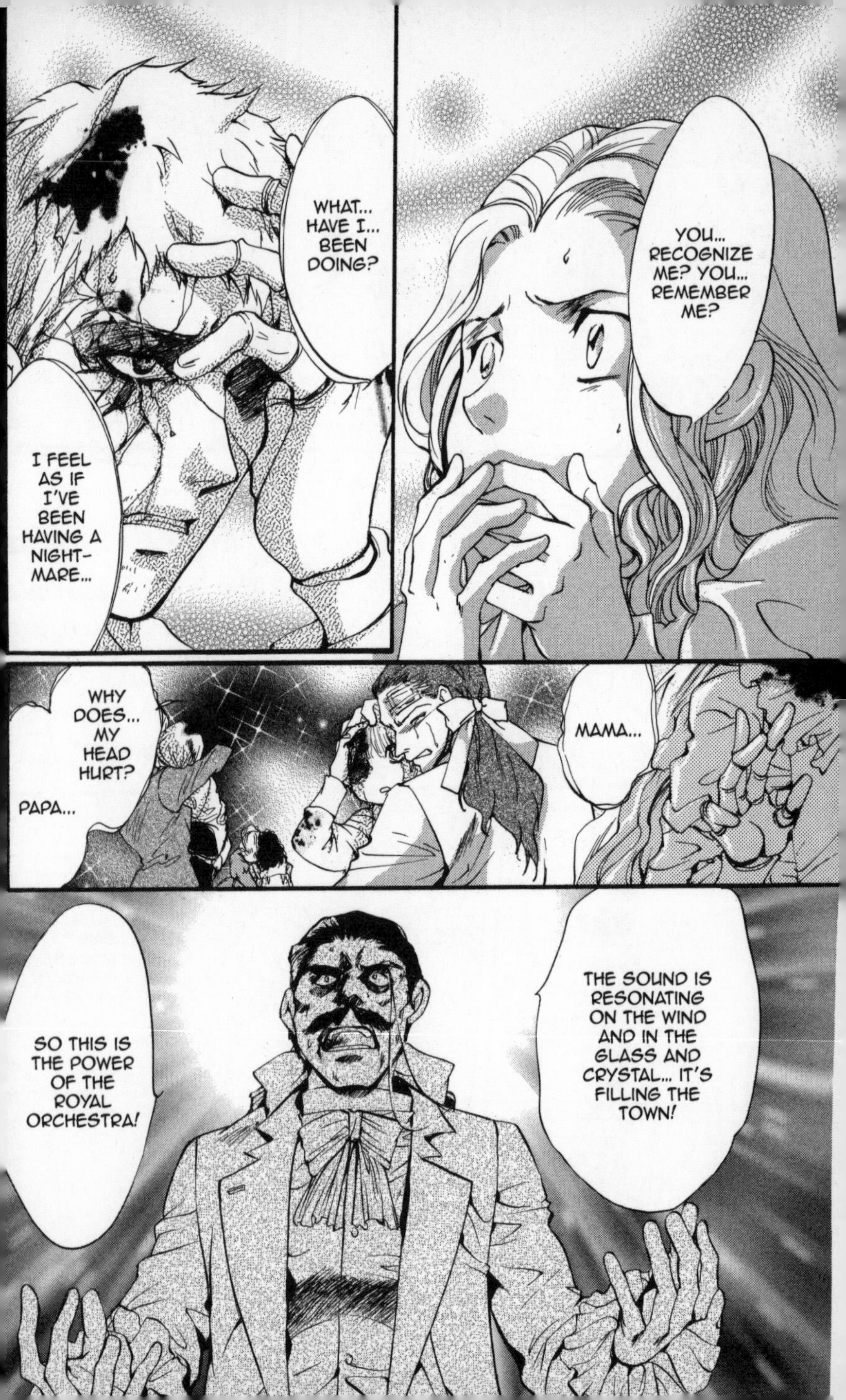
YOU... RECOGNIZE ME? YOU... REMEMBER ME?
WHAT... HAVE I... BEEN DOING?
I FEEL AS IF I'VE BEEN HAVING A NIGHT-MARE...
MAMA...
WHY DOES... MY HEAD HURT?
PAPA...
THE SOUND IS RESONATING ON THE WIND AND IN THE GLASS AND CRYSTAL... IT'S FILLING THE TOWN!
SO THIS IS THE POWER OF THE ROYAL ORCHESTRA!

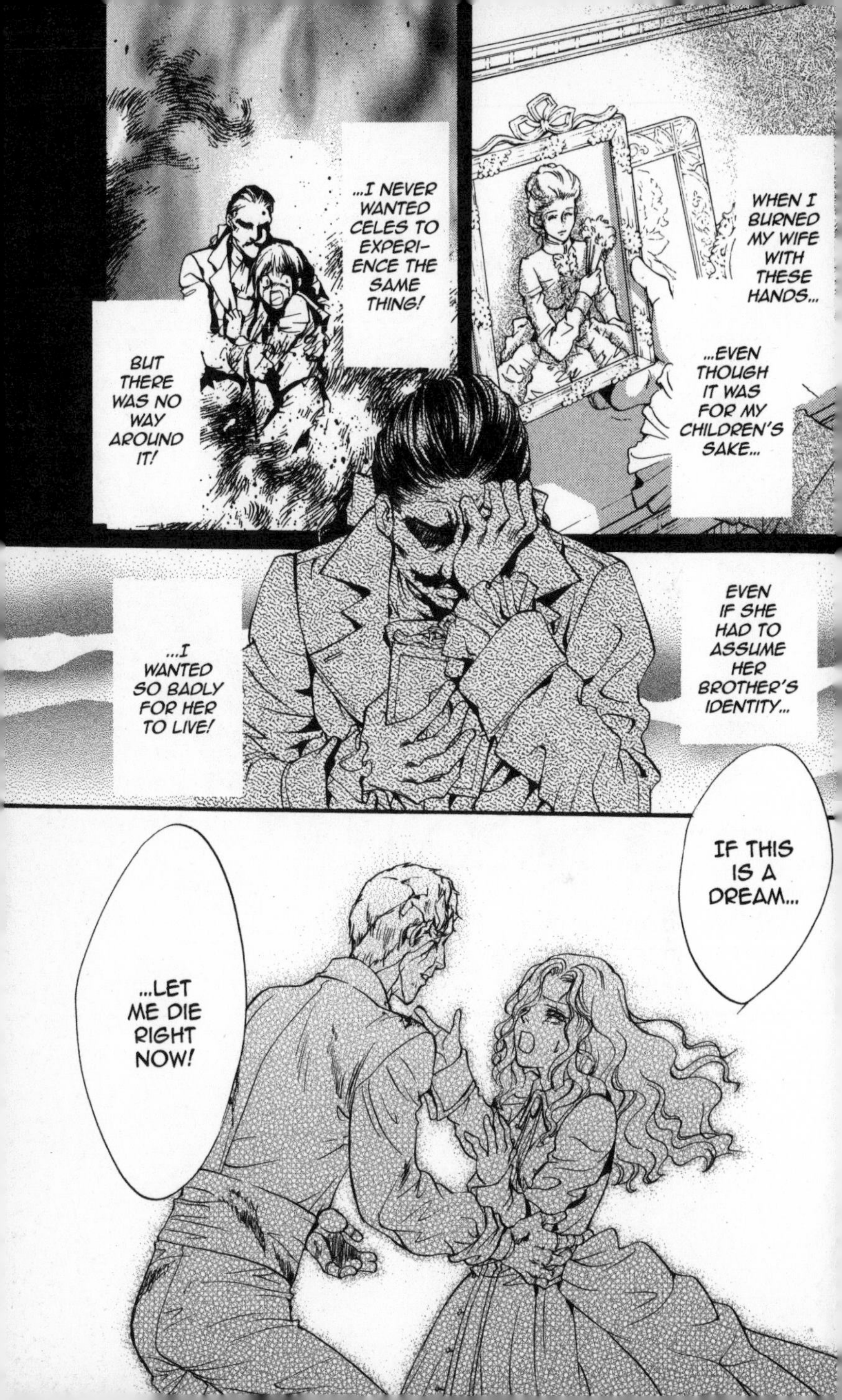
WHEN I BURNED MY WIFE WITH THESE HANDS...
...EVEN THOUGH IT WAS FOR MY CHILDREN'S SAKE...
...I NEVER WANTED CELES TO EXPERIENCE THE SAME THING!
BUT THERE WAS NO WAY AROUND IT!
EVEN IF SHE HAD TO ASSUME HER BROTHER'S IDENTITY...
...I WANTED SO BADLY FOR HER TO LIVE!
IF THIS IS A DREAM...
...LET ME DIE RIGHT NOW!

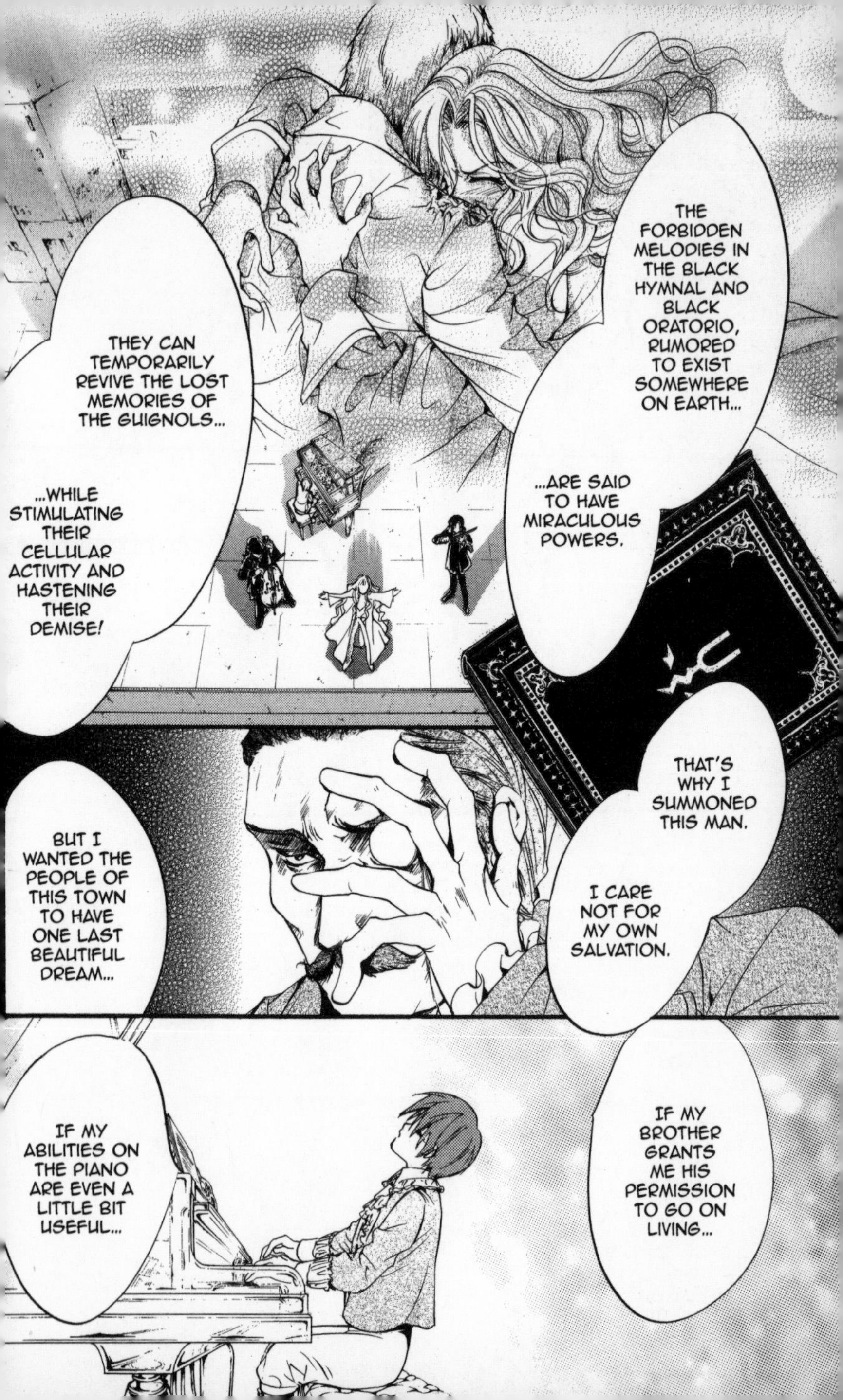
THE FORBIDDEN MELODIES IN THE BLACK HYMNAL AND BLACK ORATORIO, RUMORED TO EXIST SOMEWHERE ON EARTH...
...ARE SAID TO HAVE MIRACULOUS POWERS.
THEY CAN TEMPORARILY REVIVE THE LOST MEMORIES OF THE GUIGNOLS...
...WHILE STIMULATING THEIR CELLULAR ACTIVITY AND HASTENING THEIR DEMISE!
THAT'S WHY I SUMMONED THIS MAN.
I CARE NOT FOR MY OWN SALVATION.
BUT I WANTED THE PEOPLE OF THIS TOWN TO HAVE ONE LAST BEAUTIFUL DREAM...
IF MY BROTHER GRANTS ME HIS PERMISSION TO GO ON LIVING...
IF MY ABILITIES ON THE PIANO ARE EVEN A LITTLE BIT USEFUL...

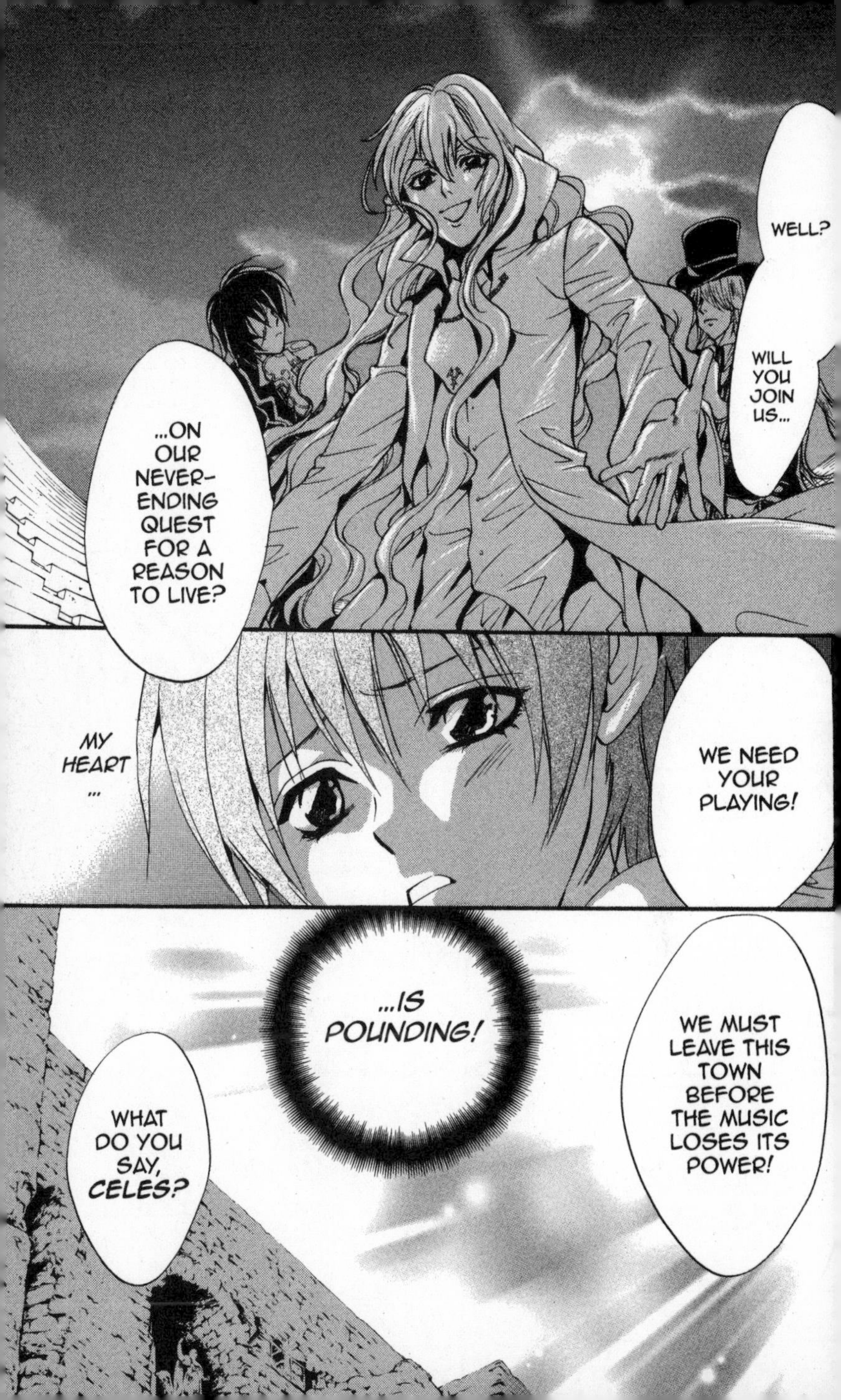
WELL?
WILL YOU JOIN US...
...ON OUR NEVER-ENDING QUEST FOR A REASON TO LIVE?
WE NEED YOUR PLAYING!
MY HEART ...
WE MUST LEAVE THIS TOWN BEFORE THE MUSIC LOSES ITS POWER!
...IS POUNDING!
WHAT DO YOU SAY, CELES?

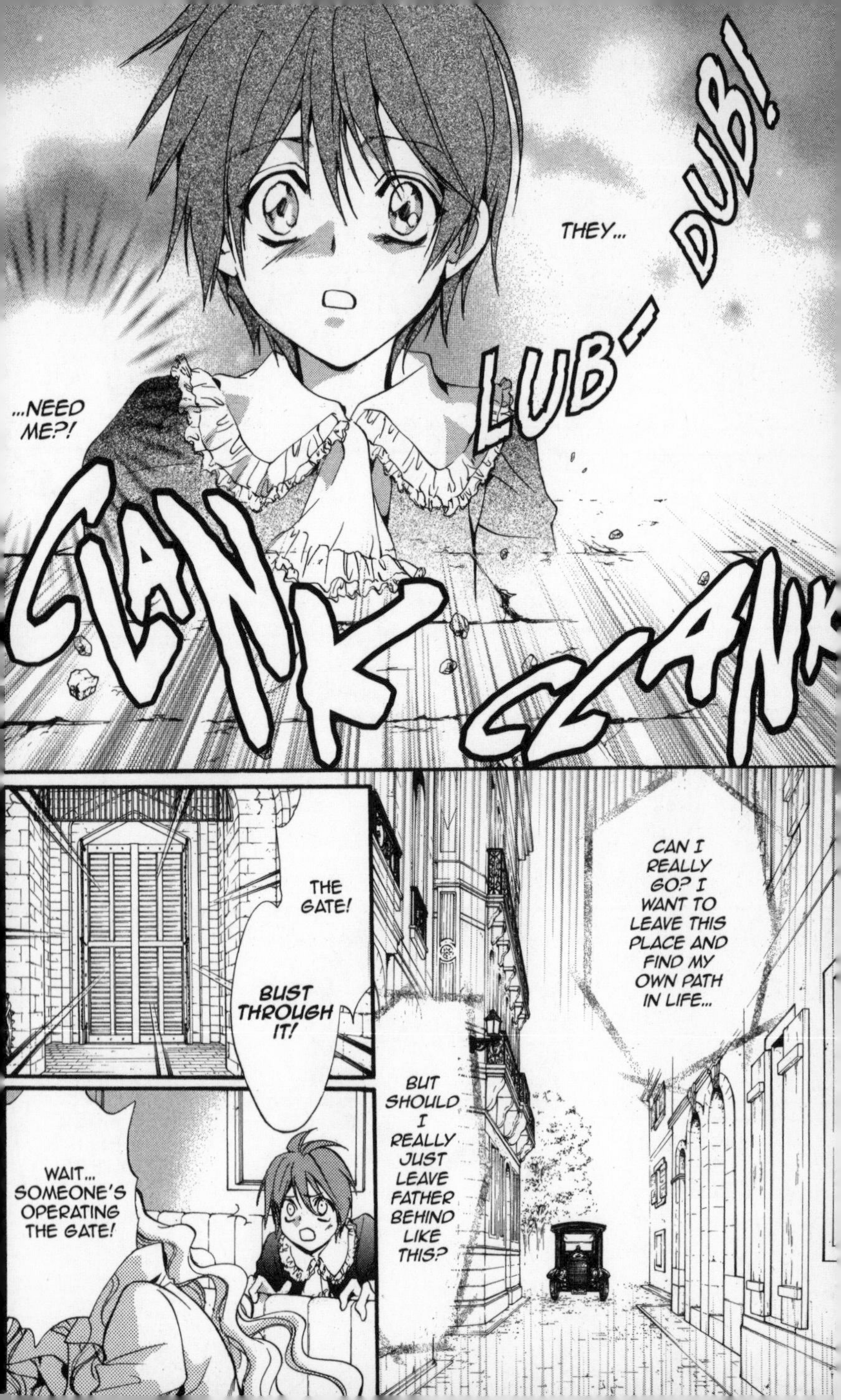
THEY...
LUB-DUB!
...NEED ME?!
CLANK
CLANK
CAN I REALLY GO? I WANT TO LEAVE THIS PLACE AND FIND MY OWN PATH IN LIFE...
BUT SHOULD I REALLY JUST LEAVE FATHER BEHIND LIKE THIS?
THE GATE!
BUST THROUGH IT!
WAIT... SOMEONE'S OPERATING THE GATE!

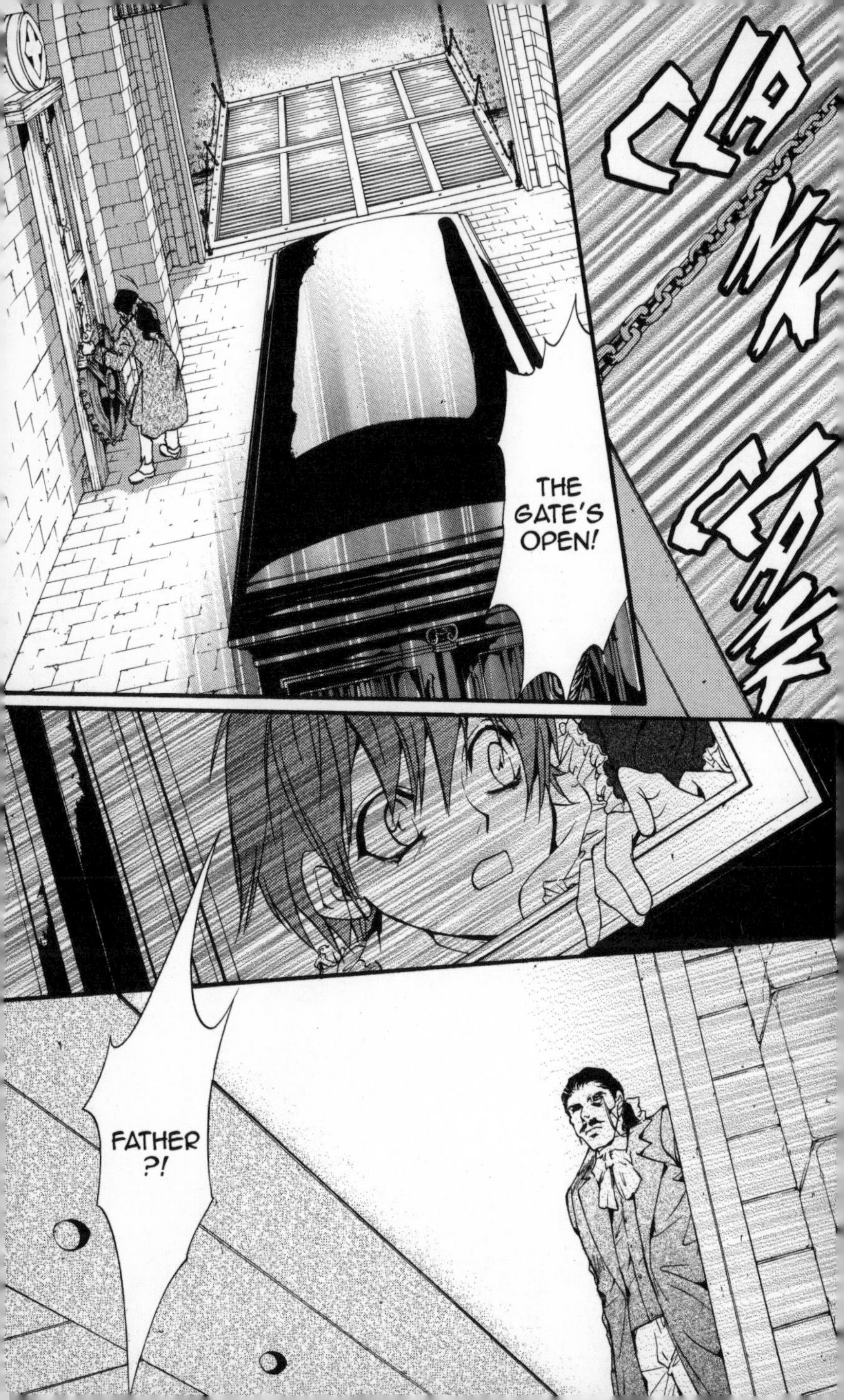
CLANK
CLANK
THE GATE'S OPEN!
FATHER ?!

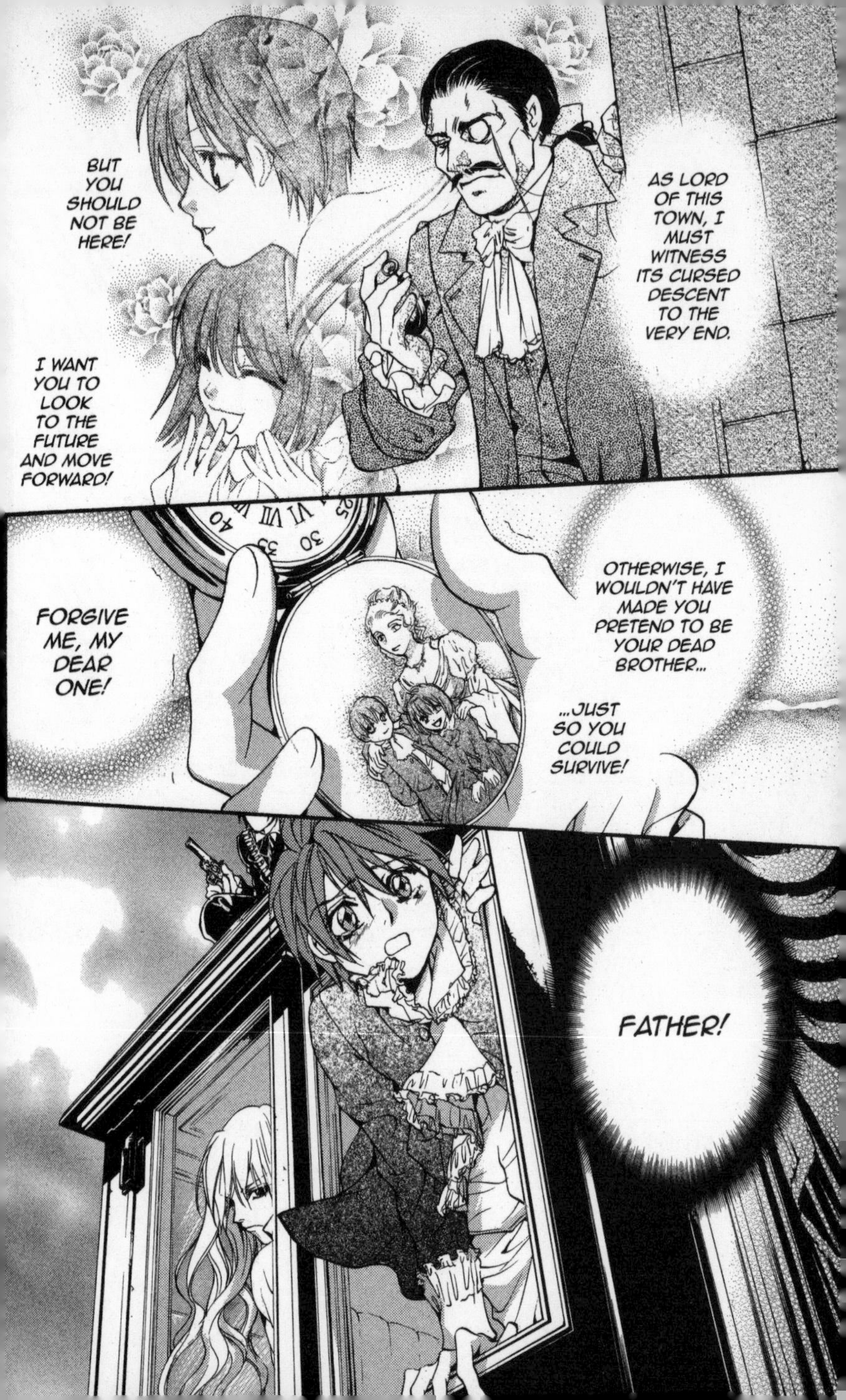
AS LORD OF THIS TOWN, I MUST WITNESS ITS CURSED DESCENT TO THE VERY END.
BUT YOU SHOULD NOT BE HERE!
I WANT YOU TO LOOK TO THE FUTURE AND MOVE FORWARD!
OTHERWISE, I WOULDN'T HAVE MADE YOU PRETEND TO BE YOUR DEAD BROTHER...
...JUST SO YOU COULD SURVIVE!
FORGIVE ME, MY DEAR ONE!
FATHER!

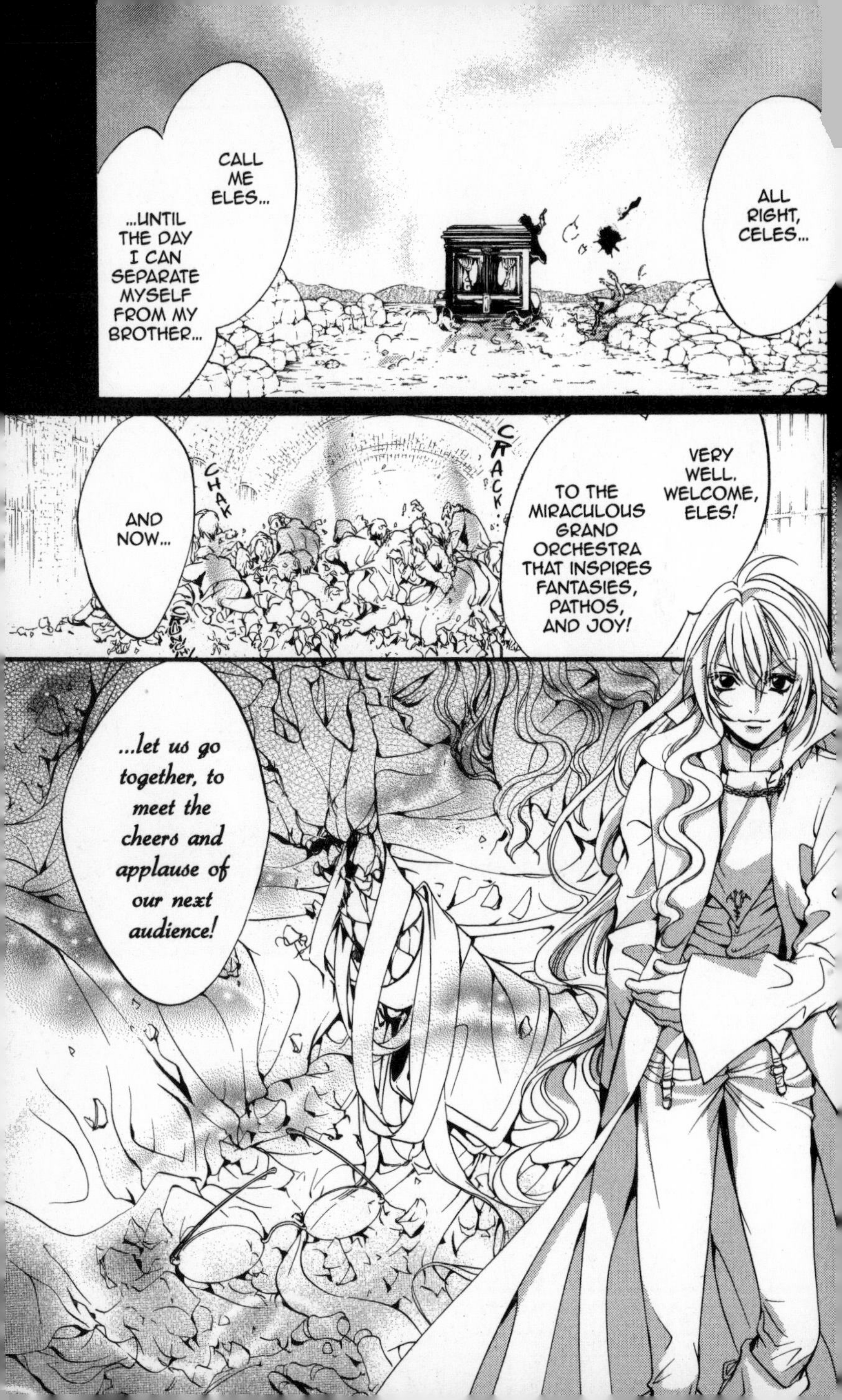
ALL RIGHT, CELES...
CALL ME ELES...
...UNTIL THE DAY I CAN SEPARATE MYSELF FROM MY BROTHER...
VERY WELL. WELCOME, ELES!
TO THE MIRACULOUS GRAND ORCHESTRA THAT INSPIRES FANTASIES, PATHOS, AND JOY!
CRACK
CHAK
AND NOW...
...let us go together, to meet the cheers and applause of our next audience!

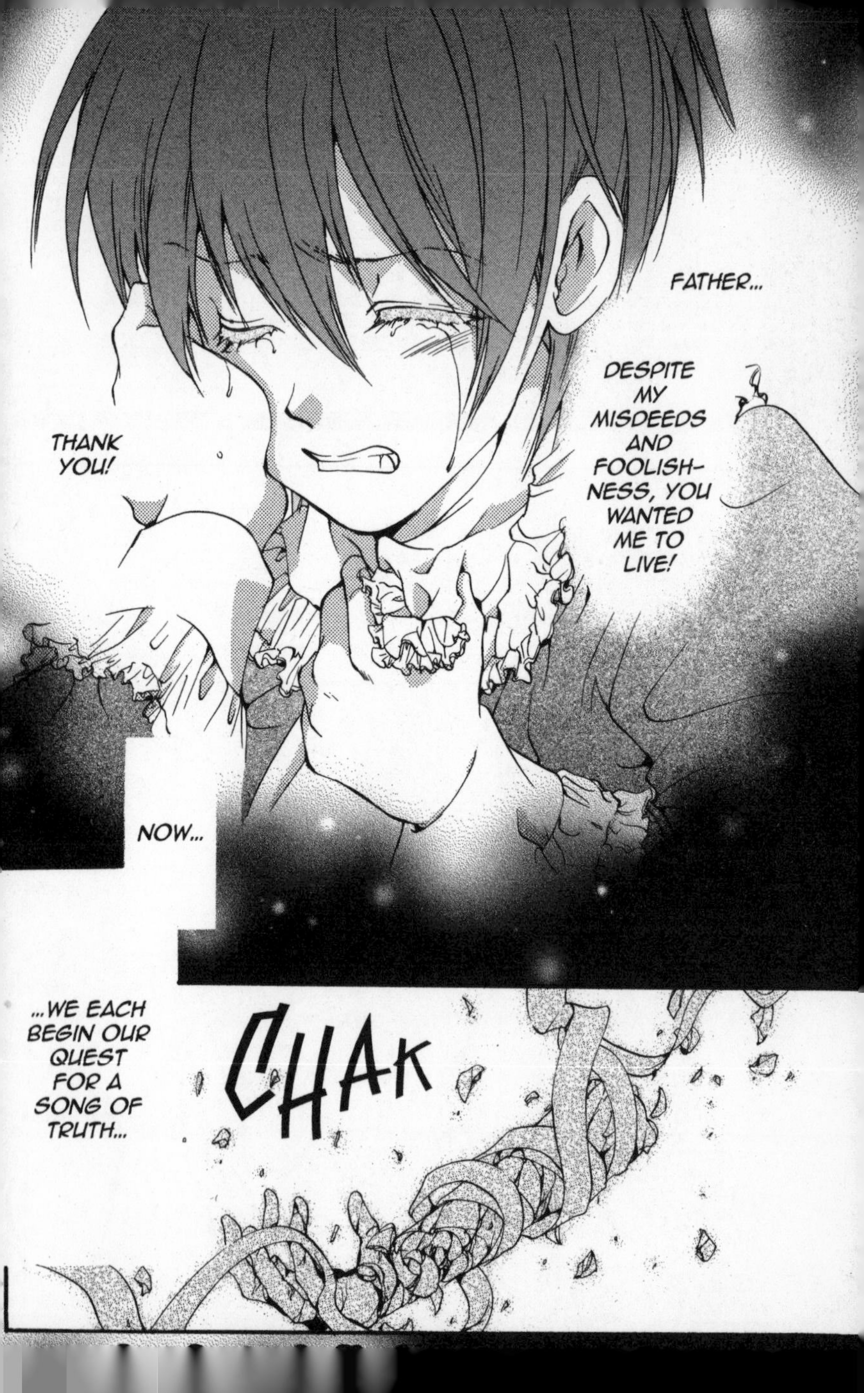
FATHER...
DESPITE MY MISDEEDS AND FOOLISHNESS, YOU WANTED ME TO LIVE!
THANK YOU!
NOW...
...WE EACH BEGIN OUR QUEST FOR A SONG OF TRUTH...
CHAK

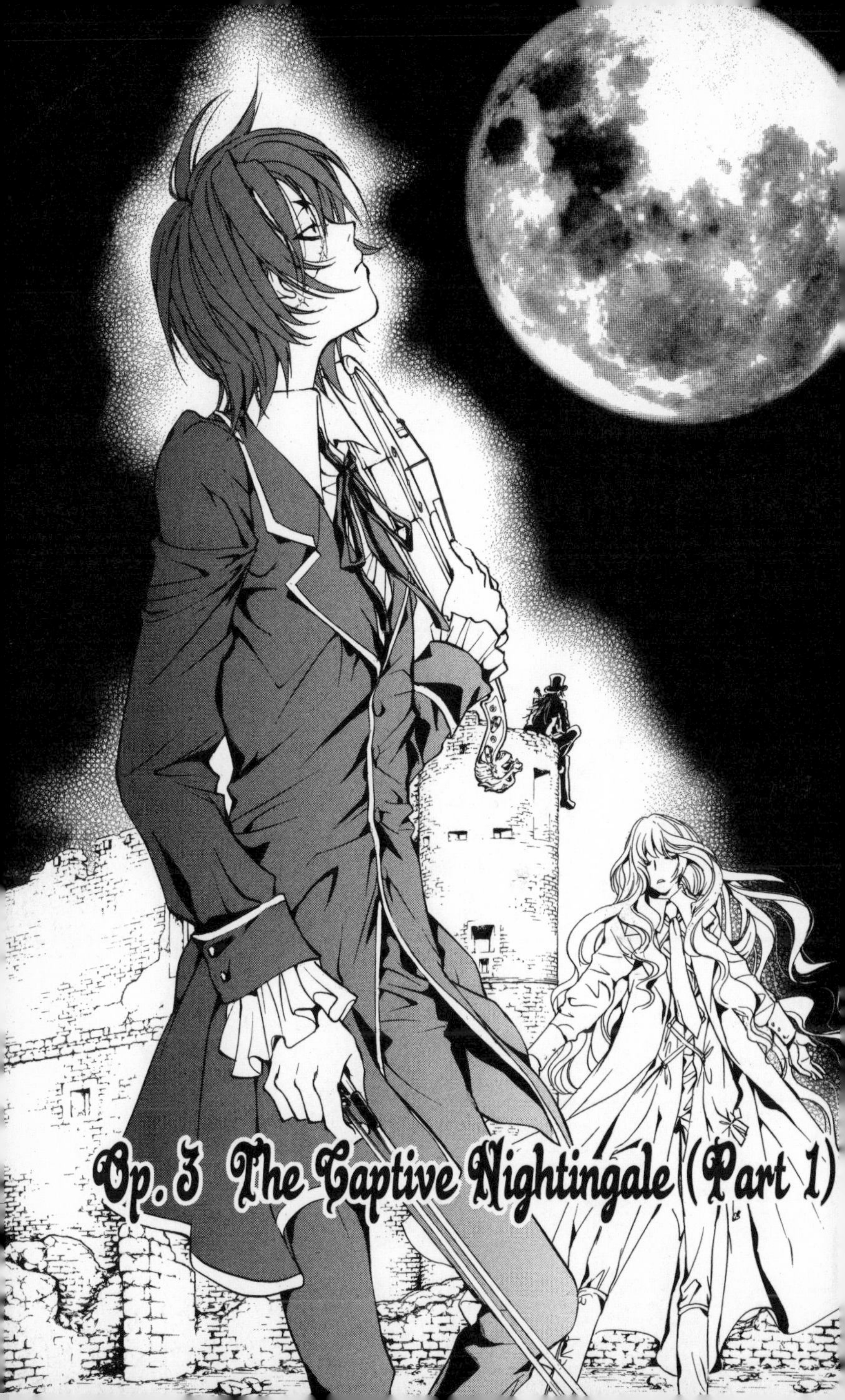
Op. 3 The Captive Nightingale (Part 1)

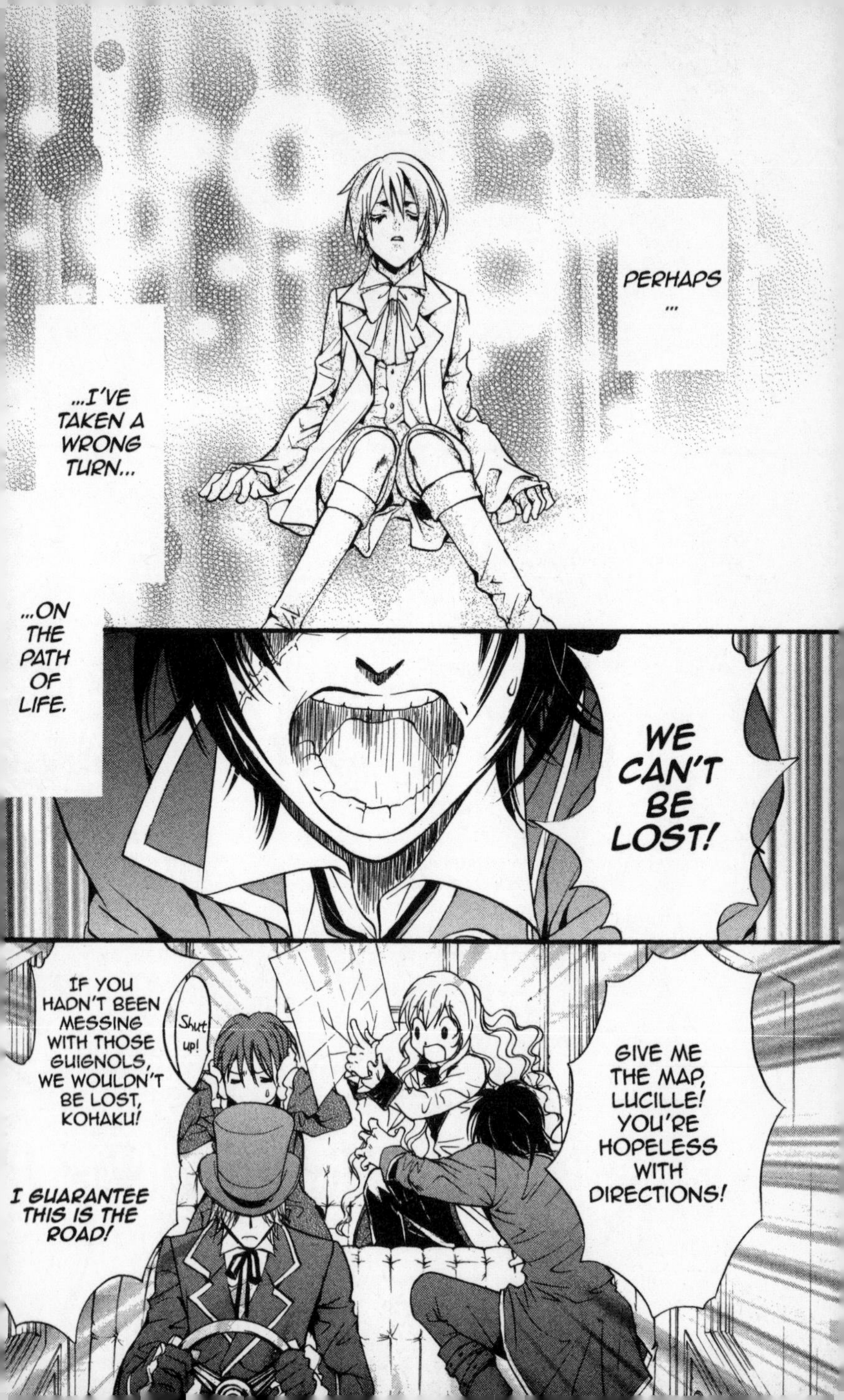
PERHAPS...
...I'VE TAKEN A WRONG TURN...
...ON THE PATH OF LIFE.
WE CAN'T BE LOST!
GIVE ME THE MAP, LUCILLE! YOU'RE HOPELESS WITH DIRECTIONS!
Shut up!
IF YOU HADN'T BEEN MESSING WITH THOSE GUIGNOLS, WE WOULDN'T BE LOST, KOHAKU!
I GUARANTEE THIS IS THE ROAD!

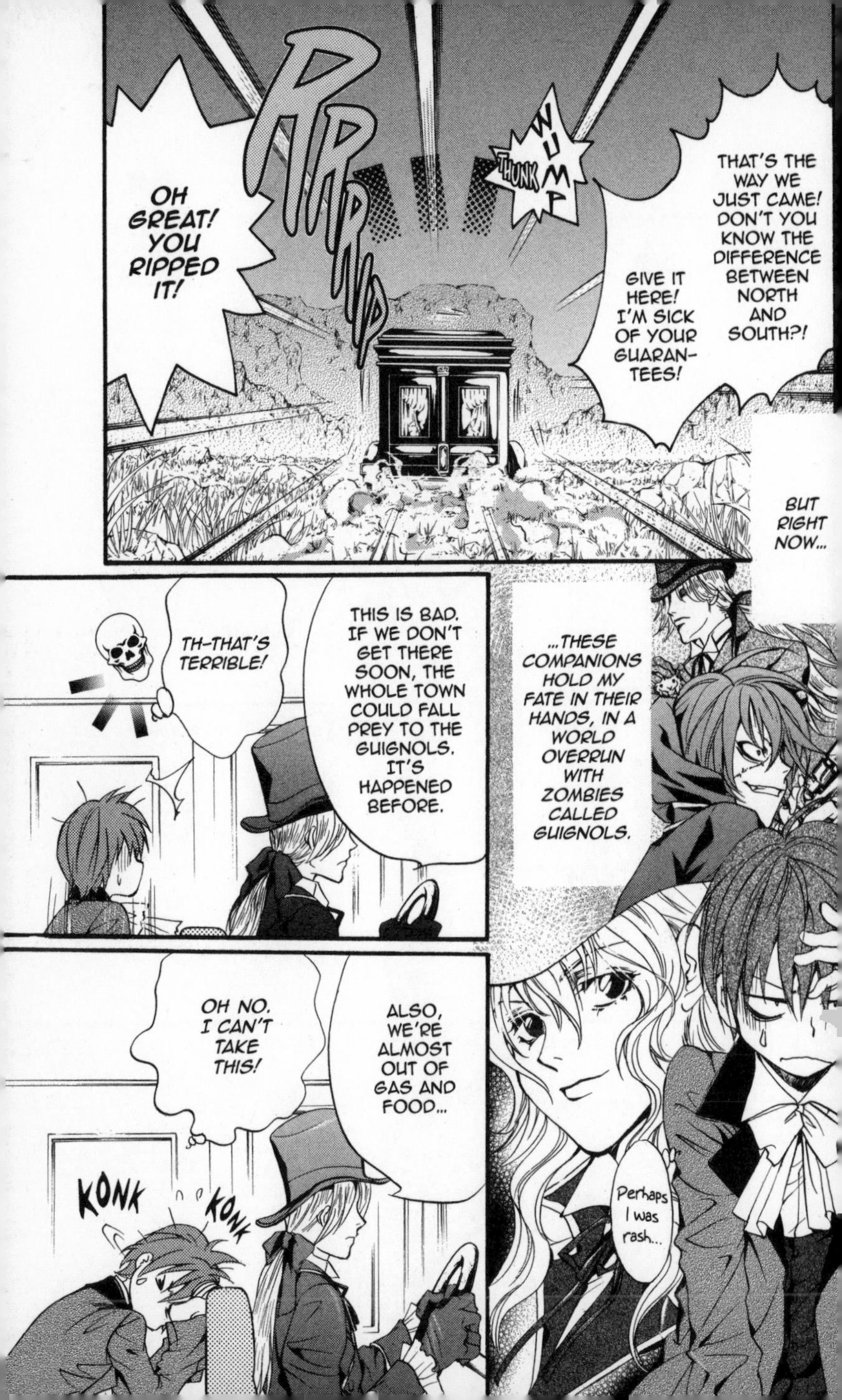
THAT'S THE WAY WE JUST CAME! DON'T YOU KNOW THE DIFFERENCE BETWEEN NORTH AND SOUTH?!
GIVE IT HERE! I'M SICK OF YOUR GUARAN-TEES!
WUMP
THUNK
OH GREAT! YOU RIPPED IT!
BUT RIGHT NOW...
...THESE COMPANIONS HOLD MY FATE IN THEIR HANDS, IN A WORLD OVERRUN WITH ZOMBIES CALLED GUIGNOLS.
Perhaps I was rash...
THIS IS BAD. IF WE DON'T GET THERE SOON, THE WHOLE TOWN COULD FALL PREY TO THE GUIGNOLS. IT'S HAPPENED BEFORE.
TH-THAT'S TERRIBLE!
ALSO, WE'RE ALMOST OUT OF GAS AND FOOD...
OH NO. I CAN'T TAKE THIS!
KONK
KONK

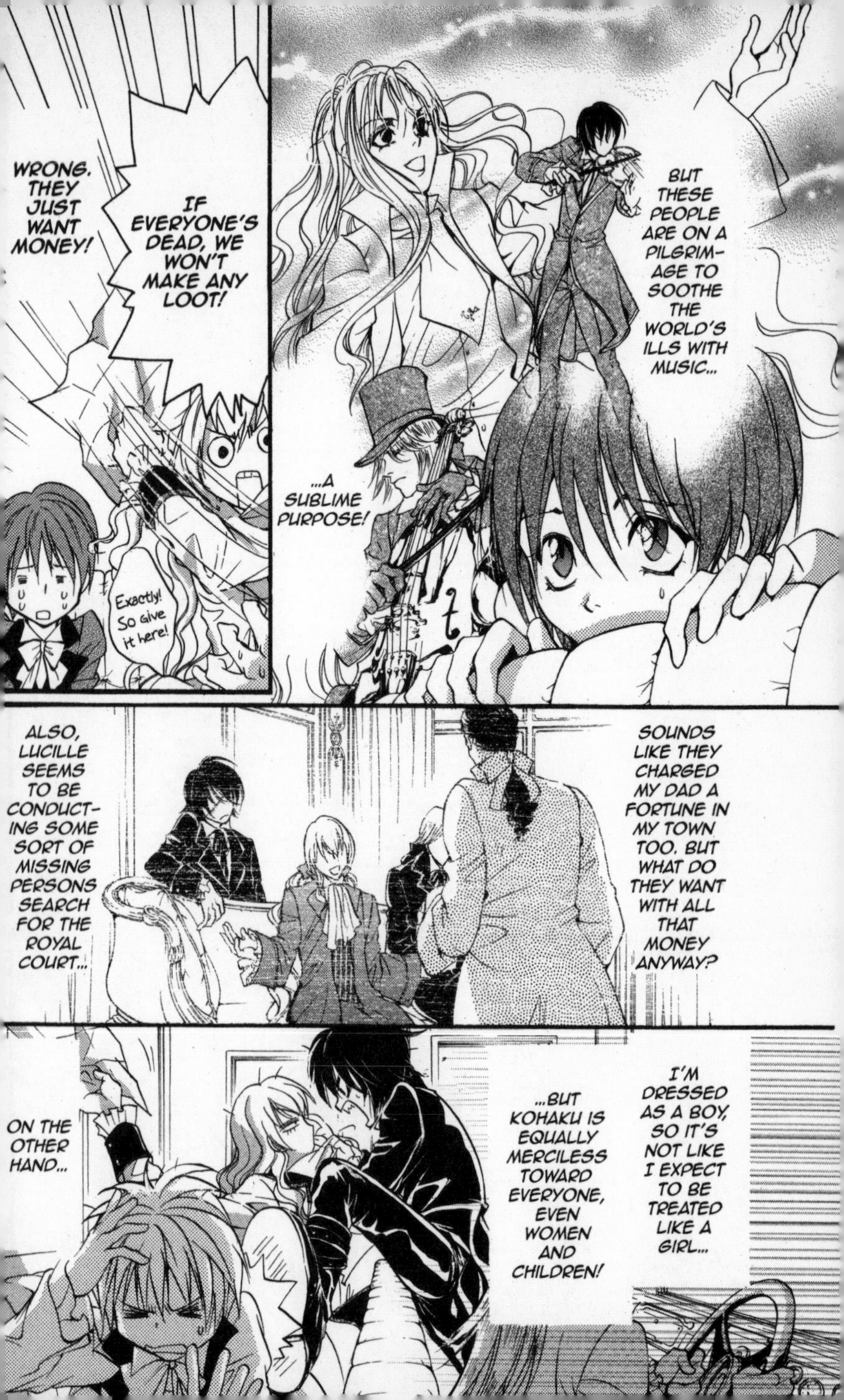
BUT THESE PEOPLE ARE ON A PILGRIM-AGE TO SOOTHE THE WORLD'S ILLS WITH MUSIC...
...A SUBLIME PURPOSE!
IF EVERYONE'S DEAD, WE WON'T MAKE ANY LOOT!
WRONG. THEY JUST WANT MONEY!
Exactly! So give it here!
SOUNDS LIKE THEY CHARGED MY DAD A FORTUNE IN MY TOWN TOO. BUT WHAT DO THEY WANT WITH ALL THAT MONEY ANYWAY?
ALSO, LUCILLE SEEMS TO BE CONDUCT-ING SOME SORT OF MISSING PERSONS SEARCH FOR THE ROYAL COURT...
I'M DRESSED AS A BOY, SO IT'S NOT LIKE I EXPECT TO BE TREATED LIKE A GIRL...
...BUT KOHAKU IS EQUALLY MERCILESS TOWARD EVERYONE, EVEN WOMEN AND CHILDREN!
ON THE OTHER HAND...

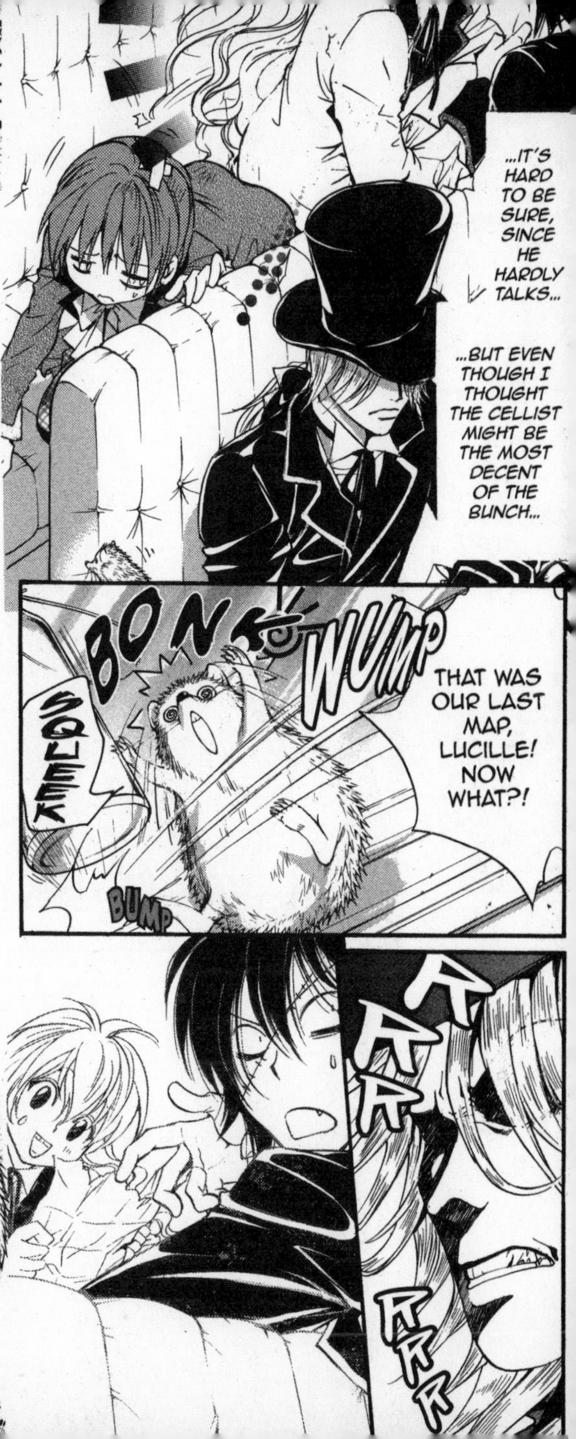
...IT'S HARD TO BE SURE, SINCE HE HARDLY TALKS...
...BUT EVEN THOUGH I THOUGHT THE CELLIST MIGHT BE THE MOST DECENT OF THE BUNCH...
BONK
WUMP
SQUEEK
THAT WAS OUR LAST MAP, LUCILLE! NOW WHAT?!
BUMP
RRRR
RRRR

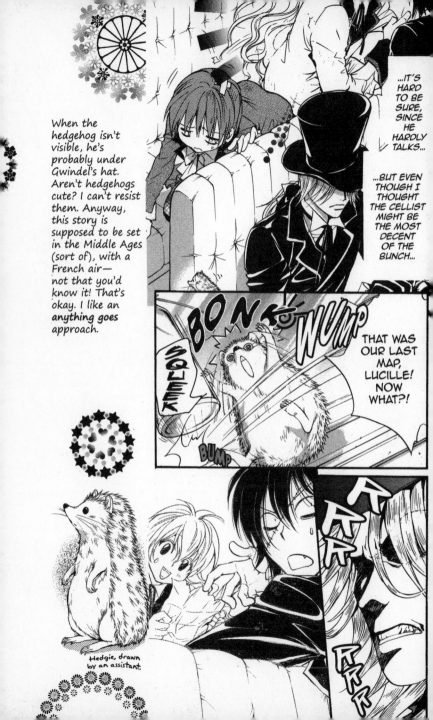

When the hedgehog isn't visible, he's probably under Gwindel's hat. Aren't hedgehogs cute? I can't resist them. Anyway, this story is supposed to be set in the Middle Ages (sort of), with a French air—not that you'd know it! That's okay. I like an **anything goes** approach.

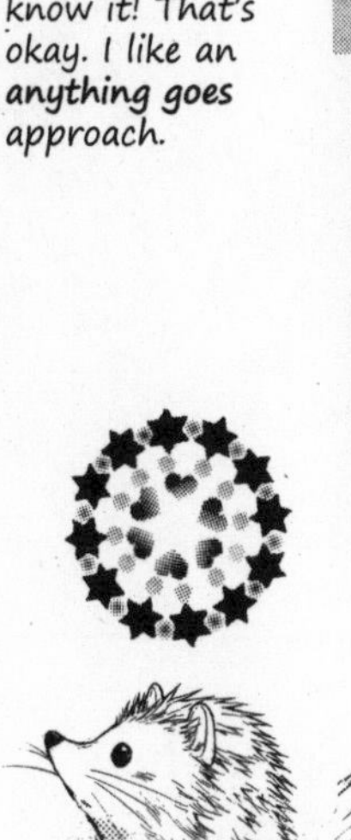

Hedgie, drawn by an assistant.

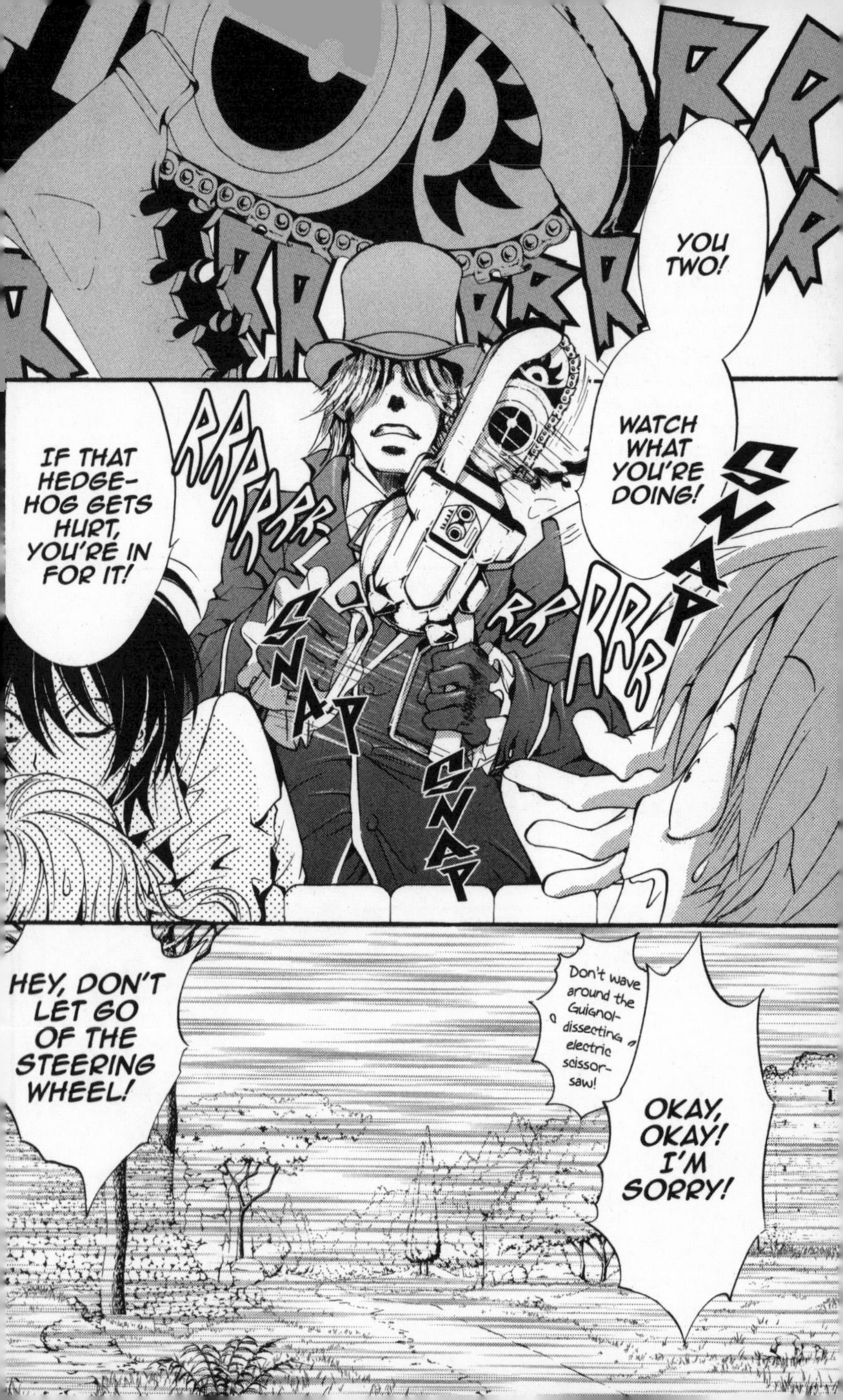
RRRR
YOU TWO!
RRRR
WATCH WHAT YOU'RE DOING!
SNAP
RRRR
IF THAT HEDGE-HOG GETS HURT, YOU'RE IN FOR IT!
SNAP
SNAP
Don't wave around the Guignol-dissecting electric scissor-saw!
OKAY, OKAY! I'M SORRY!
HEY, DON'T LET GO OF THE STEERING WHEEL!

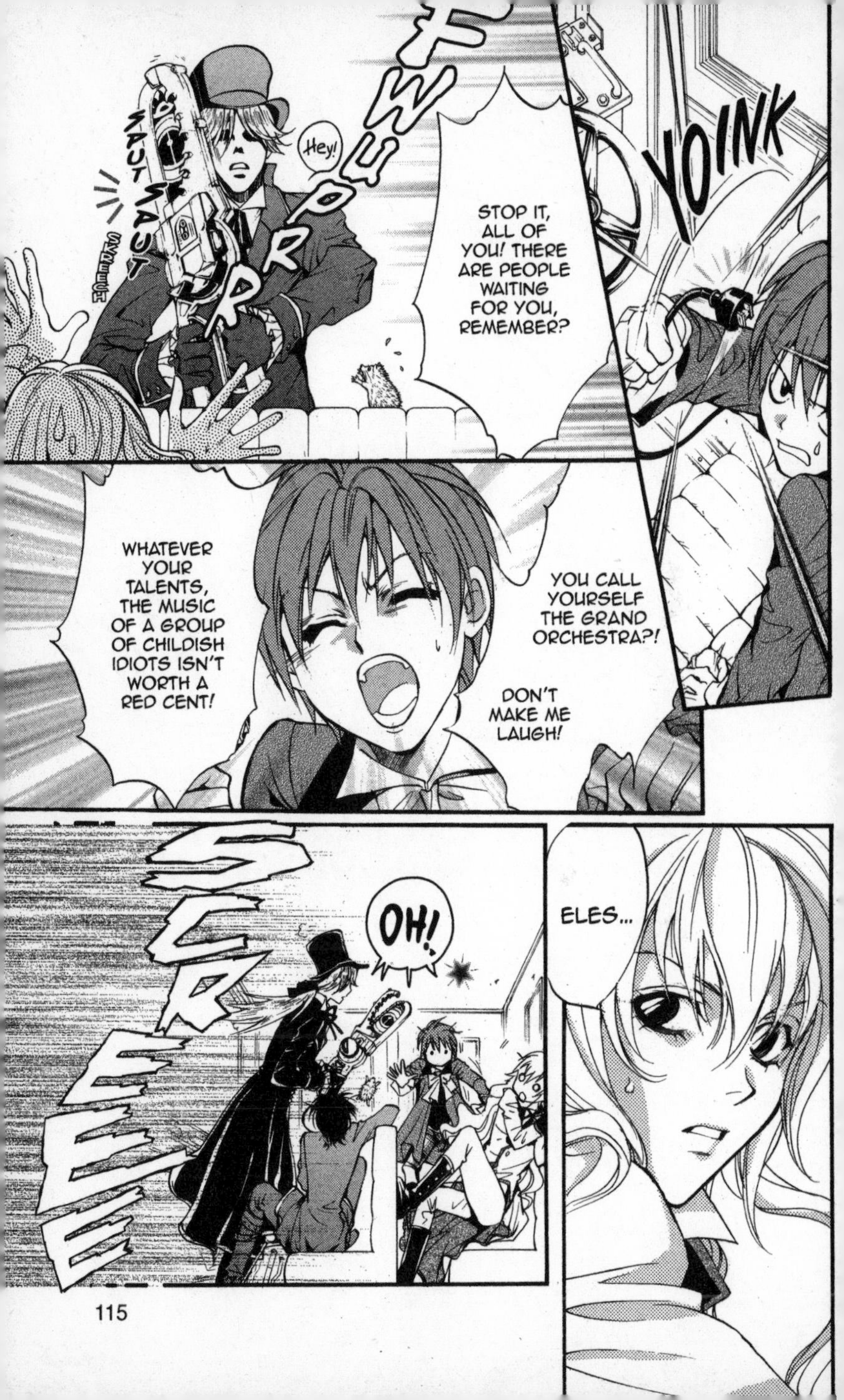
YOINK
Hey!
SPUT SPUT
SKREECH
FWUPRR
STOP IT, ALL OF YOU! THERE ARE PEOPLE WAITING FOR YOU, REMEMBER?
YOU CALL YOURSELF THE GRAND ORCHESTRA?!
DON'T MAKE ME LAUGH!
WHATEVER YOUR TALENTS, THE MUSIC OF A GROUP OF CHILDISH IDIOTS ISN'T WORTH A RED CENT!
ELES...
OH!
SCREEEE

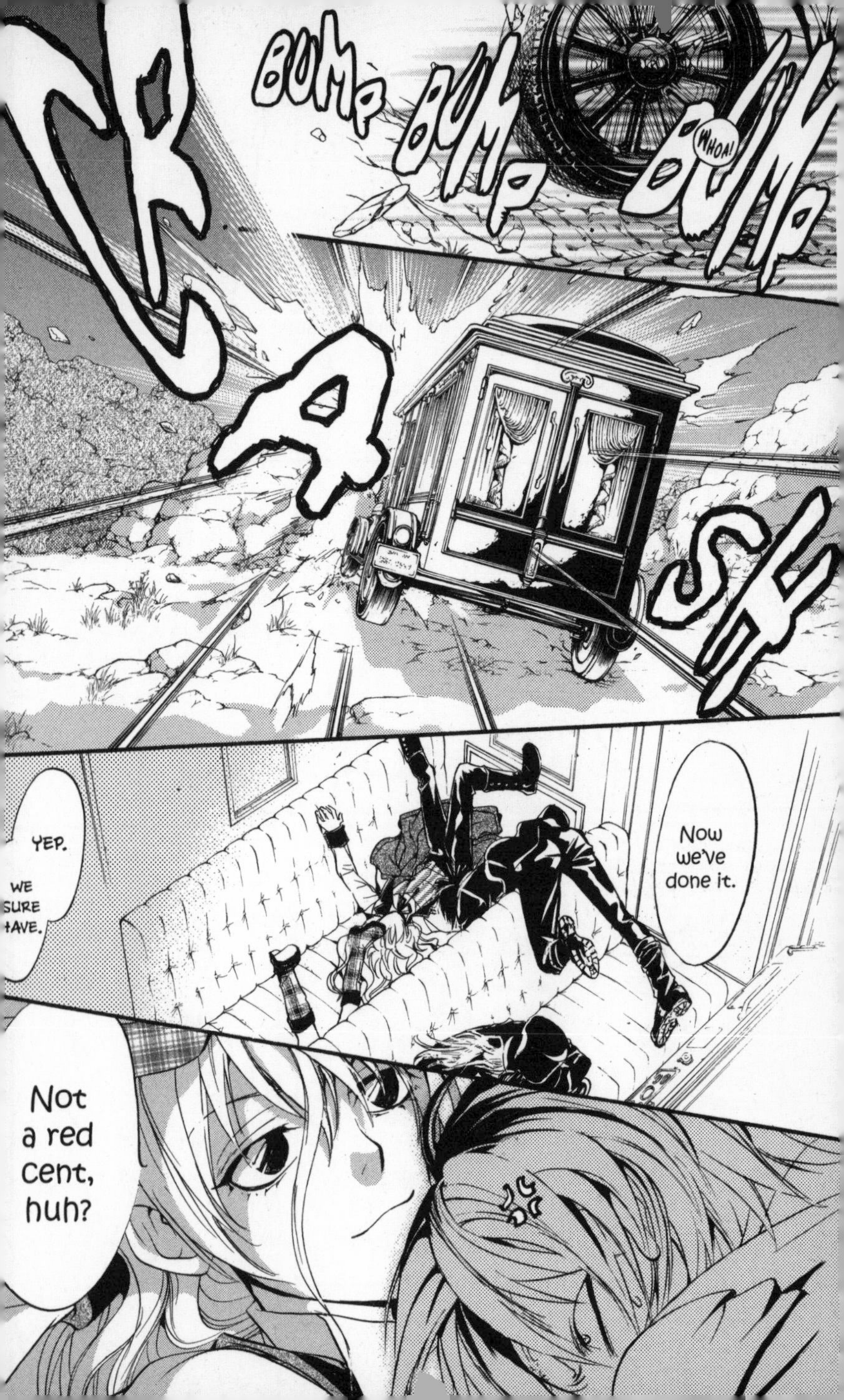
WHOA!
BUMP
BUMP
BUMP
CRASH
Now we've done it.
YEP.
WE SURE HAVE.
Not a red cent, huh?

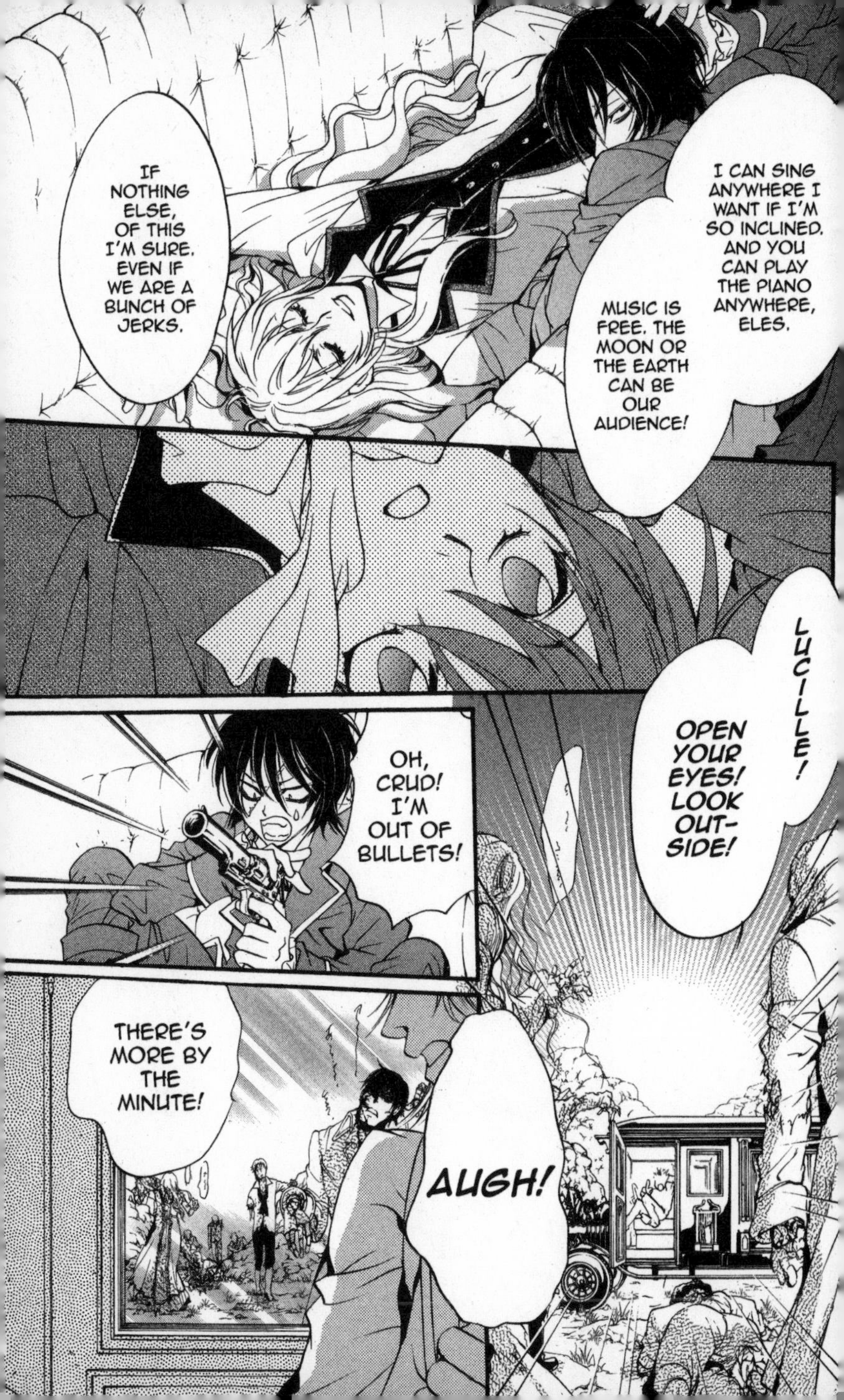
I CAN SING ANYWHERE I WANT IF I'M SO INCLINED. AND YOU CAN PLAY THE PIANO ANYWHERE, ELES.
MUSIC IS FREE. THE MOON OR THE EARTH CAN BE OUR AUDIENCE!
IF NOTHING ELSE, OF THIS I'M SURE. EVEN IF WE ARE A BUNCH OF JERKS.
LUCILLE!
OPEN YOUR EYES! LOOK OUT-SIDE!
OH, CRUD! I'M OUT OF BULLETS!
AUGH!
THERE'S MORE BY THE MINUTE!

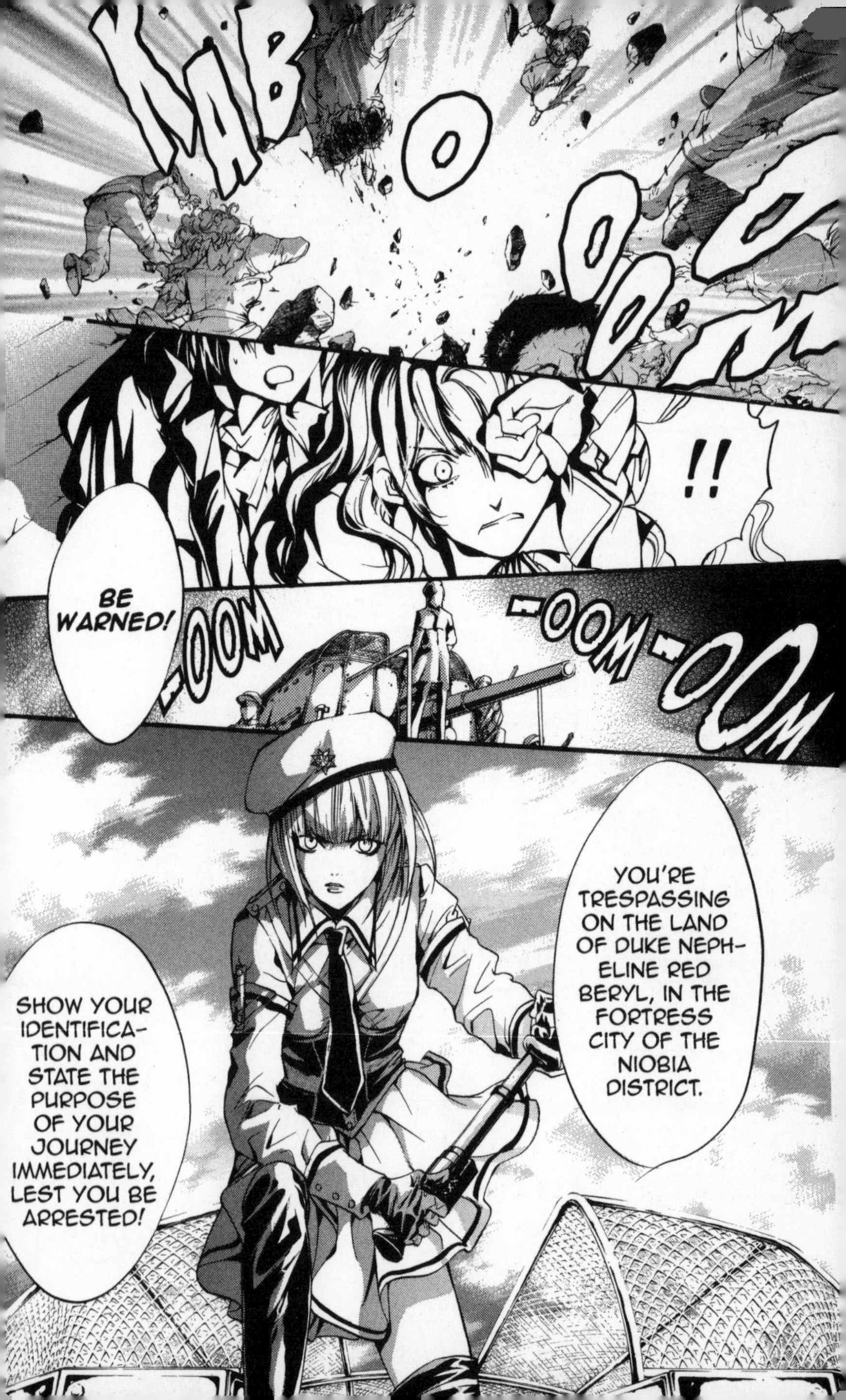
KABOOOOOM
!!
-OOM-OOM-OOM
BE WARNED!
YOU'RE TRESPASSING ON THE LAND OF DUKE NEPH-ELINE RED BERYL, IN THE FORTRESS CITY OF THE NIOBIA DISTRICT.
SHOW YOUR IDENTIFICA-TION AND STATE THE PURPOSE OF YOUR JOURNEY IMMEDIATELY, LEST YOU BE ARRESTED!

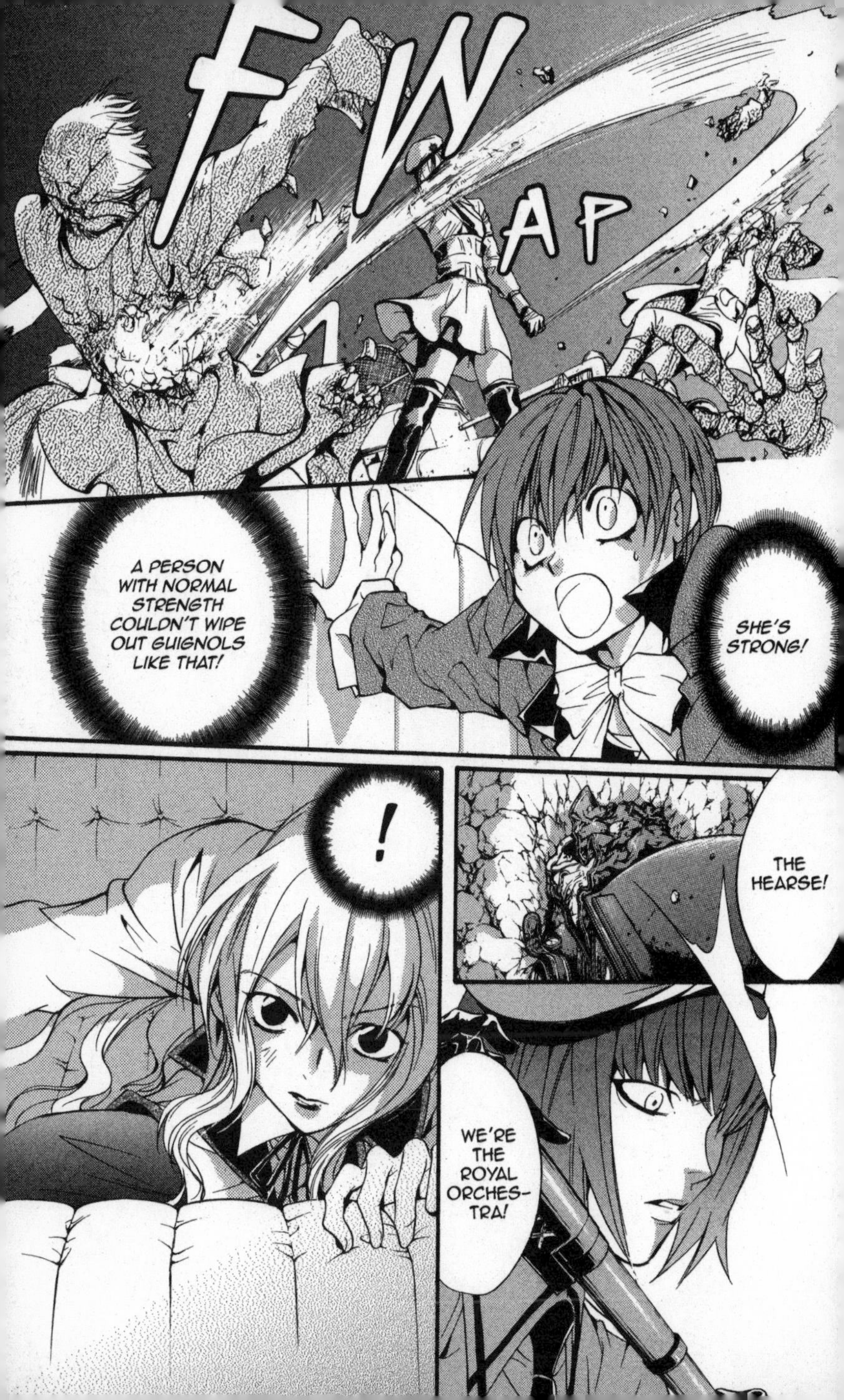
FWAP
SHE'S STRONG!
A PERSON WITH NORMAL STRENGTH COULDN'T WIPE OUT GUIGNOLS LIKE THAT!
THE HEARSE!
!
WE'RE THE ROYAL ORCHES-TRA!

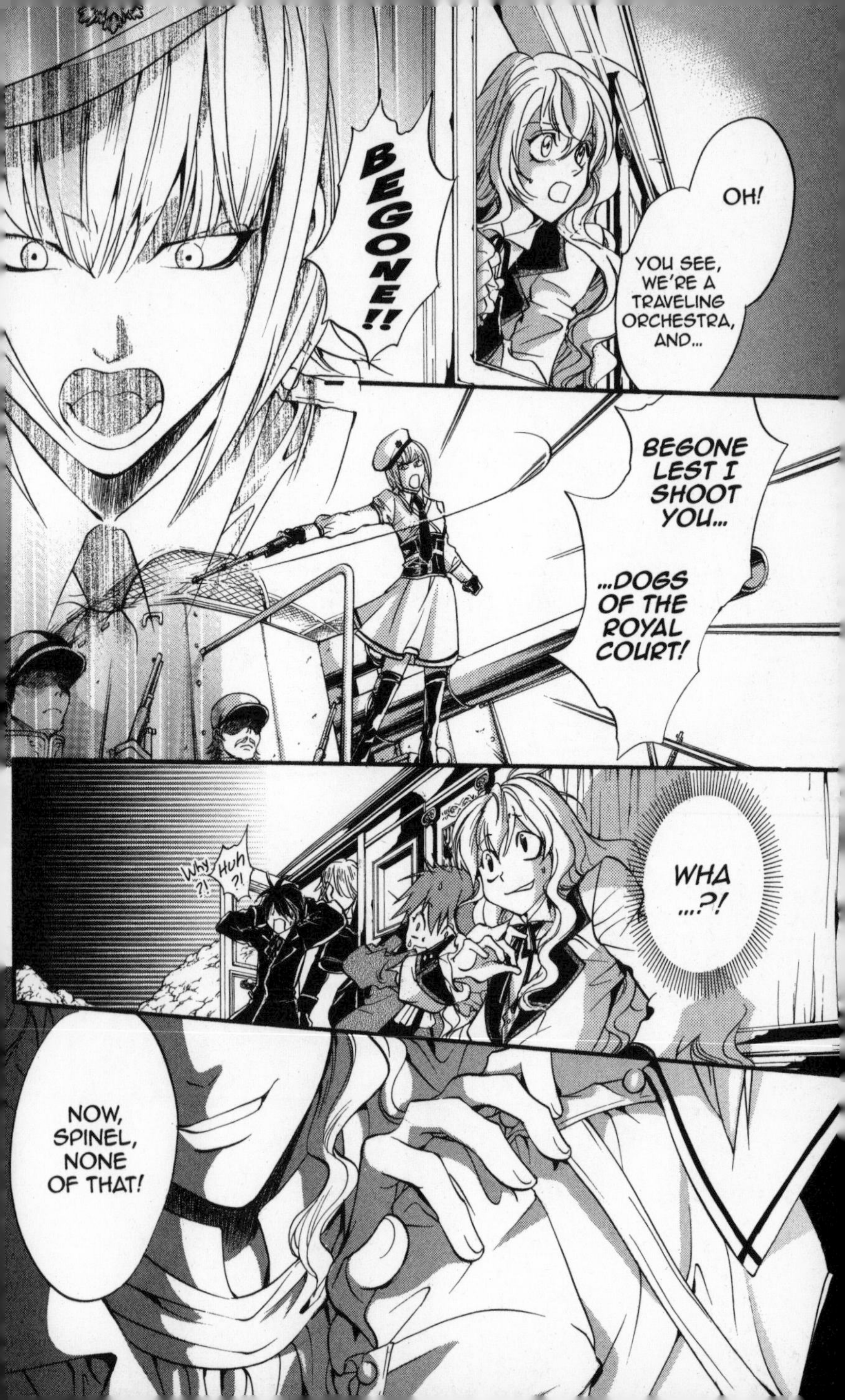
OH!
YOU SEE, WE'RE A TRAVELING ORCHESTRA, AND...
BEGONE!!
BEGONE LEST I SHOOT YOU...
...DOGS OF THE ROYAL COURT!
WHA ...?!
Huh ?!
Why ?!
NOW, SPINEL, NONE OF THAT!

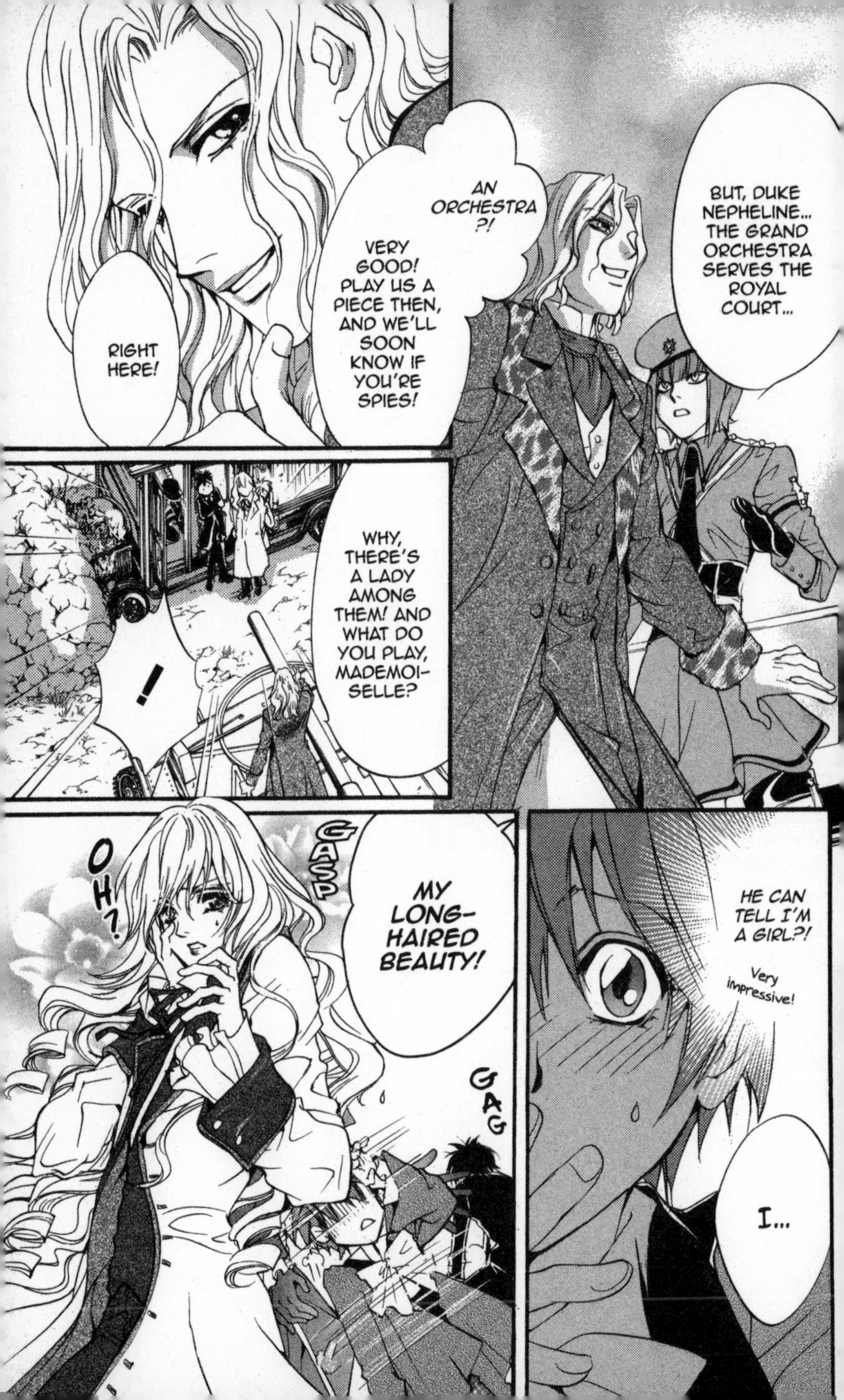
BUT, DUKE NEPHELINE... THE GRAND ORCHESTRA SERVES THE ROYAL COURT...
AN ORCHESTRA ?!
VERY GOOD! PLAY US A PIECE THEN, AND WE'LL SOON KNOW IF YOU'RE SPIES!
RIGHT HERE!
WHY, THERE'S A LADY AMONG THEM! AND WHAT DO YOU PLAY, MADEMOI-SELLE?
!
HE CAN TELL I'M A GIRL?!
Very impressive!
I...
MY LONG-HAIRED BEAUTY!
GASP
OH?
GAG

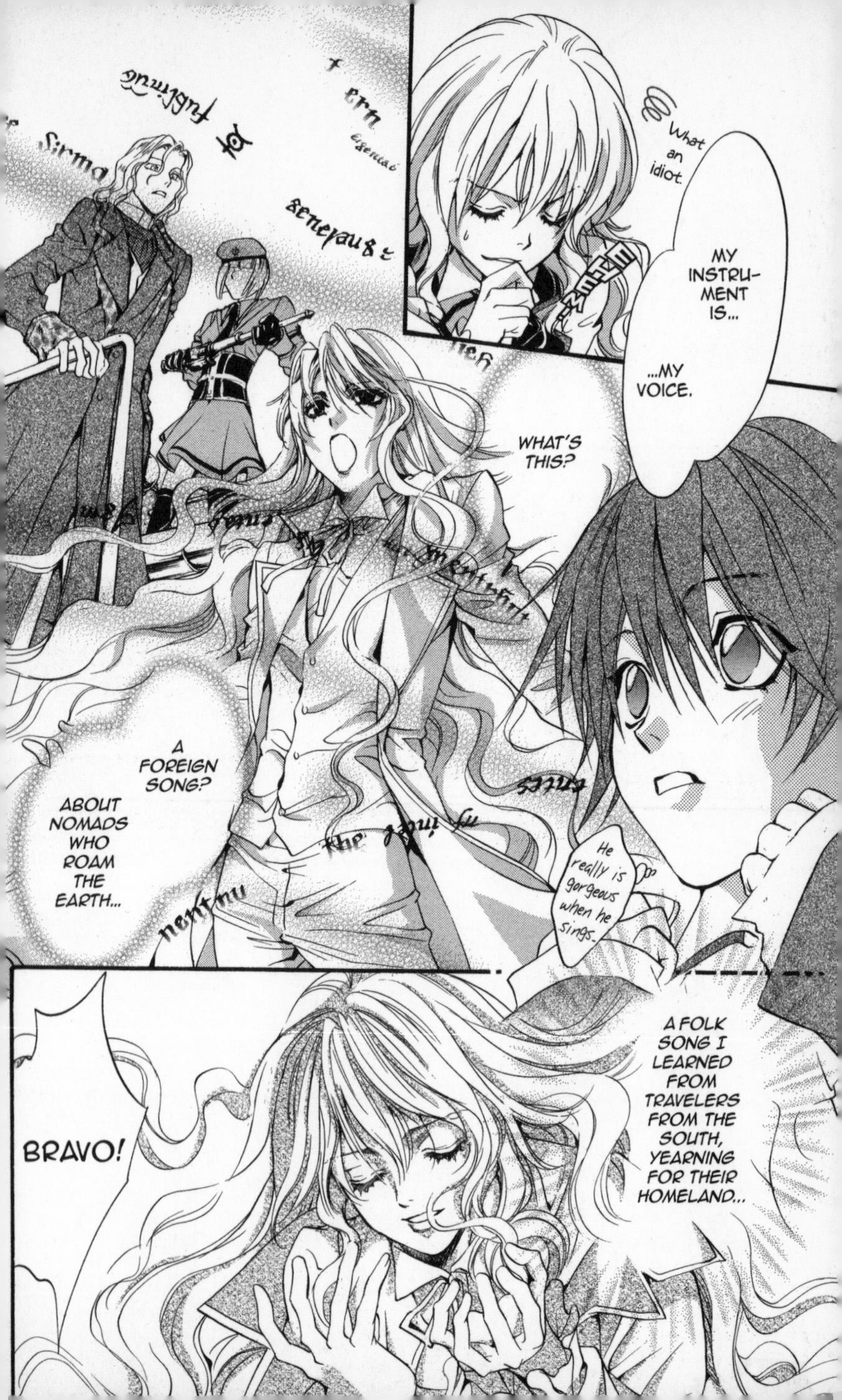
What an idiot.
MY INSTRUMENT IS...
...MY VOICE.
WHAT'S THIS?
A FOREIGN SONG?
ABOUT NOMADS WHO ROAM THE EARTH...
He really is gorgeous when he sings.
A FOLK SONG I LEARNED FROM TRAVELERS FROM THE SOUTH, YEARNING FOR THEIR HOMELAND...
BRAVO!

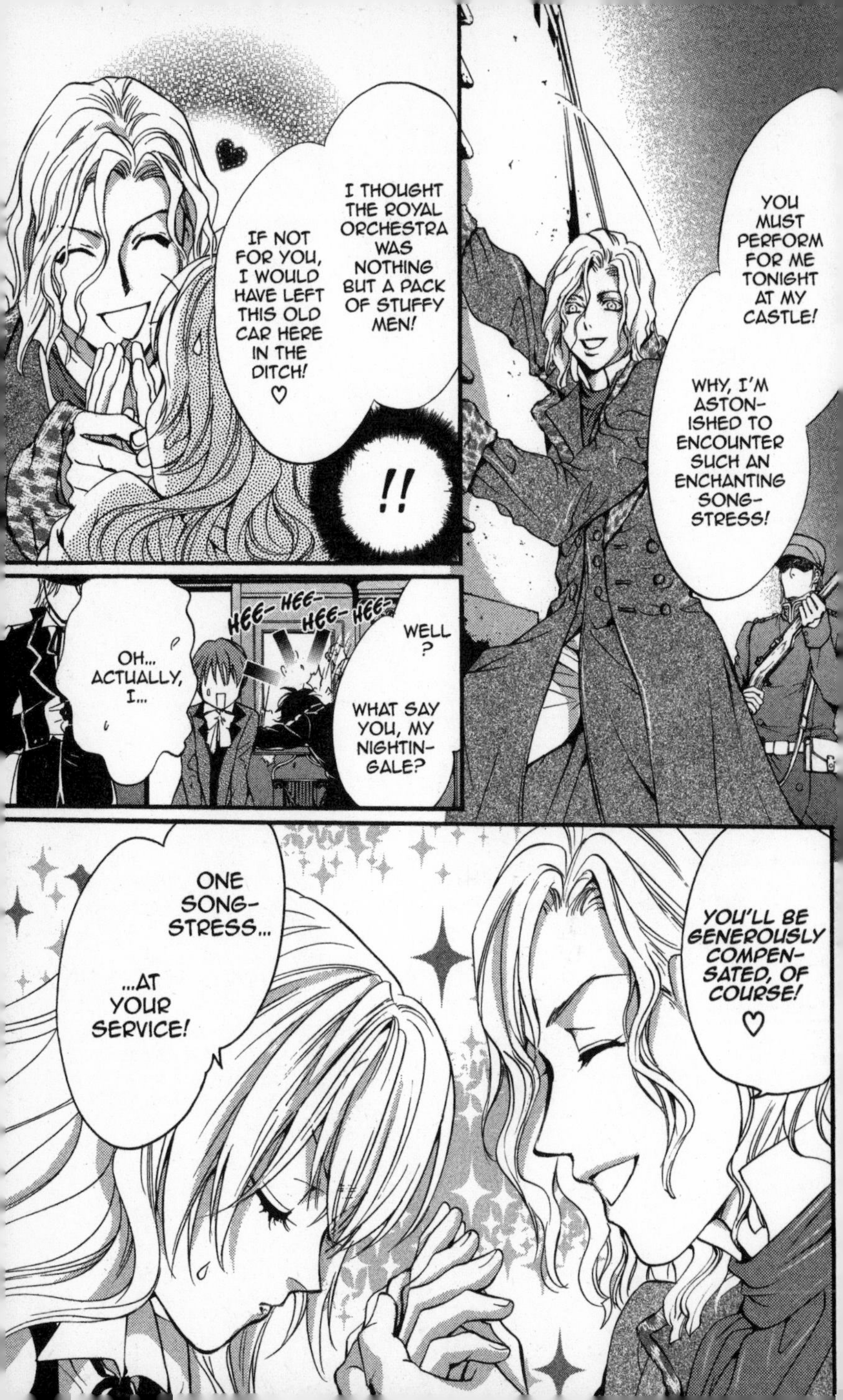
YOU MUST PERFORM FOR ME TONIGHT AT MY CASTLE!
WHY, I'M ASTON-ISHED TO ENCOUNTER SUCH AN ENCHANTING SONG-STRESS!
I THOUGHT THE ROYAL ORCHESTRA WAS NOTHING BUT A PACK OF STUFFY MEN!
IF NOT FOR YOU, I WOULD HAVE LEFT THIS OLD CAR HERE IN THE DITCH! ♡
!!
WELL? WHAT SAY YOU, MY NIGHTIN-GALE?
HEE-HEE-HEE-HEE
OH... ACTUALLY, I...
YOU'LL BE GENEROUSLY COMPEN-SATED, OF COURSE! ♡
ONE SONG-STRESS...
...AT YOUR SERVICE!

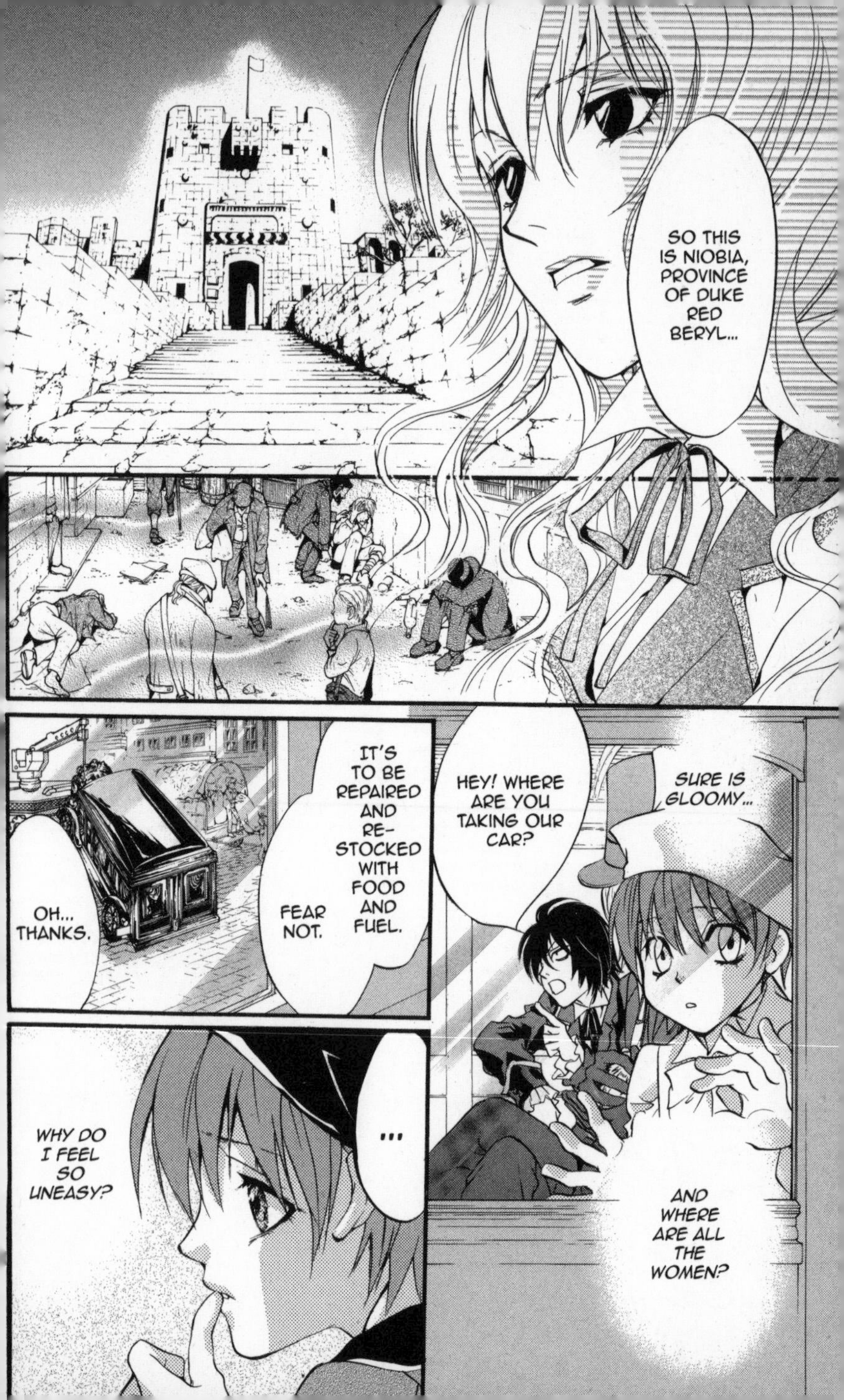
SO THIS IS NIOBIA, PROVINCE OF DUKE RED BERYL...
SURE IS GLOOMY...
HEY! WHERE ARE YOU TAKING OUR CAR?
AND WHERE ARE ALL THE WOMEN?
IT'S TO BE REPAIRED AND RE-STOCKED WITH FOOD AND FUEL.
FEAR NOT.
OH... THANKS.
...
WHY DO I FEEL SO UNEASY?

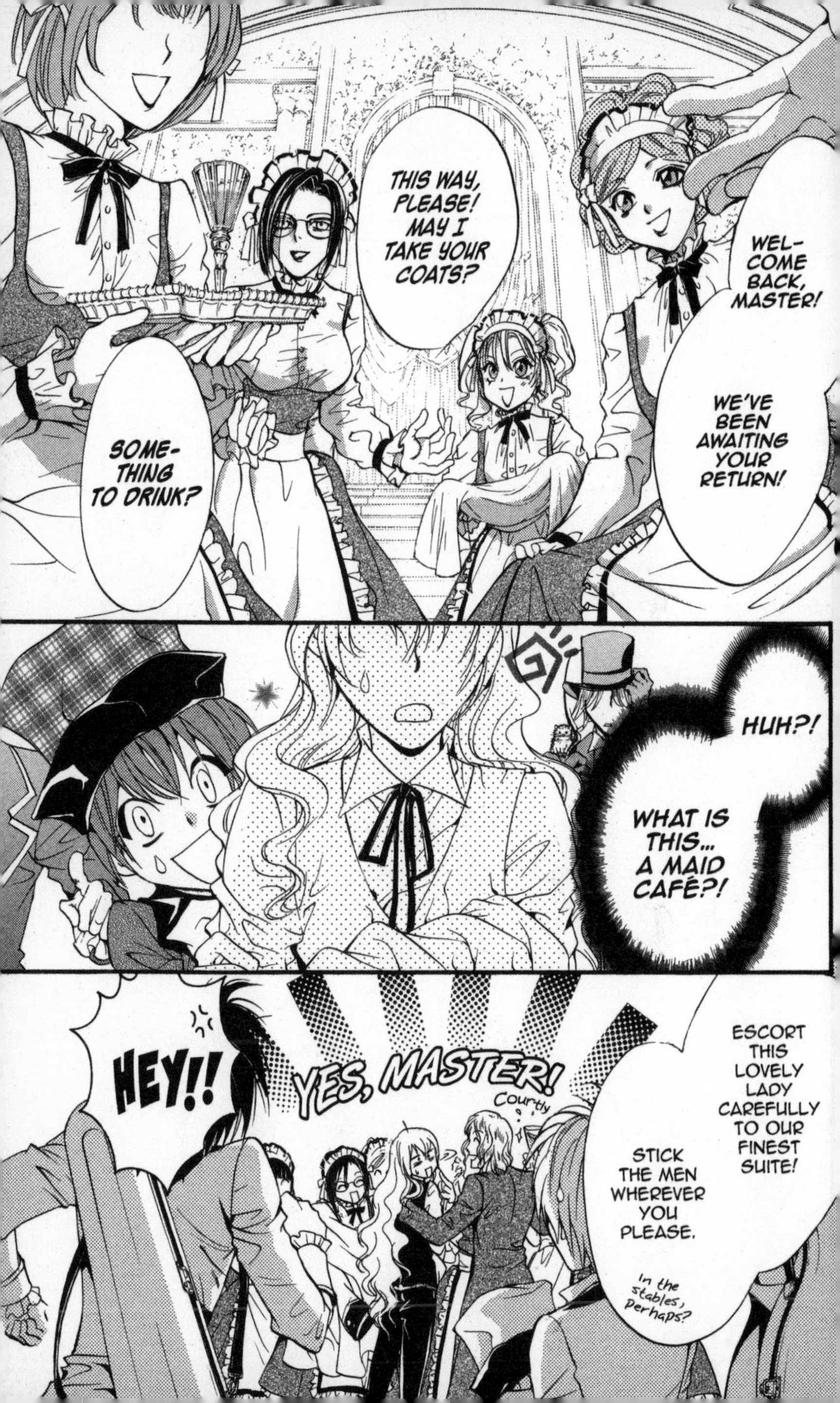
WEL-COME BACK, MASTER!
WE'VE BEEN AWAITING YOUR RETURN!
THIS WAY, PLEASE! MAY I TAKE YOUR COATS?
SOME-THING TO DRINK?
HUH?!
WHAT IS THIS... A MAID CAFÉ?!
ESCORT THIS LOVELY LADY CAREFULLY TO OUR FINEST SUITE!
STICK THE MEN WHEREVER YOU PLEASE.
In the stables, perhaps?
YES, MASTER!
Courtly
HEY!!

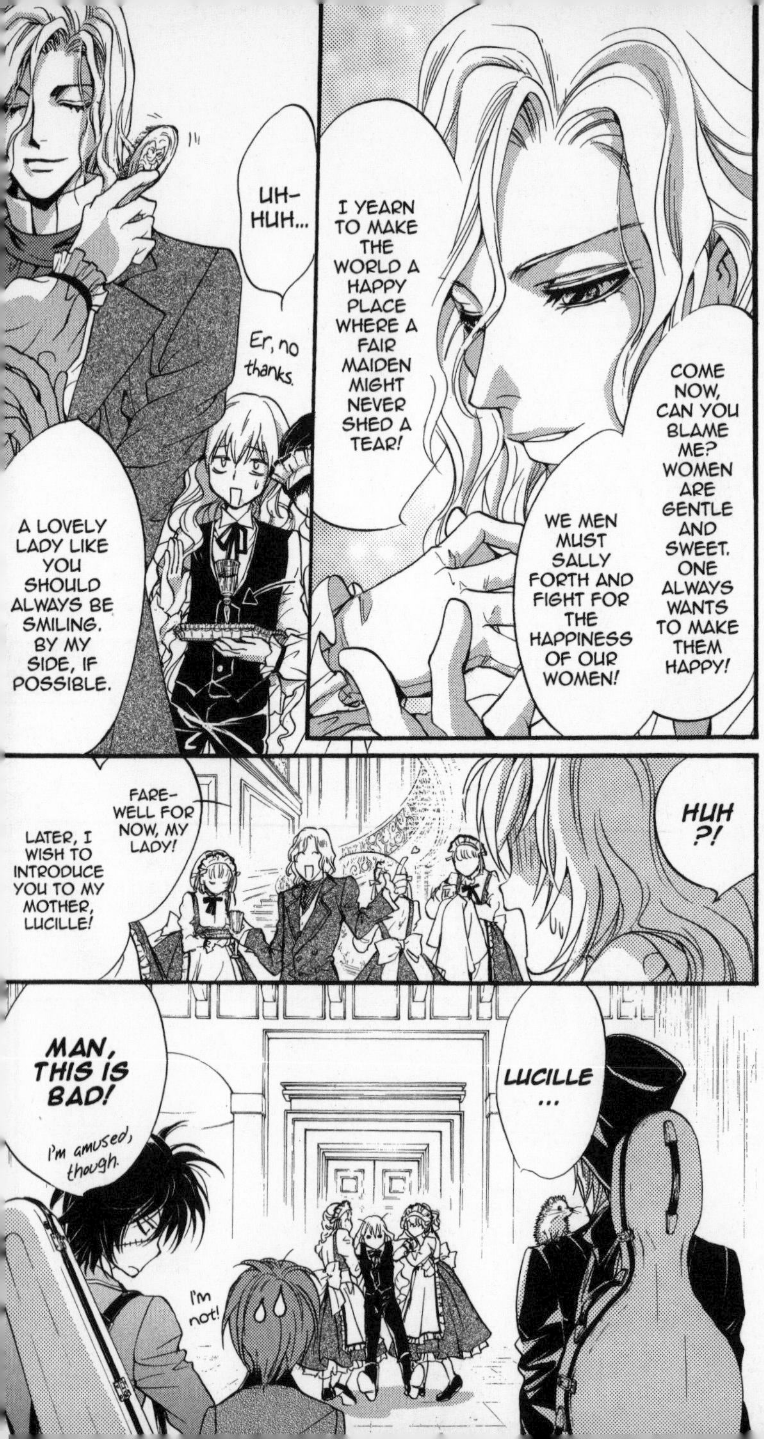
COME NOW, CAN YOU BLAME ME? WOMEN ARE GENTLE AND SWEET. ONE ALWAYS WANTS TO MAKE THEM HAPPY!
WE MEN MUST SALLY FORTH AND FIGHT FOR THE HAPPINESS OF OUR WOMEN!
I YEARN TO MAKE THE WORLD A HAPPY PLACE WHERE A FAIR MAIDEN MIGHT NEVER SHED A TEAR!
UH-HUH...
Er, no thanks.
A LOVELY LADY LIKE YOU SHOULD ALWAYS BE SMILING. BY MY SIDE, IF POSSIBLE.
HUH?!
FARE-WELL FOR NOW, MY LADY!
LATER, I WISH TO INTRODUCE YOU TO MY MOTHER, LUCILLE!
LUCILLE...
MAN, THIS IS BAD!
I'm amused, though.
I'm not!

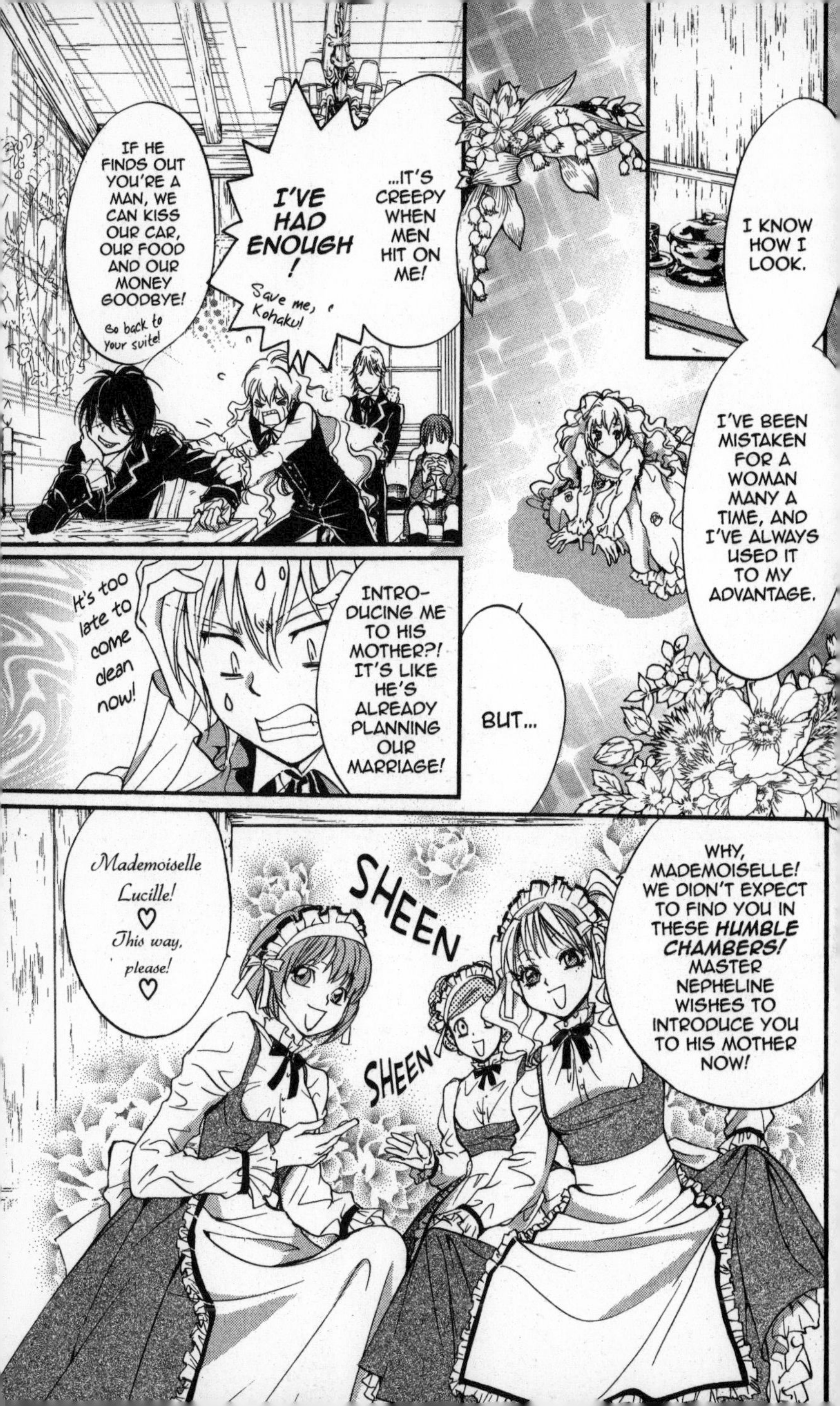
I KNOW HOW I LOOK.
I'VE BEEN MISTAKEN FOR A WOMAN MANY A TIME, AND I'VE ALWAYS USED IT TO MY ADVANTAGE.
BUT...
...IT'S CREEPY WHEN MEN HIT ON ME!
I'VE HAD ENOUGH!
Save me, Kohaku!
IF HE FINDS OUT YOU'RE A MAN, WE CAN KISS OUR CAR, OUR FOOD AND OUR MONEY GOODBYE!
Go back to your suite!
INTRO-DUCING ME TO HIS MOTHER?! IT'S LIKE HE'S ALREADY PLANNING OUR MARRIAGE!
It's too late to come clean now!
WHY, MADEMOISELLE! WE DIDN'T EXPECT TO FIND YOU IN THESE HUMBLE CHAMBERS! MASTER NEPHELINE WISHES TO INTRODUCE YOU TO HIS MOTHER NOW!
SHEEN
SHEEN
Mademoiselle Lucille! ♡ This way, please! ♡

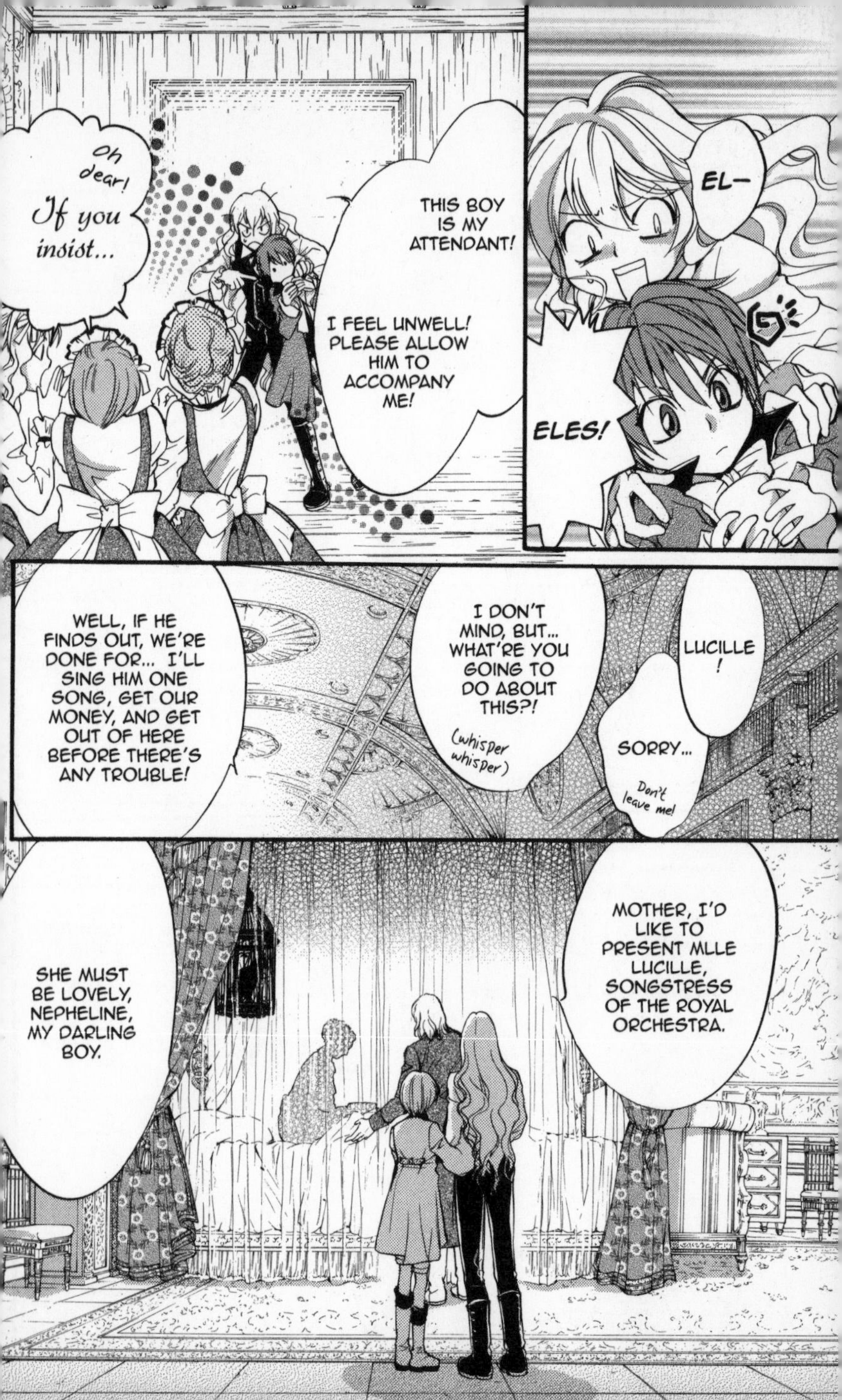
EL—
ELES!
THIS BOY IS MY ATTENDANT!
I FEEL UNWELL! PLEASE ALLOW HIM TO ACCOMPANY ME!
Oh dear!
If you insist...
LUCILLE!
SORRY...
Don't leave me!
I DON'T MIND, BUT... WHAT'RE YOU GOING TO DO ABOUT THIS?!
(whisper whisper)
WELL, IF HE FINDS OUT, WE'RE DONE FOR... I'LL SING HIM ONE SONG, GET OUR MONEY, AND GET OUT OF HERE BEFORE THERE'S ANY TROUBLE!
MOTHER, I'D LIKE TO PRESENT MLLE LUCILLE, SONGSTRESS OF THE ROYAL ORCHESTRA.
SHE MUST BE LOVELY, NEPHELINE, MY DARLING BOY.

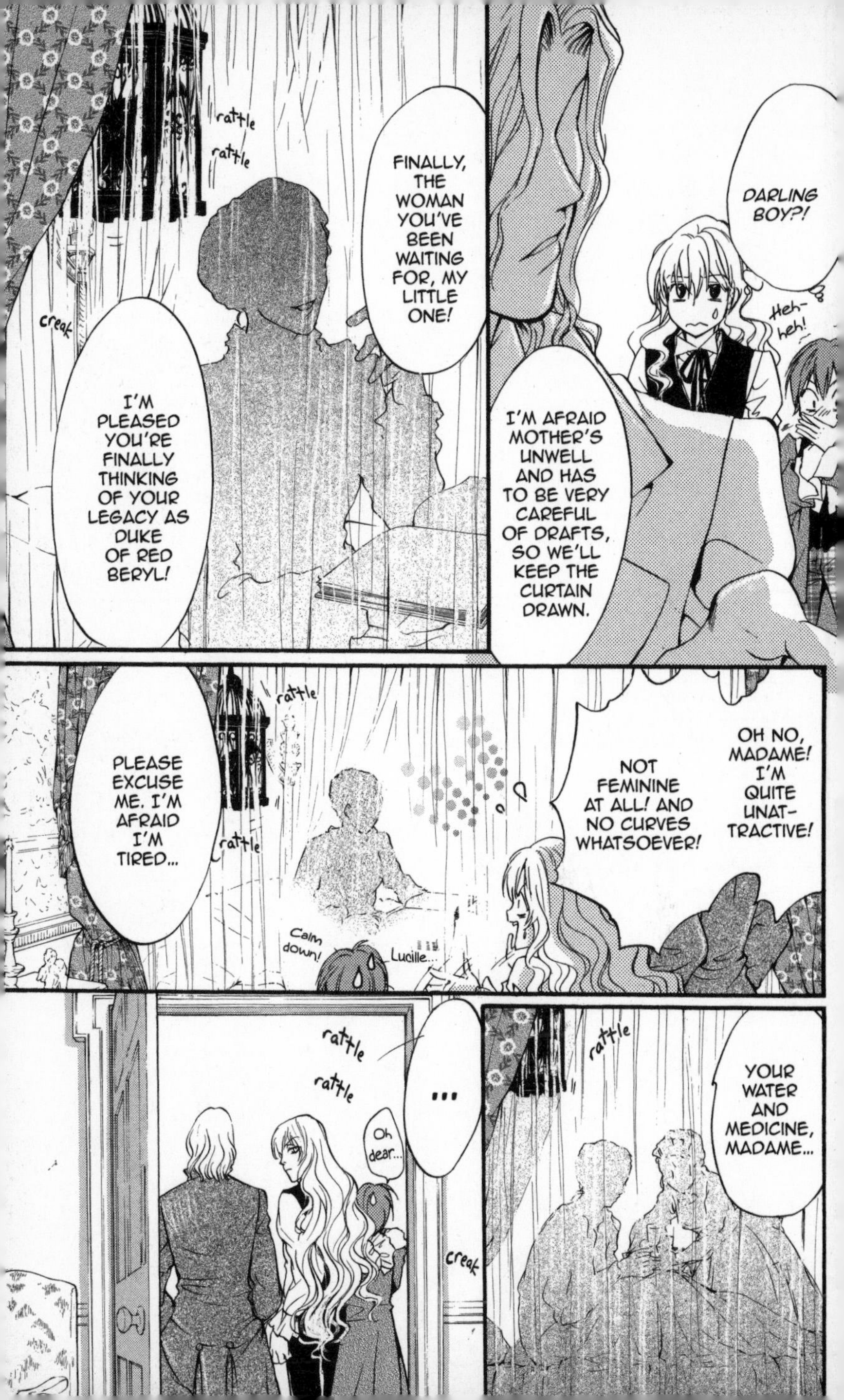
DARLING BOY?!
Heh-heh!
I'M AFRAID MOTHER'S UNWELL AND HAS TO BE VERY CAREFUL OF DRAFTS, SO WE'LL KEEP THE CURTAIN DRAWN.
FINALLY, THE WOMAN YOU'VE BEEN WAITING FOR, MY LITTLE ONE!
rattle
rattle
creak
I'M PLEASED YOU'RE FINALLY THINKING OF YOUR LEGACY AS DUKE OF RED BERYL!
OH NO, MADAME! I'M QUITE UNAT-TRACTIVE!
NOT FEMININE AT ALL! AND NO CURVES WHATSOEVER!
rattle
PLEASE EXCUSE ME. I'M AFRAID I'M TIRED...
rattle
Lucille...
Calm down!
rattle
YOUR WATER AND MEDICINE, MADAME...
...
rattle
rattle
Oh dear...
creak

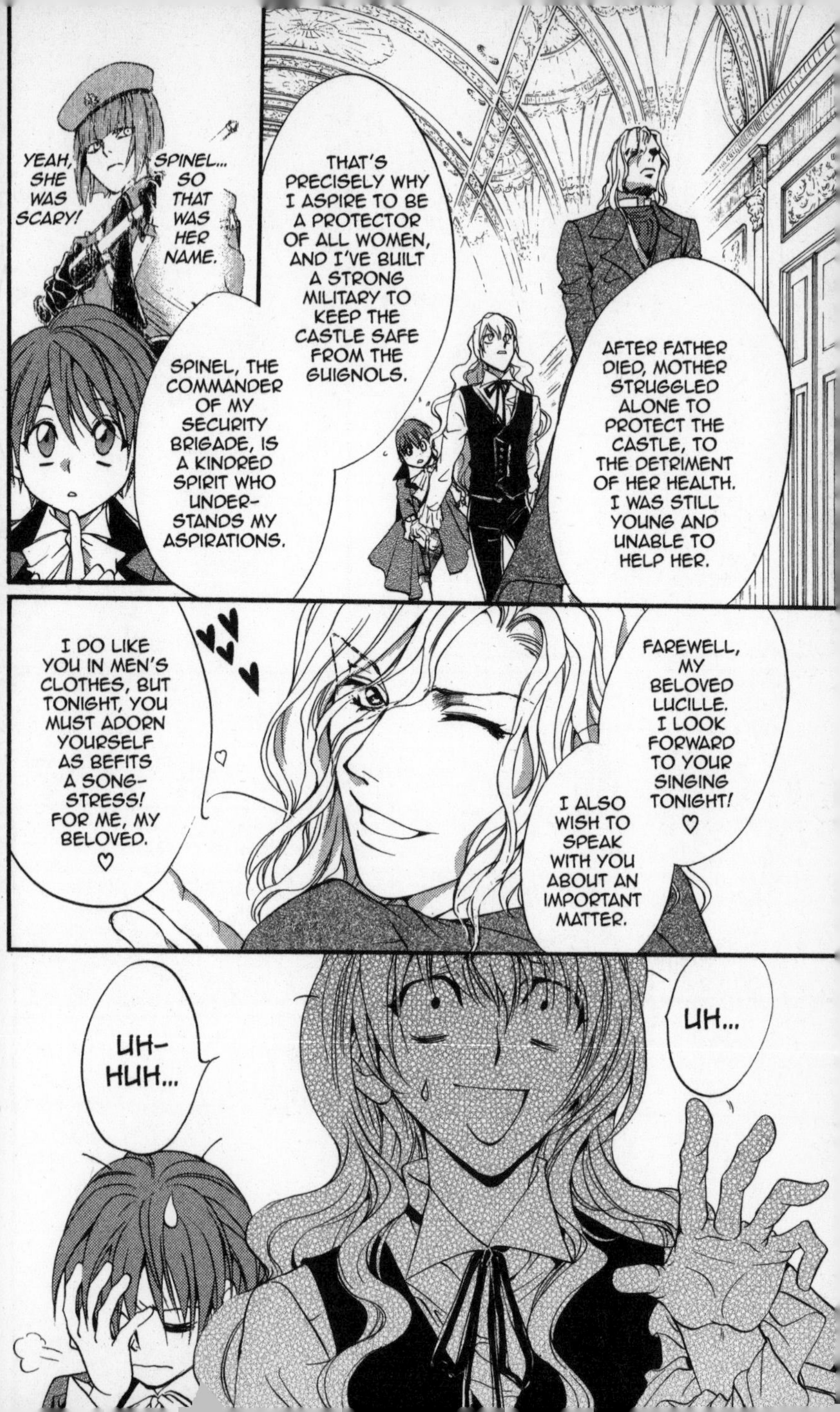
AFTER FATHER DIED, MOTHER STRUGGLED ALONE TO PROTECT THE CASTLE, TO THE DETRIMENT OF HER HEALTH. I WAS STILL YOUNG AND UNABLE TO HELP HER.
THAT'S PRECISELY WHY I ASPIRE TO BE A PROTECTOR OF ALL WOMEN, AND I'VE BUILT A STRONG MILITARY TO KEEP THE CASTLE SAFE FROM THE GUIGNOLS.
SPINEL, THE COMMANDER OF MY SECURITY BRIGADE, IS A KINDRED SPIRIT WHO UNDER-STANDS MY ASPIRATIONS.
SPINEL... SO THAT WAS HER NAME.
YEAH, SHE WAS SCARY!
FAREWELL, MY BELOVED LUCILLE. I LOOK FORWARD TO YOUR SINGING TONIGHT! ♡
I ALSO WISH TO SPEAK WITH YOU ABOUT AN IMPORTANT MATTER.
I DO LIKE YOU IN MEN'S CLOTHES, BUT TONIGHT, YOU MUST ADORN YOURSELF AS BEFITS A SONG-STRESS! FOR ME, MY BELOVED. ♡
UH...
UH-HUH...

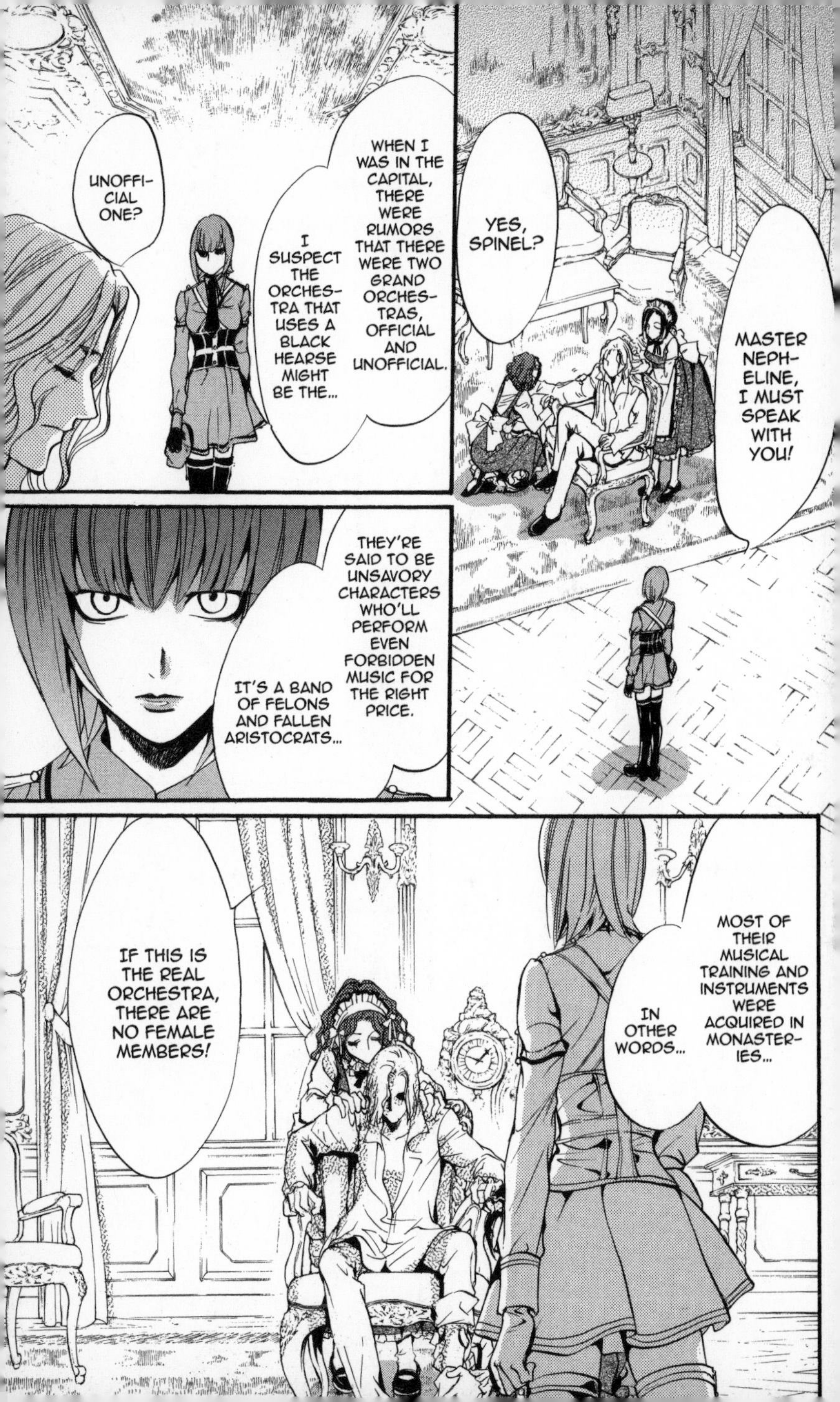
MASTER NEPHELINE, I MUST SPEAK WITH YOU!
YES, SPINEL?
WHEN I WAS IN THE CAPITAL, THERE WERE RUMORS THAT THERE WERE TWO GRAND ORCHESTRAS, OFFICIAL AND UNOFFICIAL.
I SUSPECT THE ORCHESTRA THAT USES A BLACK HEARSE MIGHT BE THE...
UNOFFICIAL ONE?
THEY'RE SAID TO BE UNSAVORY CHARACTERS WHO'LL PERFORM EVEN FORBIDDEN MUSIC FOR THE RIGHT PRICE.
IT'S A BAND OF FELONS AND FALLEN ARISTOCRATS...
MOST OF THEIR MUSICAL TRAINING AND INSTRUMENTS WERE ACQUIRED IN MONASTERIES...
IN OTHER WORDS...
IF THIS IS THE REAL ORCHESTRA, THERE ARE NO FEMALE MEMBERS!

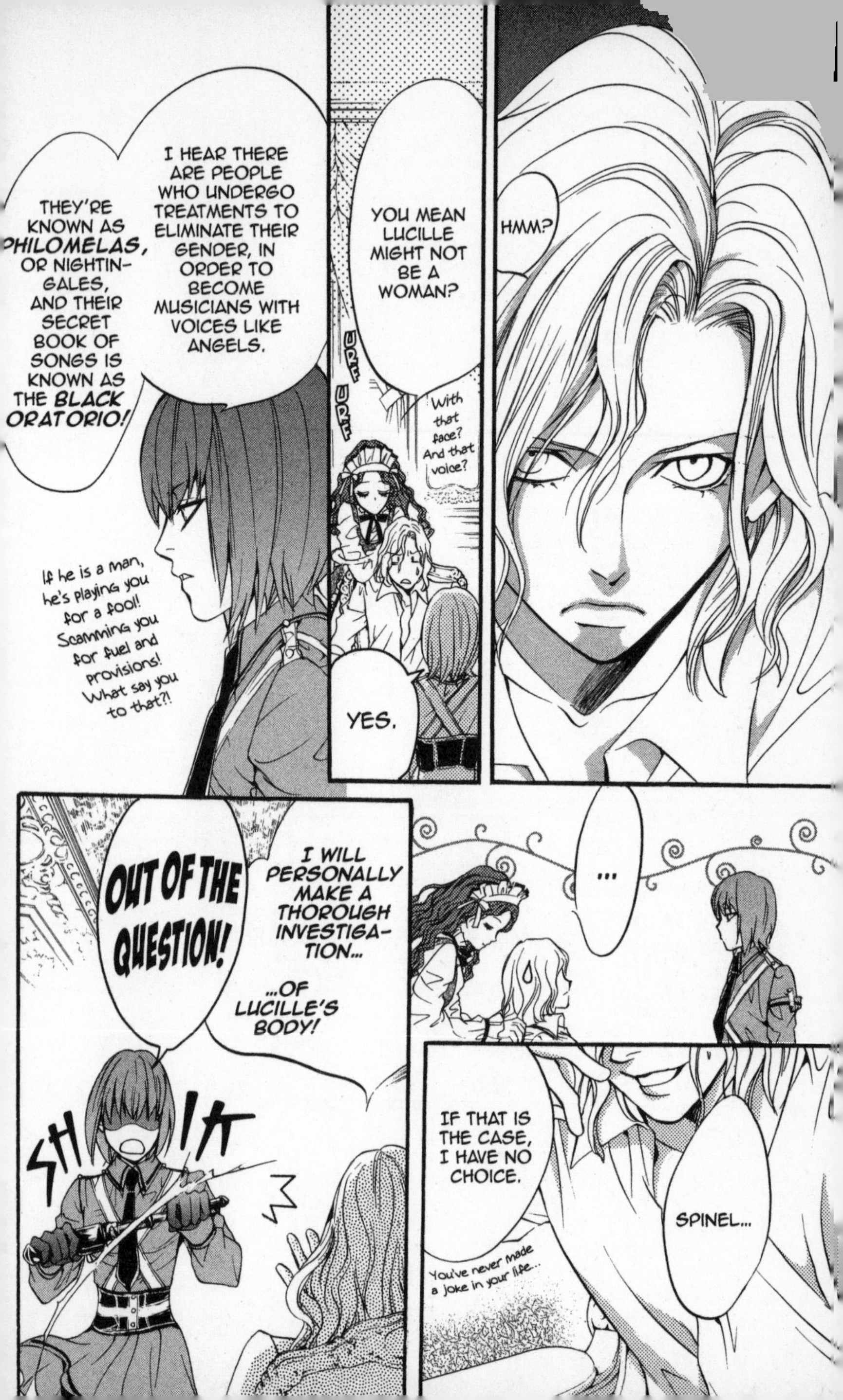
HMM?
YOU MEAN LUCILLE MIGHT NOT BE A WOMAN?
URF URF
With that face? And that voice?
YES.
I HEAR THERE ARE PEOPLE WHO UNDERGO TREATMENTS TO ELIMINATE THEIR GENDER, IN ORDER TO BECOME MUSICIANS WITH VOICES LIKE ANGELS.
THEY'RE KNOWN AS PHILOMELAS, OR NIGHTIN-GALES, AND THEIR SECRET BOOK OF SONGS IS KNOWN AS THE BLACK ORATORIO!
If he is a man, he's playing you for a fool! Scamming you for fuel and provisions! What say you to that?!
...
IF THAT IS THE CASE, I HAVE NO CHOICE.
SPINEL...
You've never made a joke in your life...
I WILL PERSONALLY MAKE A THOROUGH INVESTIGA-TION...
...OF LUCILLE'S BODY!
OUT OF THE QUESTION!
SHIK

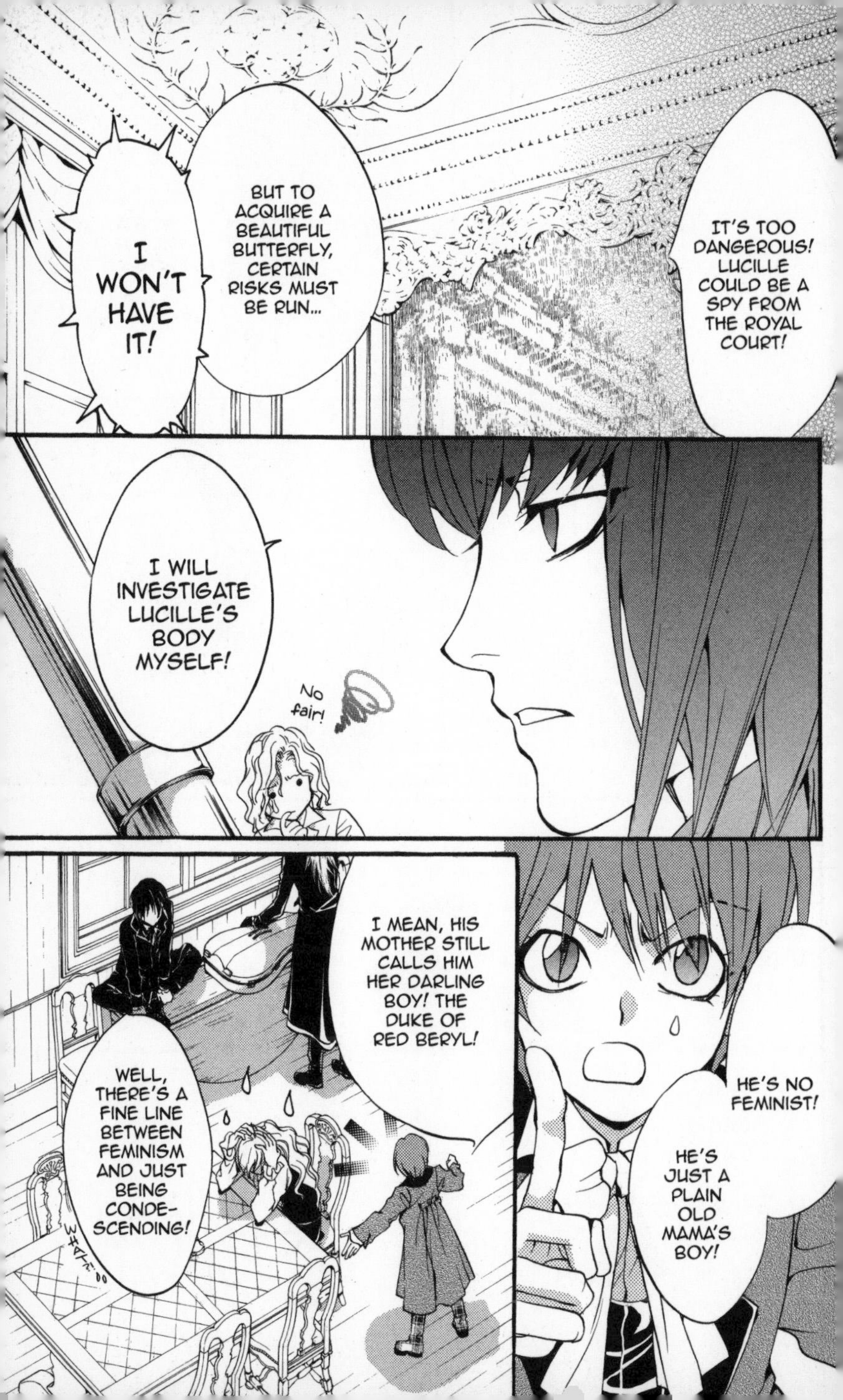
IT'S TOO DANGEROUS! LUCILLE COULD BE A SPY FROM THE ROYAL COURT!
BUT TO ACQUIRE A BEAUTIFUL BUTTERFLY, CERTAIN RISKS MUST BE RUN...
I WON'T HAVE IT!
I WILL INVESTIGATE LUCILLE'S BODY MYSELF!
No fair!
HE'S NO FEMINIST!
HE'S JUST A PLAIN OLD MAMA'S BOY!
I MEAN, HIS MOTHER STILL CALLS HIM HER DARLING BOY! THE DUKE OF RED BERYL!
WELL, THERE'S A FINE LINE BETWEEN FEMINISM AND JUST BEING CONDE-SCENDING!

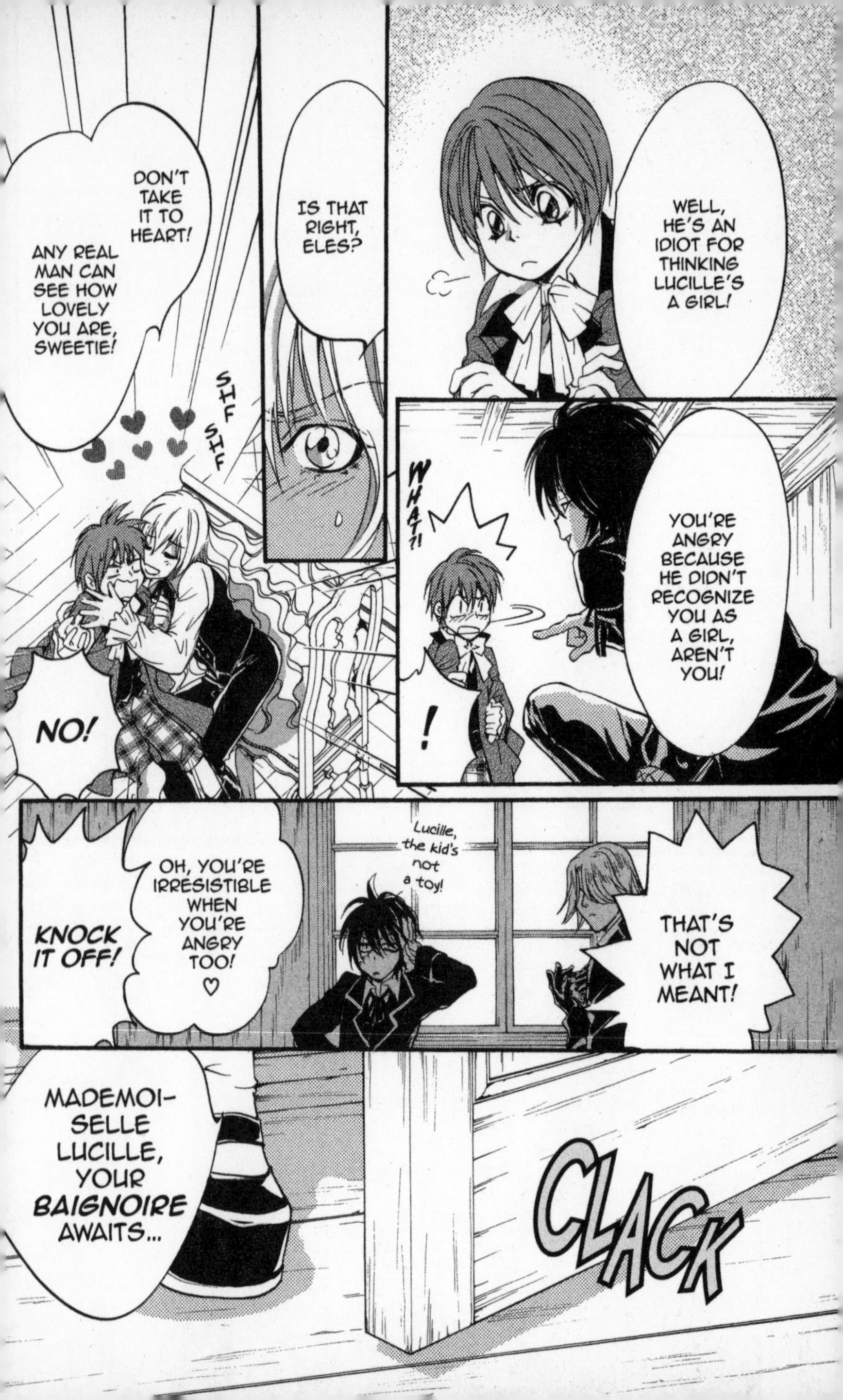
WELL, HE'S AN IDIOT FOR THINKING LUCILLE'S A GIRL!
YOU'RE ANGRY BECAUSE HE DIDN'T RECOGNIZE YOU AS A GIRL, AREN'T YOU!
WHAT?!
!
IS THAT RIGHT, ELES?
DON'T TAKE IT TO HEART!
ANY REAL MAN CAN SEE HOW LOVELY YOU ARE, SWEETIE!
SHF SHF
NO!
THAT'S NOT WHAT I MEANT!
Lucille, the kid's not a toy!
OH, YOU'RE IRRESISTIBLE WHEN YOU'RE ANGRY TOO! ♡
KNOCK IT OFF!
CLACK
MADEMOI-SELLE LUCILLE, YOUR BAIGNOIRE AWAITS...

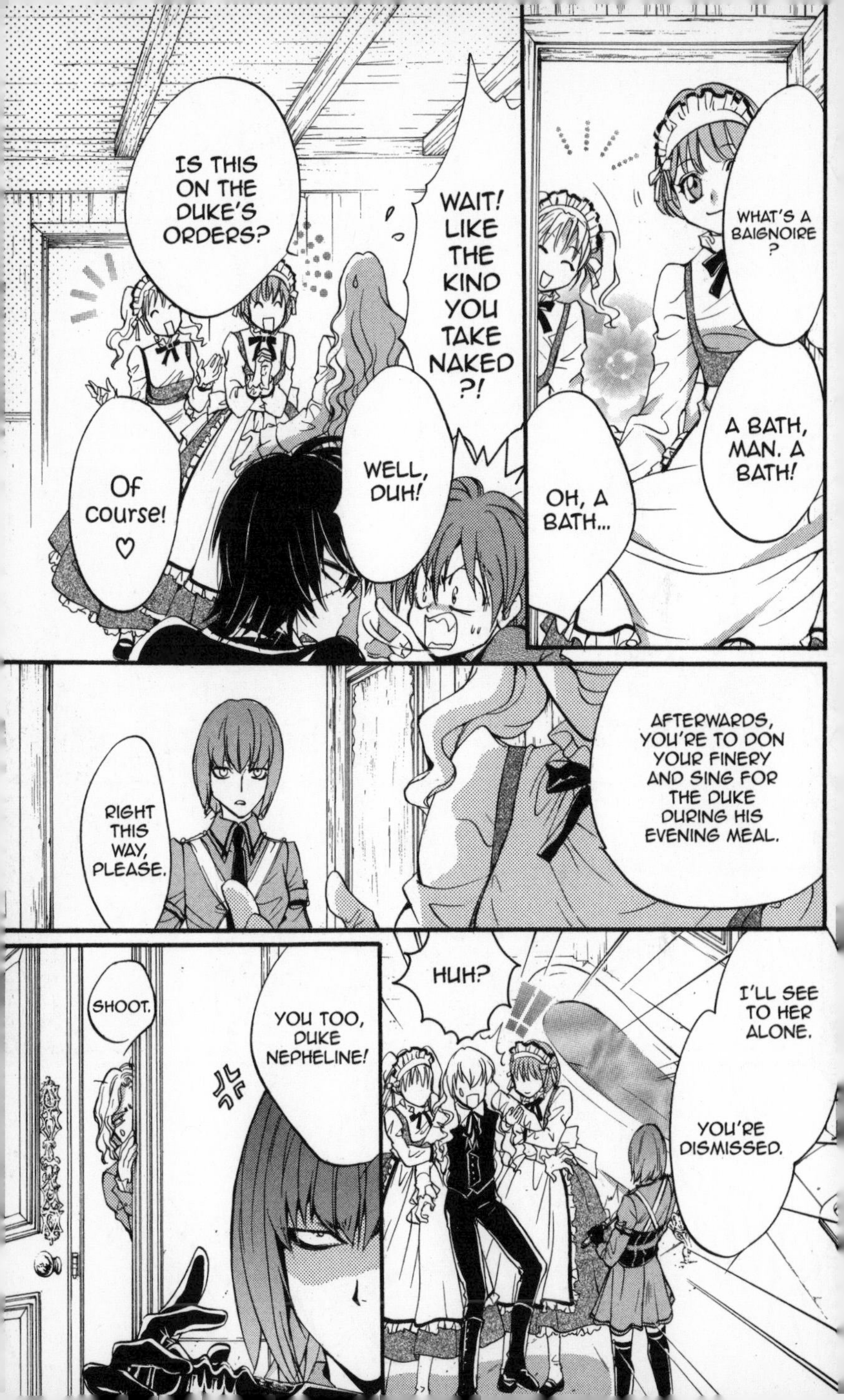
WHAT'S A BAIGNOIRE?
A BATH, MAN. A BATH!
OH, A BATH...
WAIT! LIKE THE KIND YOU TAKE NAKED?!
IS THIS ON THE DUKE'S ORDERS?
WELL, DUH!
Of course! ♡
AFTERWARDS, YOU'RE TO DON YOUR FINERY AND SING FOR THE DUKE DURING HIS EVENING MEAL.
RIGHT THIS WAY, PLEASE.
I'LL SEE TO HER ALONE.
HUH?
YOU'RE DISMISSED.
YOU TOO, DUKE NEPHELINE!
SHOOT.

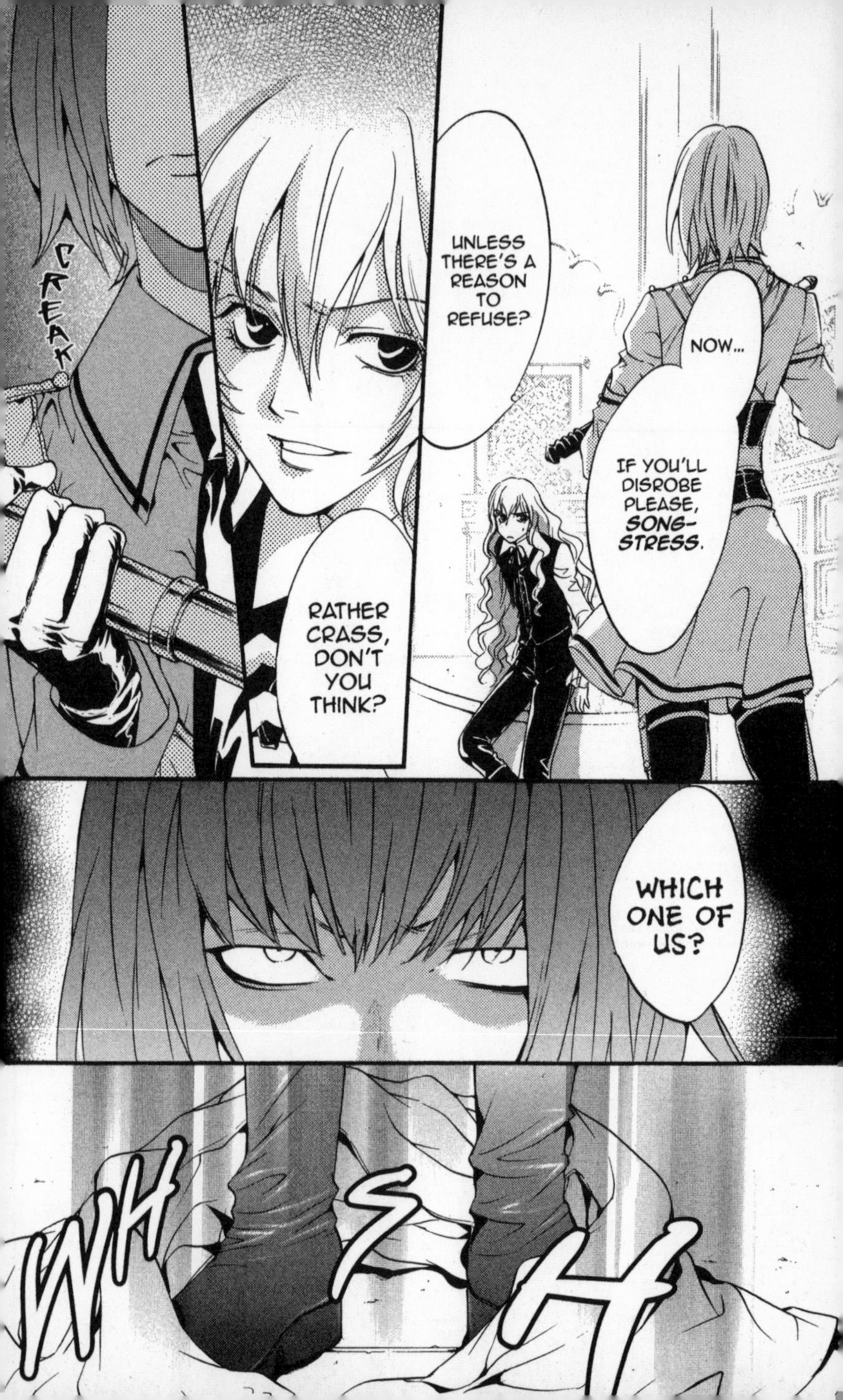
NOW...
IF YOU'LL DISROBE PLEASE, SONG-STRESS.
UNLESS THERE'S A REASON TO REFUSE?
RATHER CRASS, DON'T YOU THINK?
CREAK
WHICH ONE OF US?
WHSH

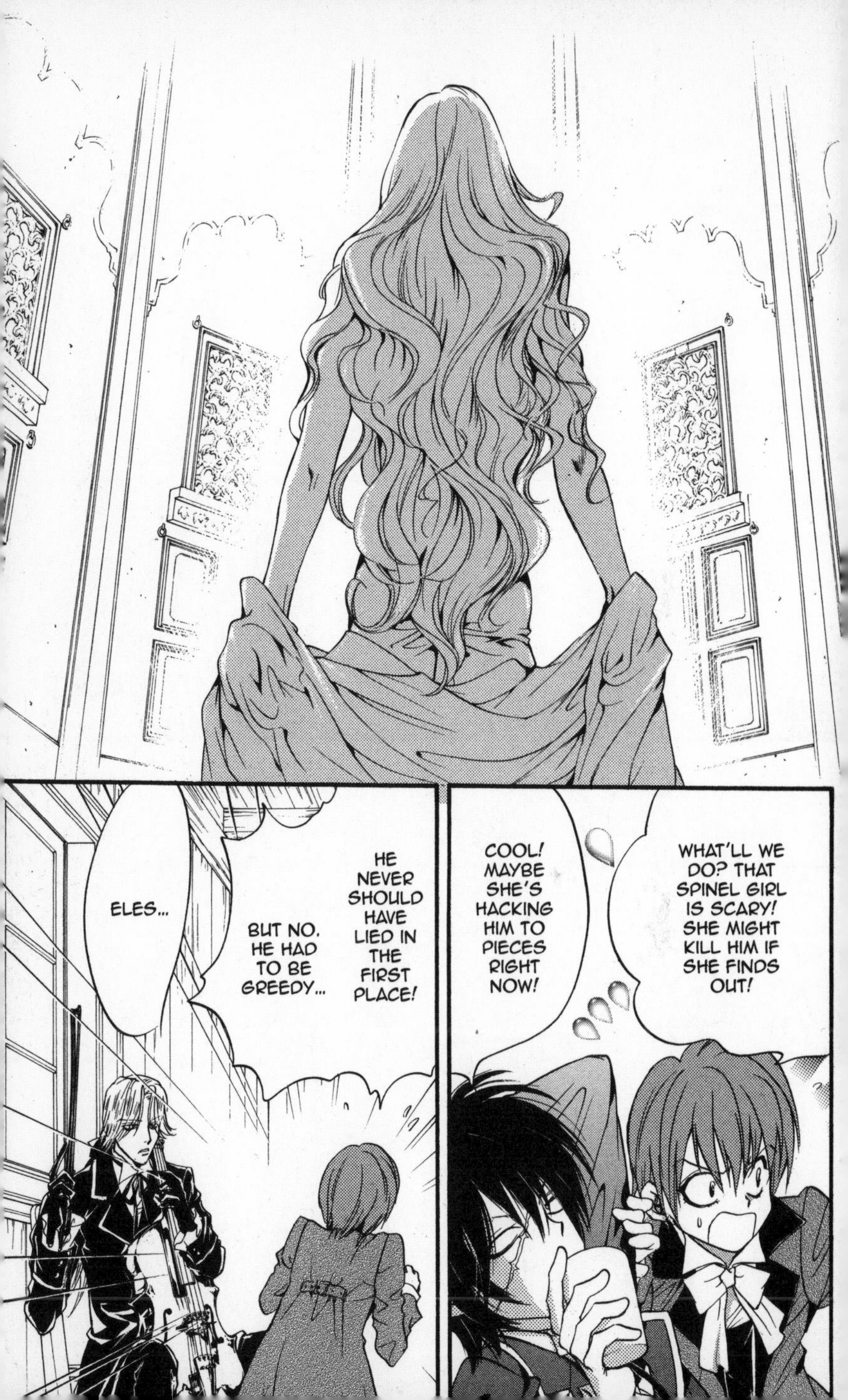
WHAT'LL WE DO? THAT SPINEL GIRL IS SCARY! SHE MIGHT KILL HIM IF SHE FINDS OUT!
COOL! MAYBE SHE'S HACKING HIM TO PIECES RIGHT NOW!
HE NEVER SHOULD HAVE LIED IN THE FIRST PLACE!
BUT NO. HE HAD TO BE GREEDY...
ELES...

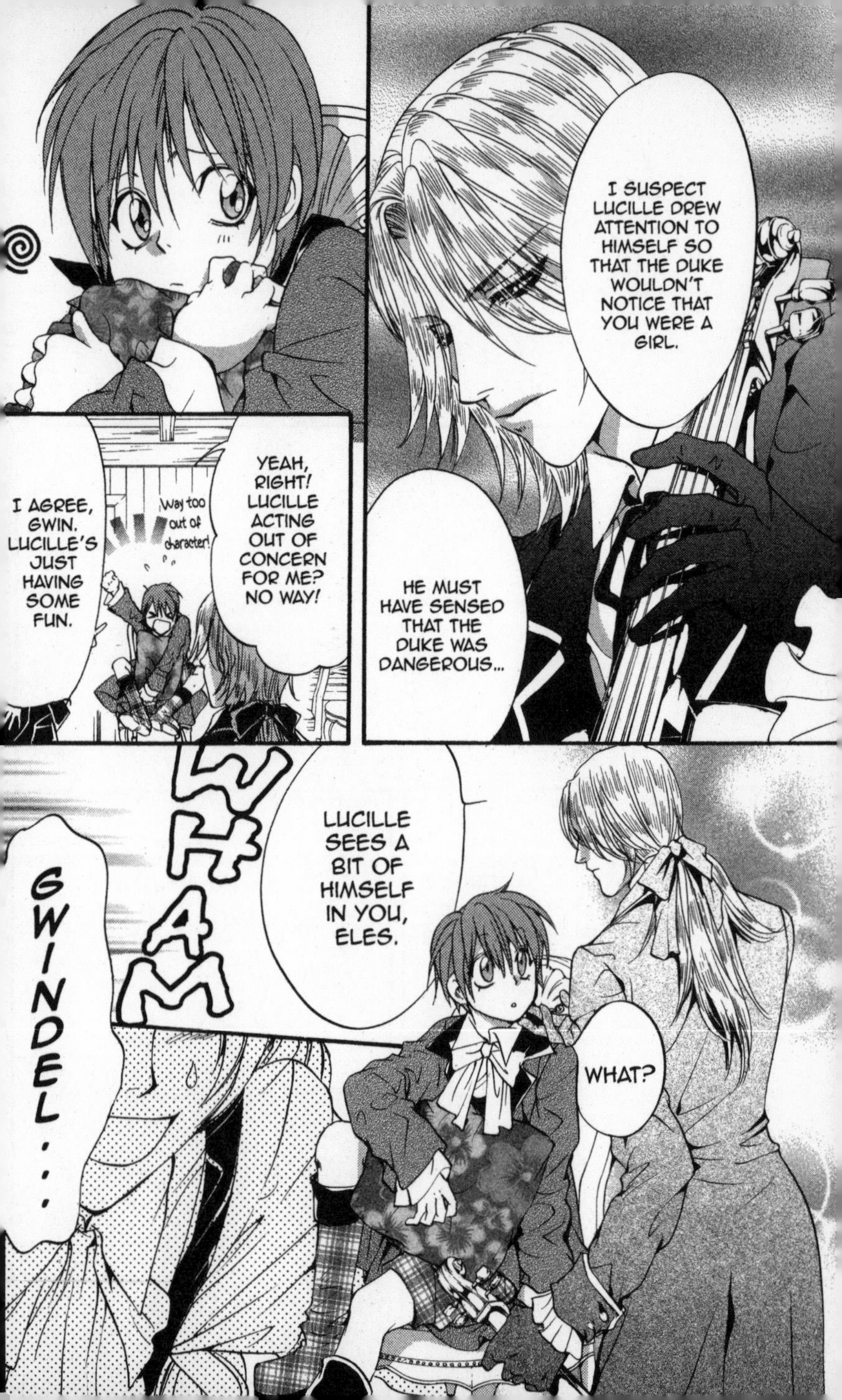
I SUSPECT LUCILLE DREW ATTENTION TO HIMSELF SO THAT THE DUKE WOULDN'T NOTICE THAT YOU WERE A GIRL.
HE MUST HAVE SENSED THAT THE DUKE WAS DANGEROUS...
YEAH, RIGHT! LUCILLE ACTING OUT OF CONCERN FOR ME? NO WAY!
Way too out of character!
I AGREE, GWIN. LUCILLE'S JUST HAVING SOME FUN.
LUCILLE SEES A BIT OF HIMSELF IN YOU, ELES.
WHAT?
WHAM
GWINDEL...

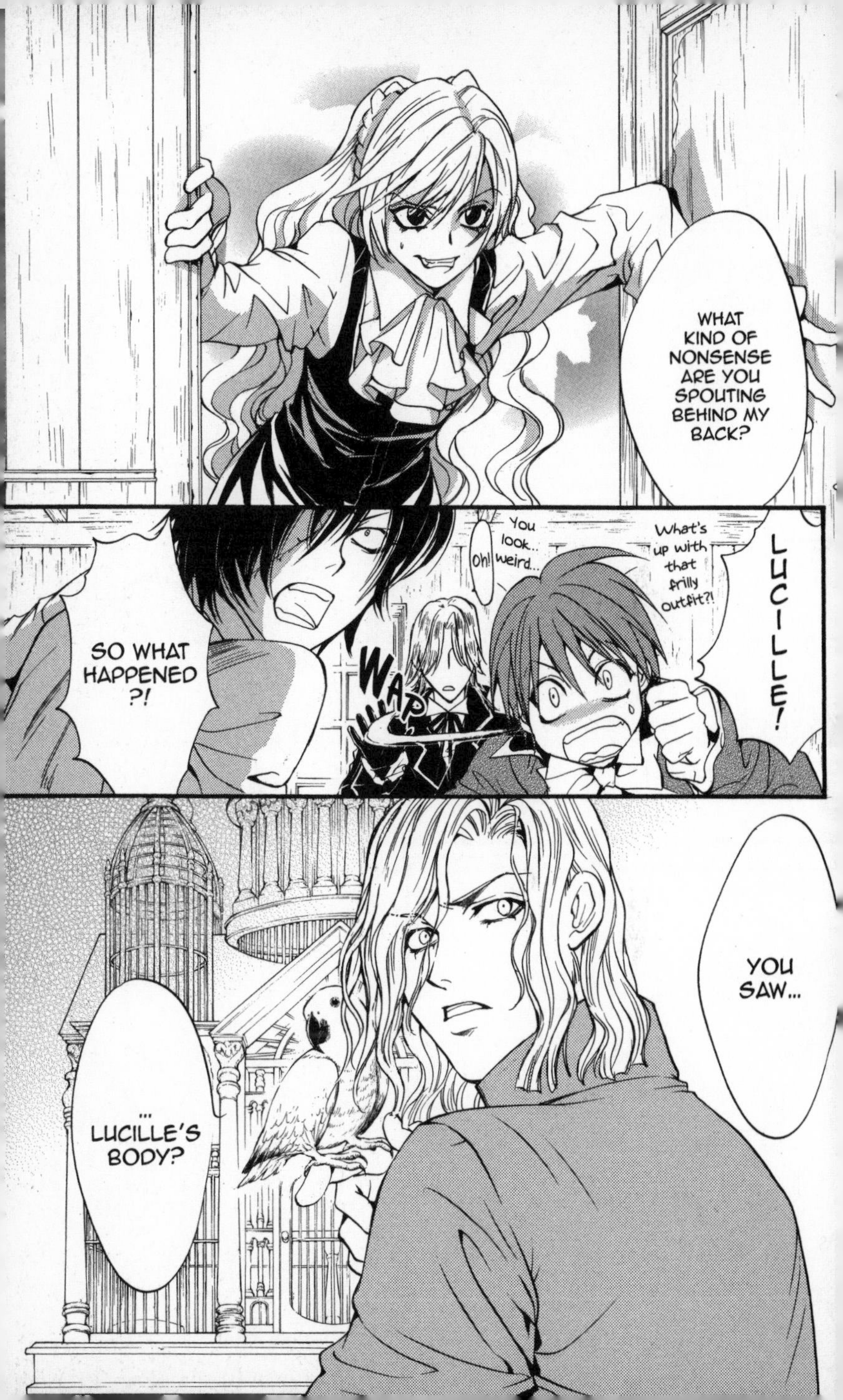
WHAT KIND OF NONSENSE ARE YOU SPOUTING BEHIND MY BACK?
LUCILLE!
What's up with that frilly outfit?!
You look.. weird...
Oh!
WAP
SO WHAT HAPPENED ?!
YOU SAW...
... LUCILLE'S BODY?

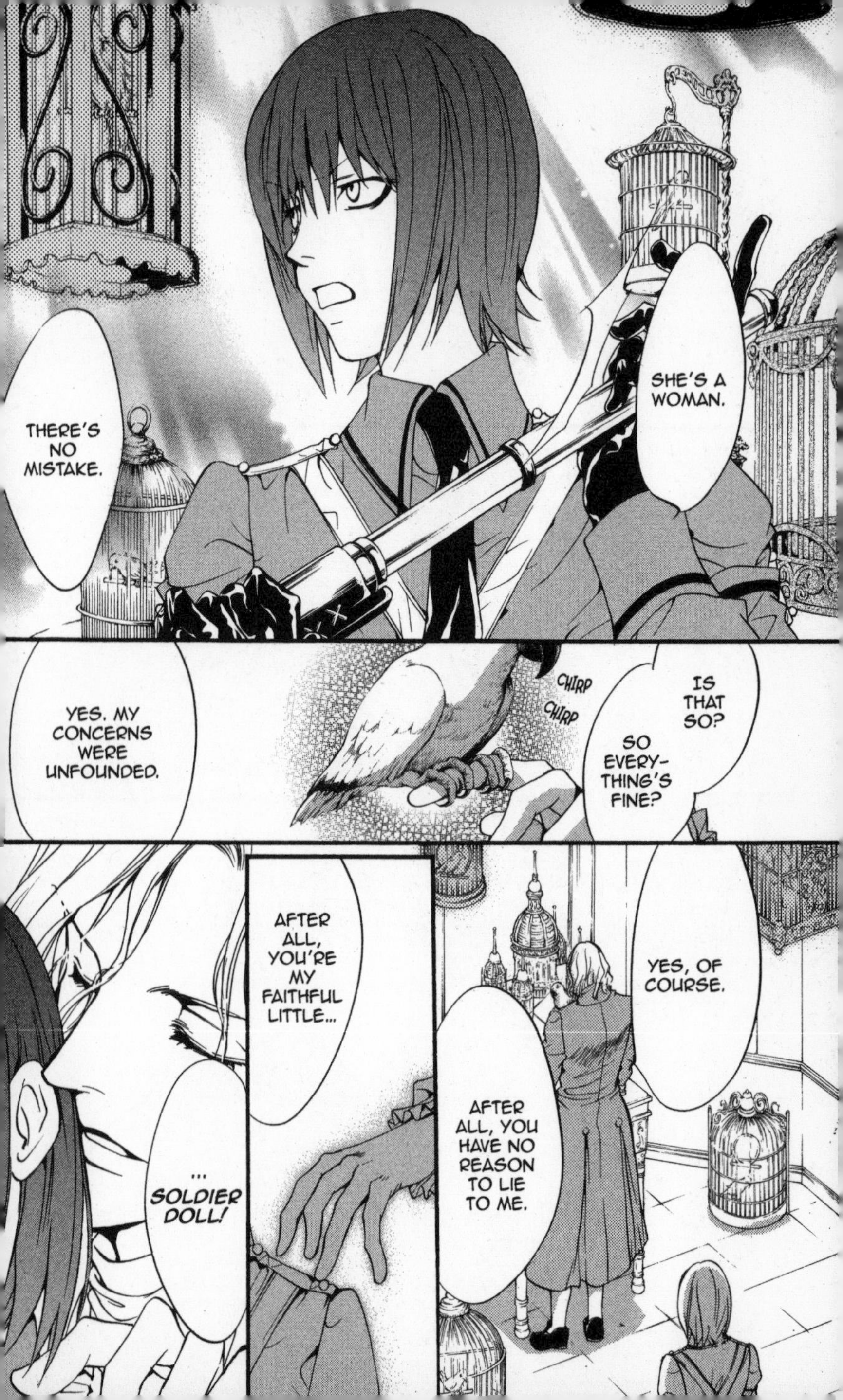
SHE'S A WOMAN.
THERE'S NO MISTAKE.
IS THAT SO?
SO EVERYTHING'S FINE?
CHIRP
CHIRP
YES. MY CONCERNS WERE UNFOUNDED.
YES, OF COURSE.
AFTER ALL, YOU HAVE NO REASON TO LIE TO ME.
AFTER ALL, YOU'RE MY FAITHFUL LITTLE...
...SOLDIER DOLL!

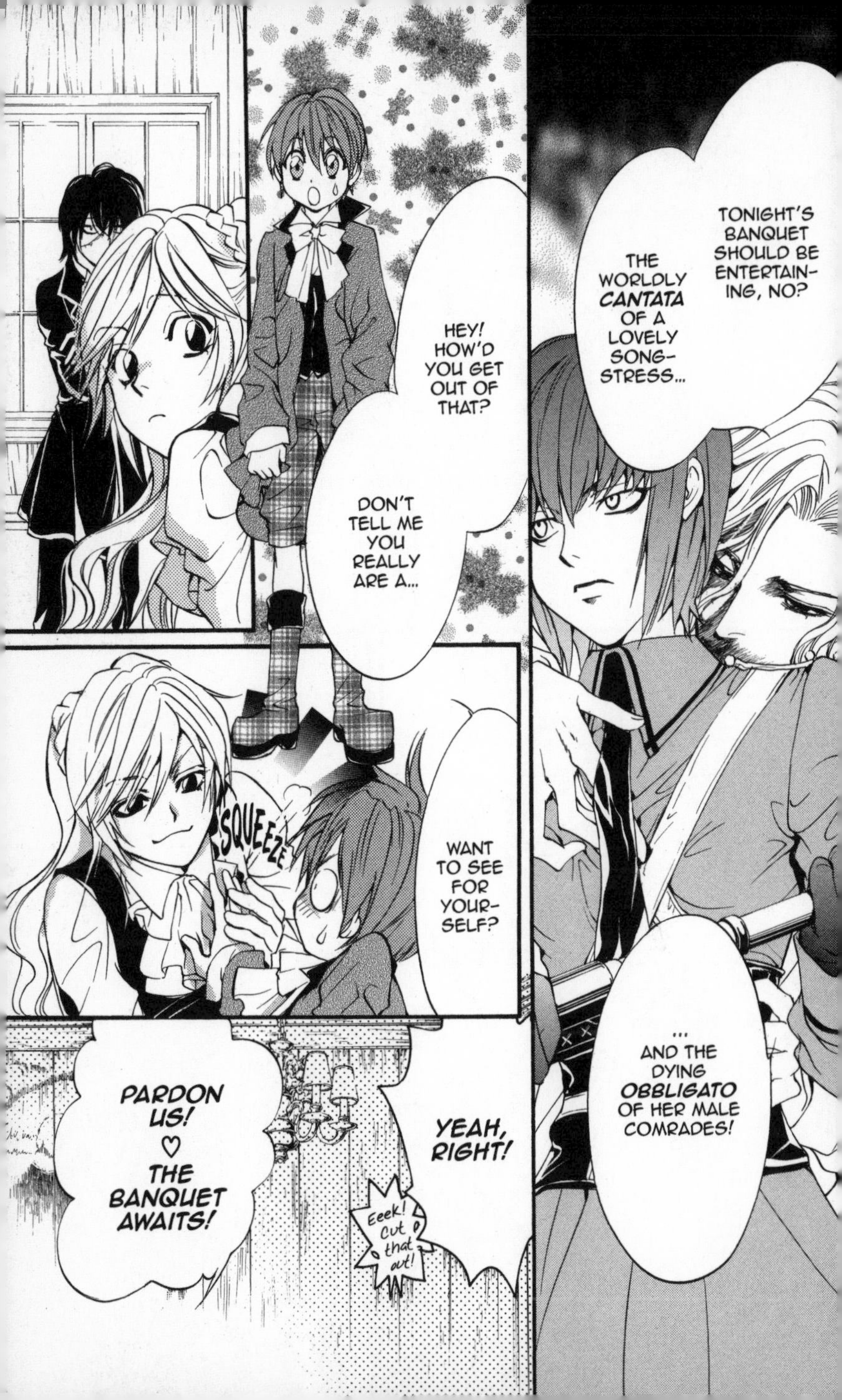

TONIGHT'S BANQUET SHOULD BE ENTERTAIN-ING, NO?
THE WORLDLY *CANTATA* OF A LOVELY SONG-STRESS...
... AND THE DYING *OBBLIGATO* OF HER MALE COMRADES!
HEY! HOW'D YOU GET OUT OF THAT?
DON'T TELL ME YOU REALLY ARE A...
WANT TO SEE FOR YOUR-SELF?
SQUEEZE
YEAH, RIGHT!
Eeek! Cut that out!
PARDON US! ♡ THE BANQUET AWAITS!

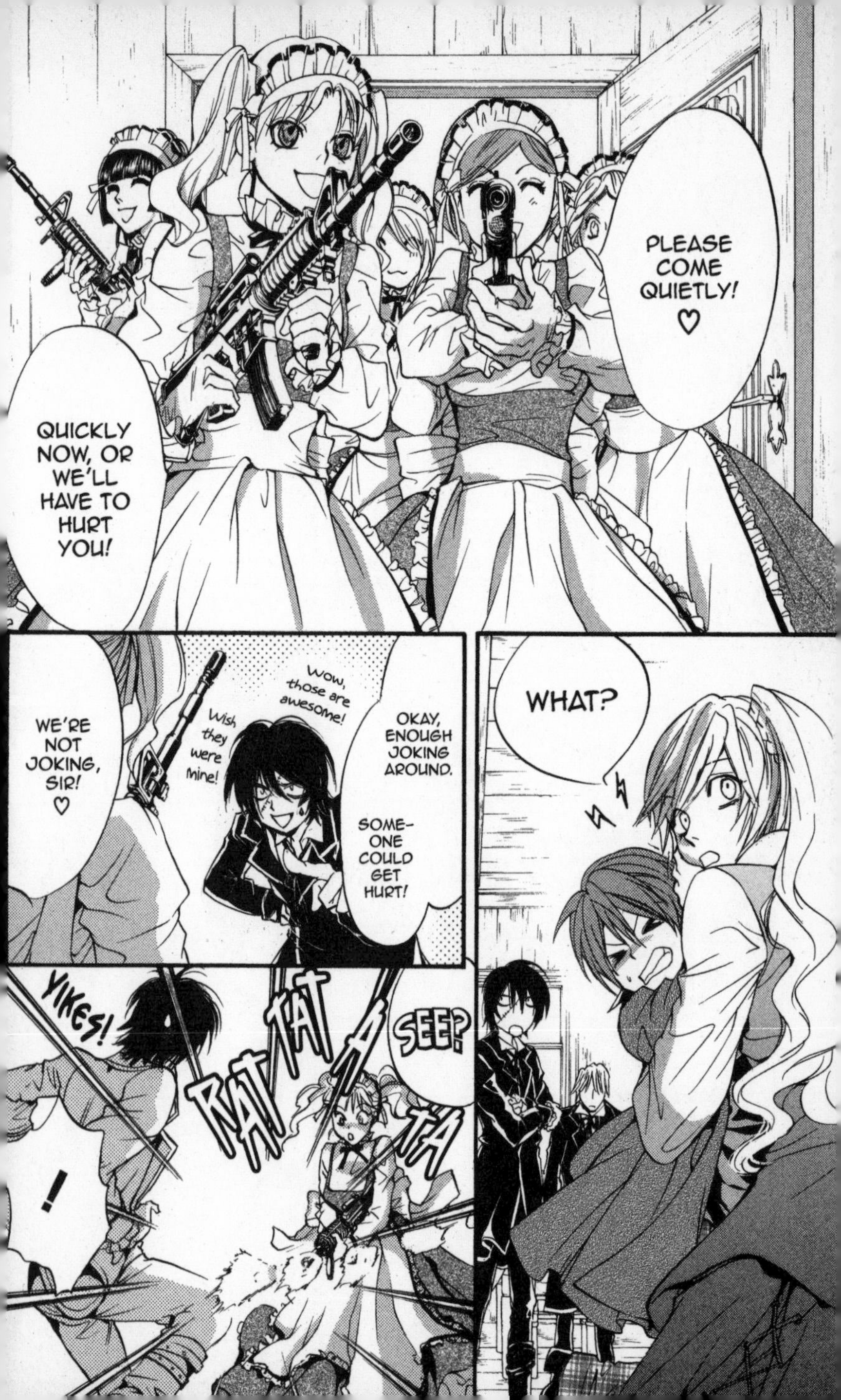
PLEASE COME QUIETLY! ♡
QUICKLY NOW, OR WE'LL HAVE TO HURT YOU!
WHAT?
OKAY, ENOUGH JOKING AROUND.
SOME-ONE COULD GET HURT!
Wow, those are awesome!
Wish they were mine!
WE'RE NOT JOKING, SIR! ♡
SEE?
RAT TAT A TA
YIKES!
!

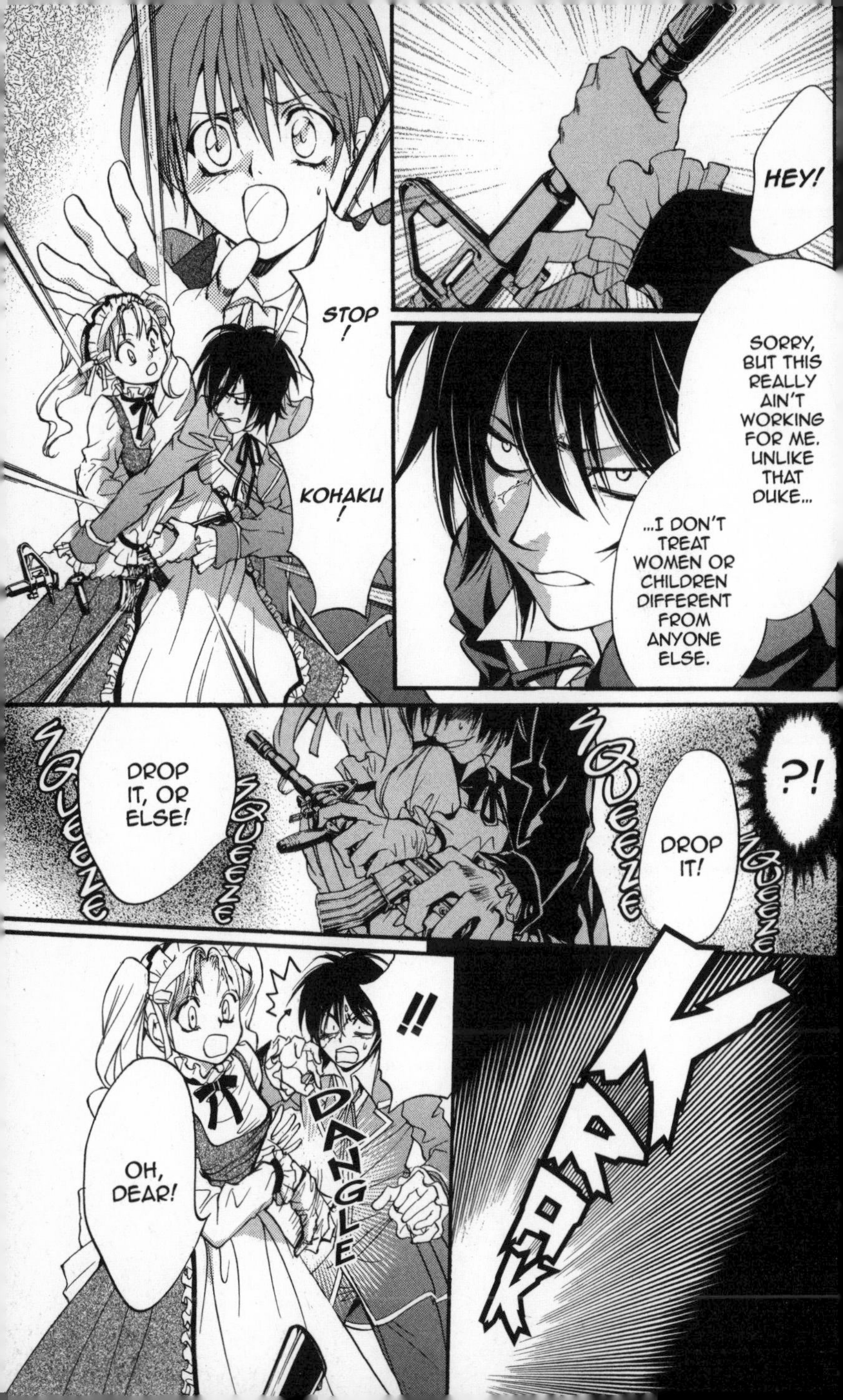
HEY!
SORRY, BUT THIS REALLY AIN'T WORKING FOR ME. UNLIKE THAT DUKE...
...I DON'T TREAT WOMEN OR CHILDREN DIFFERENT FROM ANYONE ELSE.
STOP!
KOHAKU!
?!
DROP IT!
SQUEEZE
SQUEEZE
SQUEEZE
SQUEEZE
DROP IT, OR ELSE!
KRAK
!!
DANGLE
OH, DEAR!

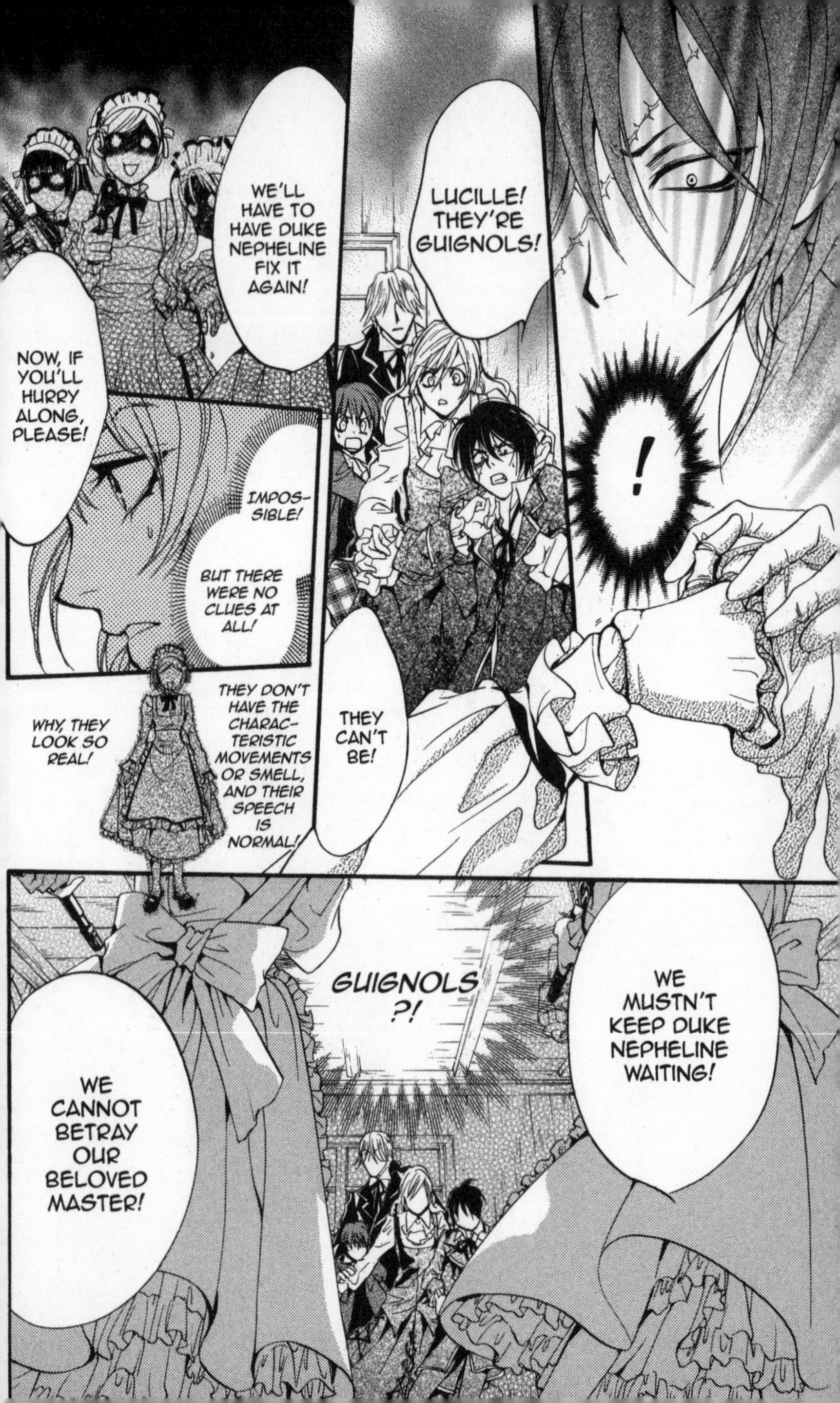
!
LUCILLE! THEY'RE GUIGNOLS!
THEY CAN'T BE!
THEY DON'T HAVE THE CHARAC-TERISTIC MOVEMENTS OR SMELL, AND THEIR SPEECH IS NORMAL!
WE'LL HAVE TO HAVE DUKE NEPHELINE FIX IT AGAIN!
NOW, IF YOU'LL HURRY ALONG, PLEASE!
IMPOS-SIBLE!
BUT THERE WERE NO CLUES AT ALL!
WHY, THEY LOOK SO REAL!
WE MUSTN'T KEEP DUKE NEPHELINE WAITING!
GUIGNOLS ?!
WE CANNOT BETRAY OUR BELOVED MASTER!

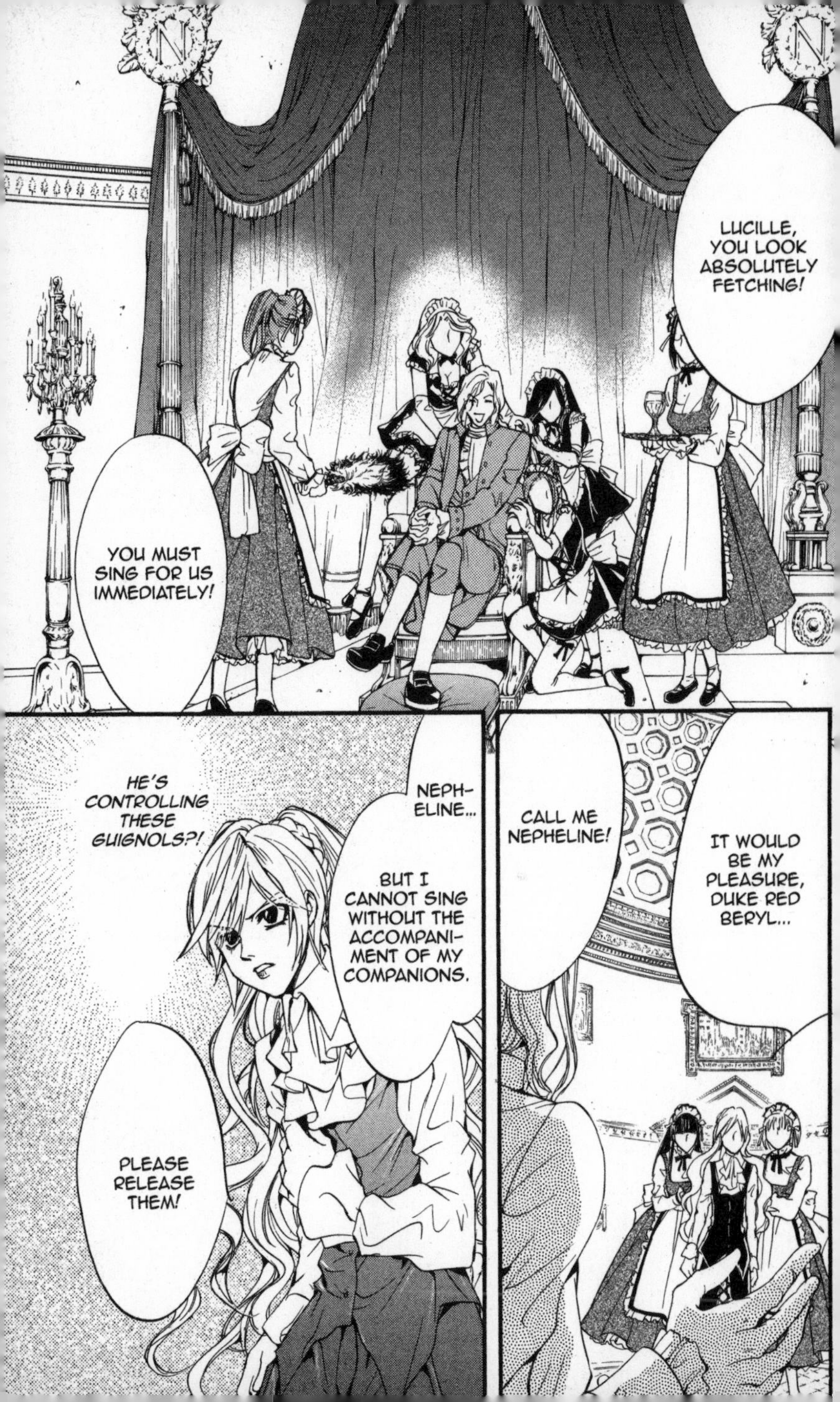
LUCILLE, YOU LOOK ABSOLUTELY FETCHING!
YOU MUST SING FOR US IMMEDIATELY!
IT WOULD BE MY PLEASURE, DUKE RED BERYL...
CALL ME NEPHELINE!
NEPH-ELINE...
BUT I CANNOT SING WITHOUT THE ACCOMPANI-MENT OF MY COMPANIONS.
HE'S CONTROLLING THESE GUIGNOLS?!
PLEASE RELEASE THEM!

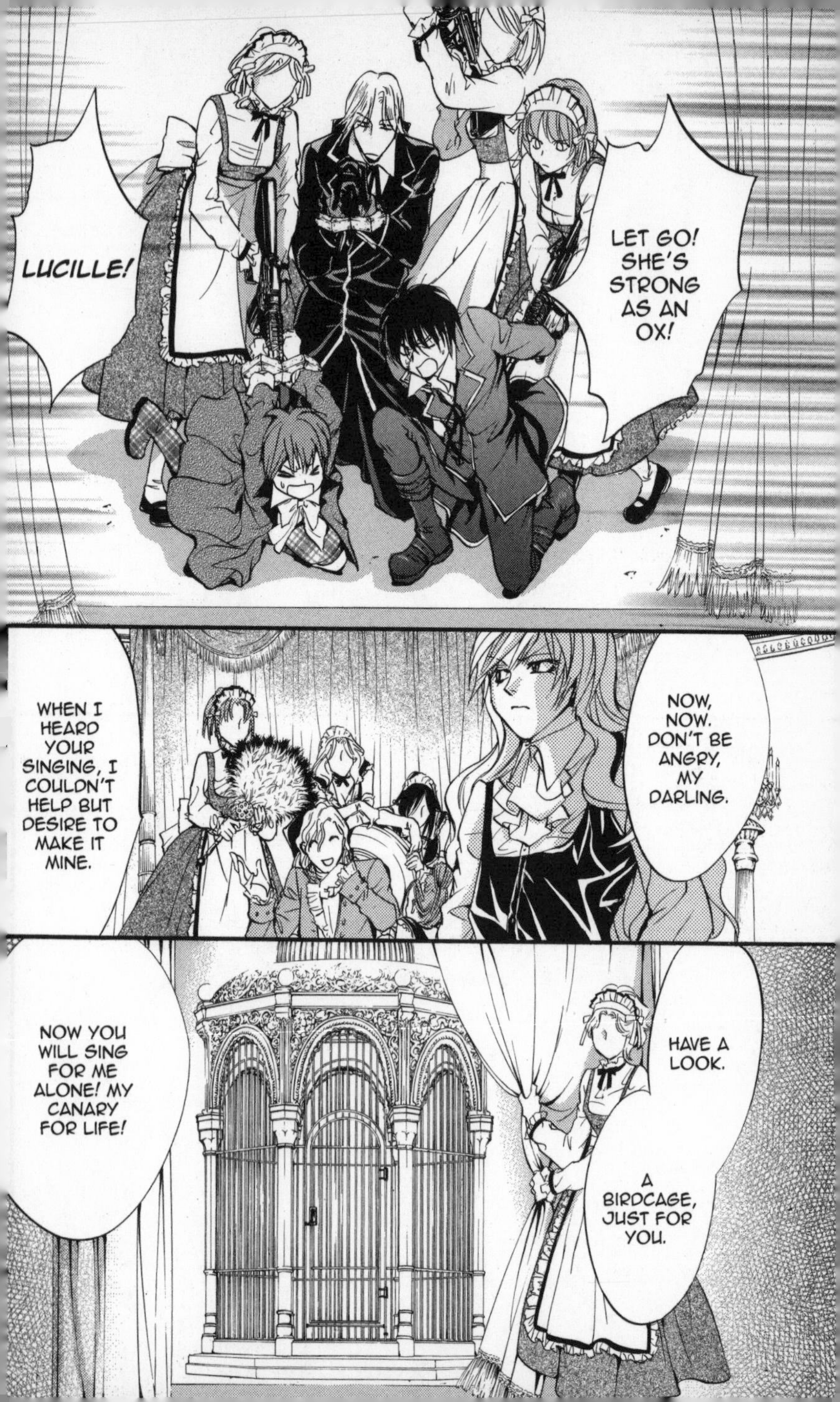
LET GO! SHE'S STRONG AS AN OX!
LUCILLE!
NOW, NOW. DON'T BE ANGRY, MY DARLING.
WHEN I HEARD YOUR SINGING, I COULDN'T HELP BUT DESIRE TO MAKE IT MINE.
HAVE A LOOK.
A BIRDCAGE, JUST FOR YOU.
NOW YOU WILL SING FOR ME ALONE! MY CANARY FOR LIFE!

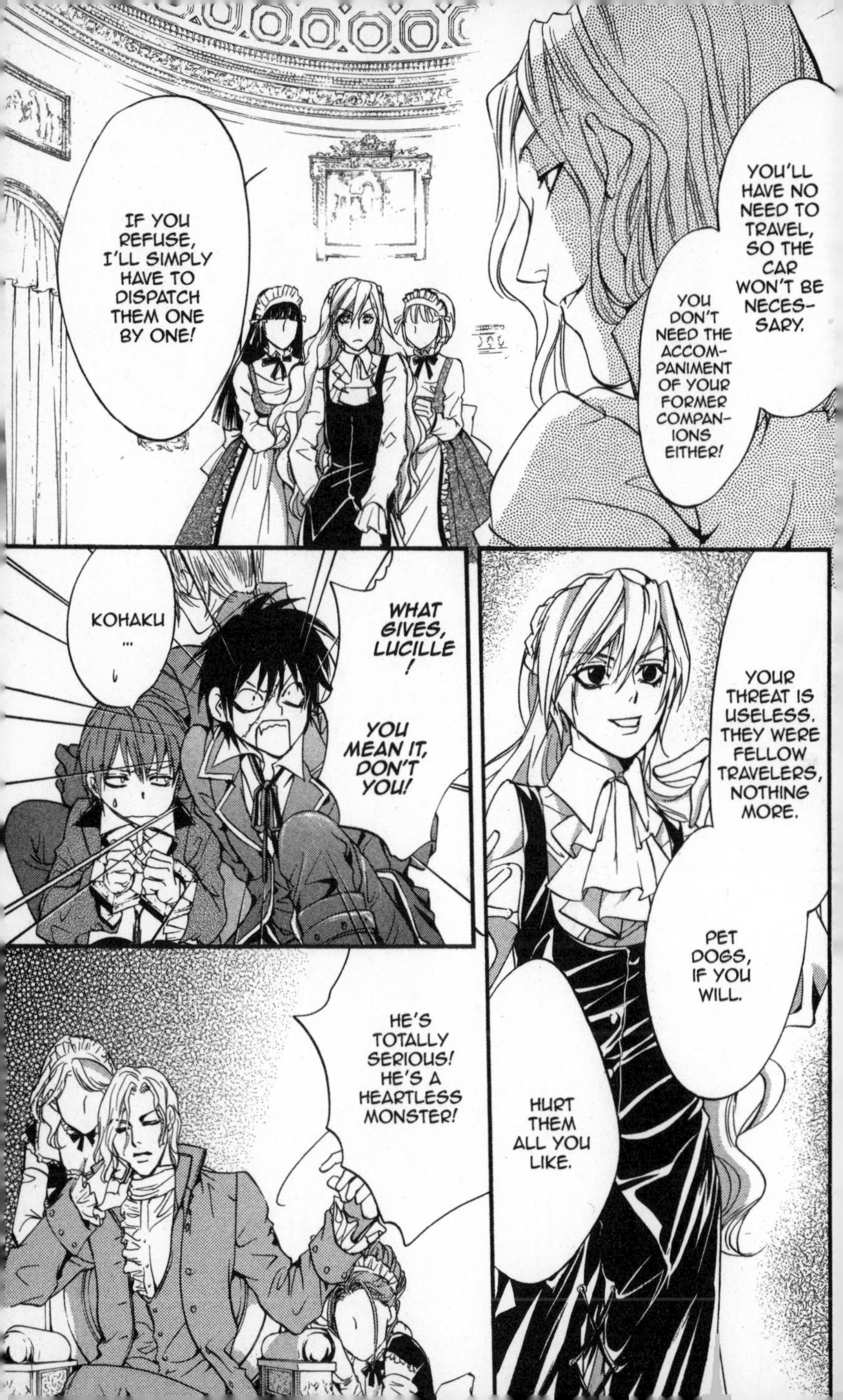
YOU'LL HAVE NO NEED TO TRAVEL, SO THE CAR WON'T BE NECES-SARY.
YOU DON'T NEED THE ACCOM-PANIMENT OF YOUR FORMER COMPAN-IONS EITHER!
IF YOU REFUSE, I'LL SIMPLY HAVE TO DISPATCH THEM ONE BY ONE!
YOUR THREAT IS USELESS. THEY WERE FELLOW TRAVELERS, NOTHING MORE.
PET DOGS, IF YOU WILL.
HURT THEM ALL YOU LIKE.
WHAT GIVES, LUCILLE!
YOU MEAN IT, DON'T YOU!
KOHAKU ...
HE'S TOTALLY SERIOUS! HE'S A HEARTLESS MONSTER!

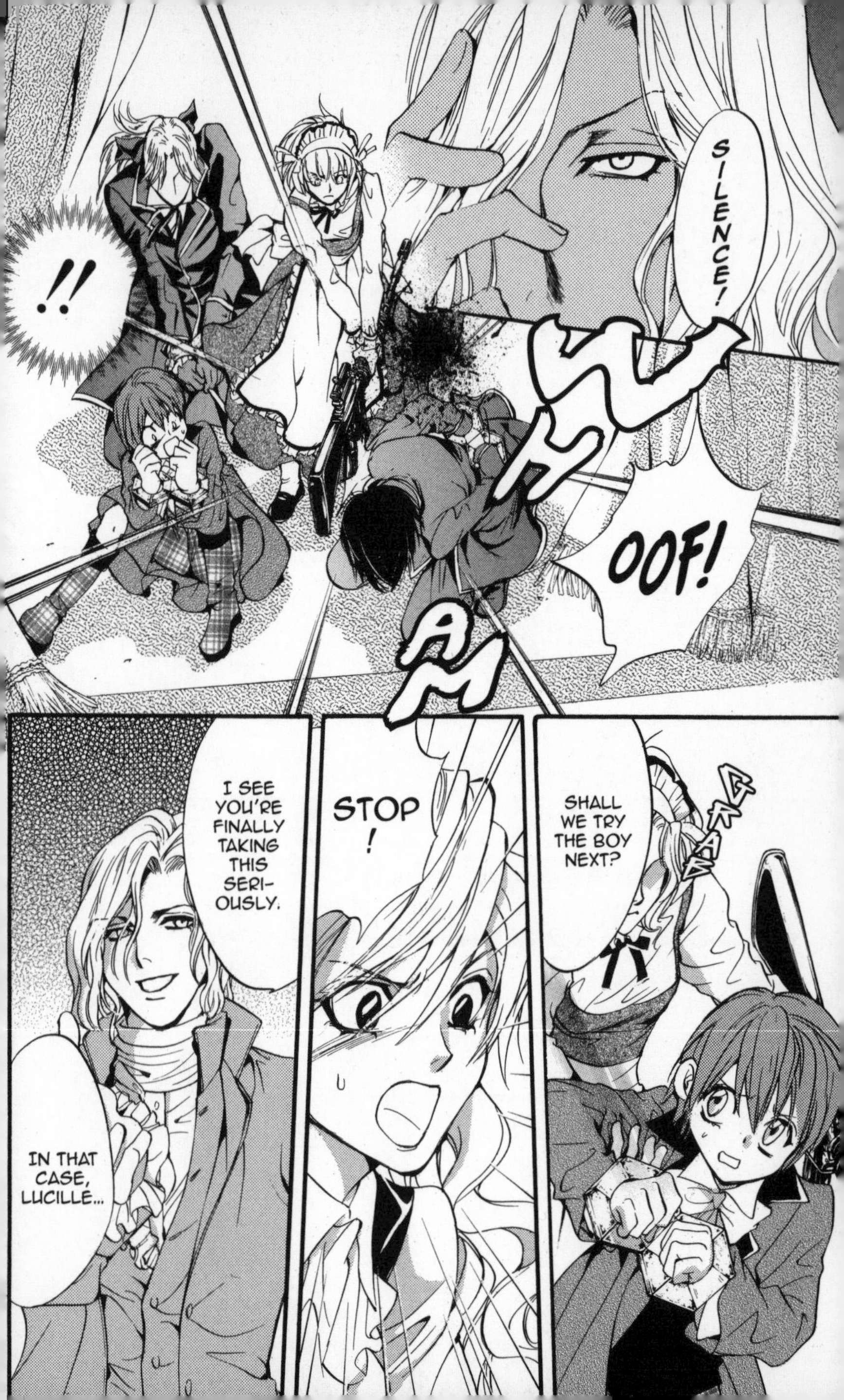

SILENCE!
WHAM
OOF!
!!
GRAB
SHALL WE TRY THE BOY NEXT?
STOP!
I SEE YOU'RE FINALLY TAKING THIS SERI-OUSLY.
IN THAT CASE, LUCILLE...

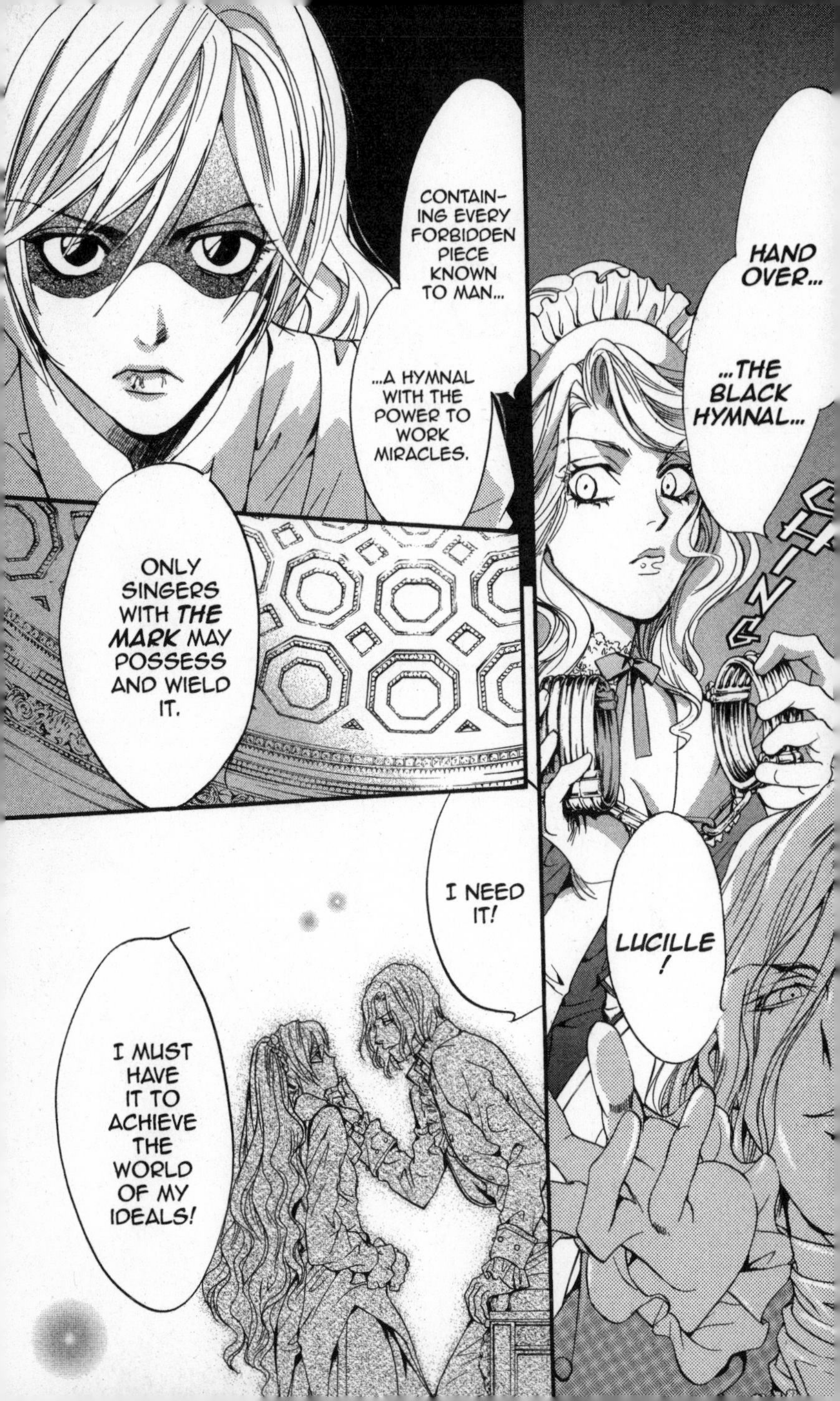
HAND OVER...
...THE BLACK HYMNAL...
CHING
LUCILLE!
CONTAINING EVERY FORBIDDEN PIECE KNOWN TO MAN...
...A HYMNAL WITH THE POWER TO WORK MIRACLES.
ONLY SINGERS WITH ***THE MARK*** MAY POSSESS AND WIELD IT.
I NEED IT!
I MUST HAVE IT TO ACHIEVE THE WORLD OF MY IDEALS!

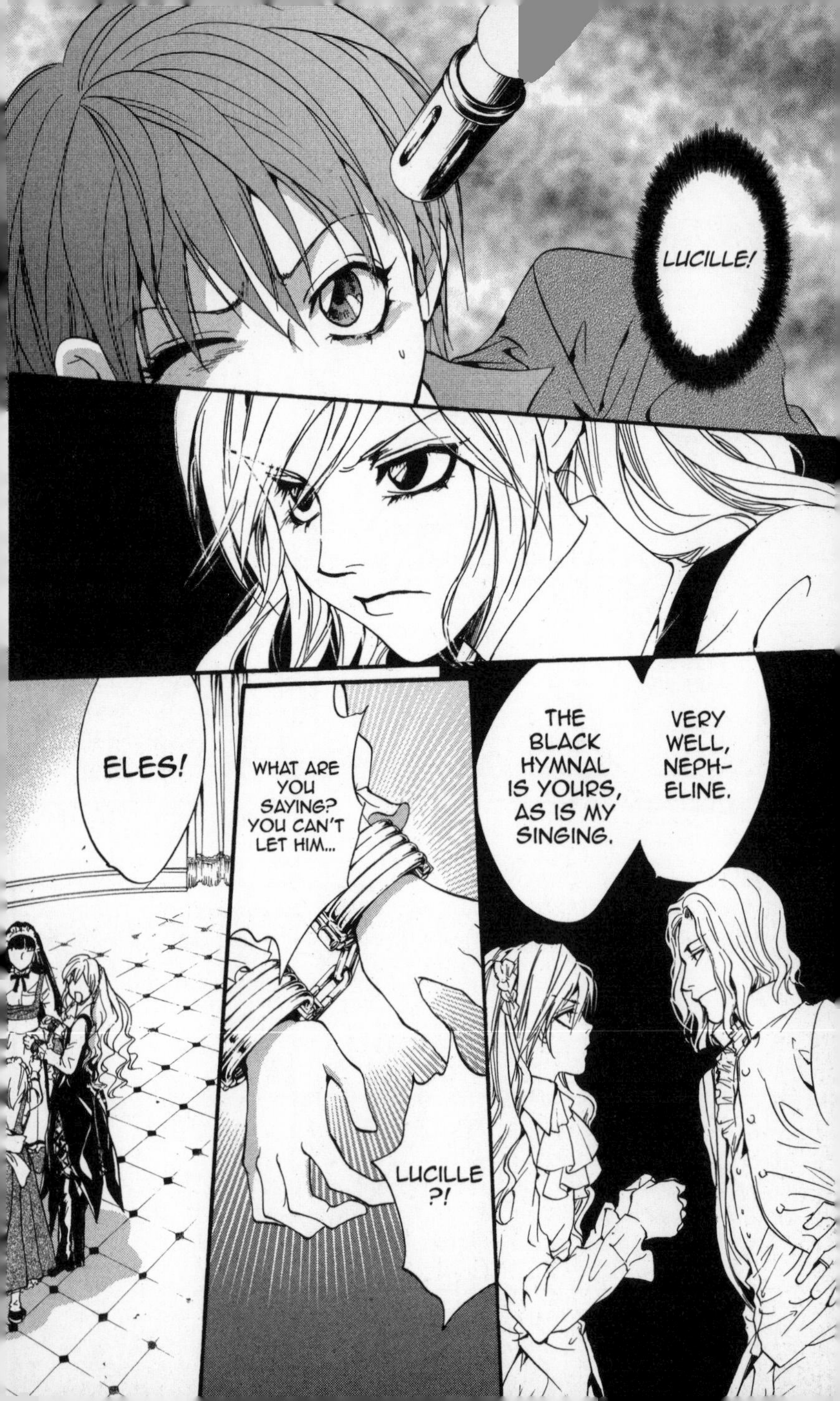
LUCILLE!
VERY WELL, NEPH-ELINE.
THE BLACK HYMNAL IS YOURS, AS IS MY SINGING.
WHAT ARE YOU SAYING? YOU CAN'T LET HIM...
LUCILLE?!
ELES!

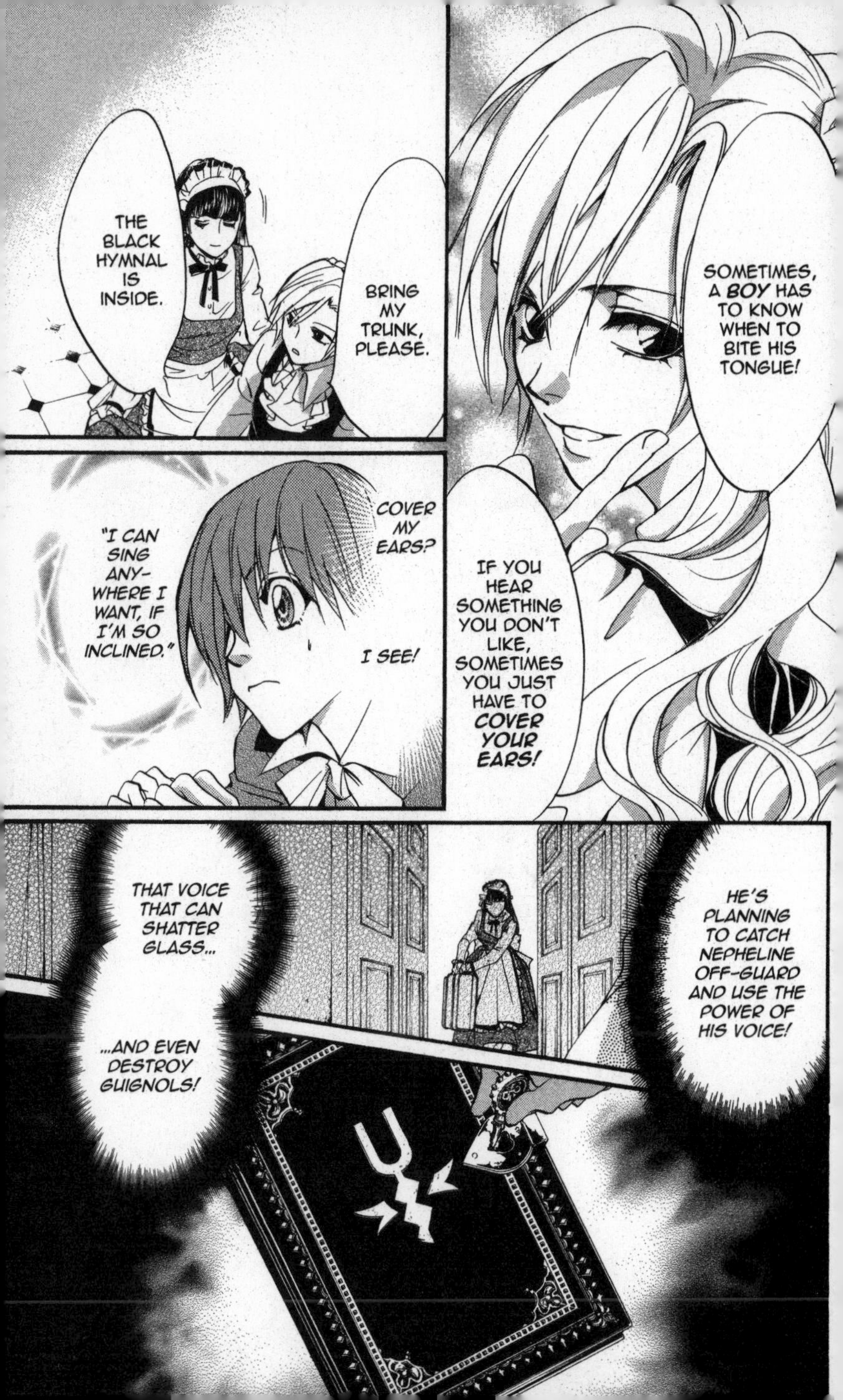
SOMETIMES, A BOY HAS TO KNOW WHEN TO BITE HIS TONGUE!
IF YOU HEAR SOMETHING YOU DON'T LIKE, SOMETIMES YOU JUST HAVE TO COVER YOUR EARS!
BRING MY TRUNK, PLEASE.
THE BLACK HYMNAL IS INSIDE.
COVER MY EARS?
I SEE!
"I CAN SING ANY-WHERE I WANT, IF I'M SO INCLINED."
HE'S PLANNING TO CATCH NEPHELINE OFF-GUARD AND USE THE POWER OF HIS VOICE!
THAT VOICE THAT CAN SHATTER GLASS...
...AND EVEN DESTROY GUIGNOLS!

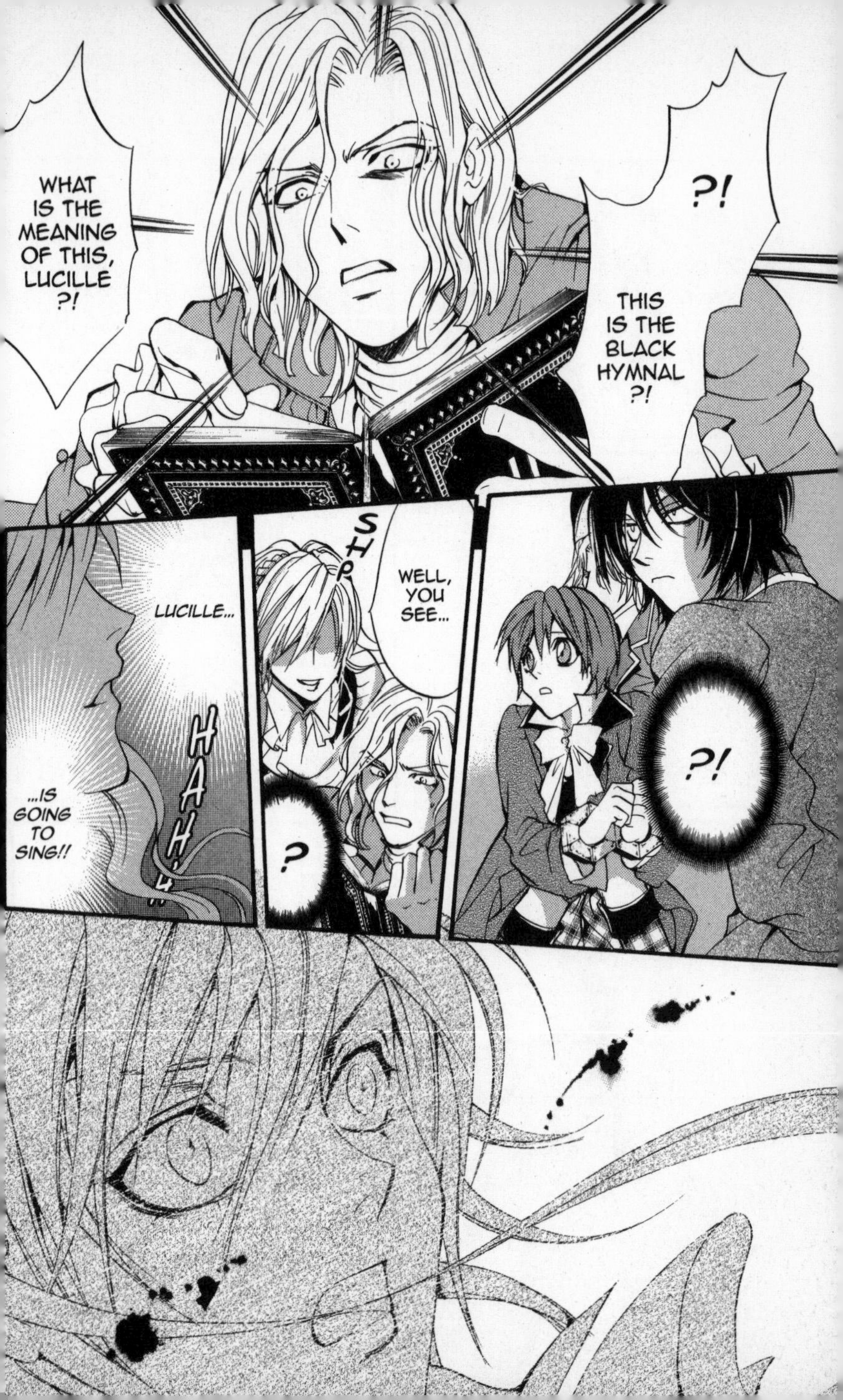
?!
THIS IS THE BLACK HYMNAL ?!
WHAT IS THE MEANING OF THIS, LUCILLE ?!
?!
SHP
WELL, YOU SEE...
?
LUCILLE...
HAAH
...IS GOING TO SING!!

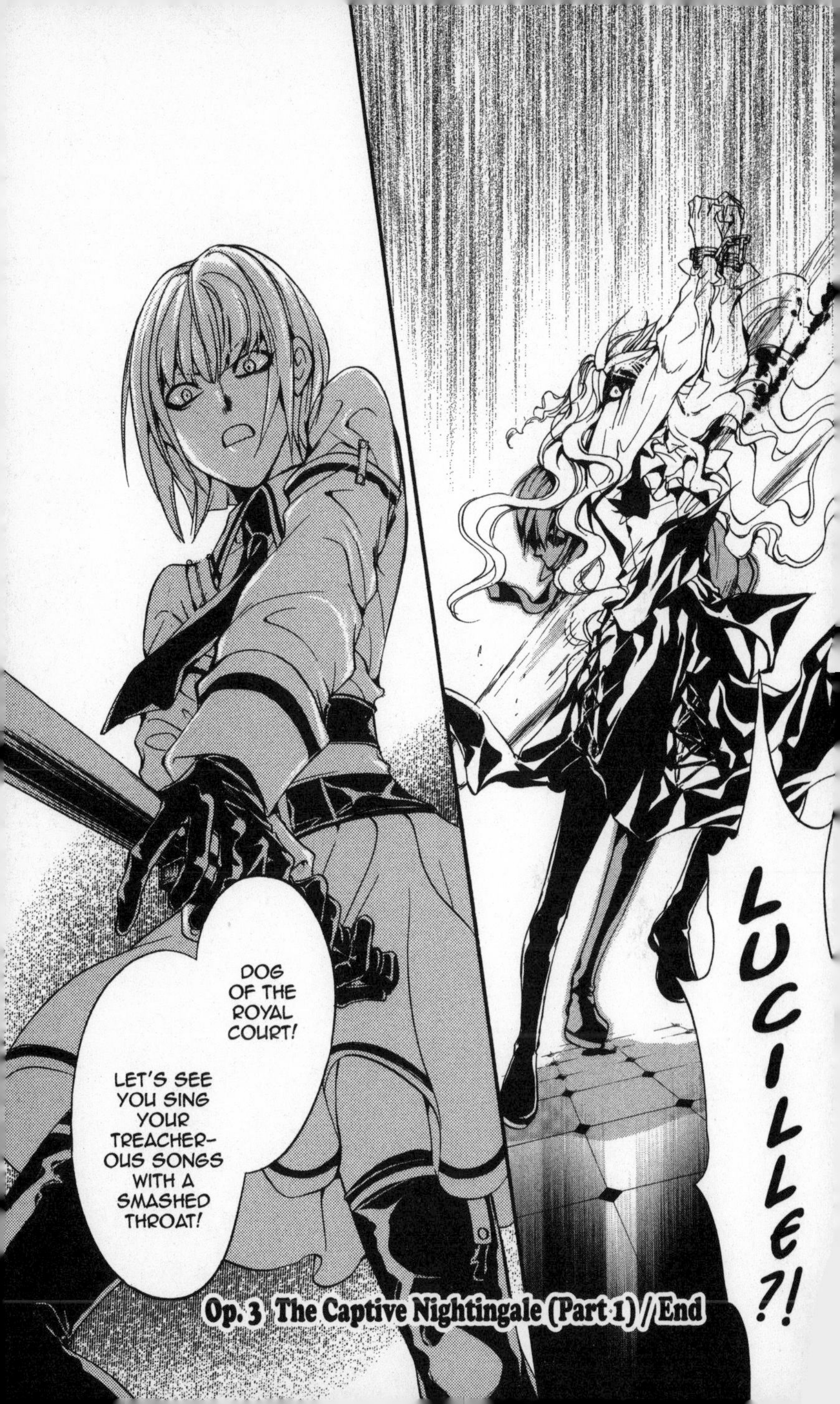
LUCILLE?!
DOG OF THE ROYAL COURT!
LET'S SEE YOU SING YOUR TREACHEROUS SONGS WITH A SMASHED THROAT!

Op. 3 The Captive Nightingale (Part 1) / End

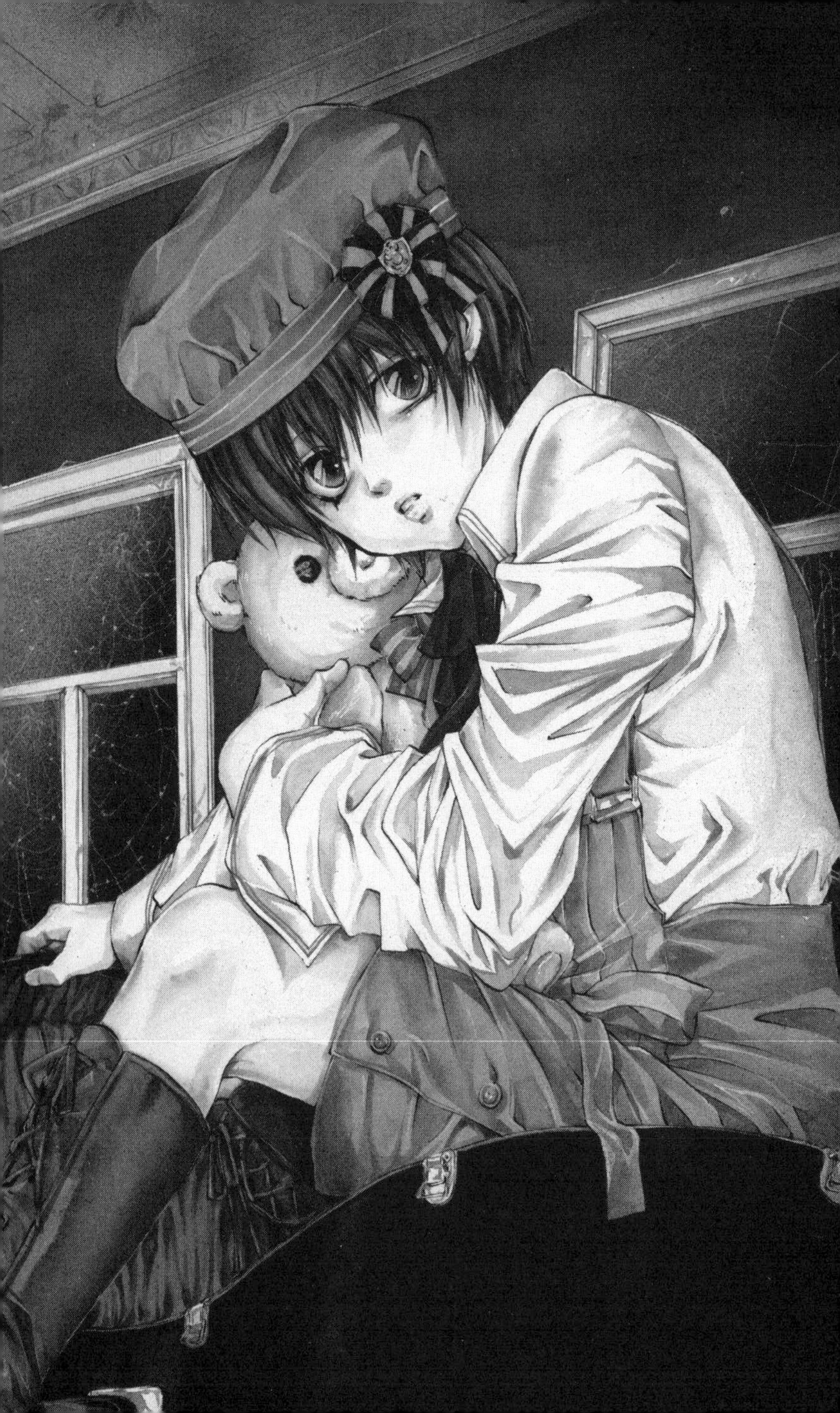

Op.4 The Captive Nightingale (Part 2

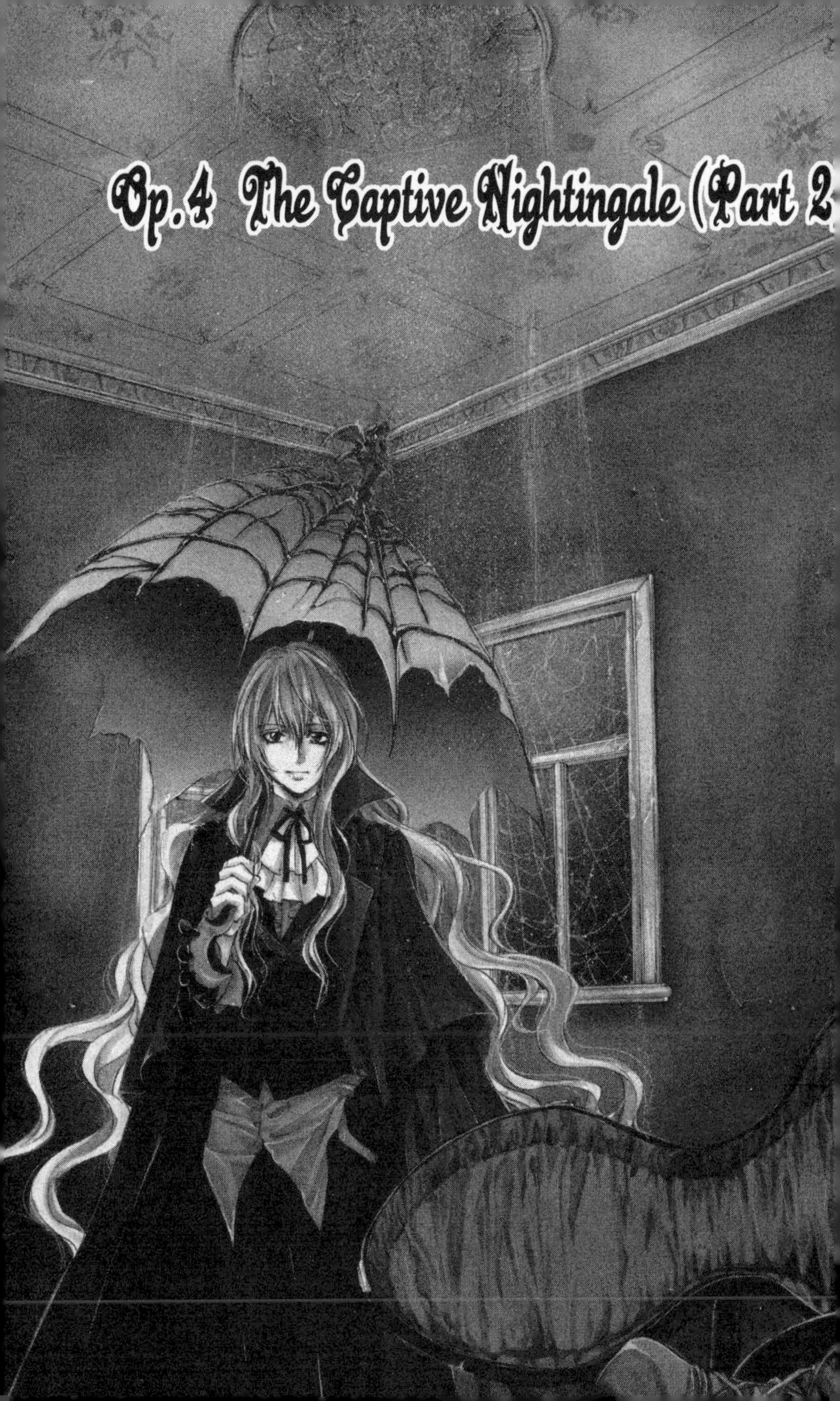

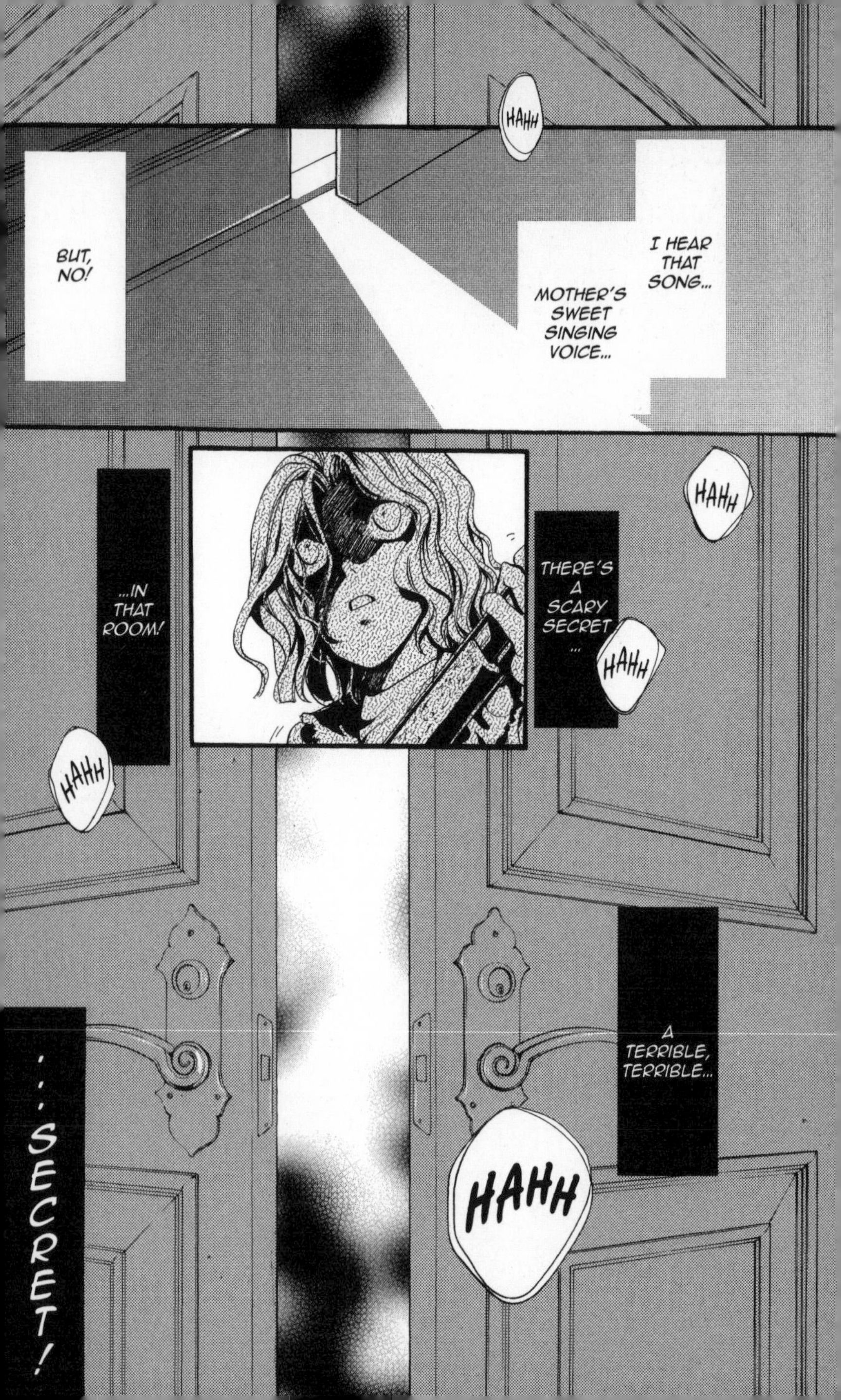
HAHH
I HEAR THAT SONG...
MOTHER'S SWEET SINGING VOICE...
BUT, NO!
HAHH
THERE'S A SCARY SECRET...
HAHH
...IN THAT ROOM!
HAHH
A TERRIBLE, TERRIBLE...
HAHH
...SECRET!

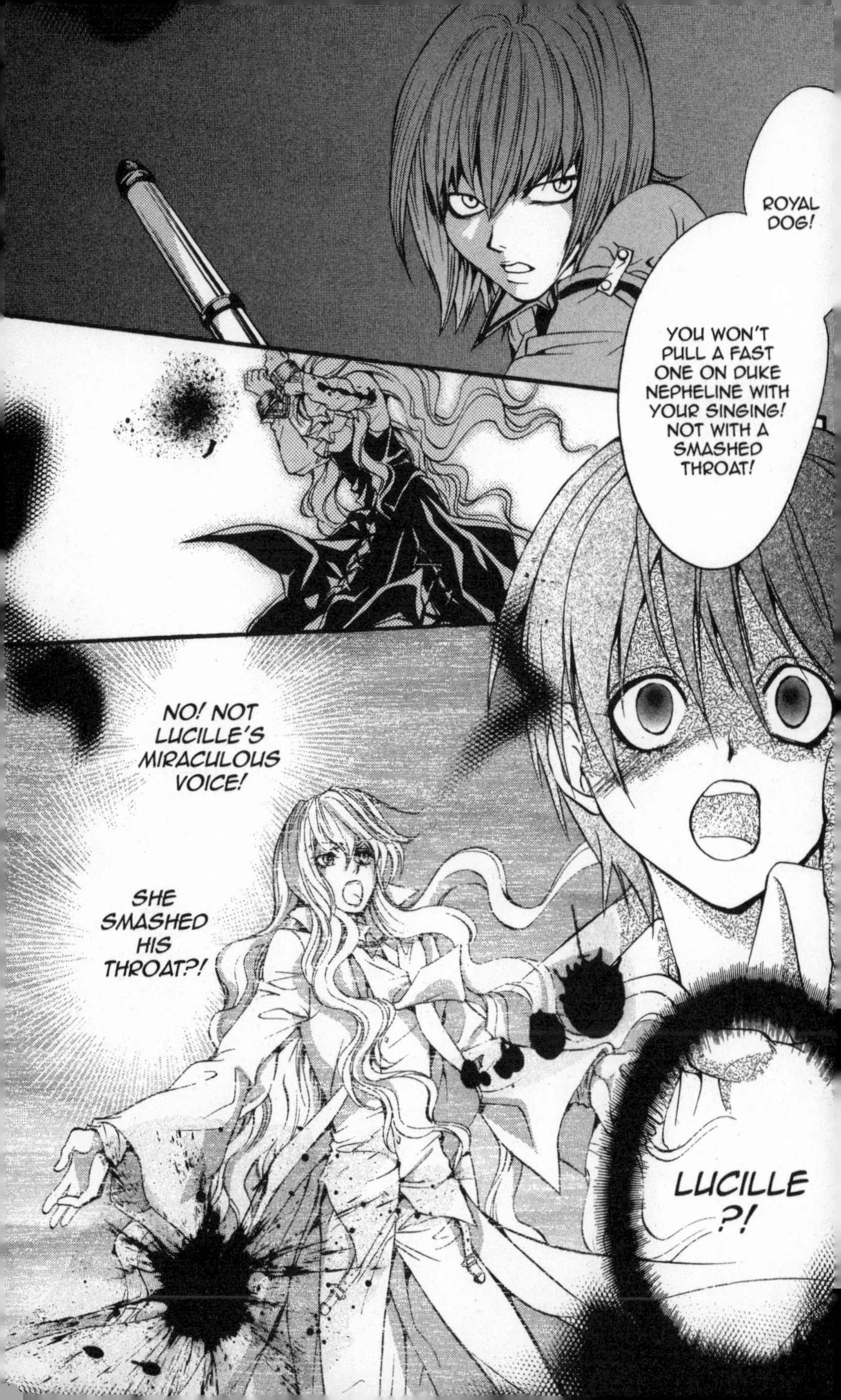
ROYAL DOG!
YOU WON'T PULL A FAST ONE ON DUKE NEPHELINE WITH YOUR SINGING! NOT WITH A SMASHED THROAT!
LUCILLE ?!
NO! NOT LUCILLE'S MIRACULOUS VOICE!
SHE SMASHED HIS THROAT?!

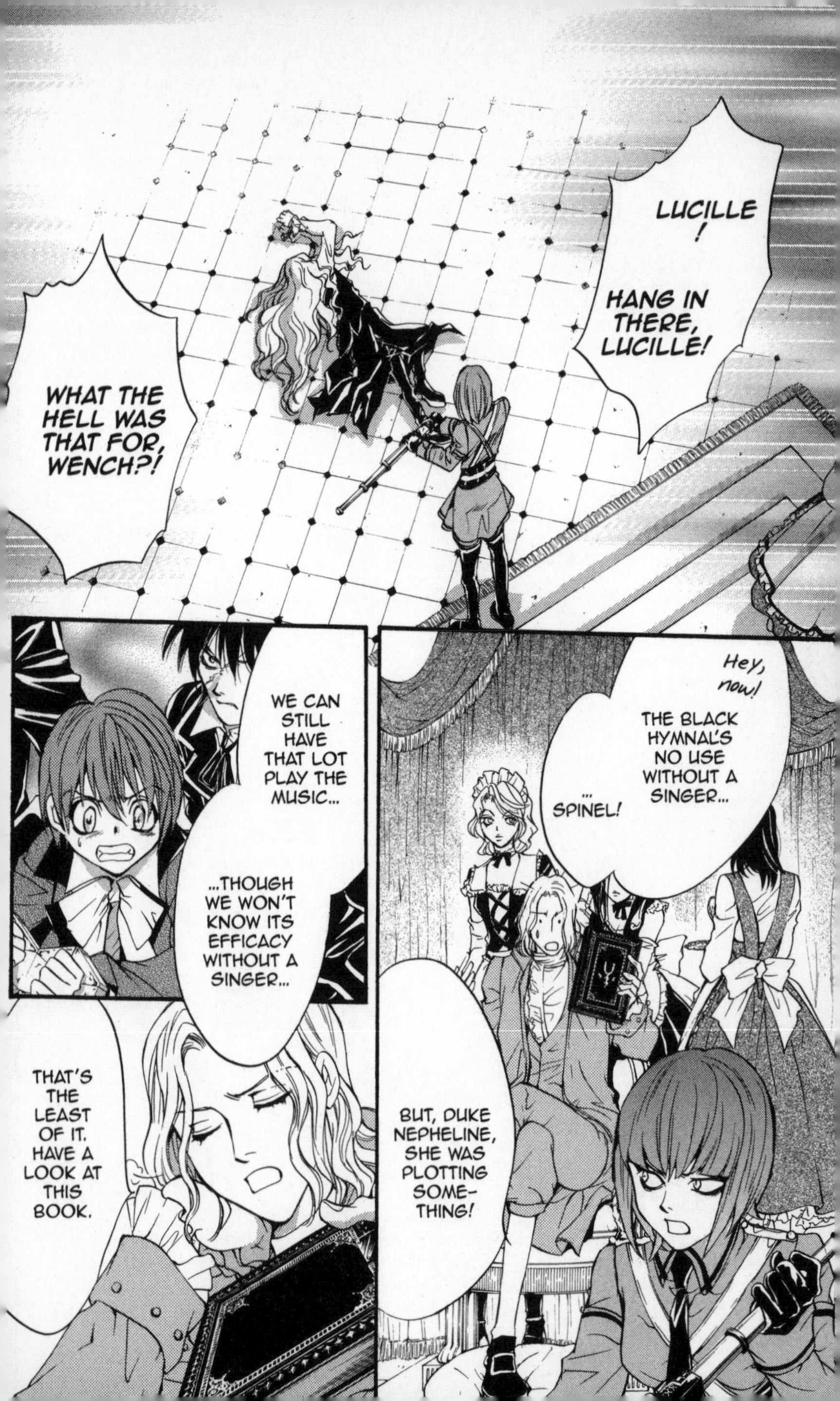
LUCILLE!
HANG IN THERE, LUCILLE!
WHAT THE HELL WAS THAT FOR, WENCH?!
Hey, now!
THE BLACK HYMNAL'S NO USE WITHOUT A SINGER...
... SPINEL!
BUT, DUKE NEPHELINE, SHE WAS PLOTTING SOME-THING!
WE CAN STILL HAVE THAT LOT PLAY THE MUSIC...
...THOUGH WE WON'T KNOW ITS EFFICACY WITHOUT A SINGER...
THAT'S THE LEAST OF IT. HAVE A LOOK AT THIS BOOK.

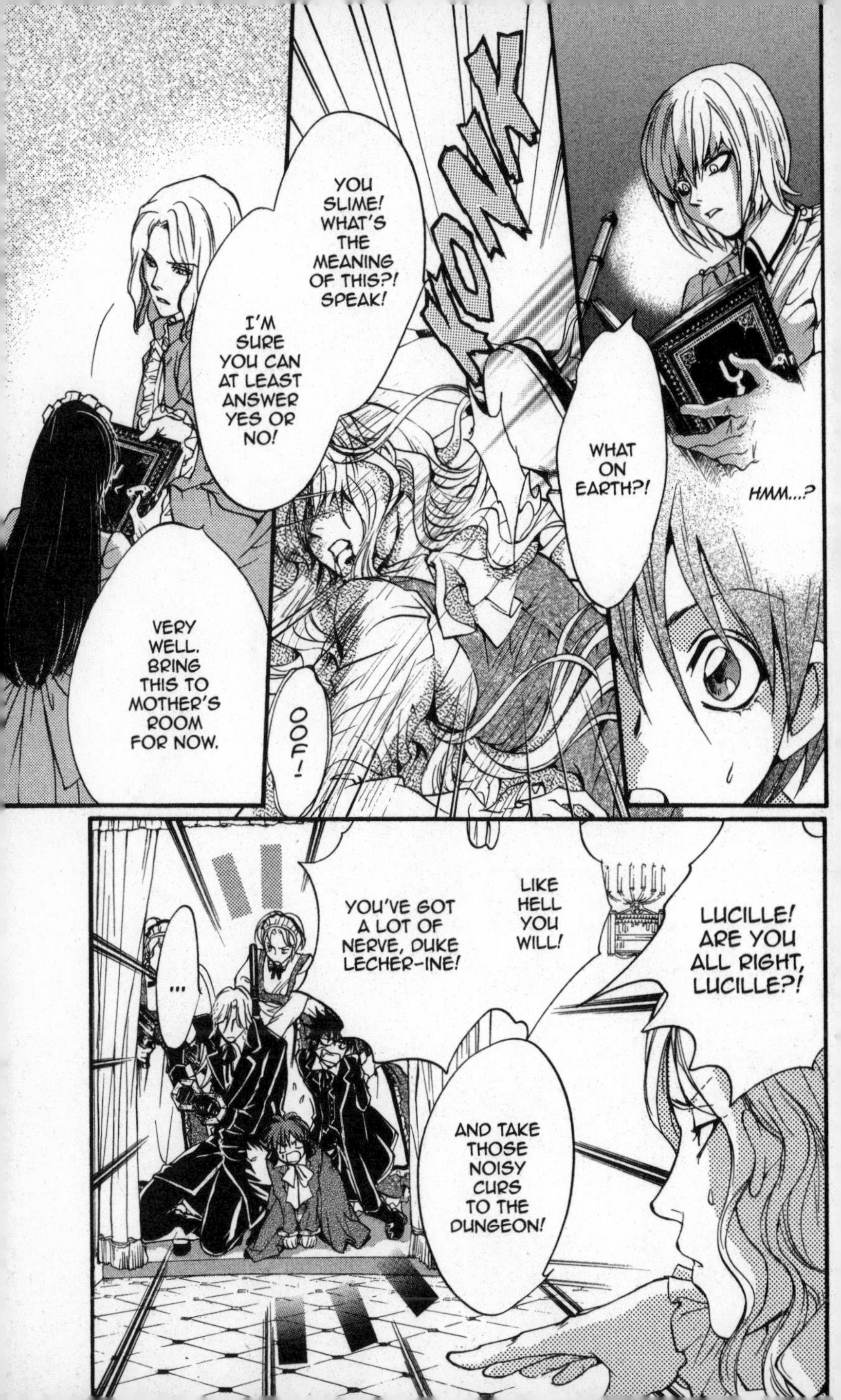
WHAT ON EARTH?!
HMM...?
TONK
OOF!
YOU SLIME! WHAT'S THE MEANING OF THIS?! SPEAK!
I'M SURE YOU CAN AT LEAST ANSWER YES OR NO!
VERY WELL. BRING THIS TO MOTHER'S ROOM FOR NOW.
LUCILLE! ARE YOU ALL RIGHT, LUCILLE?!
LIKE HELL YOU WILL!
YOU'VE GOT A LOT OF NERVE, DUKE LECHER-INE!
...
AND TAKE THOSE NOISY CURS TO THE DUNGEON!

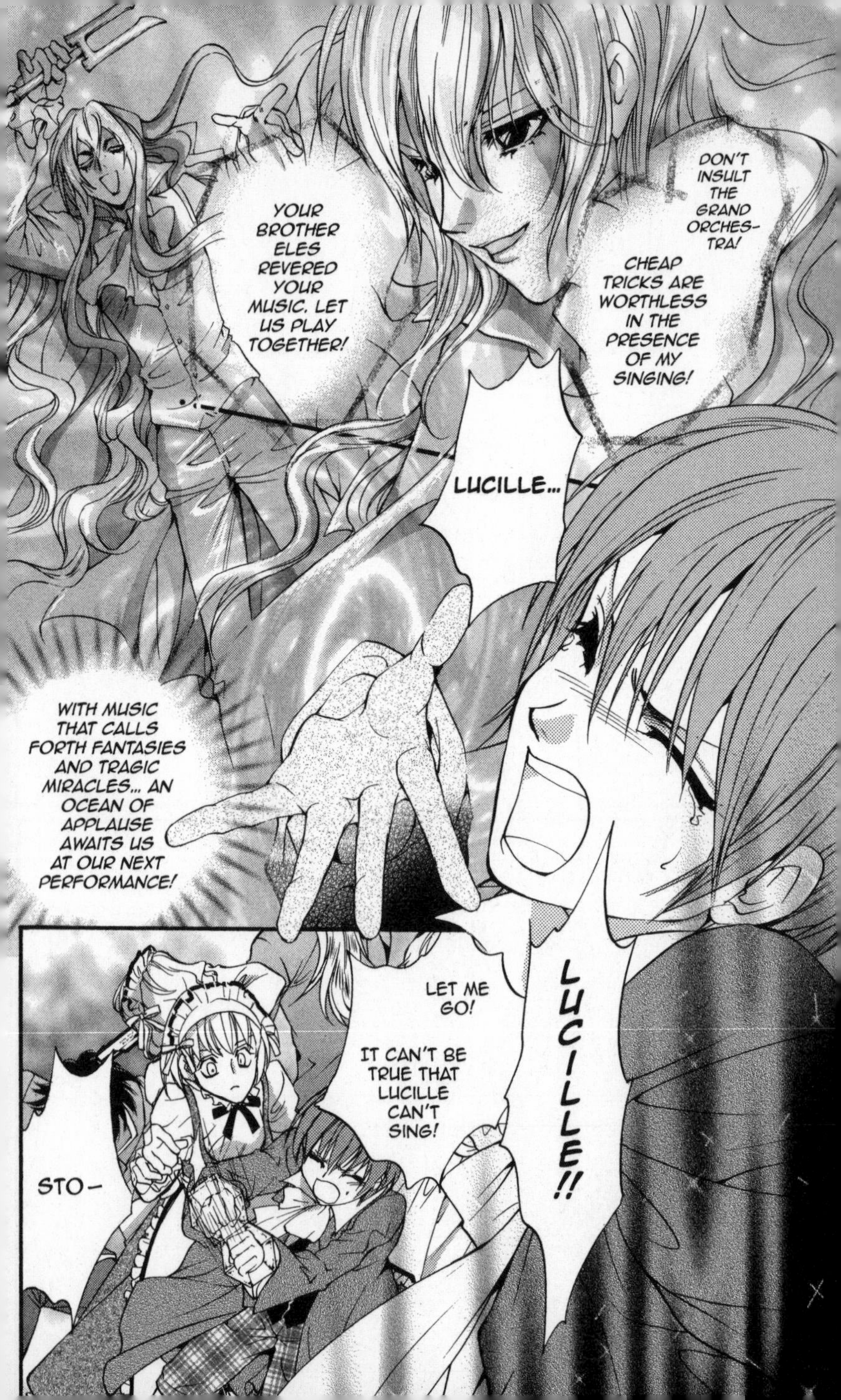
DON'T INSULT THE GRAND ORCHESTRA!
CHEAP TRICKS ARE WORTHLESS IN THE PRESENCE OF MY SINGING!
YOUR BROTHER ELES REVERED YOUR MUSIC. LET US PLAY TOGETHER!
LUCILLE...
WITH MUSIC THAT CALLS FORTH FANTASIES AND TRAGIC MIRACLES... AN OCEAN OF APPLAUSE AWAITS US AT OUR NEXT PERFORMANCE!
LUCILLE!!
LET ME GO!
IT CAN'T BE TRUE THAT LUCILLE CAN'T SING!
STO-

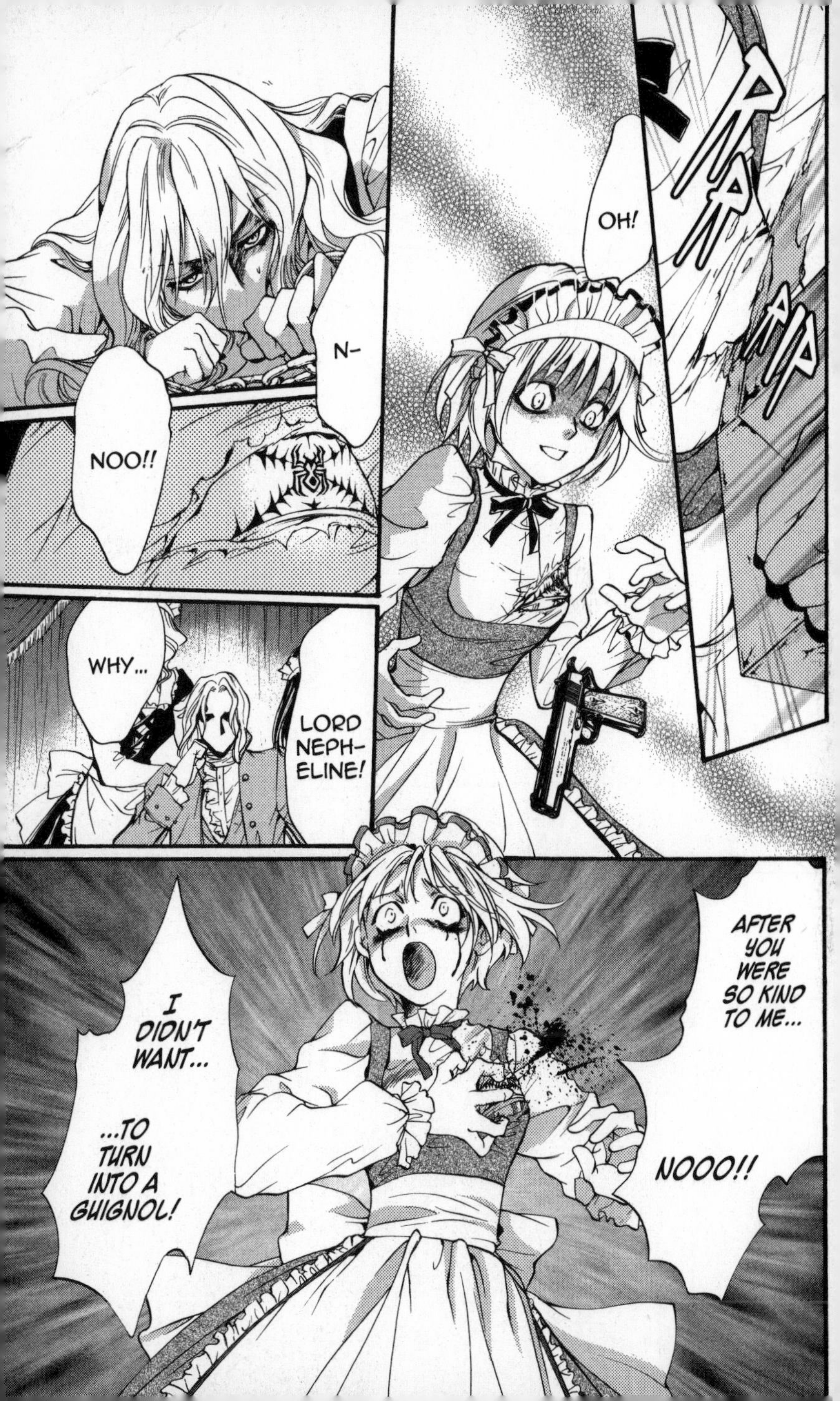
RIP
RIP
OH!
N-
NOO!!
LORD NEPHELINE!
WHY...
AFTER YOU WERE SO KIND TO ME...
I DIDN'T WANT...
...TO TURN INTO A GUIGNOL!
NOOO!!

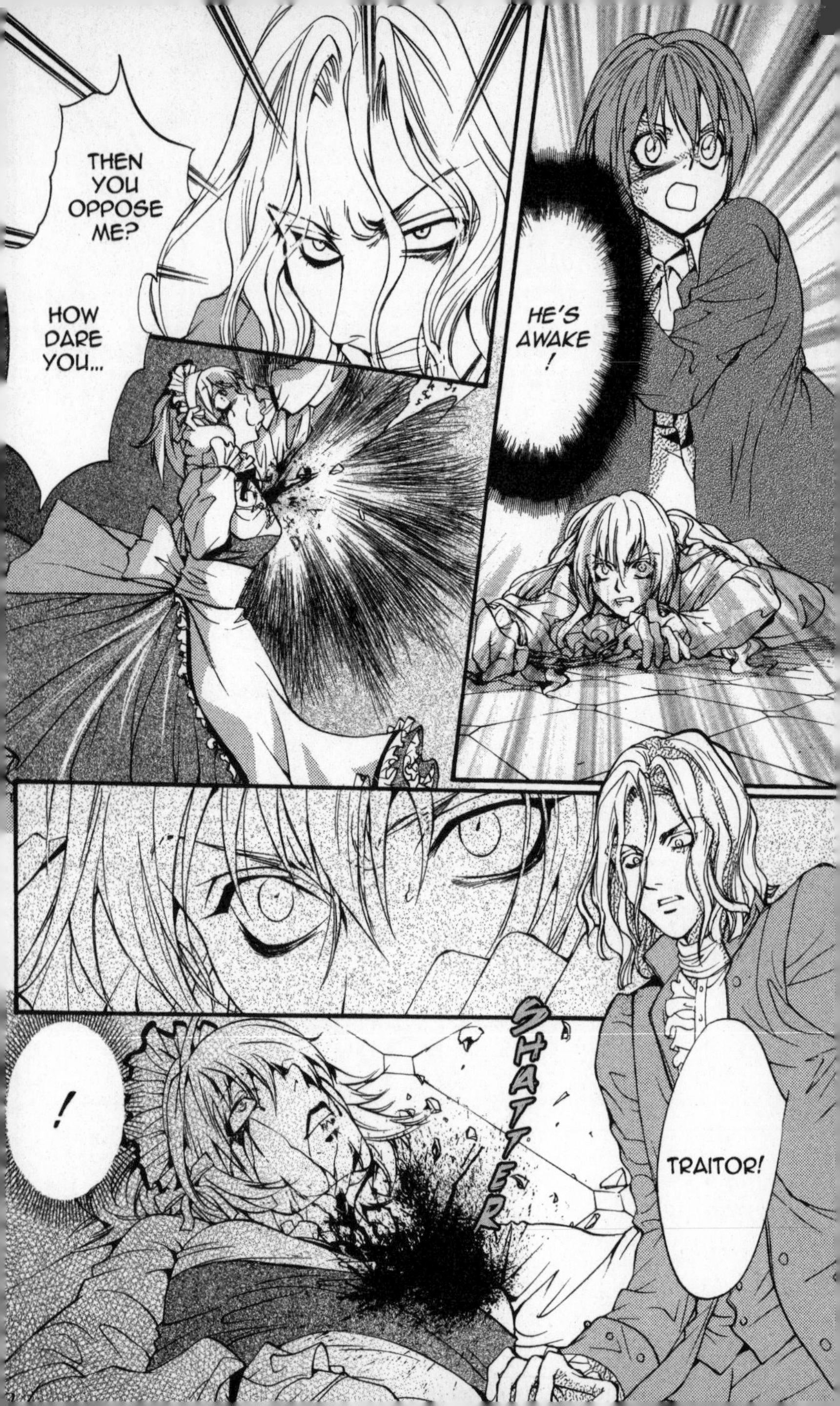
HE'S AWAKE!
THEN YOU OPPOSE ME?
HOW DARE YOU...
TRAITOR!
SHATTER
!

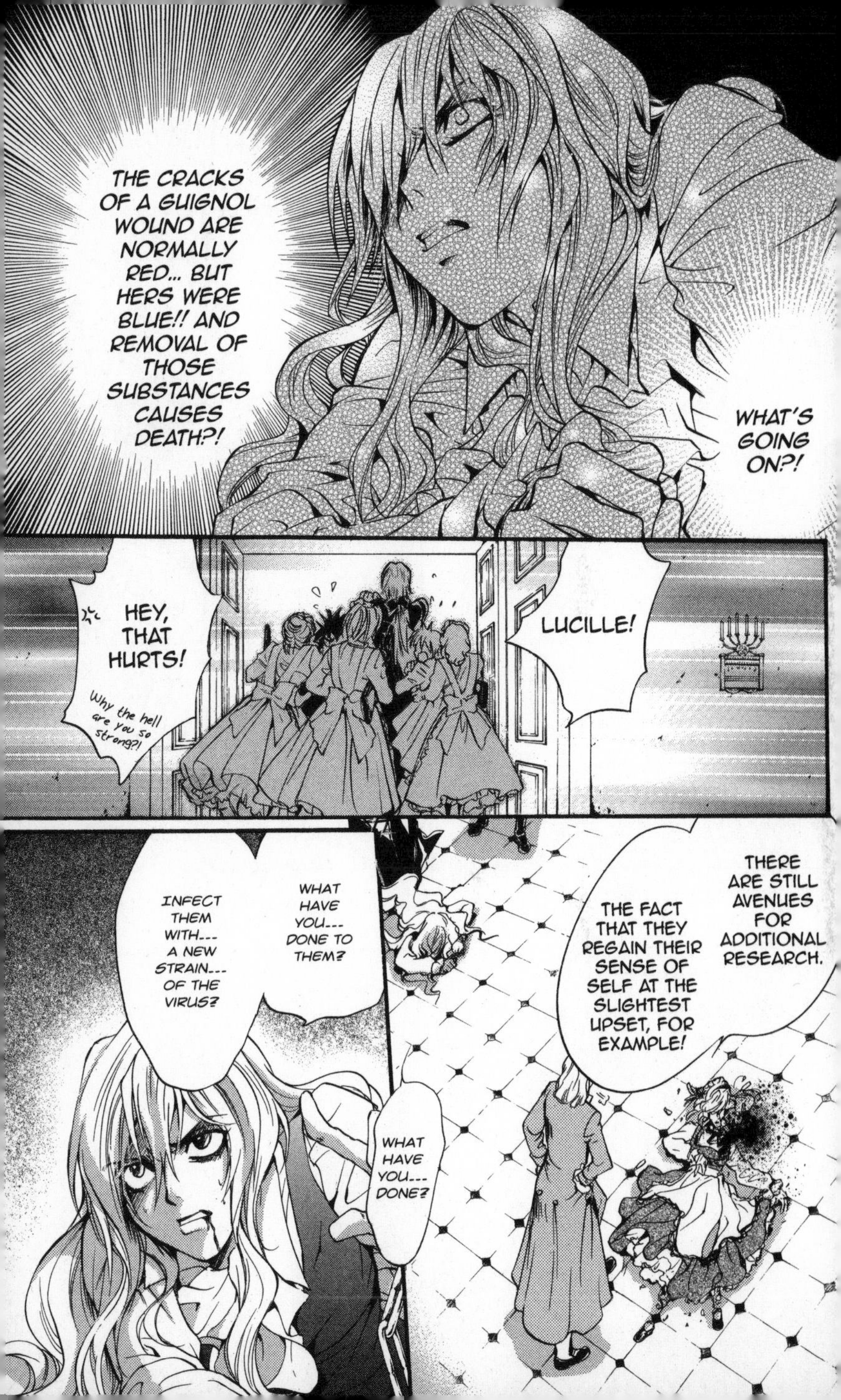
THE CRACKS OF A GUIGNOL WOUND ARE NORMALLY RED... BUT HERS WERE BLUE!! AND REMOVAL OF THOSE SUBSTANCES CAUSES DEATH?!
WHAT'S GOING ON?!
LUCILLE!
HEY, THAT HURTS!
Why the hell are you so strong?!
THERE ARE STILL AVENUES FOR ADDITIONAL RESEARCH.
THE FACT THAT THEY REGAIN THEIR SENSE OF SELF AT THE SLIGHTEST UPSET, FOR EXAMPLE!
WHAT HAVE YOU... DONE TO THEM?
INFECT THEM WITH... A NEW STRAIN... OF THE VIRUS?
WHAT HAVE YOU... DONE?

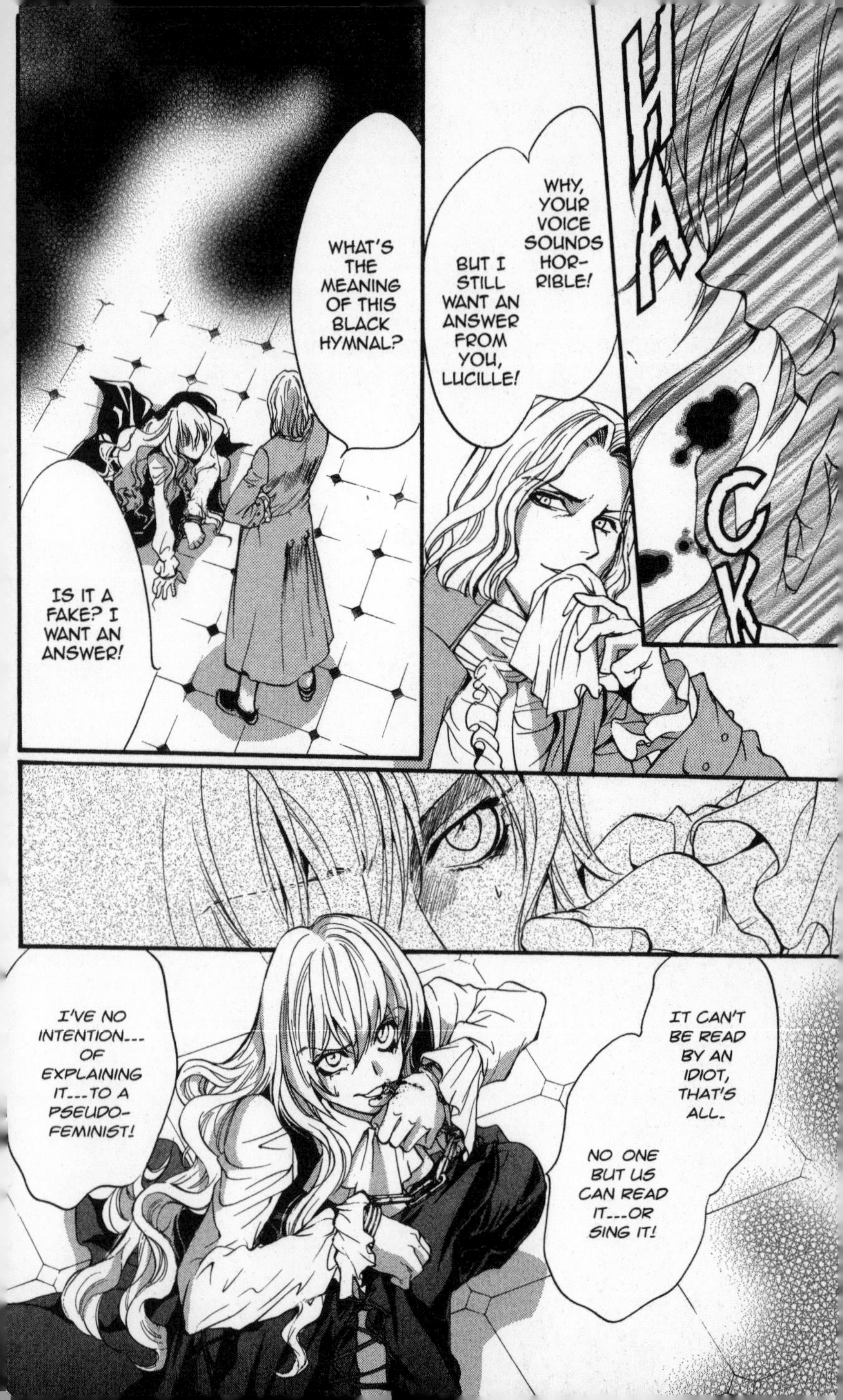
HACK
WHY, YOUR VOICE SOUNDS HOR-RIBLE!
BUT I STILL WANT AN ANSWER FROM YOU, LUCILLE!
WHAT'S THE MEANING OF THIS BLACK HYMNAL?
IS IT A FAKE? I WANT AN ANSWER!
IT CAN'T BE READ BY AN IDIOT, THAT'S ALL.
NO ONE BUT US CAN READ IT...OR SING IT!
I'VE NO INTENTION... OF EXPLAINING IT...TO A PSEUDO-FEMINIST!

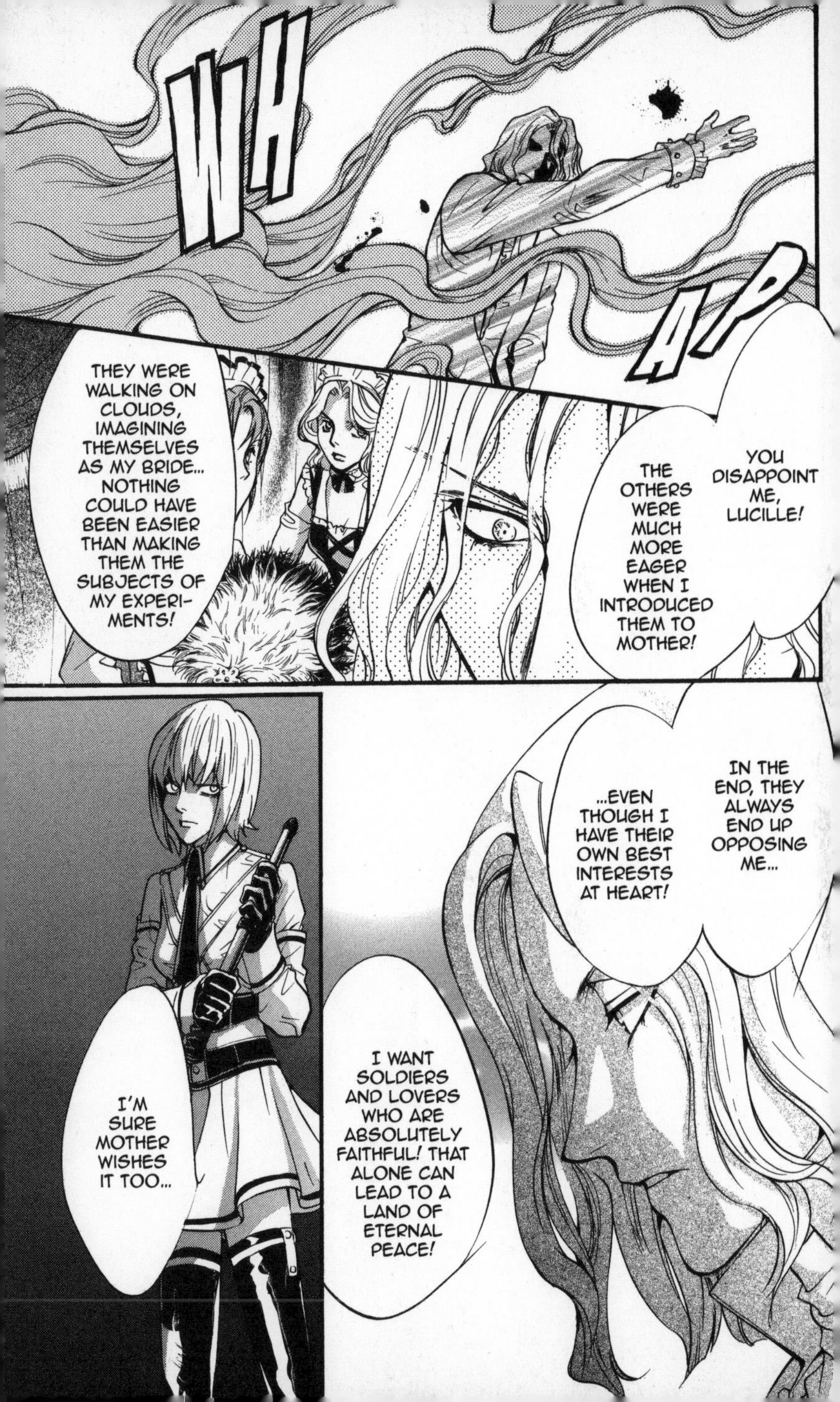
WHAP
YOU DISAPPOINT ME, LUCILLE!
THE OTHERS WERE MUCH MORE EAGER WHEN I INTRODUCED THEM TO MOTHER!
THEY WERE WALKING ON CLOUDS, IMAGINING THEMSELVES AS MY BRIDE... NOTHING COULD HAVE BEEN EASIER THAN MAKING THEM THE SUBJECTS OF MY EXPERI-MENTS!
IN THE END, THEY ALWAYS END UP OPPOSING ME...
...EVEN THOUGH I HAVE THEIR OWN BEST INTERESTS AT HEART!
I WANT SOLDIERS AND LOVERS WHO ARE ABSOLUTELY FAITHFUL! THAT ALONE CAN LEAD TO A LAND OF ETERNAL PEACE!
I'M SURE MOTHER WISHES IT TOO...

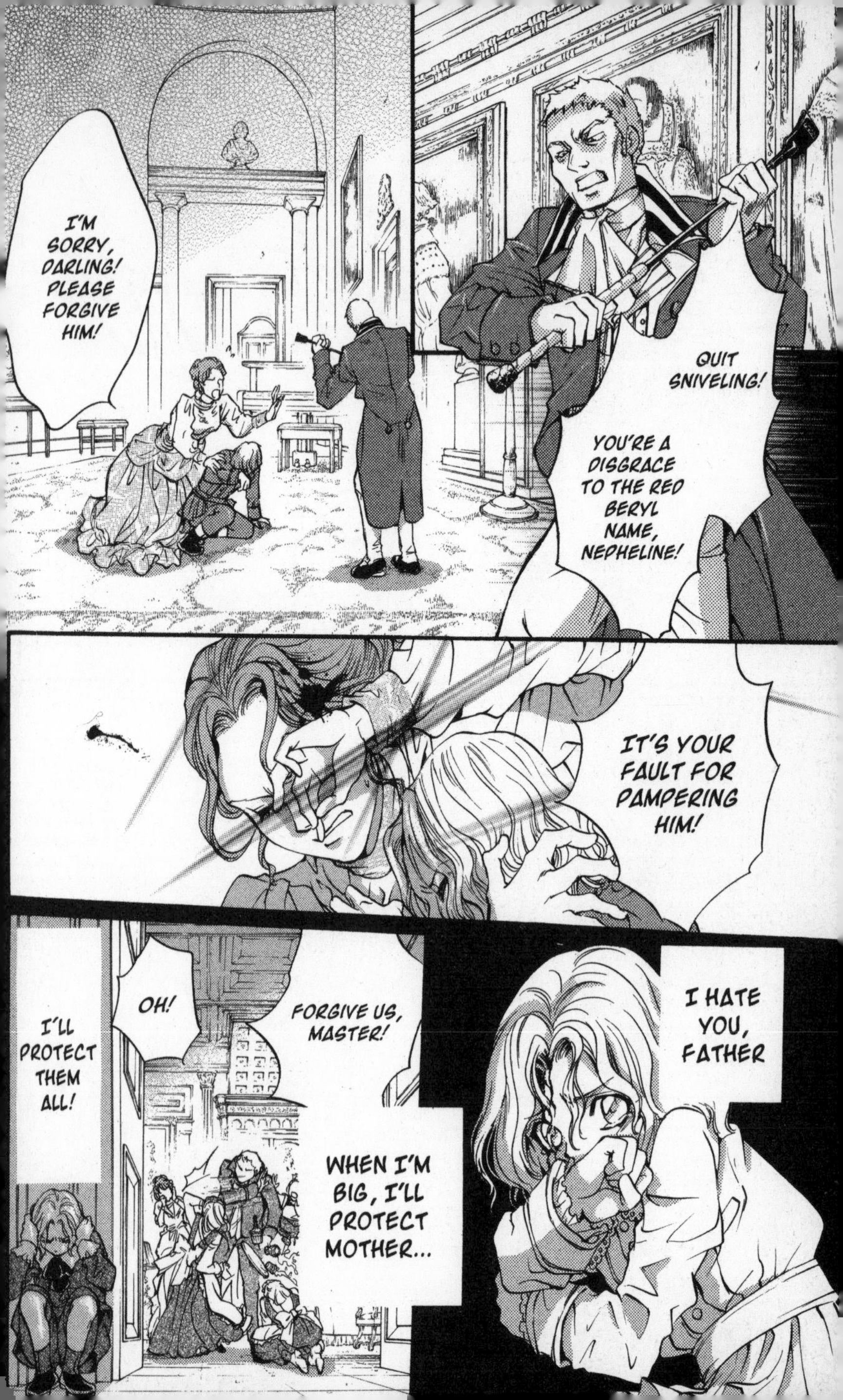
QUIT SNIVELING!
YOU'RE A DISGRACE TO THE RED BERYL NAME, NEPHELINE!
I'M SORRY, DARLING! PLEASE FORGIVE HIM!
IT'S YOUR FAULT FOR PAMPERING HIM!
I HATE YOU, FATHER
FORGIVE US, MASTER!
OH!
WHEN I'M BIG, I'LL PROTECT MOTHER...
I'LL PROTECT THEM ALL!

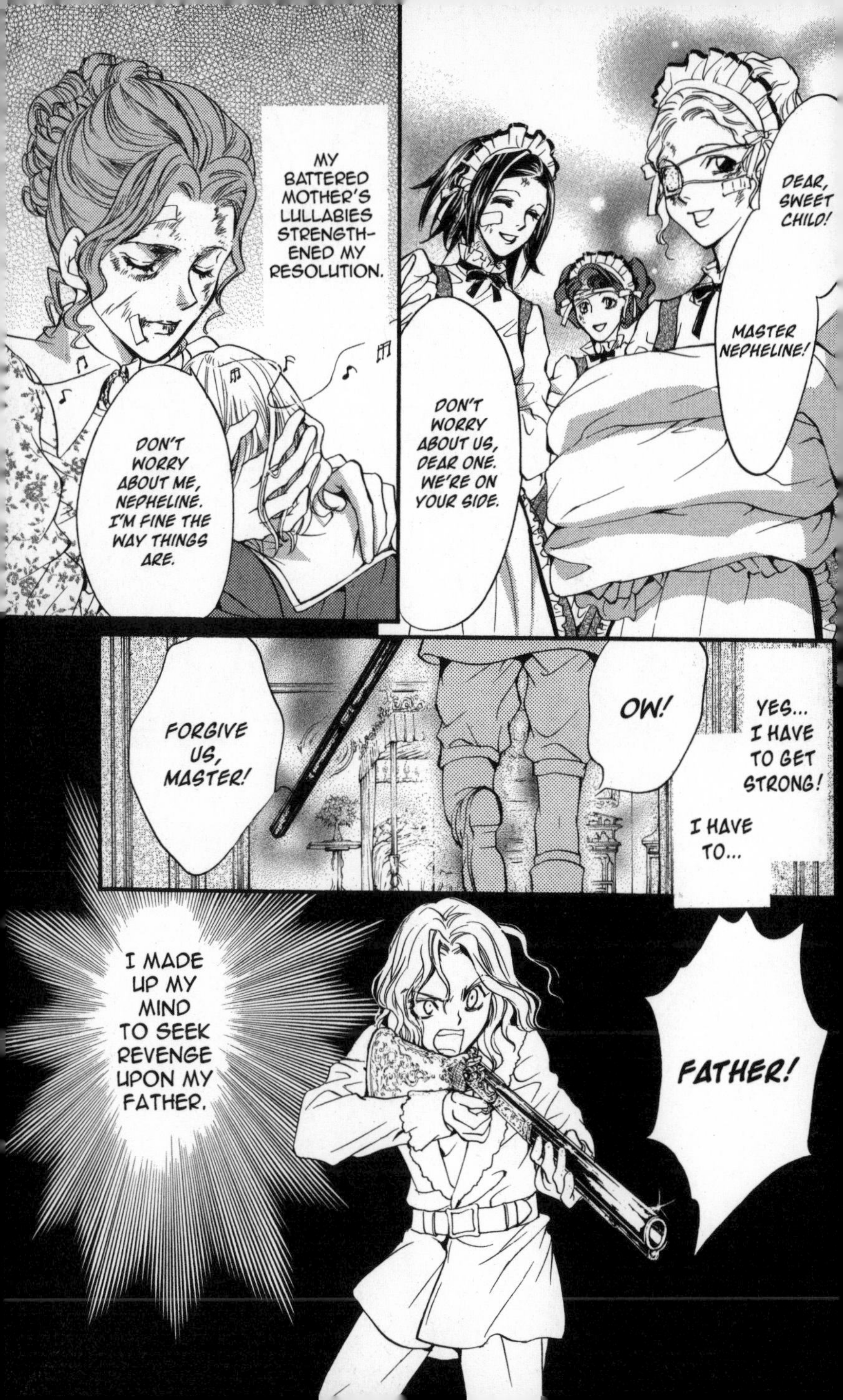
DEAR, SWEET CHILD!
MASTER NEPHELINE!
DON'T WORRY ABOUT US, DEAR ONE. WE'RE ON YOUR SIDE.
MY BATTERED MOTHER'S LULLABIES STRENGTHENED MY RESOLUTION.
DON'T WORRY ABOUT ME, NEPHELINE. I'M FINE THE WAY THINGS ARE.
YES... I HAVE TO GET STRONG!
I HAVE TO...
OW!
FORGIVE US, MASTER!
FATHER!
I MADE UP MY MIND TO SEEK REVENGE UPON MY FATHER.

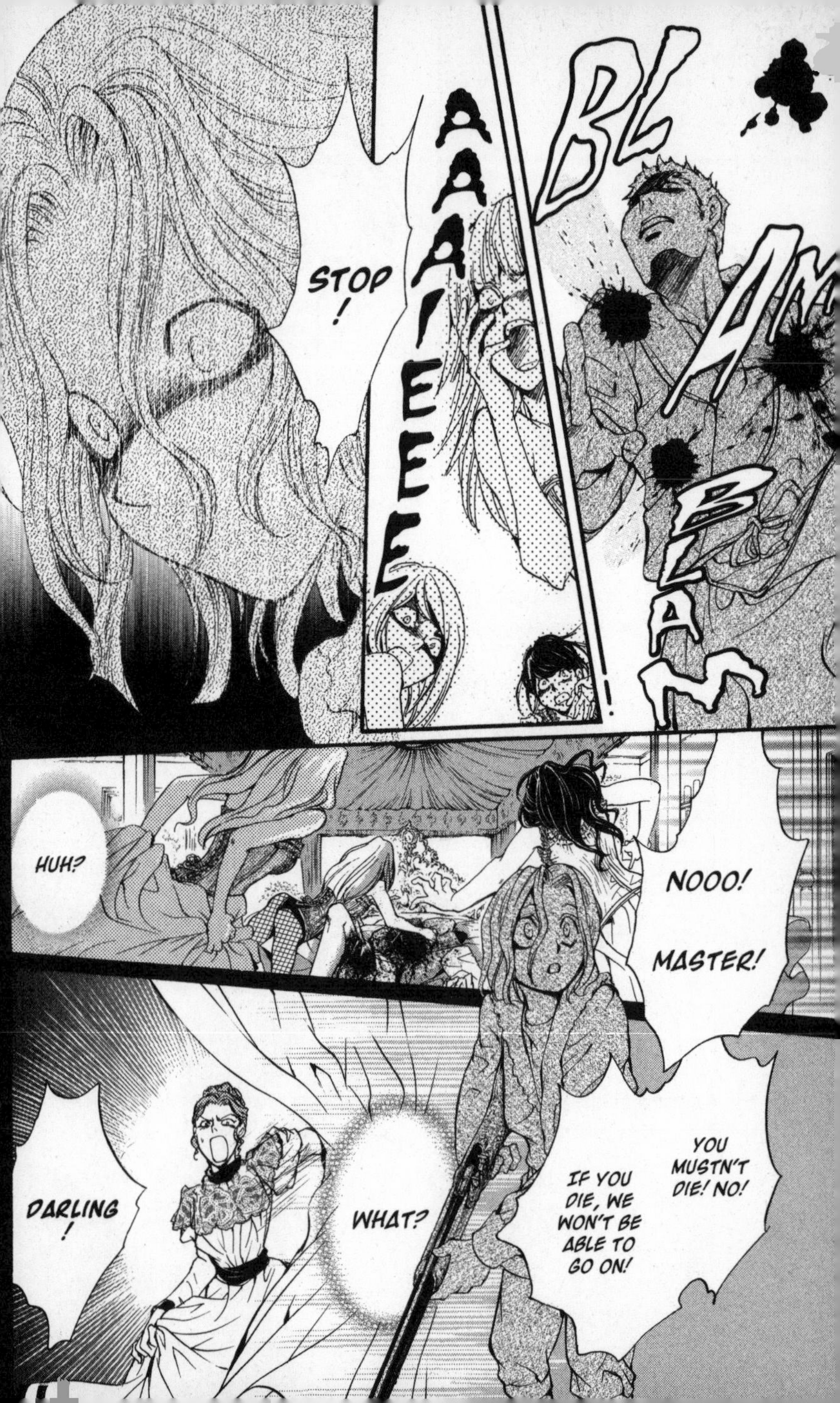
BLAM
BLAM
AAAIEEEE
STOP!
NOOO!
MASTER!
HUH?
YOU MUSTN'T DIE! NO!
IF YOU DIE, WE WON'T BE ABLE TO GO ON!
WHAT?
DARLING!

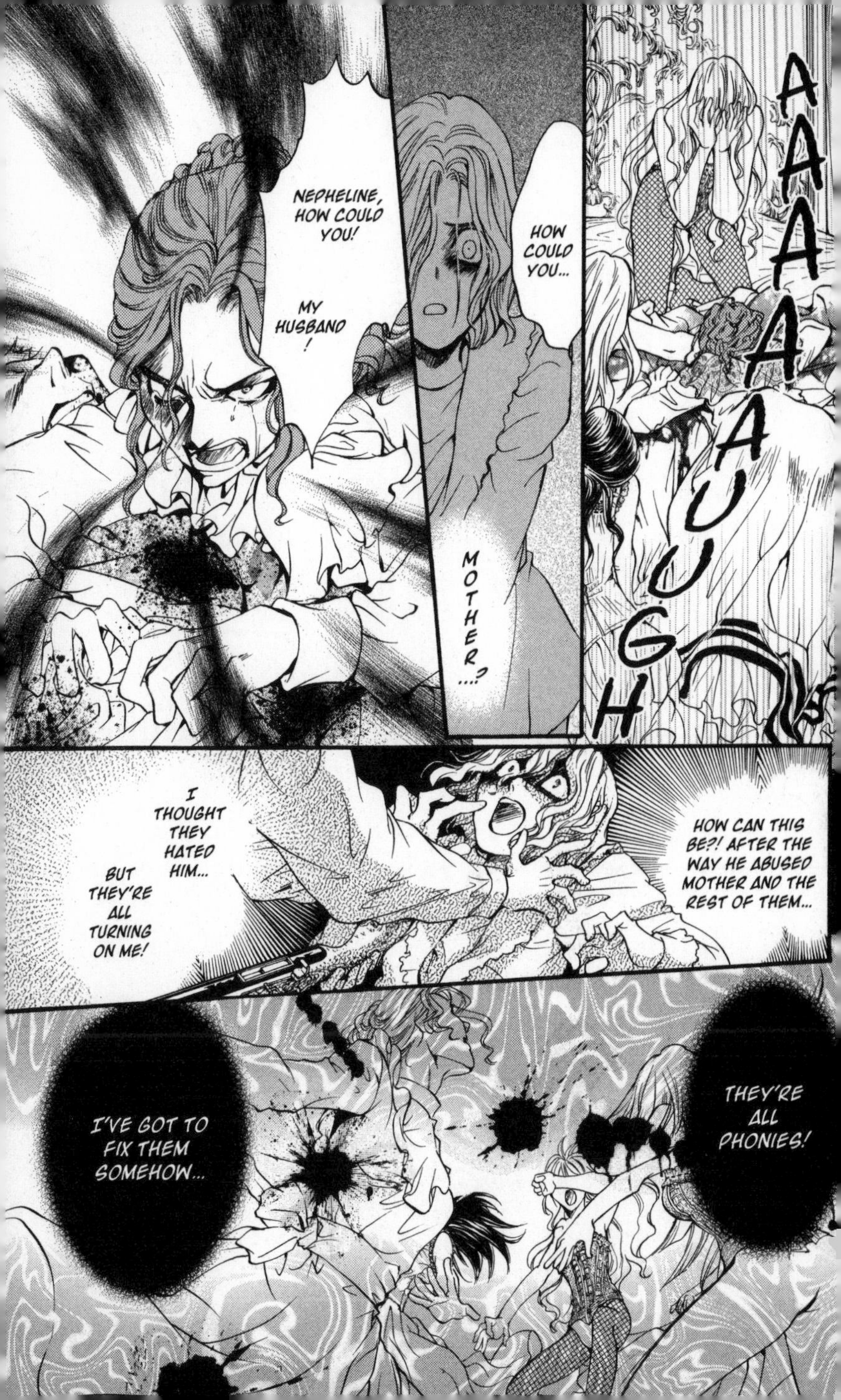
AAAAAUUGH
HOW COULD YOU...
MOTHER...?
NEPHELINE, HOW COULD YOU!
MY HUSBAND!
HOW CAN THIS BE?! AFTER THE WAY HE ABUSED MOTHER AND THE REST OF THEM...
I THOUGHT THEY HATED HIM...
BUT THEY'RE ALL TURNING ON ME!
THEY'RE ALL PHONIES!
I'VE GOT TO FIX THEM SOMEHOW...

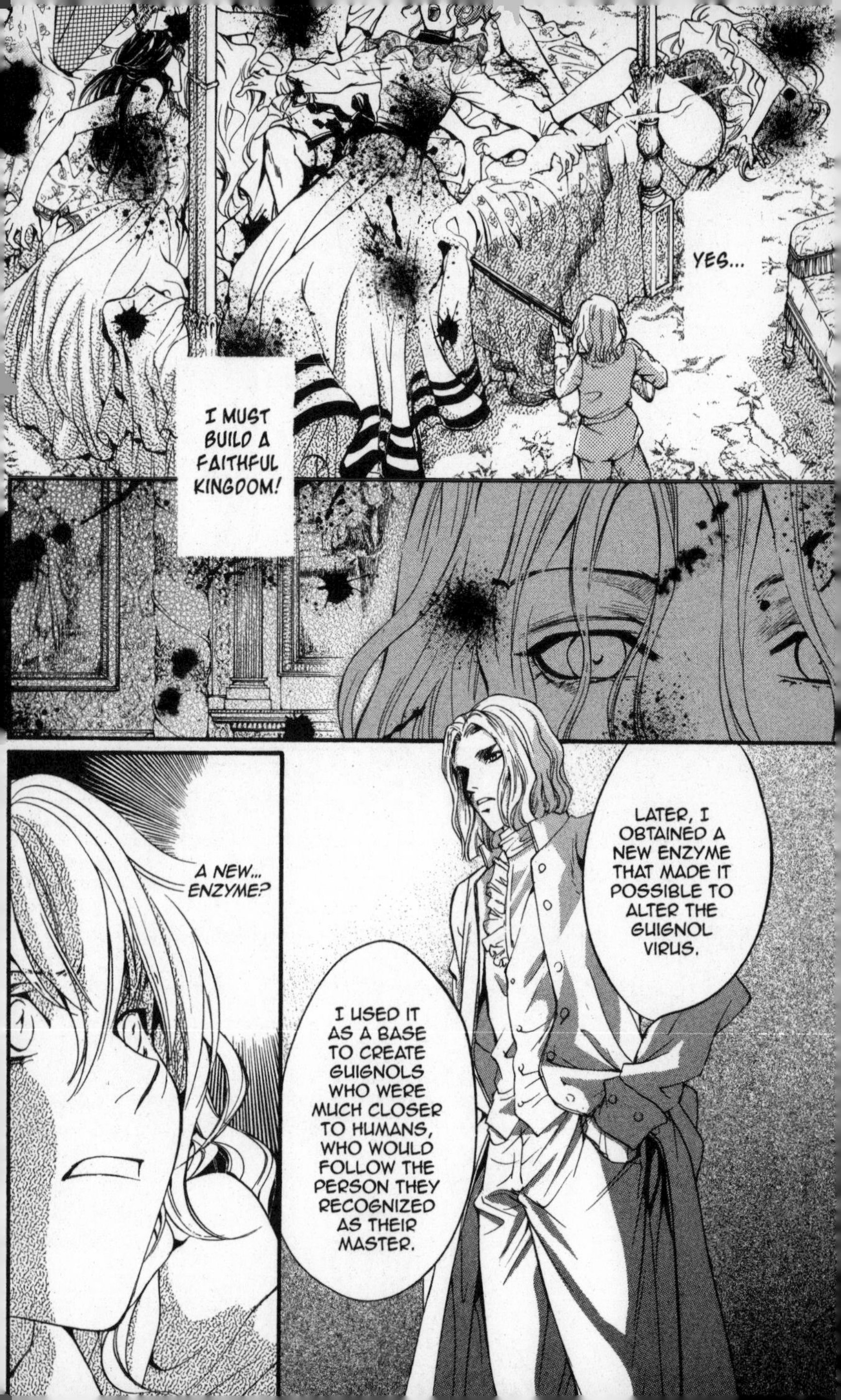
YES...
I MUST BUILD A FAITHFUL KINGDOM!
LATER, I OBTAINED A NEW ENZYME THAT MADE IT POSSIBLE TO ALTER THE GUIGNOL VIRUS.
I USED IT AS A BASE TO CREATE GUIGNOLS WHO WERE MUCH CLOSER TO HUMANS, WHO WOULD FOLLOW THE PERSON THEY RECOGNIZED AS THEIR MASTER.
A NEW... ENZYME?

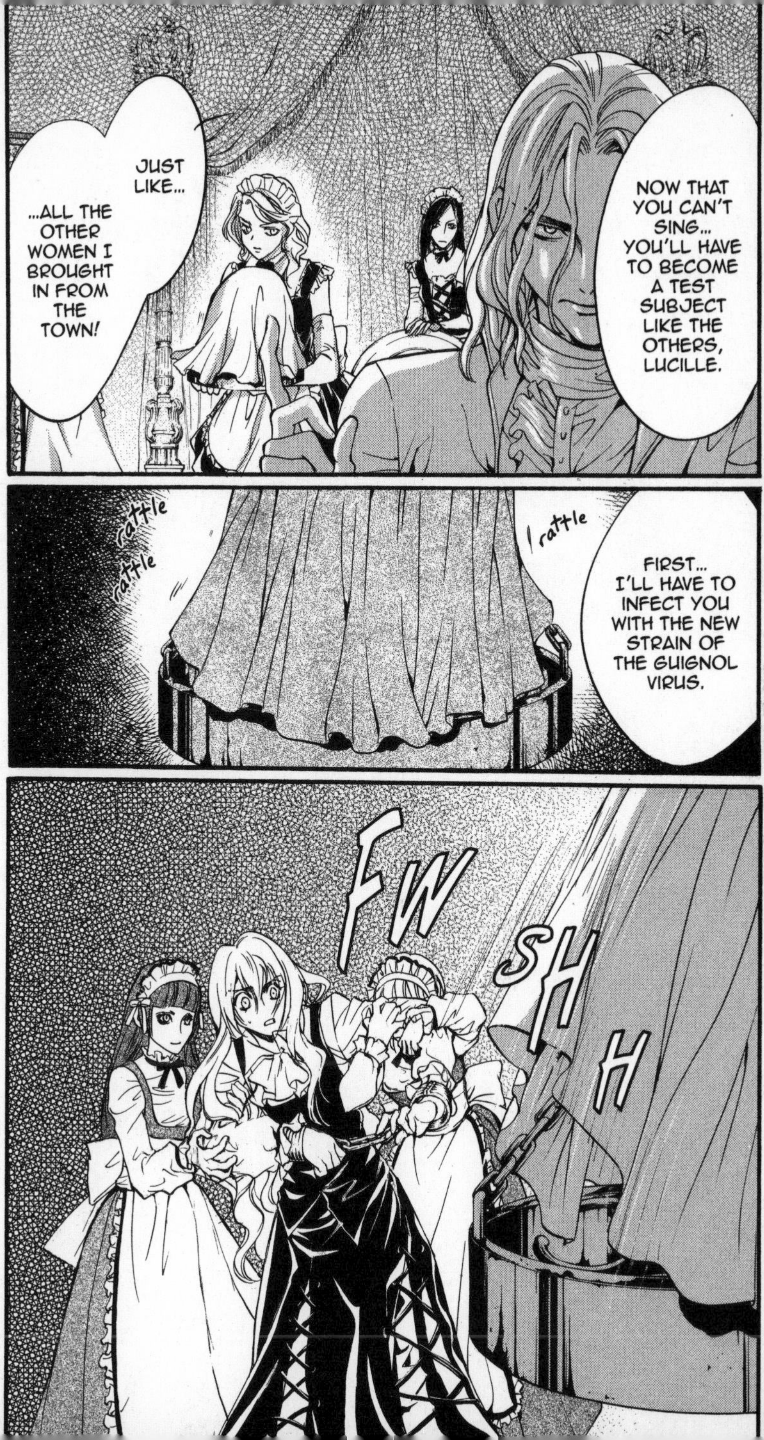
NOW THAT YOU CAN'T SING... YOU'LL HAVE TO BECOME A TEST SUBJECT LIKE THE OTHERS, LUCILLE.
JUST LIKE...
...ALL THE OTHER WOMEN I BROUGHT IN FROM THE TOWN!
FIRST... I'LL HAVE TO INFECT YOU WITH THE NEW STRAIN OF THE GUIGNOL VIRUS.
rattle
rattle
rattle
FWSHH

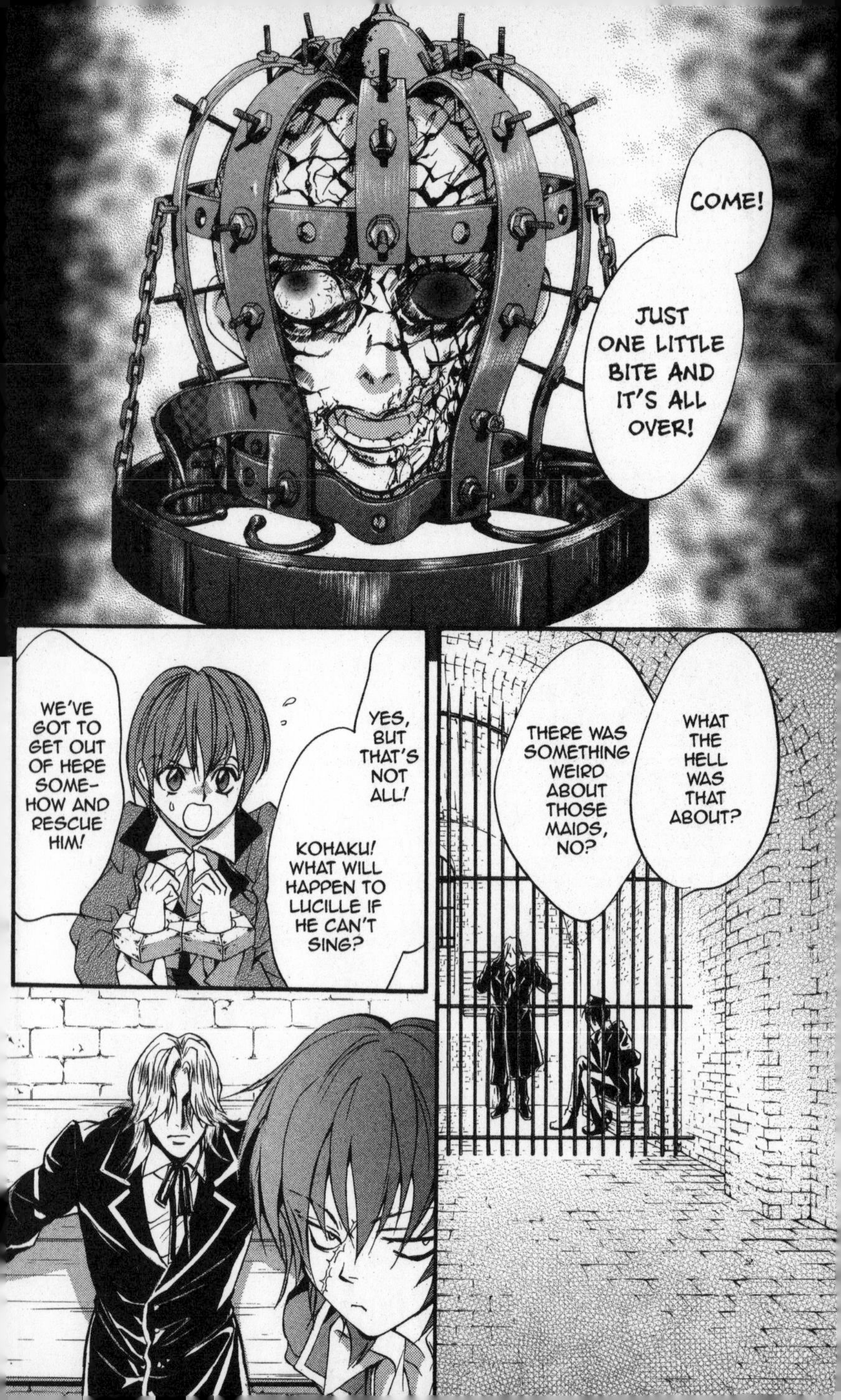

COME!
JUST ONE LITTLE BITE AND IT'S ALL OVER!
WHAT THE HELL WAS THAT ABOUT?
THERE WAS SOMETHING WEIRD ABOUT THOSE MAIDS, NO?
YES, BUT THAT'S NOT ALL!
KOHAKU! WHAT WILL HAPPEN TO LUCILLE IF HE CAN'T SING?
WE'VE GOT TO GET OUT OF HERE SOME-HOW AND RESCUE HIM!

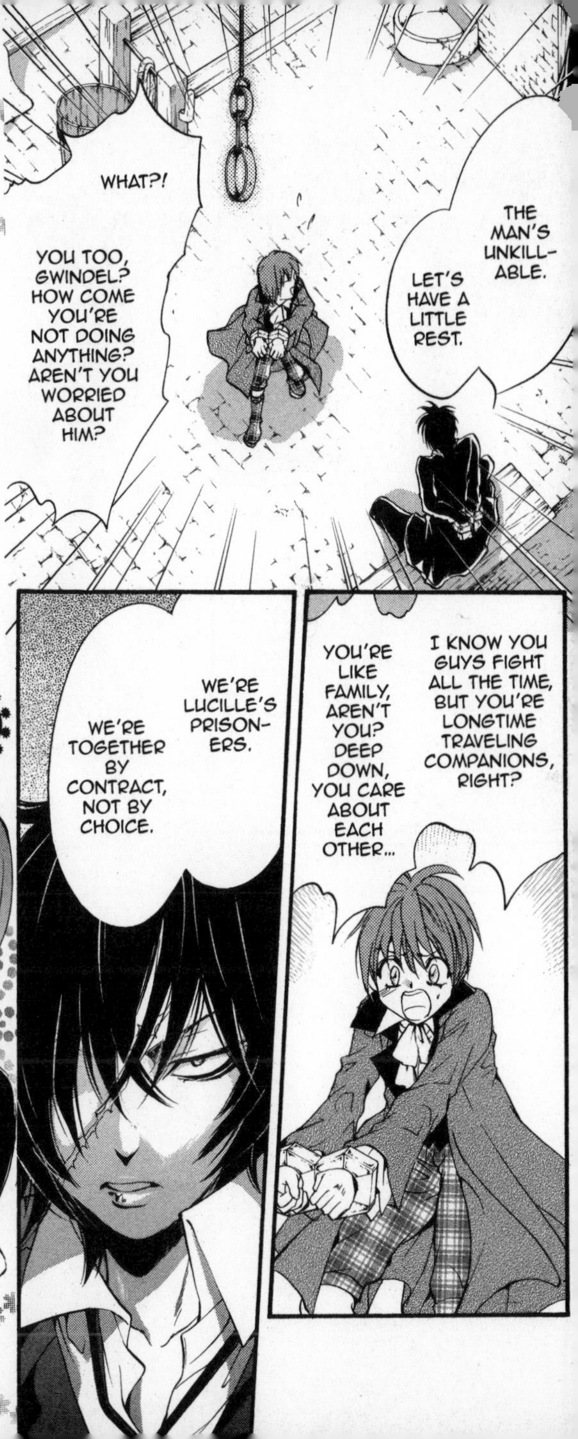
THE MAN'S UNKILLABLE.
LET'S HAVE A LITTLE REST.
WHAT?!
YOU TOO, GWINDEL? HOW COME YOU'RE NOT DOING ANYTHING? AREN'T YOU WORRIED ABOUT HIM?
I KNOW YOU GUYS FIGHT ALL THE TIME, BUT YOU'RE LONGTIME TRAVELING COMPANIONS, RIGHT?
YOU'RE LIKE FAMILY, AREN'T YOU? DEEP DOWN, YOU CARE ABOUT EACH OTHER...
WE'RE LUCILLE'S PRISONERS.
WE'RE TOGETHER BY CONTRACT, NOT BY CHOICE.

There aren't a lot of girls in the story, so it's been fun drawing Spinel. Spinel in uniform... Spinel in a sleeveless top... I like haughty girls. In my mind, she has bluish hair and red eyes. Just like spinels.

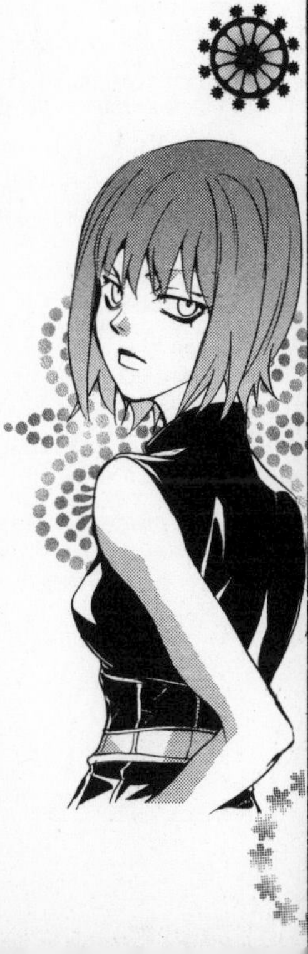

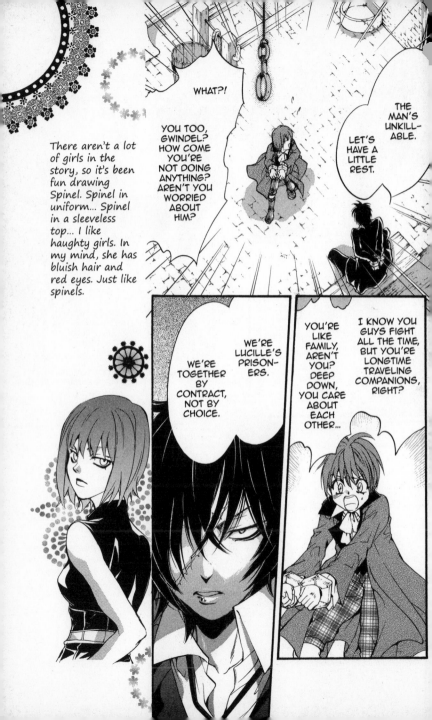

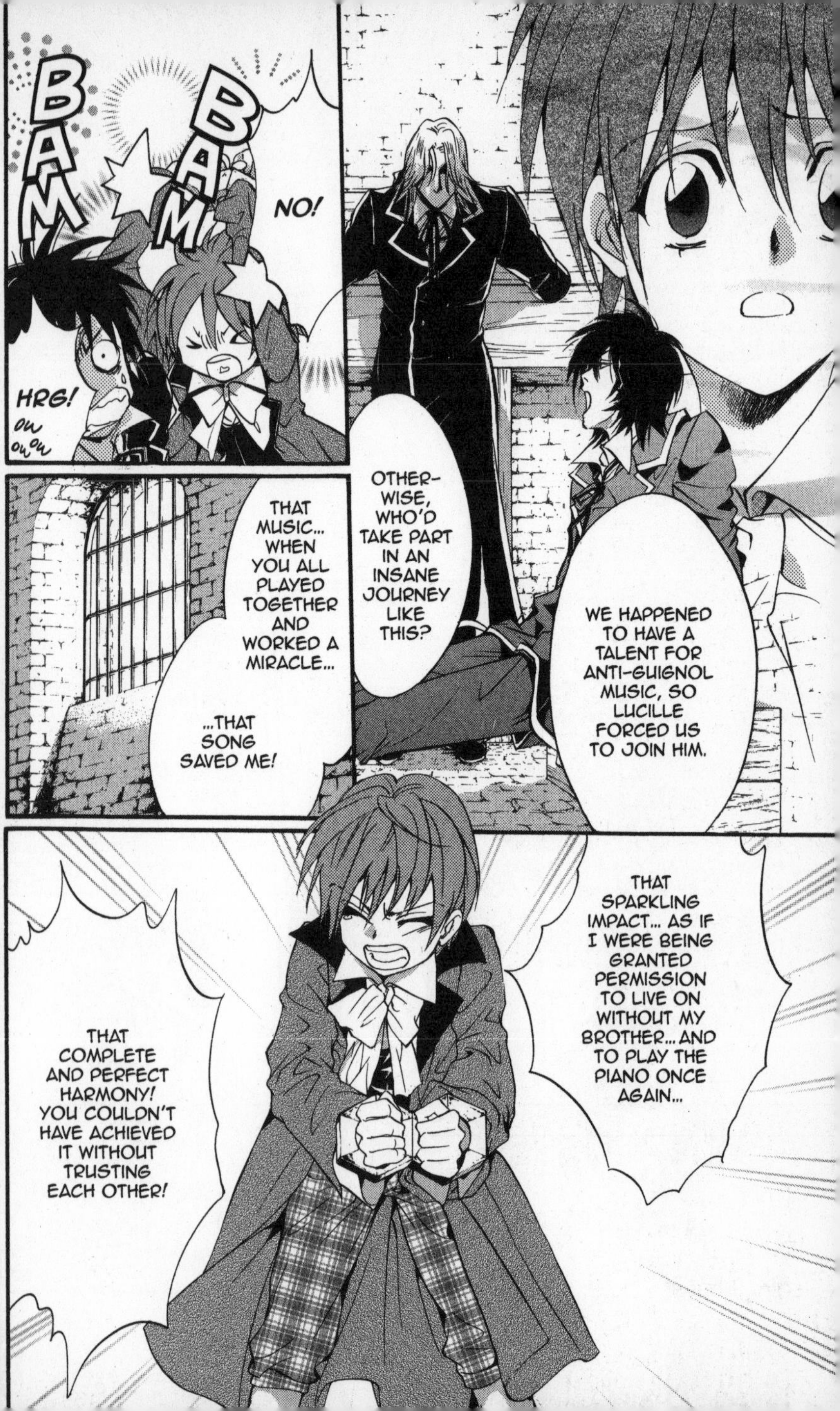

WE HAPPENED TO HAVE A TALENT FOR ANTI-GUIGNOL MUSIC, SO LUCILLE FORCED US TO JOIN HIM.
OTHER-WISE, WHO'D TAKE PART IN AN INSANE JOURNEY LIKE THIS?
BAM
BAM
NO!
HRG!
OW OW OW
THAT MUSIC... WHEN YOU ALL PLAYED TOGETHER AND WORKED A MIRACLE...
...THAT SONG SAVED ME!
THAT SPARKLING IMPACT... AS IF I WERE BEING GRANTED PERMISSION TO LIVE ON WITHOUT MY BROTHER... AND TO PLAY THE PIANO ONCE AGAIN...
THAT COMPLETE AND PERFECT HARMONY! YOU COULDN'T HAVE ACHIEVED IT WITHOUT TRUSTING EACH OTHER!

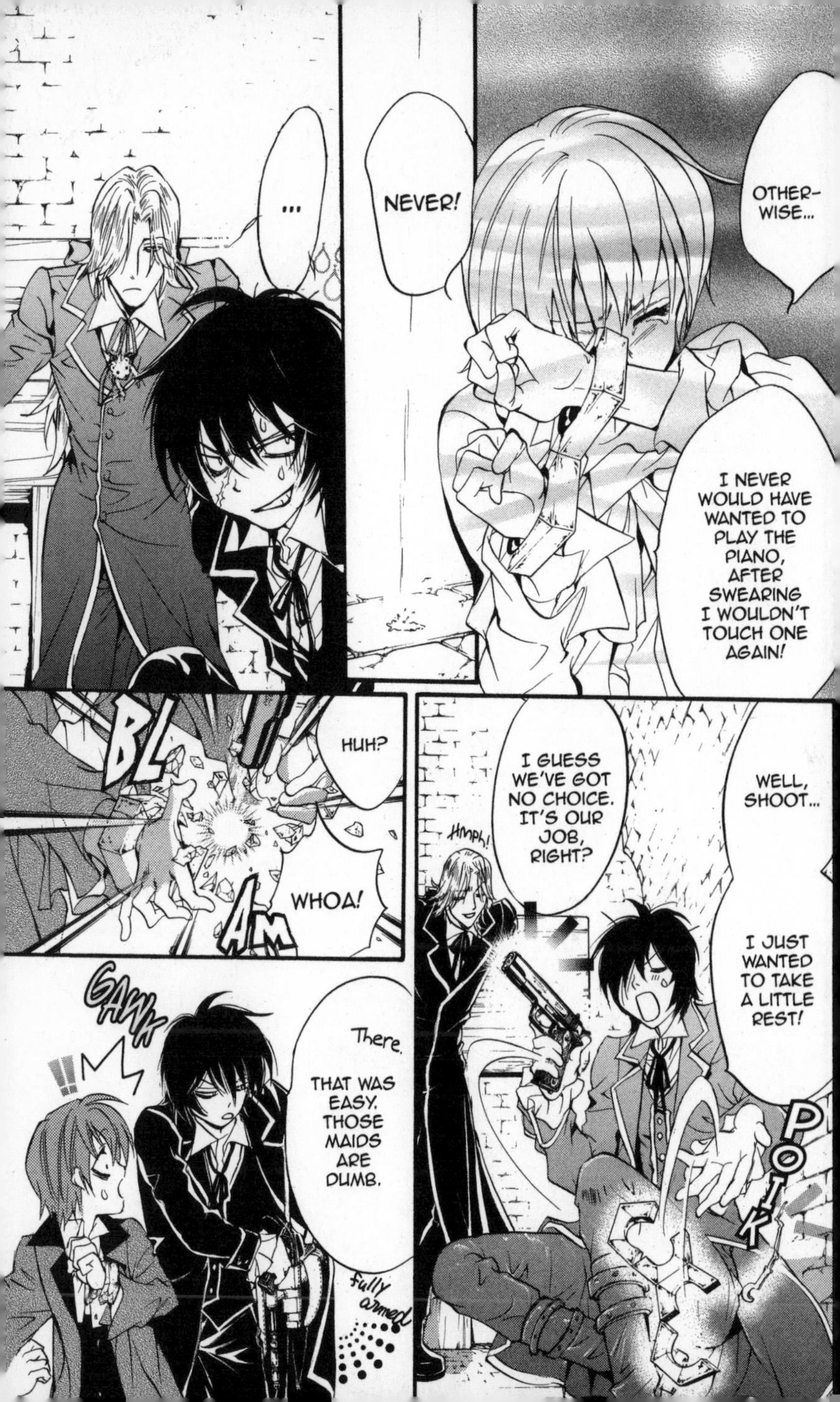
OTHER-WISE...
I NEVER WOULD HAVE WANTED TO PLAY THE PIANO, AFTER SWEARING I WOULDN'T TOUCH ONE AGAIN!
NEVER!
...
WELL, SHOOT...
I JUST WANTED TO TAKE A LITTLE REST!
I GUESS WE'VE GOT NO CHOICE. IT'S OUR JOB, RIGHT?
Hmph!
POIK
BLAM
HUH?
WHOA!
GAWK
!!
There.
THAT WAS EASY. THOSE MAIDS ARE DUMB.
fully armed

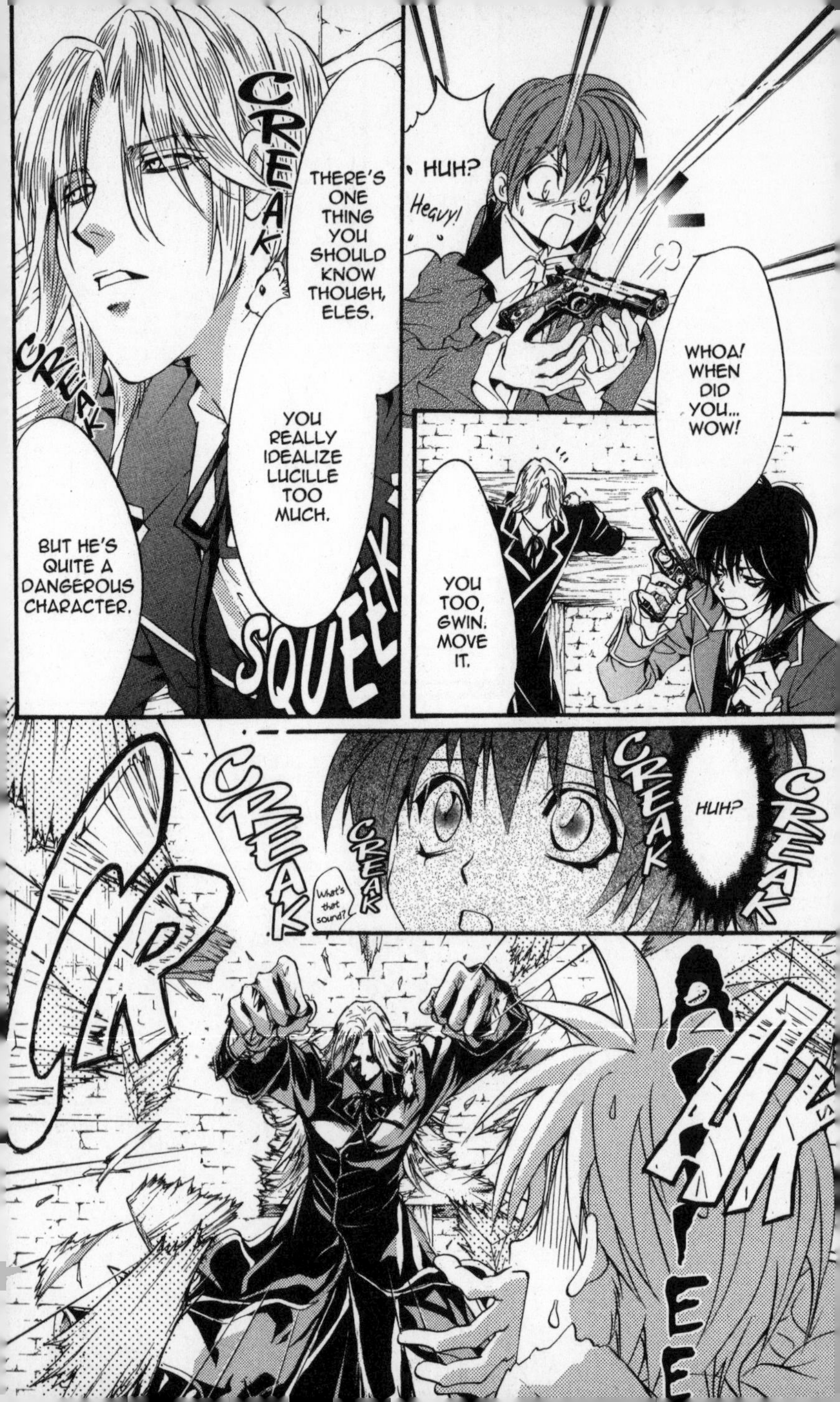
HUH?
Heavy!
WHOA! WHEN DID YOU... WOW!
YOU TOO, GWIN. MOVE IT.
CREAK
THERE'S ONE THING YOU SHOULD KNOW THOUGH, ELES.
YOU REALLY IDEALIZE LUCILLE TOO MUCH.
SQUEEK
CREAK
BUT HE'S QUITE A DANGEROUS CHARACTER.
CREAK
HUH?
CREAK
CREAK
What's that sound?
CREAK

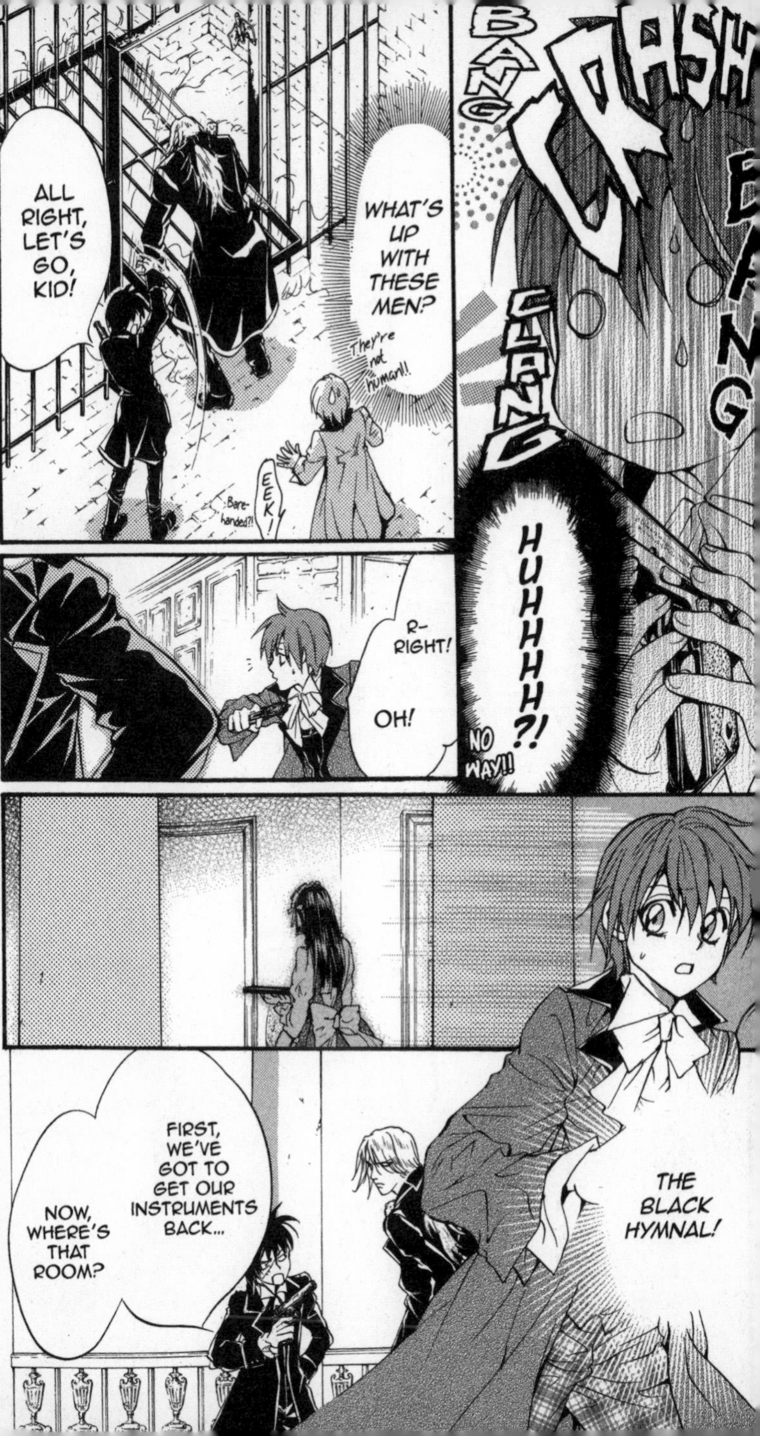
CRASH
BANG
BANG
CLANG
HUHHHHH?!
NO WAY!!
WHAT'S UP WITH THESE MEN?
They're not human!!
ALL RIGHT, LET'S GO, KID!
EEK!
Bare-handed?!
R-RIGHT!
OH!
THE BLACK HYMNAL!
FIRST, WE'VE GOT TO GET OUR INSTRUMENTS BACK...
NOW, WHERE'S THAT ROOM?

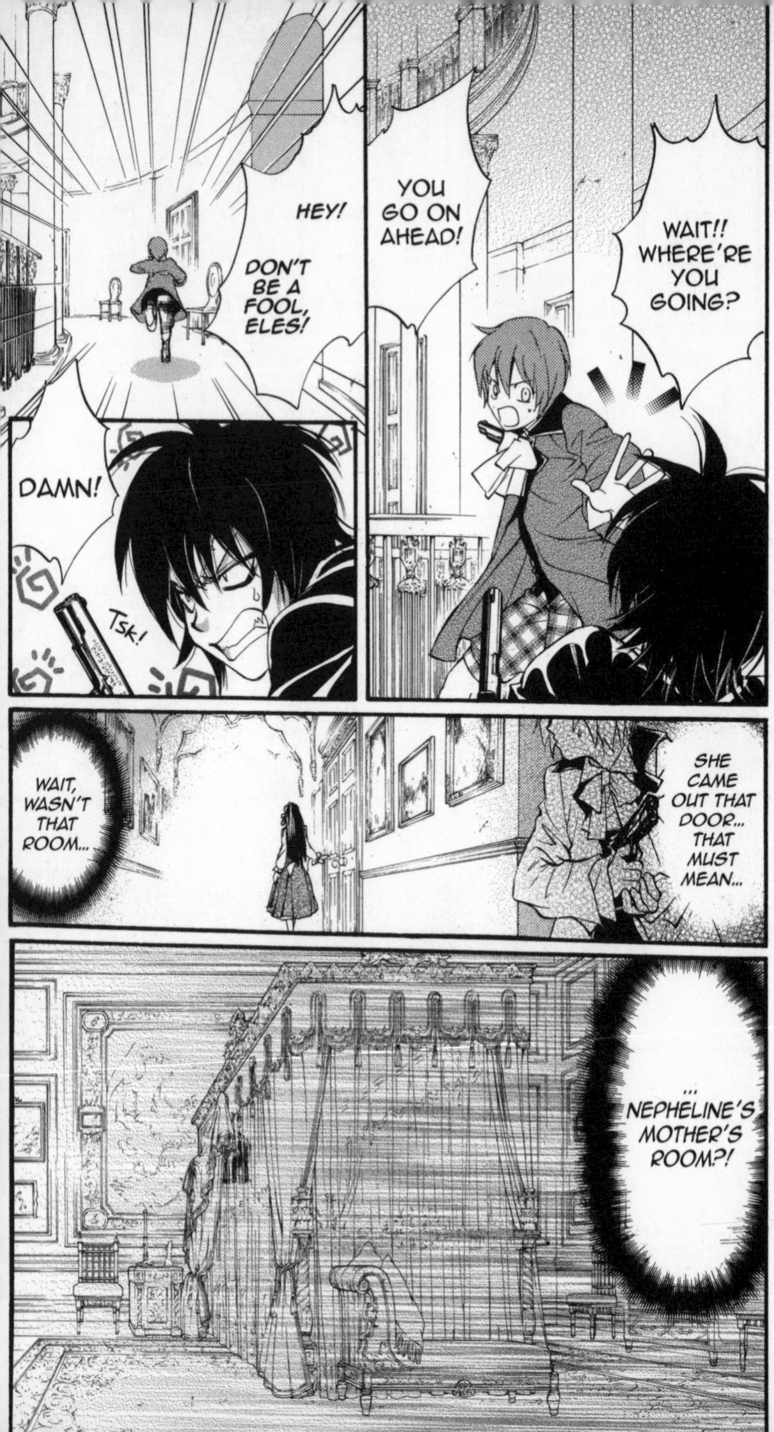
YOU GO ON AHEAD!
WAIT!! WHERE'RE YOU GOING?
HEY!
DON'T BE A FOOL, ELES!
DAMN!
Tsk!
SHE CAME OUT THAT DOOR... THAT MUST MEAN...
WAIT, WASN'T THAT ROOM...
... NEPHELINE'S MOTHER'S ROOM?!

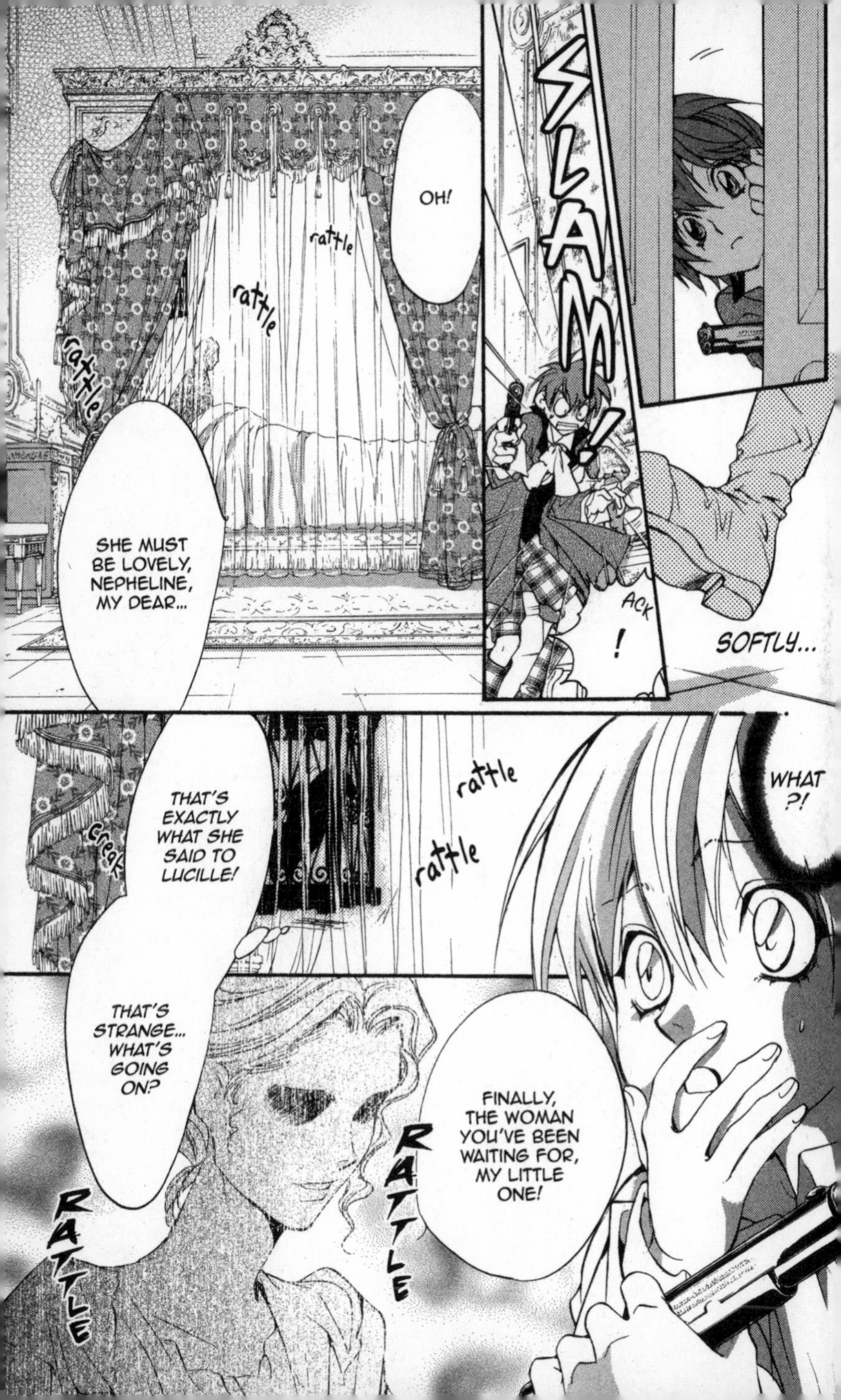
SOFTLY...
SLAM!
ACK!
OH!
rattle
rattle
rattle
SHE MUST BE LOVELY, NEPHELINE, MY DEAR...
WHAT?!
rattle
rattle
creak
THAT'S EXACTLY WHAT SHE SAID TO LUCILLE!
THAT'S STRANGE... WHAT'S GOING ON?
FINALLY, THE WOMAN YOU'VE BEEN WAITING FOR, MY LITTLE ONE!
RATTLE
RATTLE

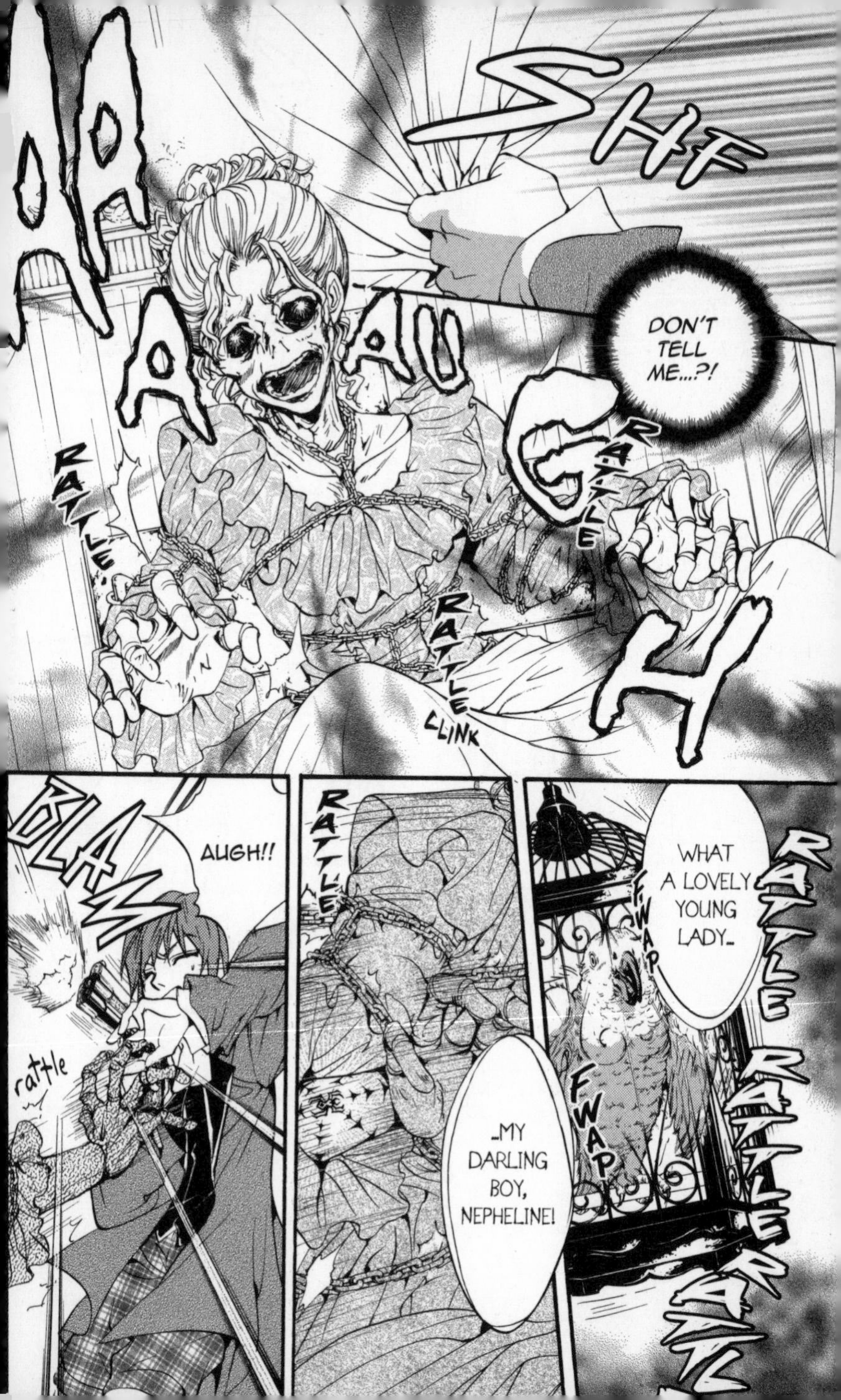
SHF
DON'T TELL ME...?!
RATTLE
AAAAUGH
RATTLE
RATTLE
CLINK
RATTLE
RATTLE
FWAP
WHAT A LOVELY YOUNG LADY...
FWAP
...MY DARLING BOY, NEPHELINE!
RATTLE
BLAM
AUGH!!
rattle

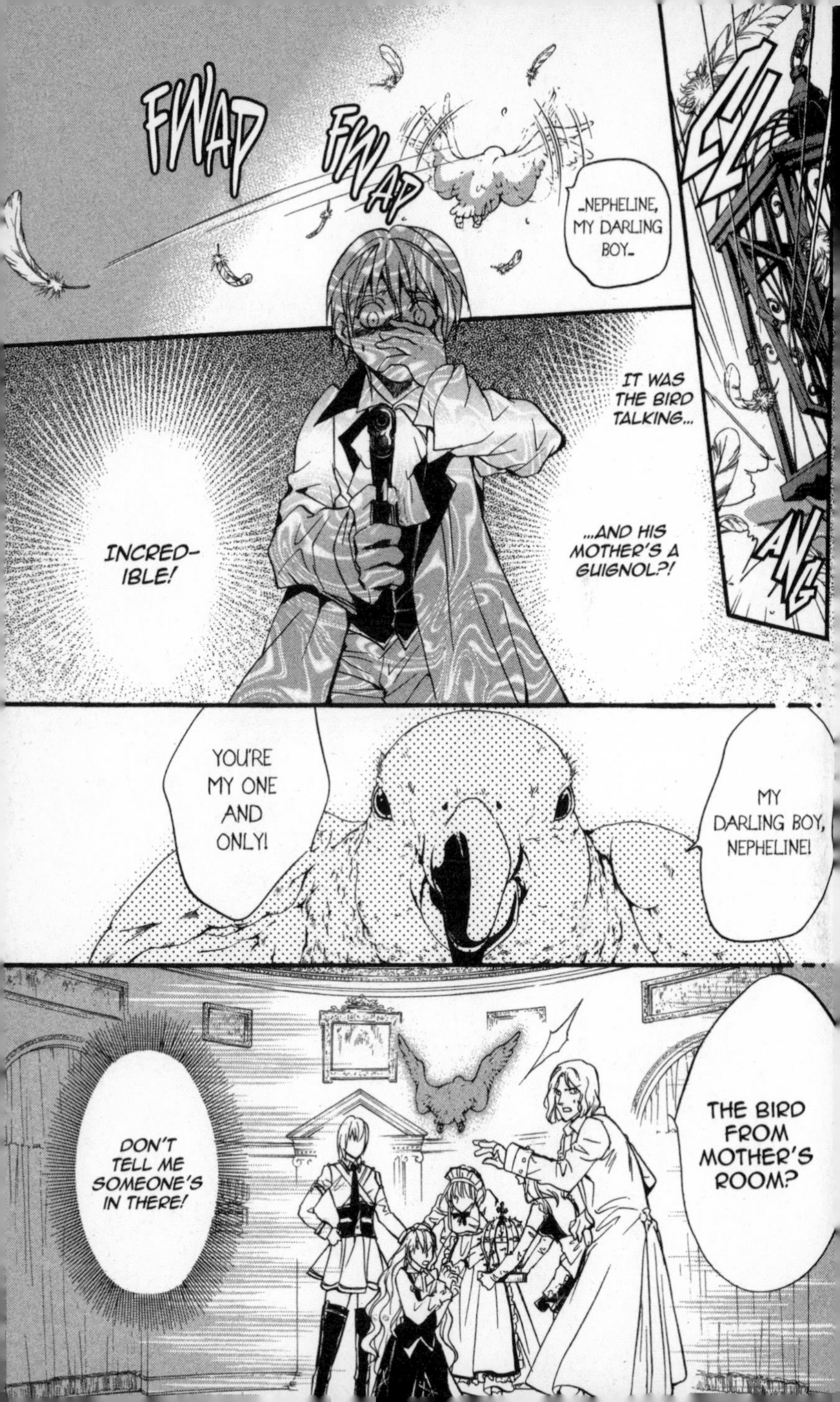
CL
ANG
...NEPHELINE, MY DARLING BOY...
FWAP
FWAP
IT WAS THE BIRD TALKING...
...AND HIS MOTHER'S A GUIGNOL?!
INCRED-IBLE!
MY DARLING BOY, NEPHELINE!
YOU'RE MY ONE AND ONLY!
THE BIRD FROM MOTHER'S ROOM?
DON'T TELL ME SOMEONE'S IN THERE!

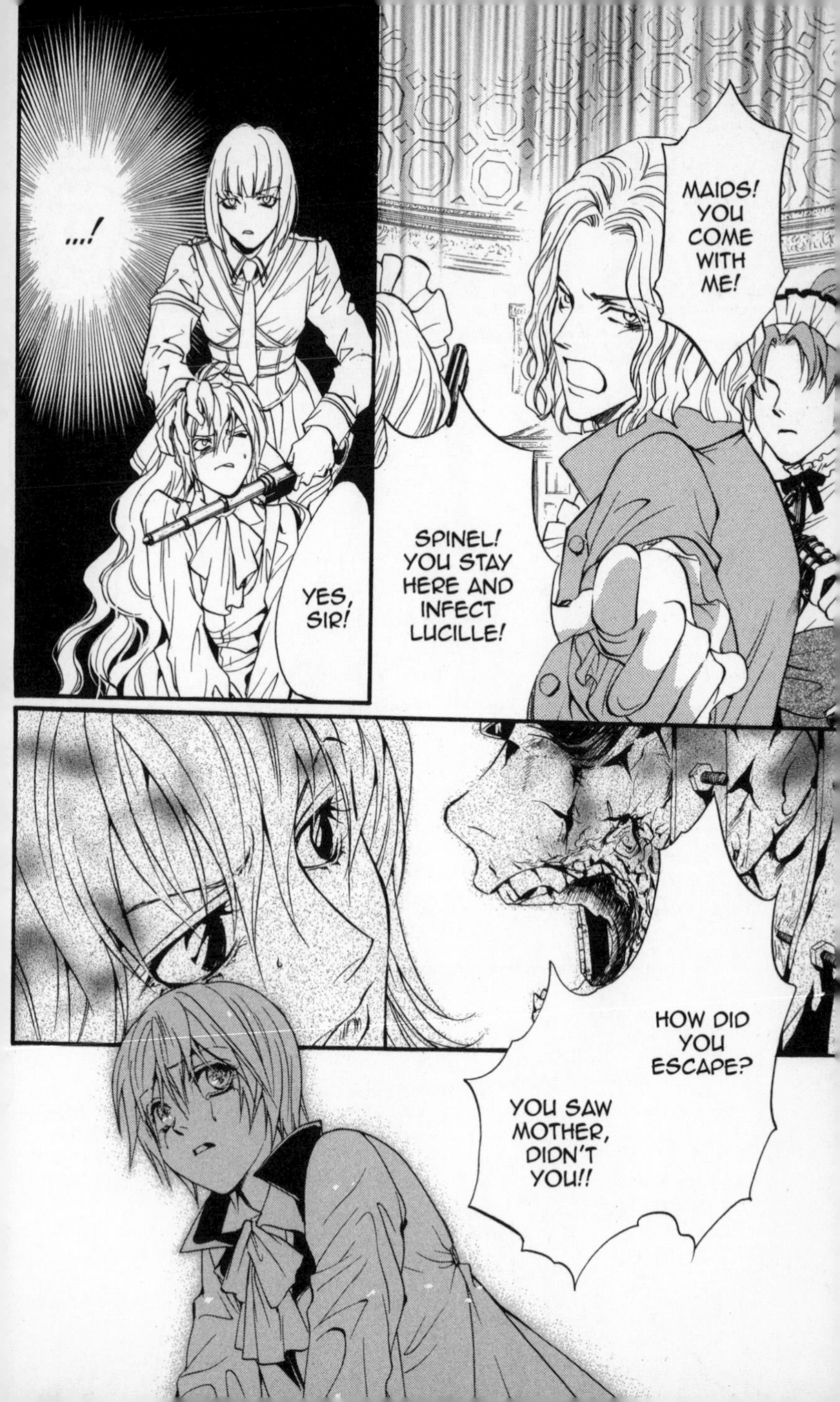
MAIDS! YOU COME WITH ME!
SPINEL! YOU STAY HERE AND INFECT LUCILLE!
YES, SIR!
...!
HOW DID YOU ESCAPE?
YOU SAW MOTHER, DIDN'T YOU!!

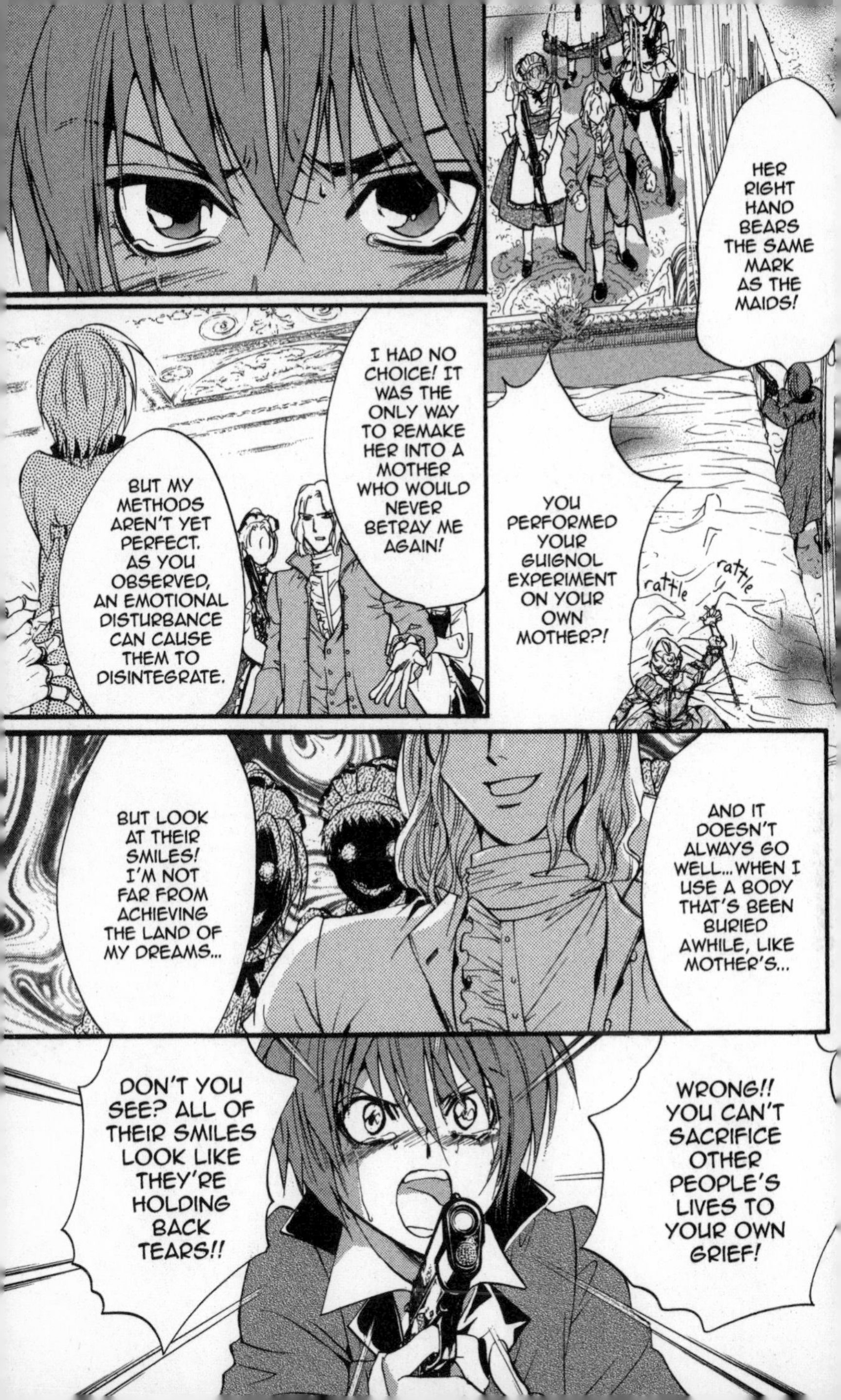
HER RIGHT HAND BEARS THE SAME MARK AS THE MAIDS!
YOU PERFORMED YOUR GUIGNOL EXPERIMENT ON YOUR OWN MOTHER?!
rattle
rattle
I HAD NO CHOICE! IT WAS THE ONLY WAY TO REMAKE HER INTO A MOTHER WHO WOULD NEVER BETRAY ME AGAIN!
BUT MY METHODS AREN'T YET PERFECT. AS YOU OBSERVED, AN EMOTIONAL DISTURBANCE CAN CAUSE THEM TO DISINTEGRATE.
AND IT DOESN'T ALWAYS GO WELL...WHEN I USE A BODY THAT'S BEEN BURIED AWHILE, LIKE MOTHER'S...
BUT LOOK AT THEIR SMILES! I'M NOT FAR FROM ACHIEVING THE LAND OF MY DREAMS...
WRONG!! YOU CAN'T SACRIFICE OTHER PEOPLE'S LIVES TO YOUR OWN GRIEF!
DON'T YOU SEE? ALL OF THEIR SMILES LOOK LIKE THEY'RE HOLDING BACK TEARS!!

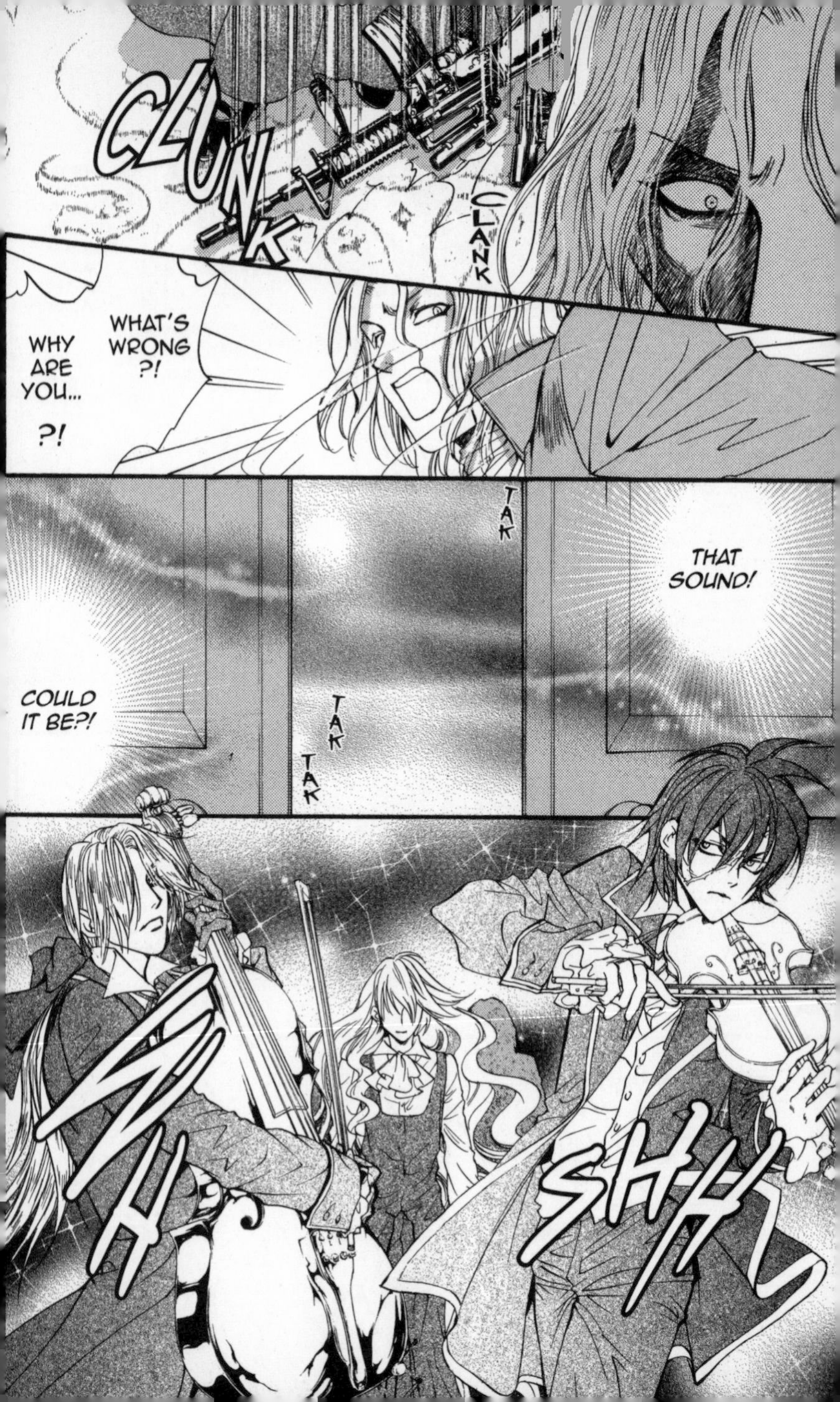
CLUNK
CLANK
WHAT'S WRONG ?!
WHY ARE YOU... ?!
THAT SOUND!
TAK
TAK
TAK
COULD IT BE?!
SHH
WHH

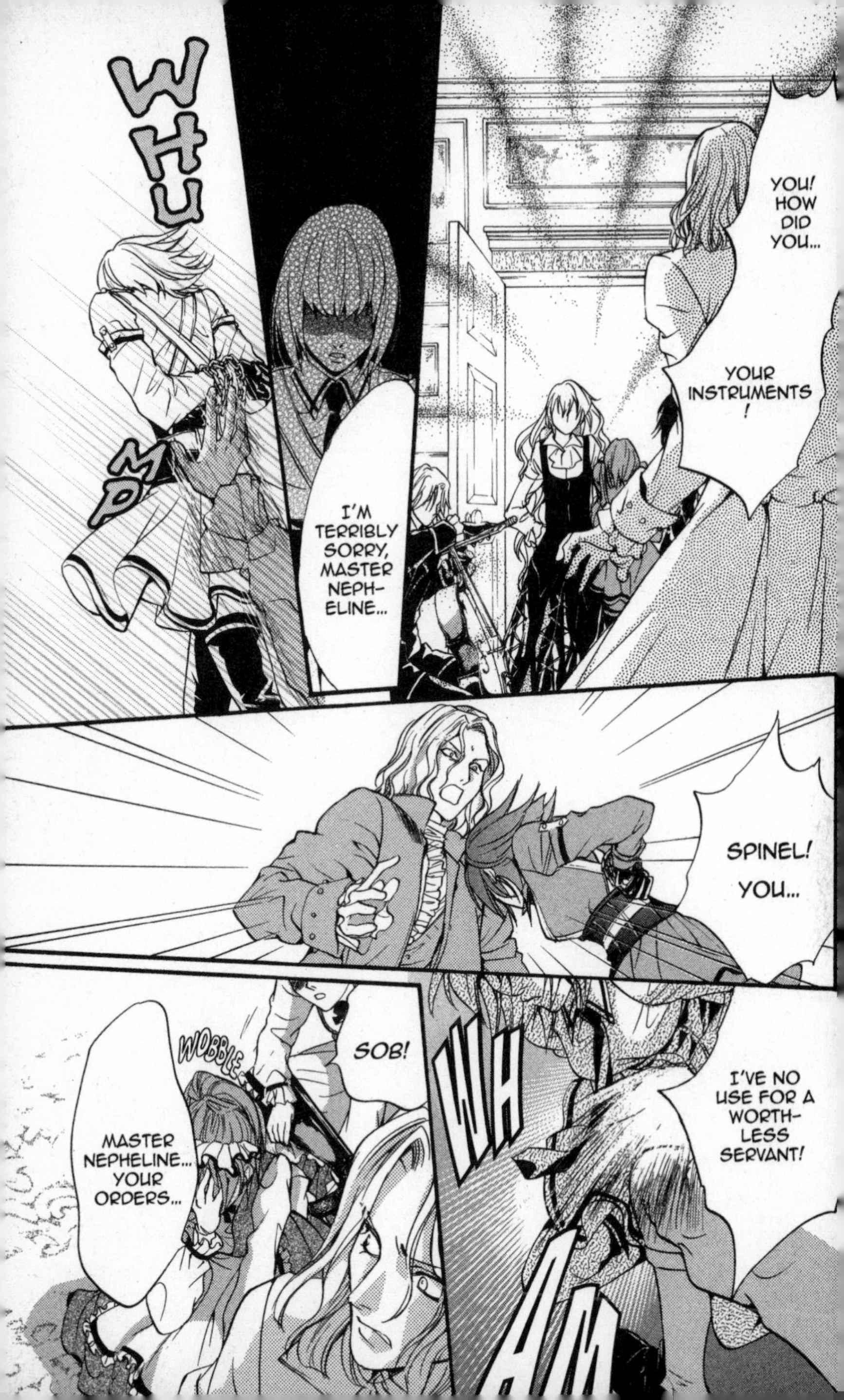

YOU! HOW DID YOU...
YOUR INSTRUMENTS!
I'M TERRIBLY SORRY, MASTER NEPHELINE...
WHUMP
SPINEL! YOU...
I'VE NO USE FOR A WORTHLESS SERVANT!
WHAM
SOB!
WOBBLE
MASTER NEPHELINE... YOUR ORDERS...

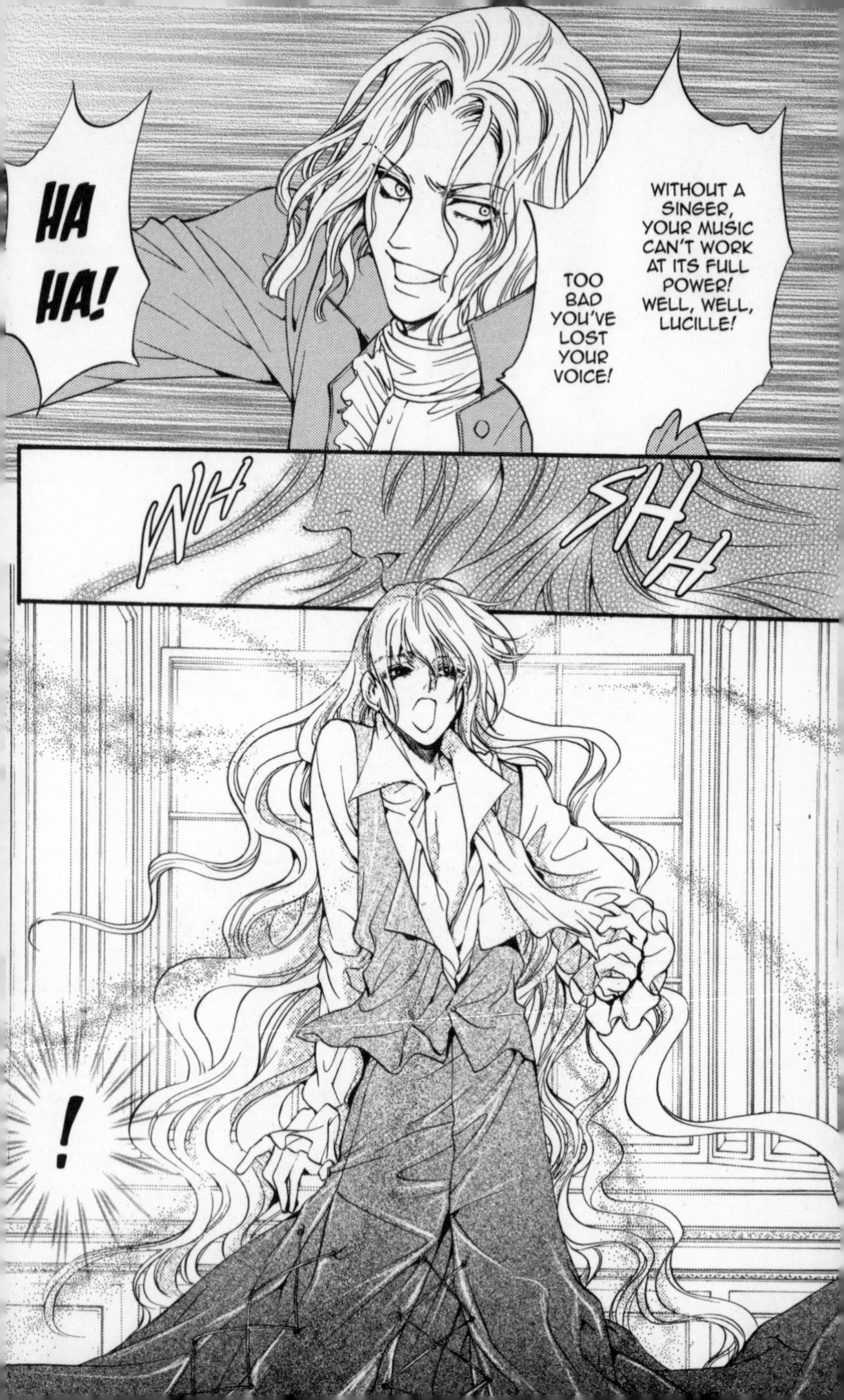
WITHOUT A SINGER, YOUR MUSIC CAN'T WORK AT ITS FULL POWER! WELL, WELL, LUCILLE!
TOO BAD YOU'VE LOST YOUR VOICE!
HA HA!
WH SHH
!

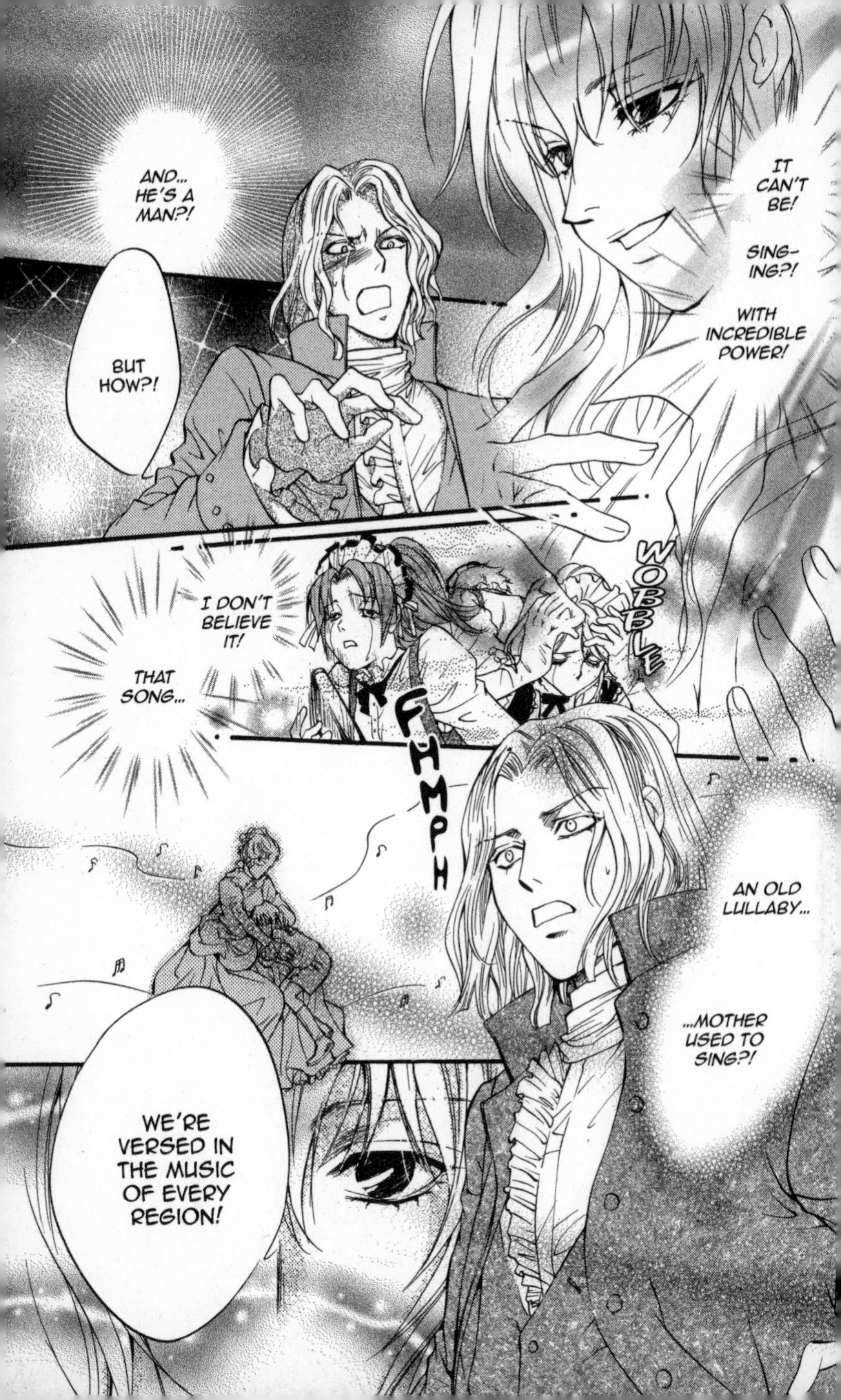
IT CAN'T BE!
SING-ING?!
WITH INCREDIBLE POWER!
AND... HE'S A MAN?!
BUT HOW?!
WOBBLE
I DON'T BELIEVE IT!
THAT SONG...
FHMPH
AN OLD LULLABY...
...MOTHER USED TO SING?!
WE'RE VERSED IN THE MUSIC OF EVERY REGION!

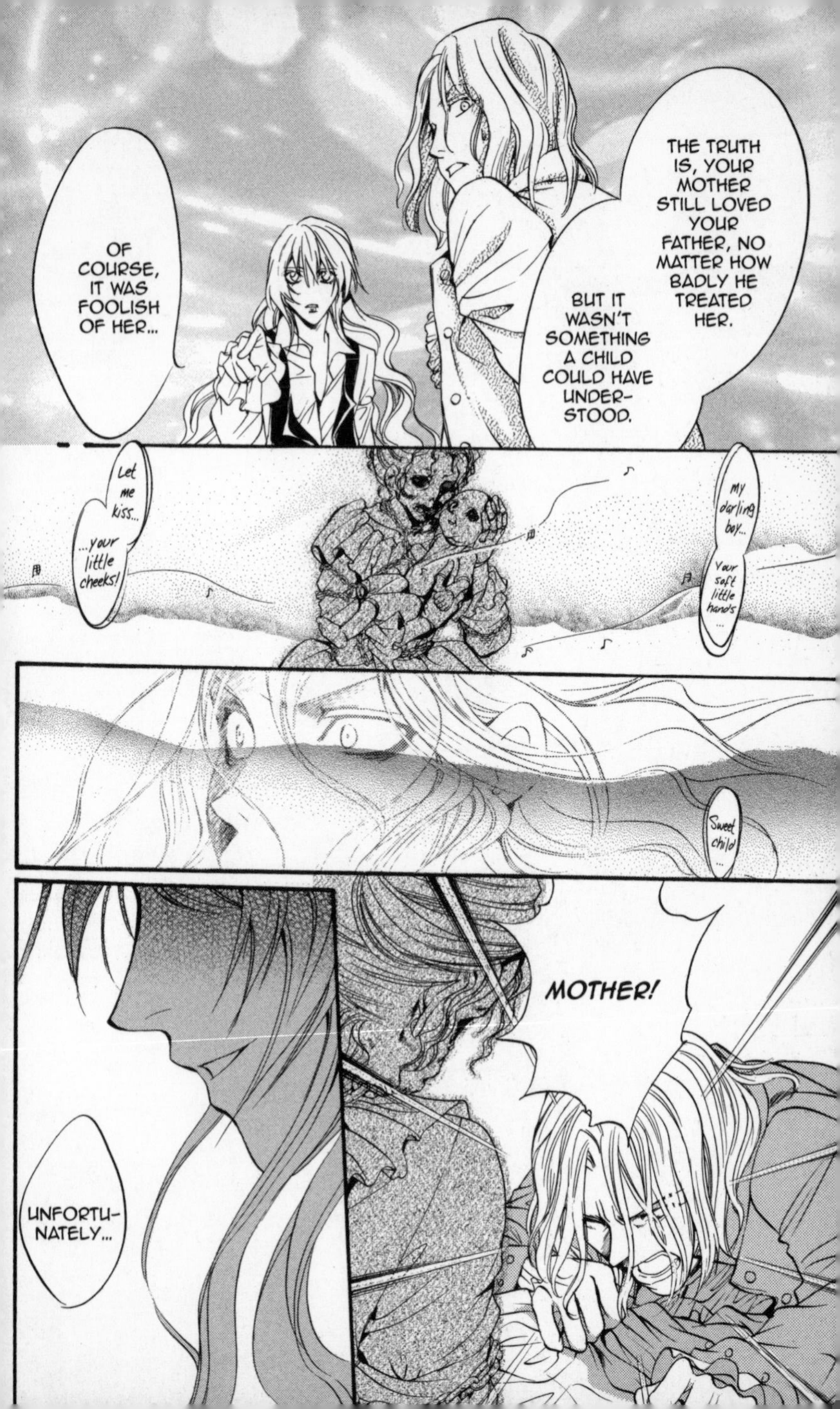
THE TRUTH IS, YOUR MOTHER STILL LOVED YOUR FATHER, NO MATTER HOW BADLY HE TREATED HER.
BUT IT WASN'T SOMETHING A CHILD COULD HAVE UNDERSTOOD.
OF COURSE, IT WAS FOOLISH OF HER...
my darling boy...
Your soft little hands...
Let me kiss...
...your little cheeks!
Sweet child...
MOTHER!
UNFORTUNATELY...

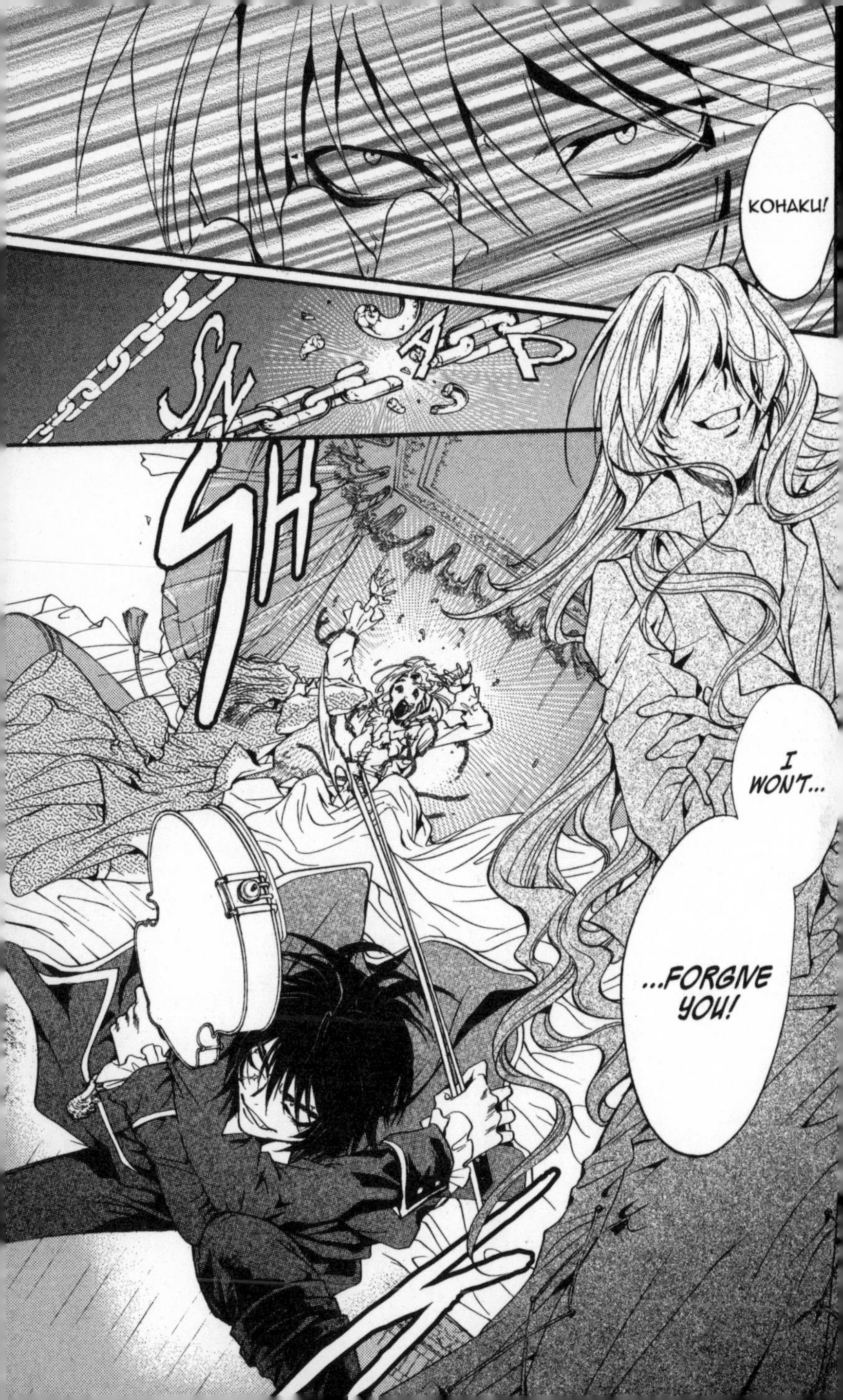
KOHAKU!
SNAP
SH
I WON'T...
...FORGIVE YOU!

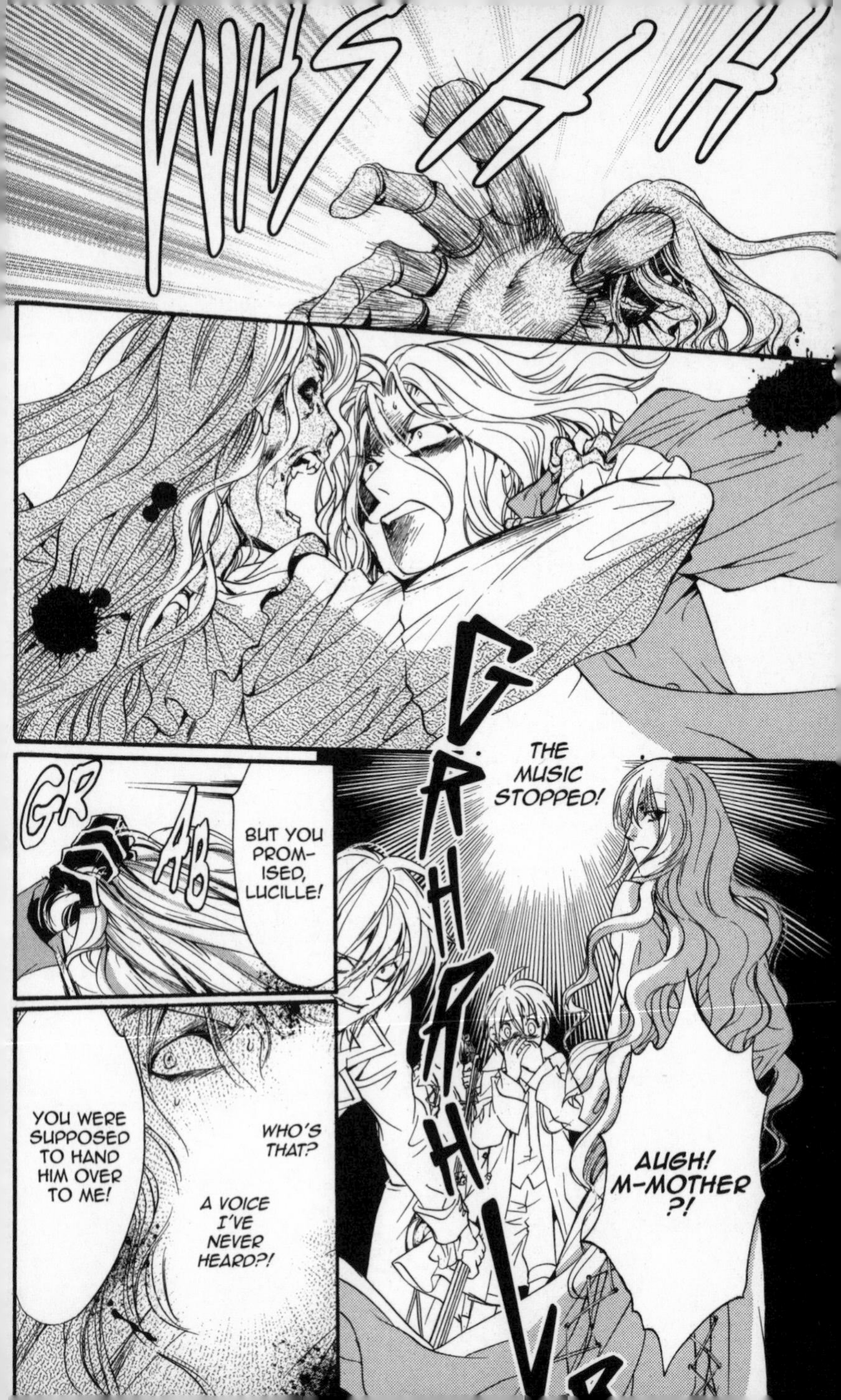
WHSHH
THE MUSIC STOPPED!
AUGH! M-MOTHER?!
GRAB
BUT YOU PROMISED, LUCILLE!
WHO'S THAT?
A VOICE I'VE NEVER HEARD?!
YOU WERE SUPPOSED TO HAND HIM OVER TO ME!

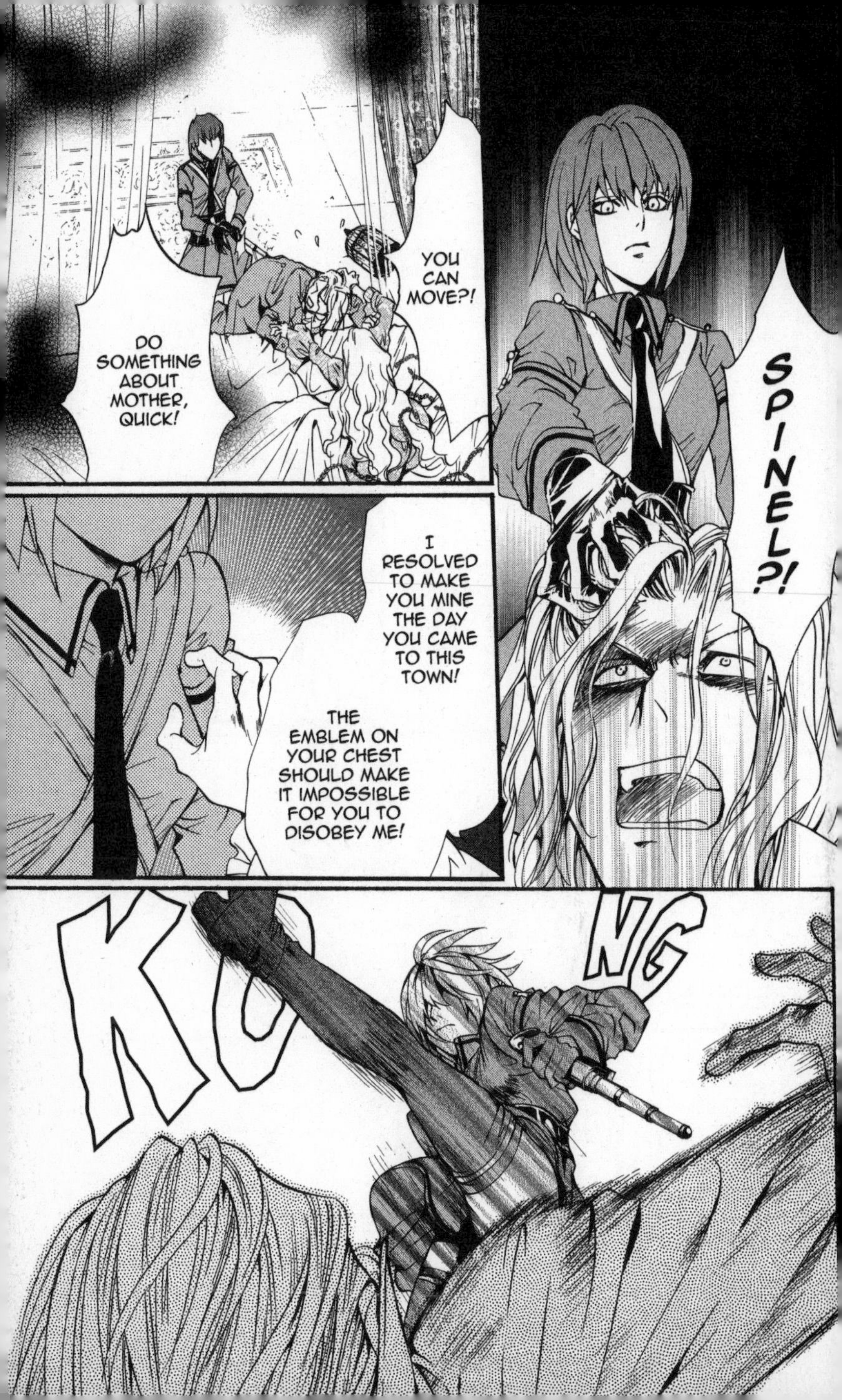
SPINEL?!
YOU CAN MOVE?!
DO SOMETHING ABOUT MOTHER, QUICK!
I RESOLVED TO MAKE YOU MINE THE DAY YOU CAME TO THIS TOWN!
THE EMBLEM ON YOUR CHEST SHOULD MAKE IT IMPOSSIBLE FOR YOU TO DISOBEY ME!
KONG

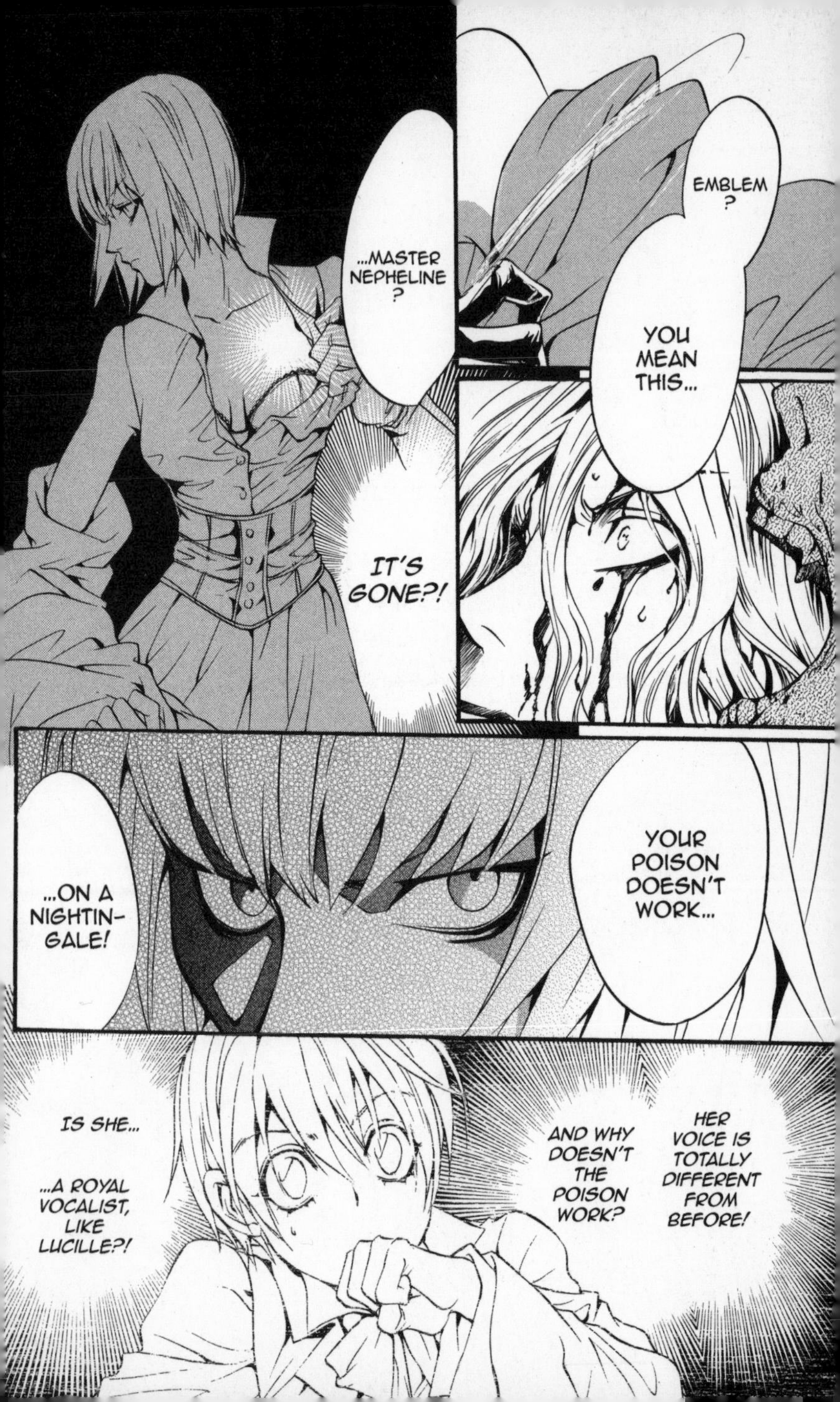
EMBLEM ?
YOU MEAN THIS...
...MASTER NEPHELINE ?
IT'S GONE?!
YOUR POISON DOESN'T WORK...
...ON A NIGHTIN-GALE!
HER VOICE IS TOTALLY DIFFERENT FROM BEFORE!
AND WHY DOESN'T THE POISON WORK?
IS SHE...
...A ROYAL VOCALIST, LIKE LUCILLE?!

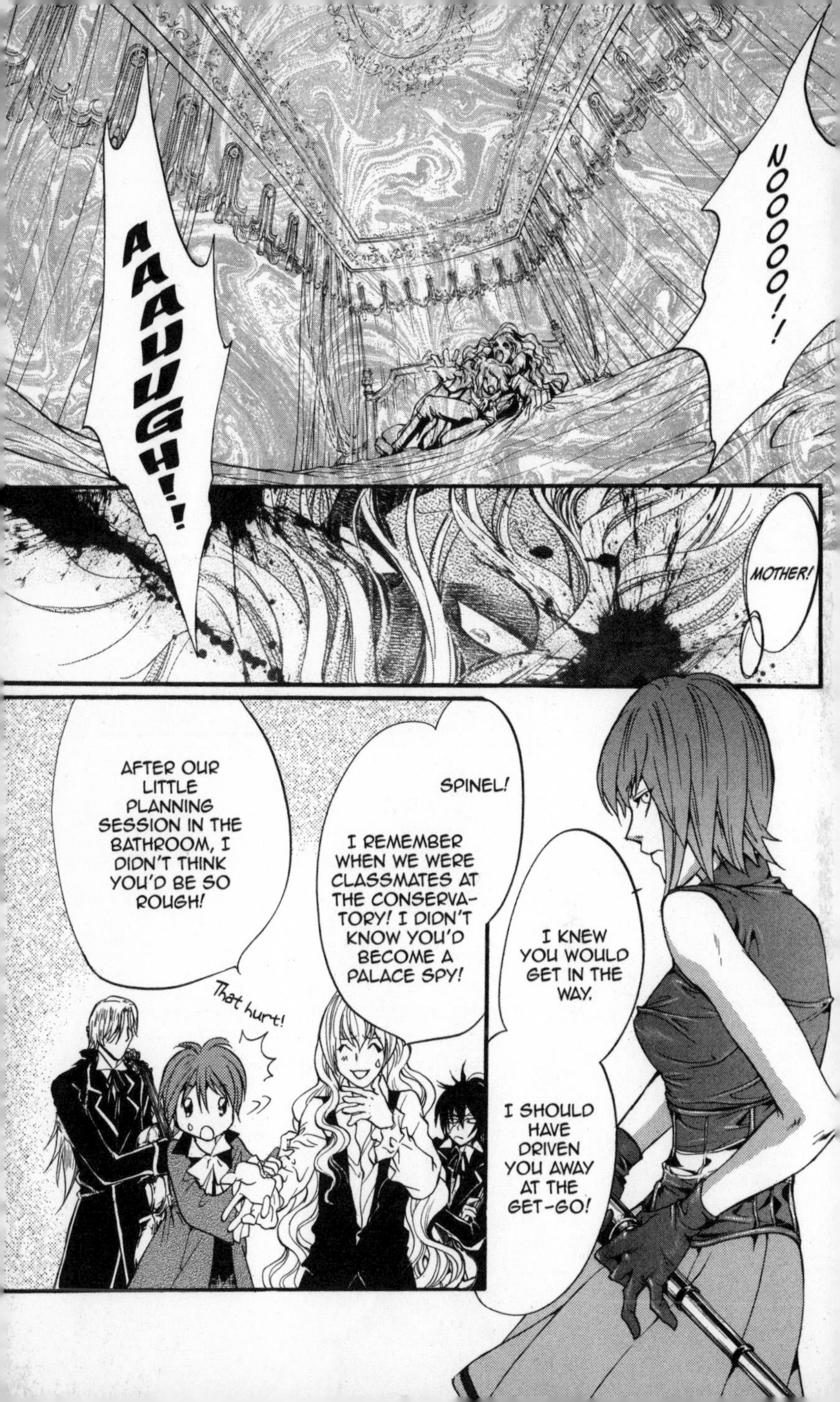
NOOOOOO!!
AAAUUGH!!
MOTHER!
I KNEW YOU WOULD GET IN THE WAY.
I SHOULD HAVE DRIVEN YOU AWAY AT THE GET-GO!
SPINEL!
I REMEMBER WHEN WE WERE CLASSMATES AT THE CONSERVA-TORY! I DIDN'T KNOW YOU'D BECOME A PALACE SPY!
AFTER OUR LITTLE PLANNING SESSION IN THE BATHROOM, I DIDN'T THINK YOU'D BE SO ROUGH!
That hurt!

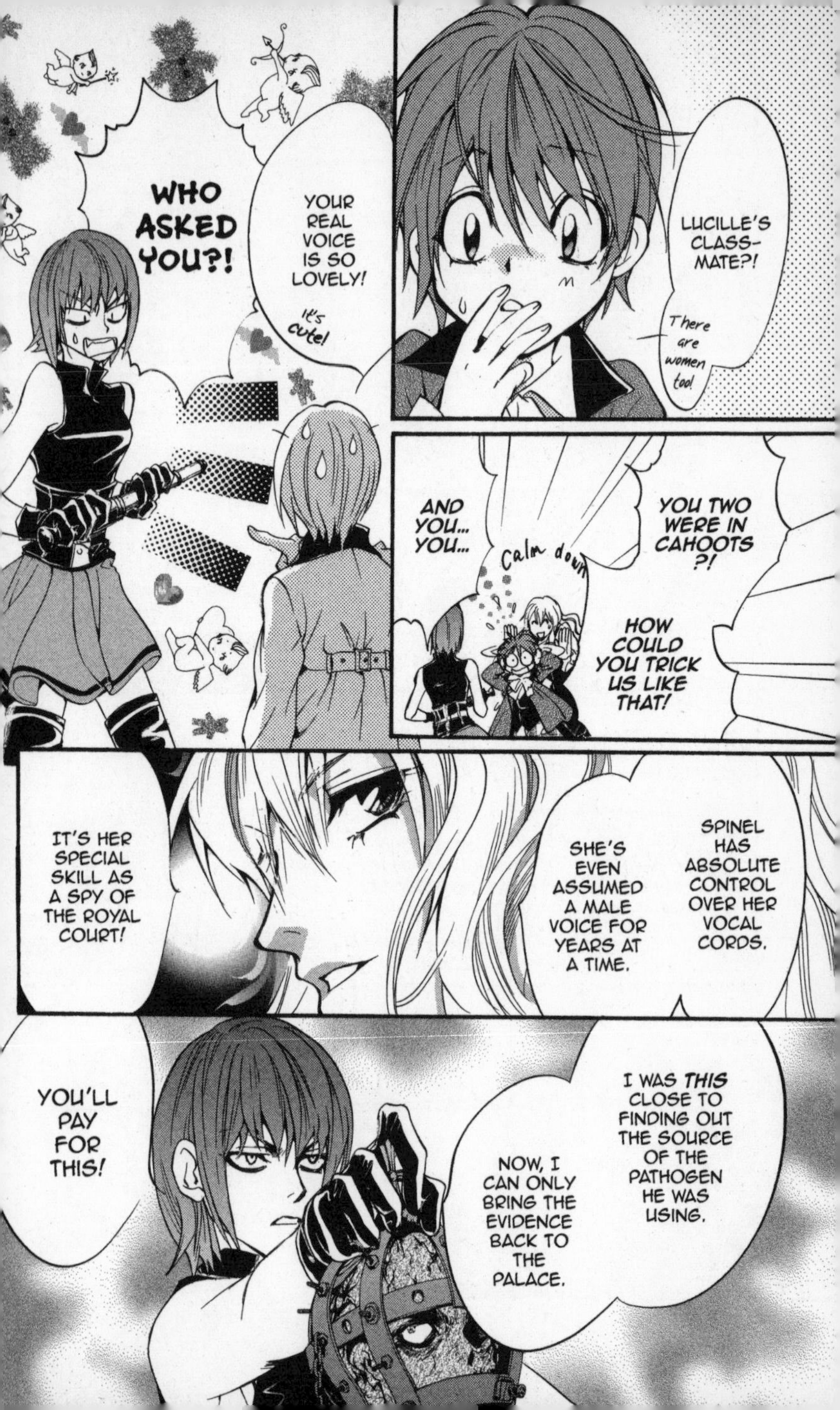
LUCILLE'S CLASSMATE?!
There are women too!
YOU TWO WERE IN CAHOOTS?!
AND YOU... YOU...
Calm down
HOW COULD YOU TRICK US LIKE THAT!
YOUR REAL VOICE IS SO LOVELY!
It's cute!
WHO ASKED YOU?!
SPINEL HAS ABSOLUTE CONTROL OVER HER VOCAL CORDS.
SHE'S EVEN ASSUMED A MALE VOICE FOR YEARS AT A TIME.
IT'S HER SPECIAL SKILL AS A SPY OF THE ROYAL COURT!
I WAS *THIS* CLOSE TO FINDING OUT THE SOURCE OF THE PATHOGEN HE WAS USING.
NOW, I CAN ONLY BRING THE EVIDENCE BACK TO THE PALACE.
YOU'LL PAY FOR THIS!

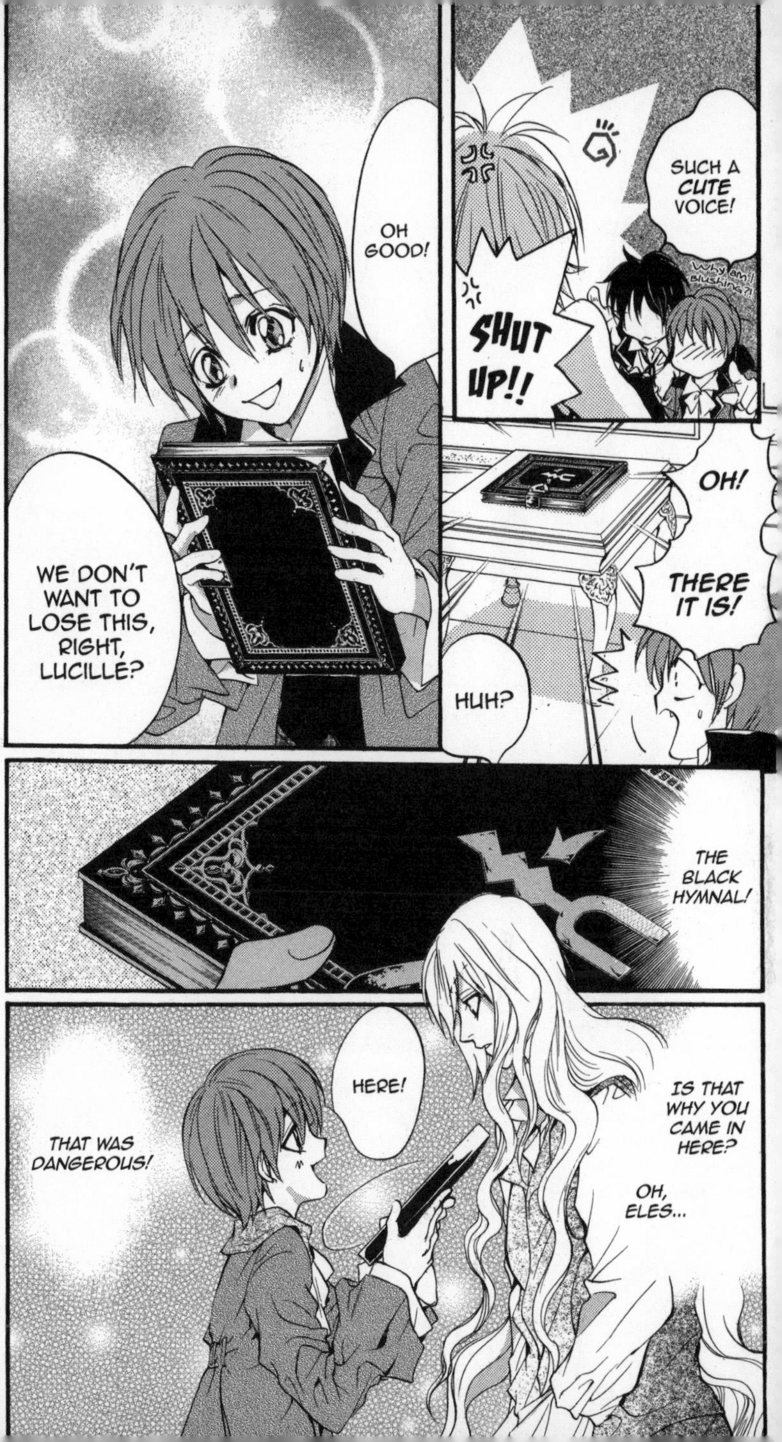
SUCH A CUTE VOICE!
Why am I blushing?!
SHUT UP!!
OH! THERE IT IS!
HUH?
OH GOOD!
WE DON'T WANT TO LOSE THIS, RIGHT, LUCILLE?
THE BLACK HYMNAL!
IS THAT WHY YOU CAME IN HERE?
OH, ELES...
HERE!
THAT WAS DANGEROUS!

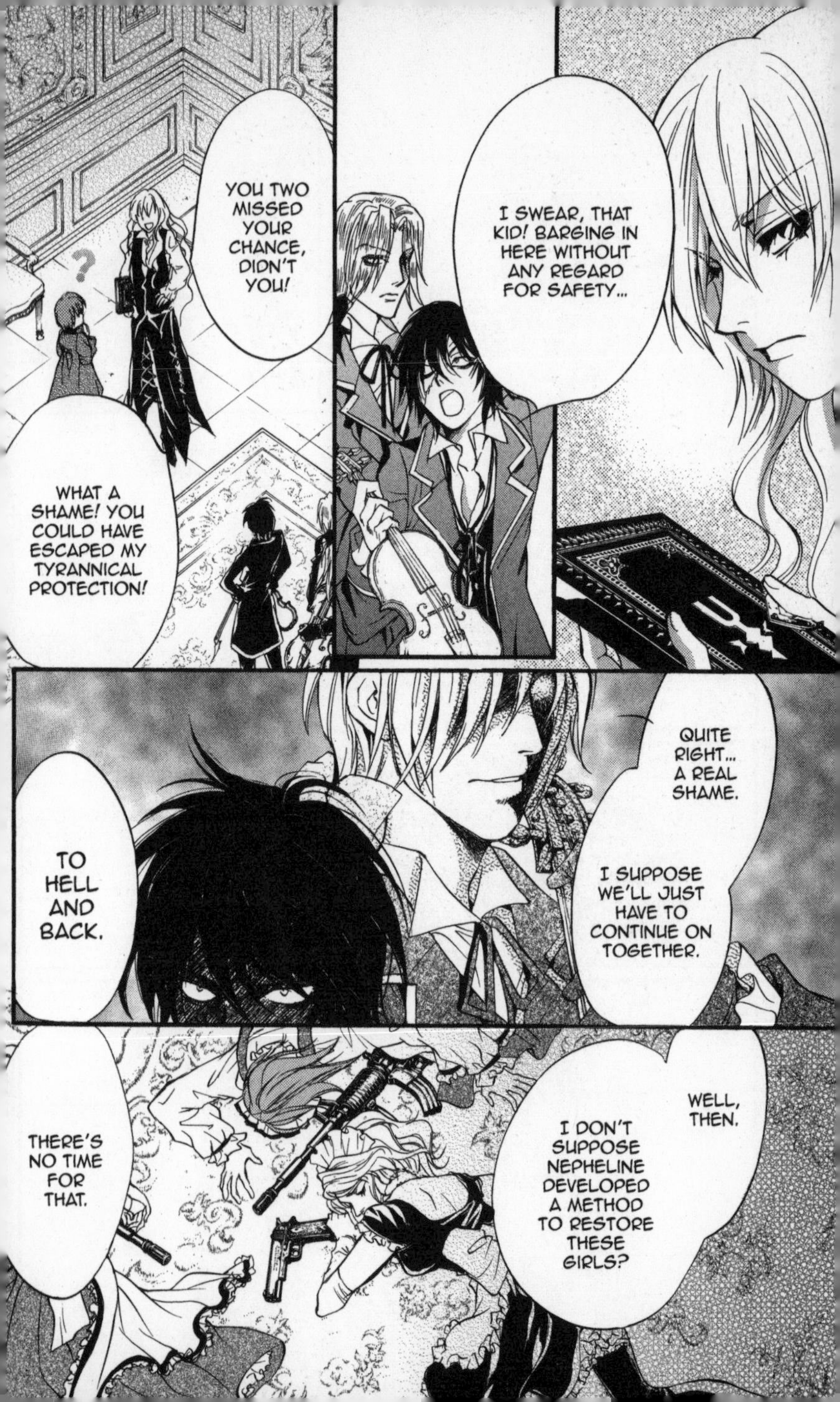
I SWEAR, THAT KID! BARGING IN HERE WITHOUT ANY REGARD FOR SAFETY...
YOU TWO MISSED YOUR CHANCE, DIDN'T YOU!
WHAT A SHAME! YOU COULD HAVE ESCAPED MY TYRANNICAL PROTECTION!
QUITE RIGHT... A REAL SHAME.
I SUPPOSE WE'LL JUST HAVE TO CONTINUE ON TOGETHER.
TO HELL AND BACK.
WELL, THEN.
I DON'T SUPPOSE NEPHELINE DEVELOPED A METHOD TO RESTORE THESE GIRLS?
THERE'S NO TIME FOR THAT.

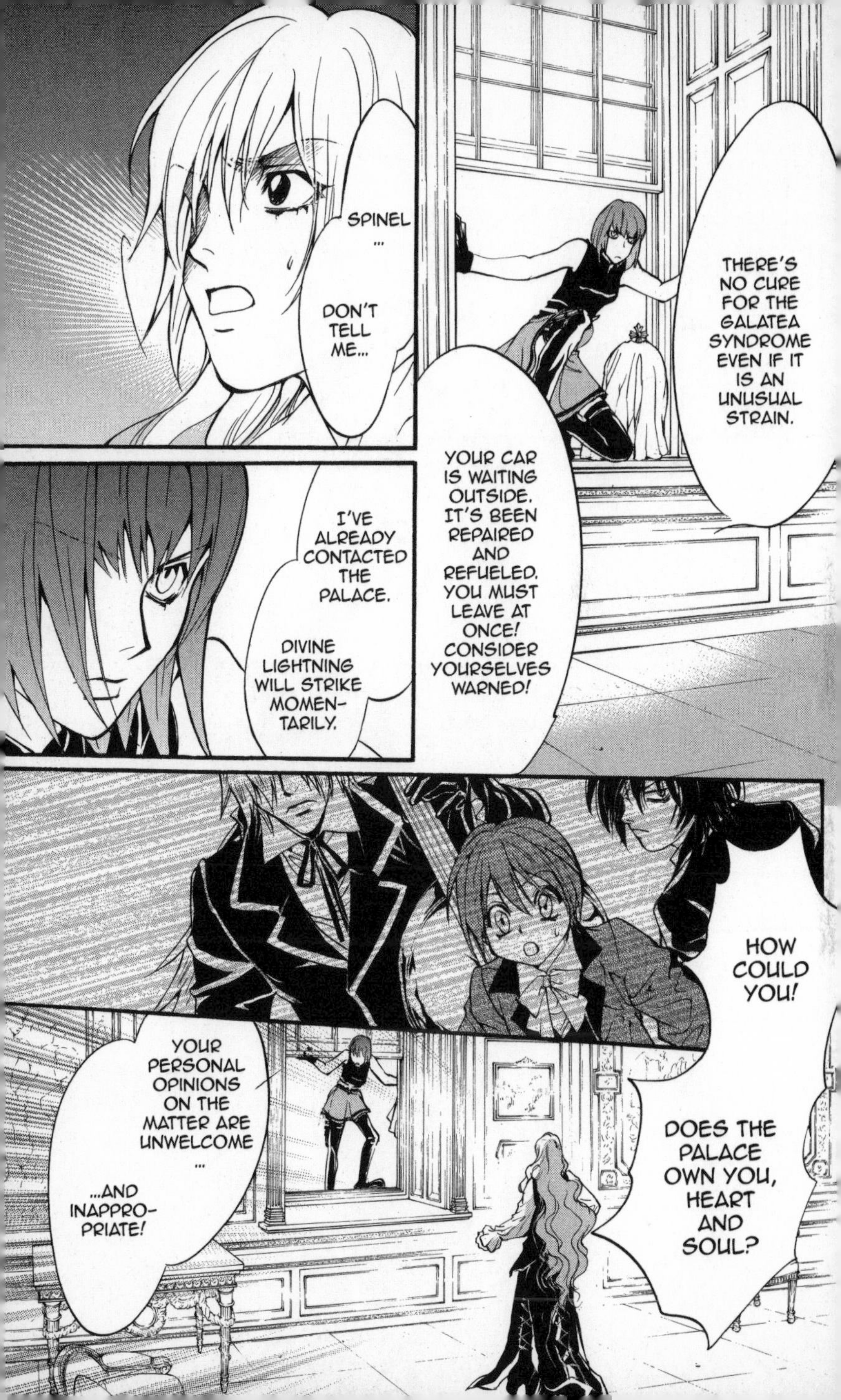

THERE'S NO CURE FOR THE GALATEA SYNDROME EVEN IF IT IS AN UNUSUAL STRAIN.
SPINEL ...
DON'T TELL ME...
I'VE ALREADY CONTACTED THE PALACE.
DIVINE LIGHTNING WILL STRIKE MOMENTARILY.
YOUR CAR IS WAITING OUTSIDE. IT'S BEEN REPAIRED AND REFUELED. YOU MUST LEAVE AT ONCE! CONSIDER YOURSELVES WARNED!
HOW COULD YOU!
DOES THE PALACE OWN YOU, HEART AND SOUL?
YOUR PERSONAL OPINIONS ON THE MATTER ARE UNWELCOME ...
...AND INAPPROPRIATE!

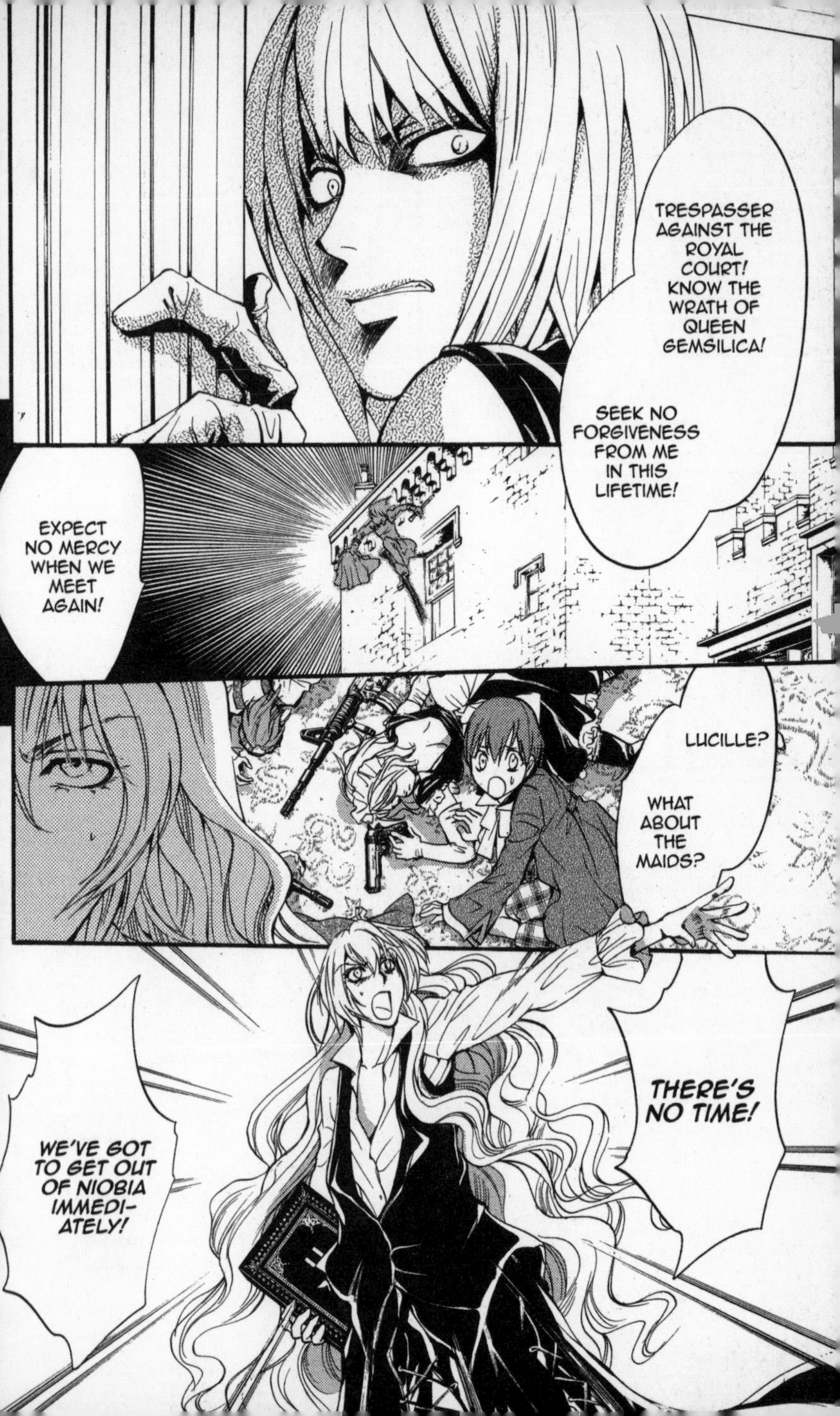
TRESPASSER AGAINST THE ROYAL COURT! KNOW THE WRATH OF QUEEN GEMSILICA!
SEEK NO FORGIVENESS FROM ME IN THIS LIFETIME!
EXPECT NO MERCY WHEN WE MEET AGAIN!
LUCILLE?
WHAT ABOUT THE MAIDS?
THERE'S NO TIME!
WE'VE GOT TO GET OUT OF NIOBIA IMMEDI-ATELY!

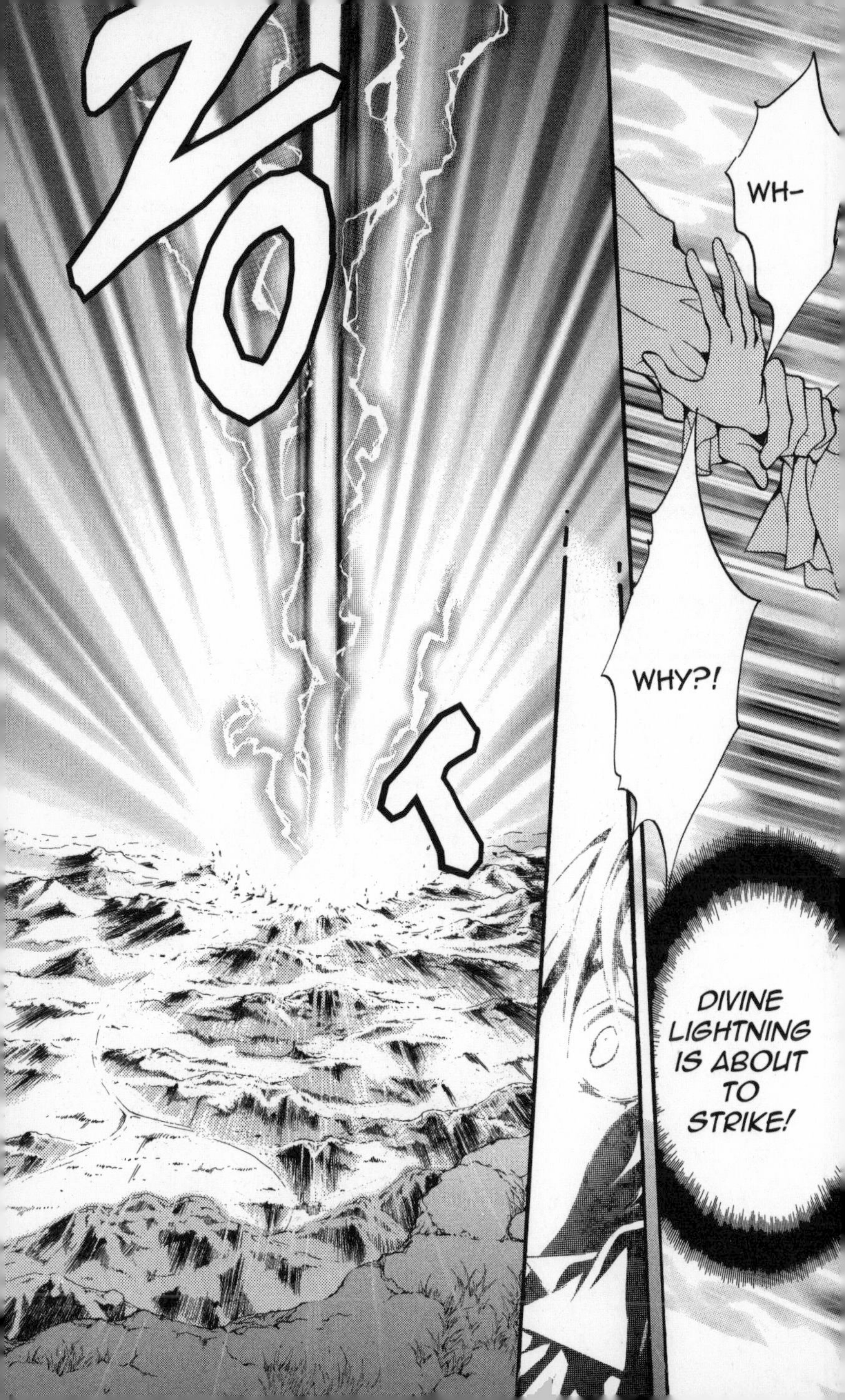
WH-
WHY?!
DIVINE LIGHTNING IS ABOUT TO STRIKE!
ZOT

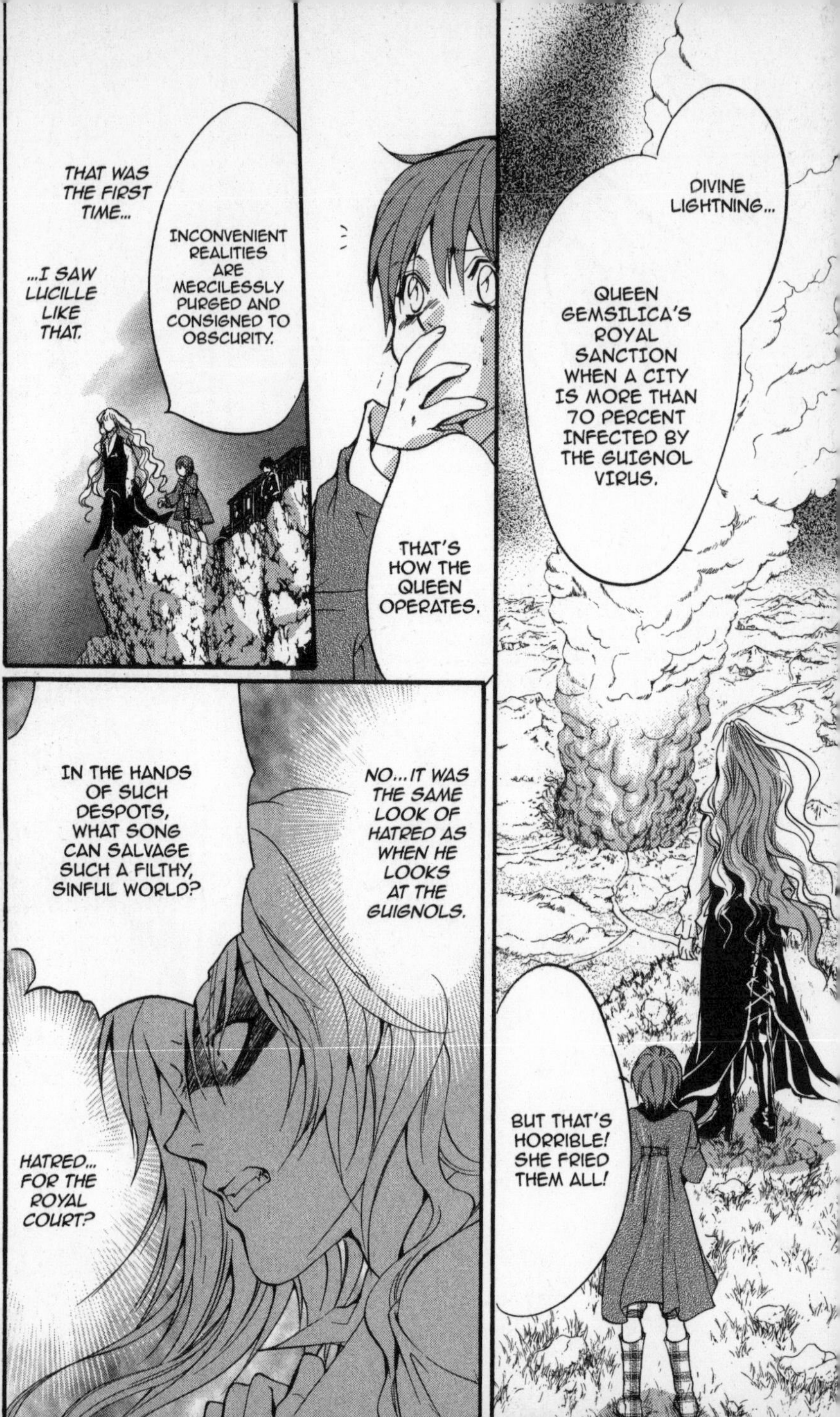
DIVINE LIGHTNING...
QUEEN GEMSILICA'S ROYAL SANCTION WHEN A CITY IS MORE THAN 70 PERCENT INFECTED BY THE GUIGNOL VIRUS.
BUT THAT'S HORRIBLE! SHE FRIED THEM ALL!
THAT'S HOW THE QUEEN OPERATES.
INCONVENIENT REALITIES ARE MERCILESSLY PURGED AND CONSIGNED TO OBSCURITY.
THAT WAS THE FIRST TIME...
...I SAW LUCILLE LIKE THAT.
NO... IT WAS THE SAME LOOK OF HATRED AS WHEN HE LOOKS AT THE GUIGNOLS.
IN THE HANDS OF SUCH DESPOTS, WHAT SONG CAN SALVAGE SUCH A FILTHY, SINFUL WORLD?
HATRED... FOR THE ROYAL COURT?

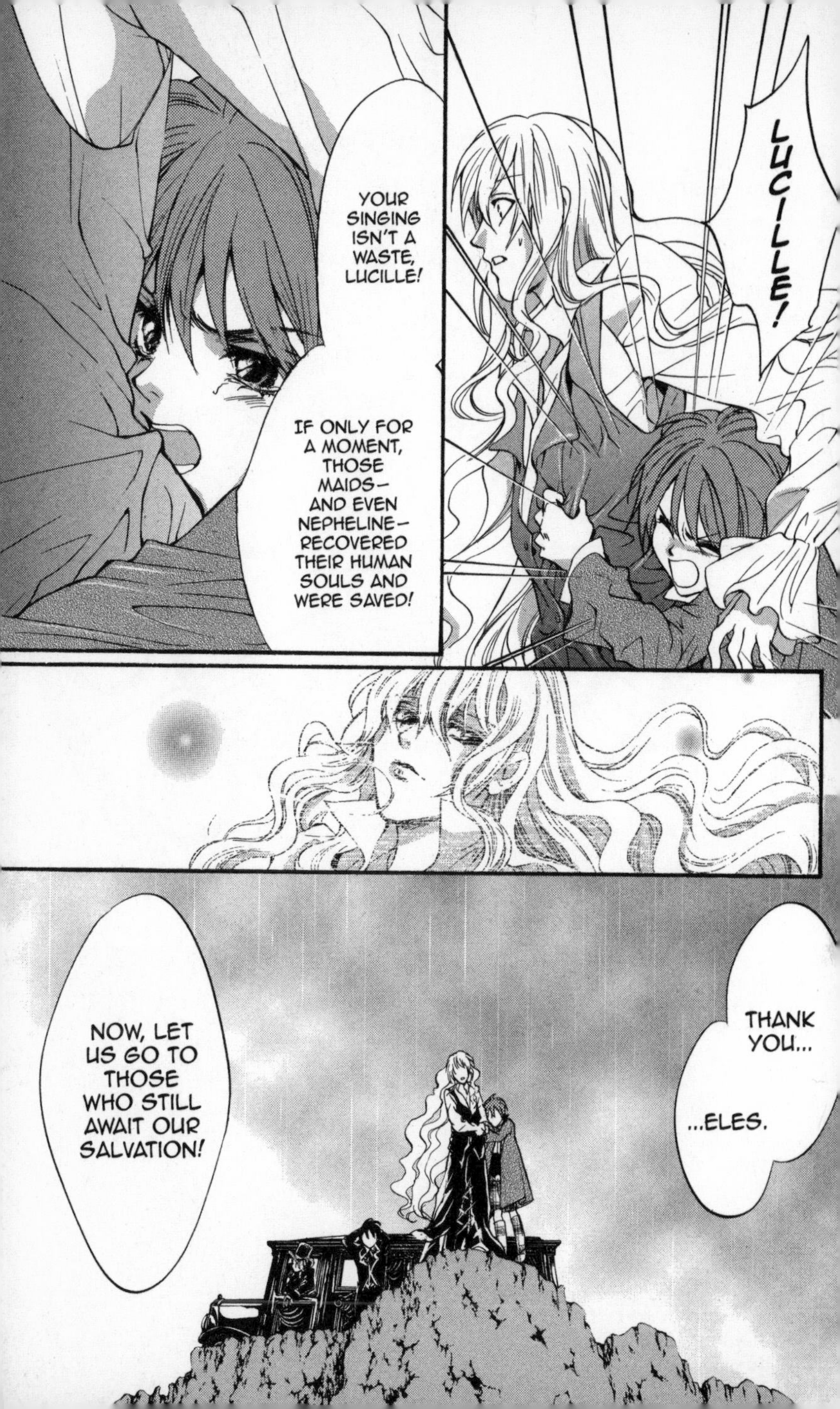
LUCILLE!
YOUR SINGING ISN'T A WASTE, LUCILLE!
IF ONLY FOR A MOMENT, THOSE MAIDS— AND EVEN NEPHELINE— RECOVERED THEIR HUMAN SOULS AND WERE SAVED!
THANK YOU...
...ELES.
NOW, LET US GO TO THOSE WHO STILL AWAIT OUR SALVATION!

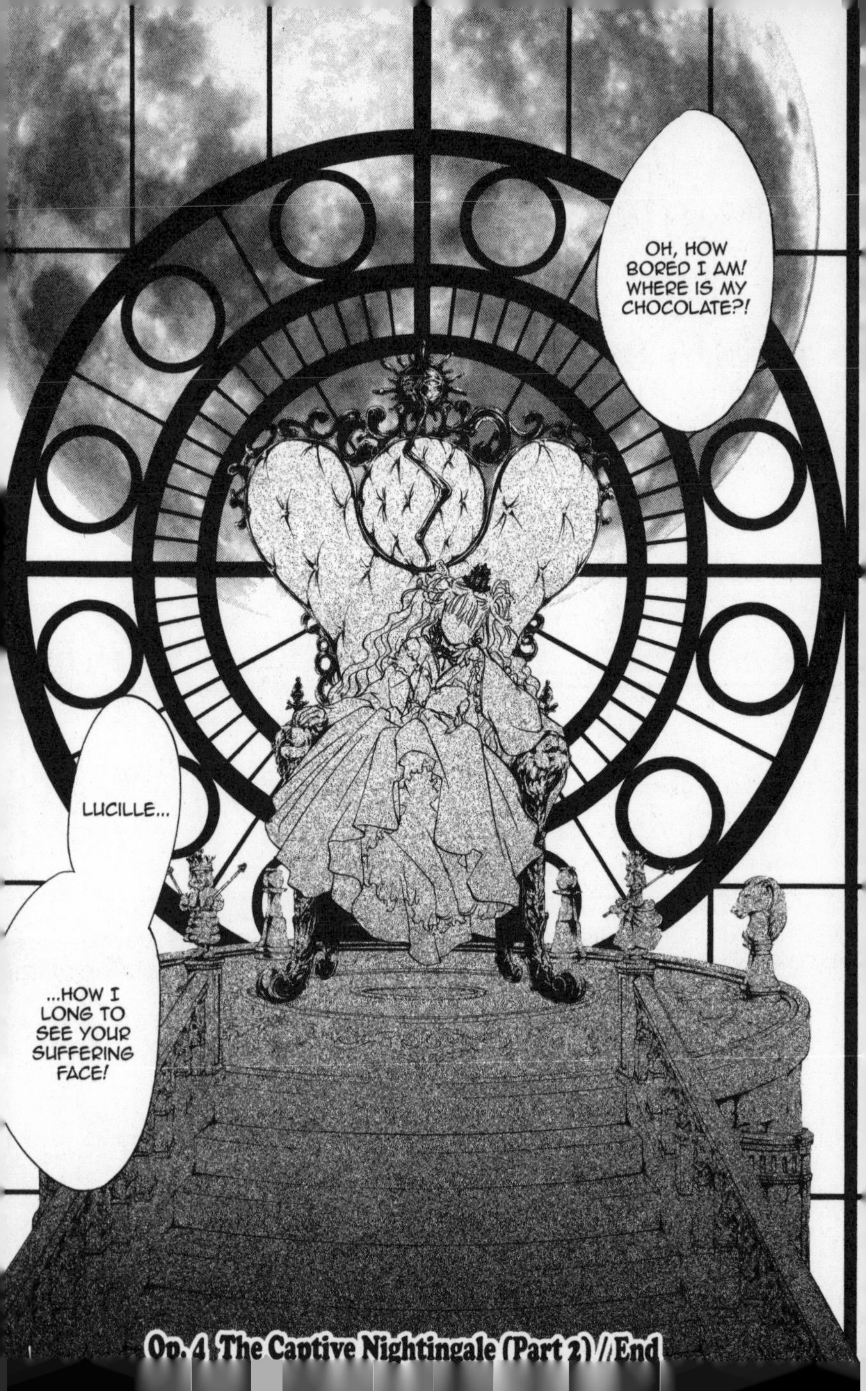
OH, HOW BORED I AM! WHERE IS MY CHOCOLATE?!
LUCILLE...
...HOW I LONG TO SEE YOUR SUFFERING FACE!

Op. 4 The Captive Nightingale (Part 2) // End

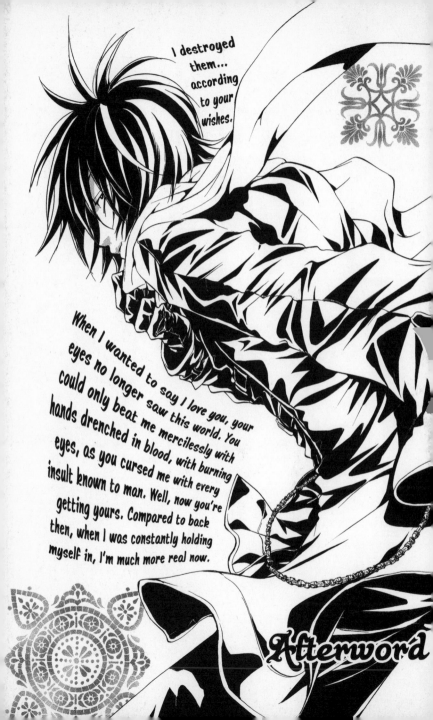

I destroyed them... according to your wishes.

When I wanted to say I love you, your eyes no longer saw this world. You could only beat me mercilessly with hands drenched in blood, with burning eyes, as you cursed me with every insult known to man. Well, now you're getting yours. Compared to back then, when I was constantly holding myself in, I'm much more real now.

Afterword

Creator:
Kaori Yuki

Date of Birth:
December 18

Blood Type:
B

Major Works:
Angel Sanctuary and *The Cain Saga*

 aori Yuki was born in Tokyo and started drawing at a very early age. Following her debut work, *Natsufuku no Erie* (Ellie in Summer Clothes), in the Japanese magazine *Bessatsu Hana to Yume*, she wrote a compelling series of short stories: *Zankoku na Douwatachi* (Cruel Fairy Tales), *Neji* (Screw) and *Sareki Ôkoku* (Gravel Kingdom).

As proven by her best-selling series *Angel Sanctuary*, *Godchild* and *Fairy Cube*, her celebrated body of work has etched an indelible mark on the Gothic comics genre. She likes mysteries and British films and is a fan of the movie *Dead Poets Society* and the show *Twin Peaks*.

GRAND GUIGNOL ORCHESTRA
Vol. 1
Shojo Beat Edition

STORY AND ART BY KAORI YUKI

Translation Camellia Nieh
Touch-up Art & Lettering Eric Erbes
Design Fawn Lau
Editor Joel Enos, Pancha Diaz

GUIGNOL KYUTEI GAKUDAN by Kaori Yuki
© Kaori Yuki 2009
All rights reserved.
First published in Japan in 2009 by HAKUSENSHA, Inc., Tokyo.
English language translation rights arranged with HAKUSENSHA, Inc., Tokyo.

The rights of the author(s) of the work(s) in this publication to be so identified
have been asserted in accordance with the Copyright, Designs and Patents Act 1988.
A CIP catalogue record for this book is available from the British Library.

Printed in the U.S.A.

Published by VIZ Media, LLC
P.O. Box 77010
San Francisco, CA 94107

10 9 8 7 6 5 4 3 2 1
First printing, October 2010

www.viz.com

www.shojobeat.com

Love Kaori Yuki?

Read the rest of VIZ Media's Kaori Yuki collection!

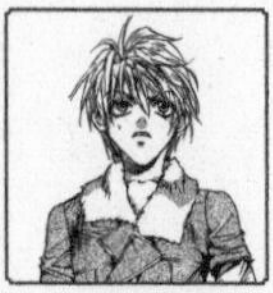

Angel Sanctuary • Rated T+ for Older Teen • 20 Volumes

The angel Alexiel loved God, but she rebelled against Heaven. As punishment, she is sent to Earth to live an endless series of tragic lives. She now inhabits the body of Setsuna Mudo, a troubled teen wrought with forbidden love.

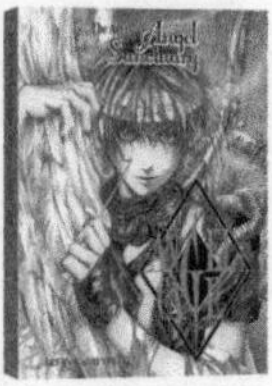

The Art of Angel Sanctuary: Angel Cage

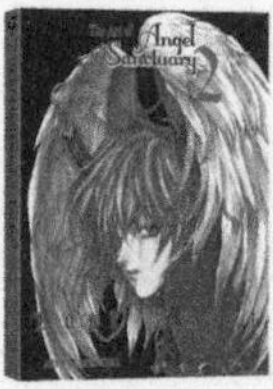

The Art of Angel Sanctuary 2: Lost Angel

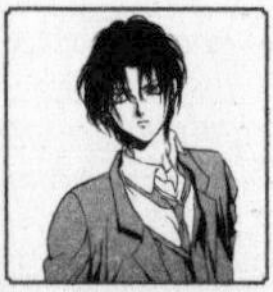

The Cain Saga • Rated M for Mature Readers • 5 Volumes

The prequel to the *Godchild* series, *The Cain Saga* follows the young Cain as he attempts to unravel the secrets of his birth. Delve into the tortured past of Earl Cain C. Hargreaves! Plus bonus short stories in each volume!

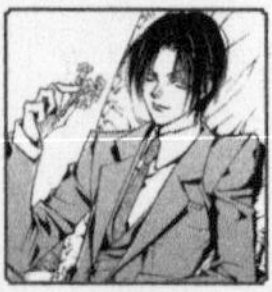

Godchild • Rated T+ for Older Teen • 8 Volumes

In 19th century London, dashing young nobleman Earl Cain Hargreaves weaves his way through the shadowy cobblestone streets that hide the dark secrets of aristocratic society. His mission is to solve the mystery of his shrouded lineage.

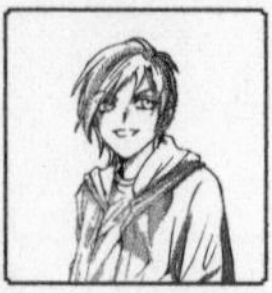

Fairy Cube • Rated T+ for Older Teen • 3 Volumes

Ian and Rin used to just *see* spirits. Now Ian *is* one. Using the Fairy Cube, Ian must figure out how to stop the lizard-spirit Tokage from taking over his life and destroying any chance he has of resurrection.

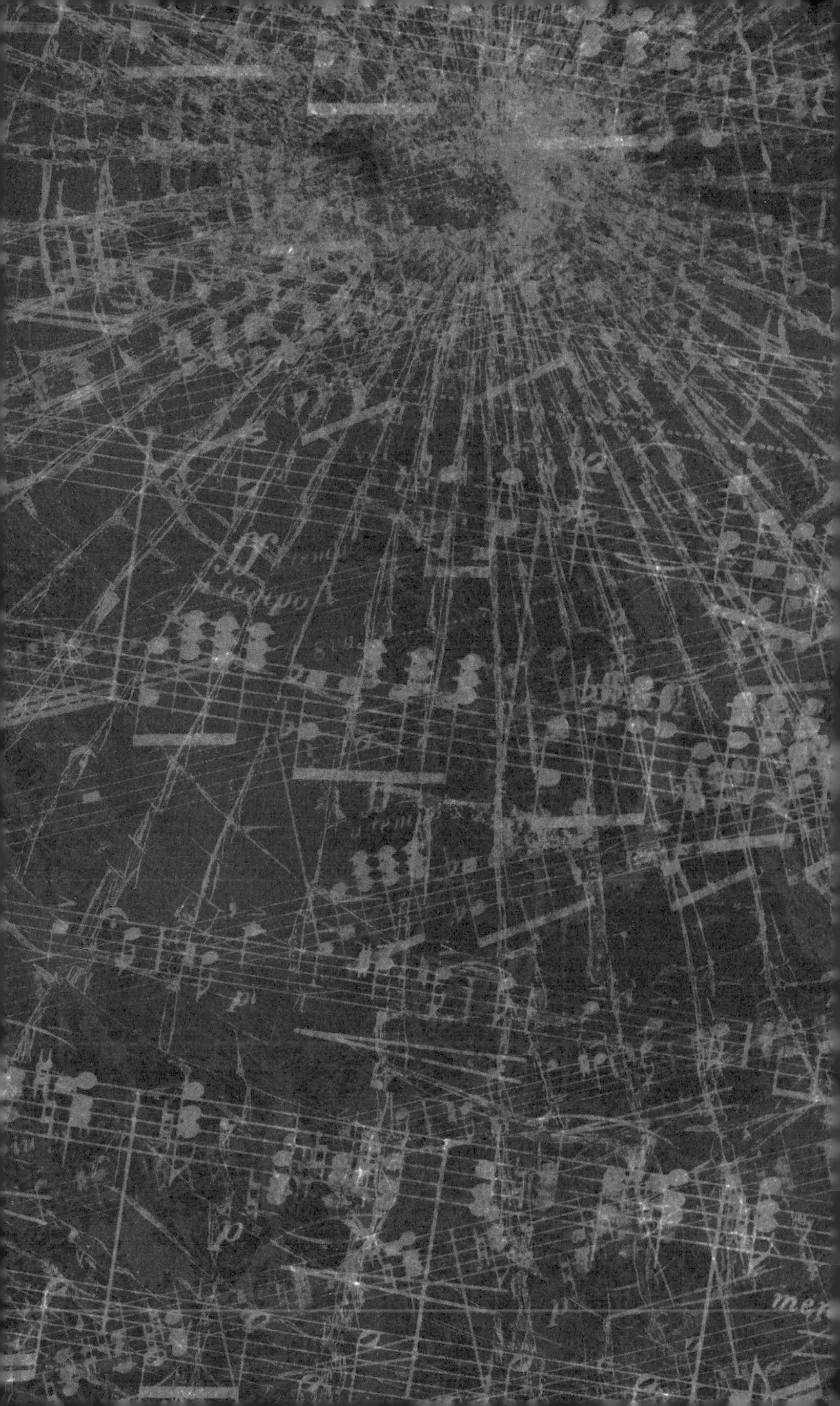